The New Science
of Dreaming

The New Science
of Dreaming

Volume 2
Content, Recall, and Personality
Correlates

EDITED BY DEIRDRE BARRETT
AND PATRICK McNAMARA

Praeger Perspectives

Westport, Connecticut
London

Library of Congress Cataloging-in-Publication Data

The new science of dreaming / edited by Deirdre Barrett and Patrick McNamara.

   p. cm.

   Includes bibliographical references and index.

   ISBN 978-0-275-99045-9 (set : alk. paper) — ISBN 978-0-275-99046-6 (v. 1 : alk. paper) — ISBN 978-0-275-99047-3 (v. 2 : alk. paper) — ISBN 978-0-275-99048-0 (v. 3 : alk. paper) 1. Dreams. I. Barrett, Deirdre. II. McNamara, Patrick, 1956–

   BF1078.N454 2007

   154.6'3—dc22   2007008458

British Library Cataloguing in Publication Data is available.

Library of Congress Catalog Card Number: 2007008458
ISBN-13: 978-0-275-99045-9 (set)
ISBN-10: 0-275-99045-1
ISBN-13: 978-0-275-99046-6 (vol 1)
ISBN-10: 0-275-99046-X
ISBN-13: 978-0-275-99047-3 (vol 2)
ISBN-10: 0-275-99047-8
ISBN-13: 978-0-275-99048-0 (vol 3)
ISBN-10: 0-275-99048-6

First published in 2007

Praeger Publishers, 88 Post Road West, Westport, CT 06881
An imprint of Greenwood Publishing Group, Inc.
www.praeger.com

Printed in the United States of America

The paper used in this book complies with the Permanent Paper Standard issued by the National Information Standards Organization (Z39.48-1984).

10 9 8 7 6 5 4 3 2 1

Contents

Acknowledgments

We would like to thank Debora Carvalko from Greenwood Press for her advocacy of this project, for her help at every step of the way, and for her advice and encouragement at critical junctures of the project.

We would also like to thank our advisory board members John S. Antrobus, G. William Domhoff, Ernest Hartmann, J. Allan Hobson, and Charles Stewart. In addition to their help in identifying topics to be covered, they also helped us to find the best authors to cover them! These advisers have immeasurably increased the quality of these volumes.

We would also like to thank the International Association for the Study of Dreams, www.asdreams.org, whose conference, Web site, and publications have connected us with many of the authors in these volumes.

We would also like to thank Emily Abrams, Chris Dallas-Koziol, Jessica George, Anna Kookoolis, and Sarah Varghese for their help with editing and formatting the references for all the chapters in the series—a thankless task at best, but these assistants did it both conscientiously and carefully.

Finally, we would like to thank Erica Harris, who helped out on all aspects of this project. Her organizational help has meant all the difference throughout. She kept track of correspondence with authors, helped edit the chapters, and generally kept the project running smoothly and on schedule.

Introduction

"What are dreams?" has been a perennial question for philosophers and for ordinary dreamers throughout history. Over the last century, it has also become a focus of scientific inquiry. In 1985, Tore Nielsen surveyed scholarly dream articles published over the previous one hundred years and found that they contained two large waves of activity (Nielsen, 1985). The first began immediately after the publication of Freud's *The Interpretation of Dreams* (1900/1965). This surge consisted of clinical articles. Though Freud's ideas about dreams are often said to be "discredited," he actually introduced the characterization that dreams are predominately visual, metaphoric thought often linked to mental processes outside conscious awareness. This is now widely accepted and not thought of as "Freudian." It was Freud's emphasis on "wish fulfillment" of primitive sexual and aggressive urges as the overriding motivations in dreams that psychology has discarded. Freud also believed that dreams occurred only when a conflict arose, whereas research has come to show that we dream regularly through the night and recall only a fraction of this. Research showing the average dream is the negative side of neutral (Hall & Van de Castle, 1966) similarly made a central role for wish fulfillment more vulnerable to Occam's razor. The more extreme and obviously erroneous psychoanalytic assertions are often cited as having discouraged scientific researchers from exploring dream content and clinical issues.

The next wave of publications came as a physiologic one when rapid eye movement (REM) sleep was discovered. Aserinsky and Kleitman (1953) observed that the brain, cardiovascular, and respiratory systems became more active at approximately 90-minute intervals through the night. This corresponded with the timing of awakenings likeliest to result in a dream report. There were high hopes that this discovery might shed light not only on dreaming but on personality and mind/brain controversies in general. Though subsequent studies added much detail to the portrait of REM and its cycling with other stages of sleep, initially they did not impact clinical or cognitive knowledge of dreaming, much less other aspects of psychology. The physiologic researchers didn't combine their research with the type of detailed content studies in which clinicians are interested. The tone of their articles often implied that all interesting questions about dreams had been solved by describing the physiological processes of REM. In 1979, dream researcher Harry Fiss observed:

> The fact that sleep researchers have thus emphasized the biological substratum of dreaming and by and large neglected the psychological experience of dreaming has given rise to a curious paradox: despite the monumental achievements in sleep research in recent years, our prevalent notions of dreaming continue to be derived principally from clinical practice and psychoanalysis—as if REM had never been discovered. In brief, the technological breakthrough of the fifties and sixties has had relatively little impact on our understanding of dreaming. (Fiss, 1979, p. 41)

Over the last two decades, however, there has been more cross-fertilization of content and physiologic studies of dreaming. The technology has advanced so that researchers can identify the biochemistry and neuroimaging of the dreaming brain in enough detail to relate it to what is known about the psychological functions of these specific areas. Clinical and cognitive researchers have also begun comprehensive studies that tie into physiological findings. The subjective and physiologic data on dreaming are finally beginning to inform each other. New dream research has become relevant to helping clinicians treat posttraumatic stress and anxiety disorders. It is becoming a tool for cognitive psychologists studying the orienting response and memory. Dream studies are beginning to tell us more about brain development—both across species and across the human lifetime.

The New Science of Dreaming brings together this exciting new body of research. The volumes are organized around three broad themes: neurophysiological research, dream content and clinical approaches, and theoretical and cultural perspectives.

Volume 1 presents the recent physiological studies of dreaming—mostly characterizing REM sleep but also including non-REM (NREM) dreams and the differential aspects of REM most linked to dream characteristics. In Chapter 1, Claude Gottesmann surveys the history of research on the physiology of dreaming sleep. He begins with researchers some two centuries ago who noted isolated signs of REM without fully identifying it and follows this through the latest discoveries on biological characteristics of the state. In Chapter 2, Patrick McNamara, Charles Nunn, Robert Barton, Erica Harris, and Isabella Capellini describe the phylogeny of REM and NREM and at what point in evolution a process analogous to dreaming may have arisen. Using REM sleep as a proxy for the dreaming brain/mind, McNamara et al. find that REM is most prominent in terrestrial, placental mammals and only occurs bihemispherically. NREM, on the other hand, can occur in a single hemisphere. Thus, the evolution of REM sleep may be tied to the evolution of brain structures like the corpus collosum that facilitate interhemispheric transfer of information. In Chapter 3, J. Allan Hobson discusses cellular and molecular models of dreaming and how they account for such formal dream features as sensorimotor hallucinosis, delusional errors of state identification, emotional intensification, and memory loss. In Chapter 4, Hobson explores how drugs alter these to affect dreaming.

In Chapter 5, Thien Thanh Dang-Vu, Manuel Schabus, Martin Desseilles, Sophie Schwartz, and Pierre Maquet review neuroimaging studies of REM sleep. The emerging picture reveals activation of the pons, the thalamus, temporo-occipital and limbic/paralimbic areas (including the amygdala), along with a relative quiescence of dorsolateral prefrontal and inferior parietal cortices. The authors note that these correlate well with observed cognition during dreaming. In Chapter 6, Edward F. Pace-Schott focuses in more detail on one of these findings—the frontal lobes' diminished activation during REM—to account for many dream characteristics. In Chapter 7, Erin J. Wamsley and John S. Antrobus describe their "Dual Rhythm" model of dreaming, which suggests that both the REM-NREM cycle and changes in cortical activation across the 24-hour cycle are sources of nonspecific brain activation supporting mentation during sleep. Maria Livia Fantini and Luigi Ferini-Strambi's Chapter 8 describes REM Behavior Disorder and other REM parasomnias in which movement is disinhibited during REM and people often thrash around—apparently acting out dreams. They discuss how the dream content interacts with the disorder. In Chapter 9, Patrick McNamara, Deirdre McLaren, Sara Kowalczyk, and Edward F. Pace-Schott describe the contrasting physiologies of REM and NREM sleep states and then report new data on dreams associated with these two sleep states. They find that while attributions of mental states to dream characters by the dreamer occurs in both sleep states, these "theory of mind" abilities are much more robust in REM than in NREM sleep. In Chapter 10, Sanford Auerbach reviews changes in dream recall and dream content in association with various neurologic disorders. Finally, in Chapter 11, David Kahn discusses how biochemical differences during REM decrease access to episodic memory and diminish the tendency to reflect on implausibility, incongruity, discontinuity, and illogical thinking.

Volume 2 presents cognitive, personality, and clinical research on dreams. In Chapter 1, G. William Domhoff reviews content studies and finds they do not support the common stereotype of dreams as highly emotional, bizarre, or similar in structure or content to schizophrenia or delirium. He concludes that most dreams are reasonable simulations of waking life containing occasional rare features, such as distorted settings and objects, unusual characters, inexplicable activities, strange images and metamorphoses, and sudden scene shifts. In Chapter 2, Michael Schredl examines the literature on gender differences in dreaming, summarizing the major findings: women recall dreams more often than men, men's dreams have more physical aggression and work settings, and women's dreams contain more people and household objects. He discusses how these findings map onto differences between gender roles in waking life and suggests this is supportive of the continuity hypothesis of dreaming.

In Chapter 3, Roar Fosse and G. William Domhoff present a model of dreams as "non-executive orienting"—suggesting that dynamic oscillations of the dreaming networks cause them to self-organize into narrow but spatially extended corridors of attention that reach conscious awareness. In Chapter 4, Michael Schredl reviews the literature on dream recall and proposes a model by which major correlates—stress, personality, attitudes toward dreams, sleep arousal and retrieval effects, and memory (especially visual memory)—all interact to produce the variations we observe in dream recall. In Chapter 5, Mark Blagrove looks in more detail at the effects of personality on recall and dream content differences. In Chapter 6, Clara E. Hill and Patricia Spangler review the history of dreams in psychotherapy and modern empirical evidence on outcomes of dream work, including differential predictors of who benefits most. They conclude that there is strong evidence that working with dreams in therapy is beneficial but that more research is needed to determine the effective components. The next few chapters explore nightmares. In Chapter 7, Mehmet Yücel Agargün describes these as terrifying REM dreams. He distinguishes between spontaneous nightmares, as opposed to posttraumatic ones, and explores a possible relationship between suicidality and nightmares. In Chapter 8, Raija-Leena Punamäki reviews the effects of trauma on dreaming. She describes posttraumatic nightmares and discusses how other dream parameters—frequency of recall, tendency toward recurring dreams, dreaming about the trauma or not—can predict who will recover better from trauma versus who goes on to experience long-lasting posttraumatic stress disorder (PTSD). In Chapter 9, Tore Nielsen and Jessica Lara-Carrasco suggest that dreaming serves an emotional regulation function and that nightmares are expressions of this function. They propose several possible mechanisms that may be central to emotion regulation during dreaming, especially during nightmares, including desomatization, contextualization, progressive emotional problem-solving, and fear memory extinction.

The last two chapters of Volume 2 are devoted to special types of dreams. In Chapter 10, Stanley Krippner describes reports of strange, extraordinary, and unexplained experiences related to dreams, which have fascinated people throughout the millennia. He gives examples of beliefs in dream precognition and divine guidance in Ancient Egypt Assyrian, Babylonian, and Sumerian cultures, follows these beliefs through Tibetan Buddhist, Hindu, and Native American traditions, and then reviews modern parapsychology research on dreaming. In Chapter 11, Stephen LaBerge reviews the research on "lucid dreaming"—dreams in which the dreamer realizes that they are dreaming. He describes the first volitional signaling by eye movements from a lucid dream, which established that they were indeed occurring in REM, and he reviews the research on characteristics of REM that make lucidity more or less likely, as well as intentional strategies to elicit the state.

Volume 3 presents cultural and theoretical perspectives on dreaming. This includes the perspectives of disciplines quite distinct from psychology. It also covers new psychological theories—many of which arise from the new field of evolutionary psychology. It begins with a look at the perspectives of ethnography, religion, and literature. In Chapter 1, Carol Schreier Rupprecht suggests that dreaming is the earliest form of human creativity and that literature made its first appearance when dreams went from being narrated orally to being written down. In Chapter 2, Roger Ivar Lohmann describes how ethnography views dream content, interpretation, and use in terms of cultural values, categories, expectations, and social conventions. In Chapter 3, Kelly Bulkeley surveys the role of dreams in Christianity, Islam, Buddhism, Judaism, Hinduism, and the local spiritualities of Africa, Oceania, and the Americas. He then presents his own research on dreams that the dreamer identifies as a mystical or religious experience. He concludes that mystical dreams may serve as "spirit simulations," provoking greater awareness of nonhuman beings and powers with whom humans may form beneficial relationships.

The next several chapters present different functional and evolutionary theories of dreaming. In Chapter 4, Katja Valli and Antti Revonsuo suggest that the function of dreams is "threat simulation" and perhaps simulation of other categories of events linked to survival. In Chapter 5, Patrick McNamara, Erica Harris, and Anna Kookoolis propose that REM and dreaming are best explained by the evolutionary concept of "costly signaling." While most characteristics and behaviors are adaptive, some are ironically selected exactly because they handicap the individual—indicating a robustness of all other survival mechanisms. Dreams and the sharing of dreams with others may involve emotional signaling. Chapter 6 by Deirdre Barrett posits that dreams are thinking or problem solving in a different biochemical state from that of waking. She reviews research on dreams and problem solving and proposes that specific characteristics of dream mentation are determined by which sensory modalities we must monitor (the need to remain still and quiet during sleep, she suggests), but other aspects of the state seems to be fine-tuned to certain psychological purposes.

In Chapter 7, Robert G. Kunzendorf proposes an alternative to Freud's position that dreams represent wish fulfillment to account for the same symbolic phenomena of dream imagery that Freud described. Kunzendorf's model is a continuum of decreasing symbolism from nocturnal dreaming to normal daydreaming to wakeful self-talk, and also a continuum of decreasing symbolism across individual development as people mature. In Chapter 8, Ernest Hartmann characterizes dreams as hyperconnective compared to waking thought. He says these connections are guided by emotions, which can be identified by identifying the "Central Image" of the dream. In Chapter 9, Jennifer Michelle Windt and Thomas Metzinger trace philosophical perspectives on dream consciousness from Aristotle's *On Dreams* through Descartes' first *Meditation*, Bertrand Russell's *Human Knowledge*, and finally Daniel Dennett's modern musings on dreams. They assert that philosophers' skepticism about dream awareness is more than an armchair exercise of theoretical doubt—that dreaming is a paradigm for questions about consciousness, truth, and reality. In Chapter 10, Alan T. Lloyd critically reviews several evolutionary theories of dreaming and then integrates insights from evolutionary theory with psychoanalytic theory into a fresh and clinically relevant approach to dreams. In Chapter 11, Richard Schweickert applies new mathematical techniques from complexity theory and network theory to social interconnections of characters in and among dreams. He reports that many dreams can be described formally as "small world networks," which are networks that are connected in such a way as to facilitate transfer of optimal amounts of information between nodes in the network. Interestingly, the famous "engine man's dreams" may be an exception to this rule.

Altogether, these essays provide a summary of the contemporary knowledge of dreaming. They integrate cognitive, personality, and clinical issues with physiology and prioritize questions about dreams that we want to answer over the next couple of decades.

We believe that a real science of dreams is now on the agenda and that the essays in these books support this belief.

REFERENCES

Aserinsky, E., & Kleitman, N. (1953). Regularly occurring periods of eye motility, and concomitant phenomena during sleep. *Science, 118*, 273–274.

Fiss, H. (1979). Current dream research: A psychobiological perspective. In B. Wolman (Ed.), *Handbook of dreams* (pp. 20–75). New York: Van Nostrand Reinhold.

Freud, S. (1965). *The interpretation of dreams* (J. Strachey, Trans.). London: Oxford University Press. (Original work published 1900)

Hall, C., & Van de Castle, R. (1966). *The content analysis of dreams.* New York: Appleton-Century-Crofts.

Nielsen, T. (1985). One century of dream research. *ASD Newsletter, 2*(3), 1 and 3.

One

Realistic Simulation and Bizarreness in Dream Content: Past Findings and Suggestions for Future Research

G. William Domhoff

INTRODUCTION

According to age-old stereotypes that are constantly reinforced by breathless stories in the modern mass media, the content of dreams is extremely bizarre, with little apparent rhyme or reason. *Newsweek* began an August, 9, 2004, feature story on "What Dreams Are Made Of" with the following lines:

> In the middle of the night, we are all Fellini—the creator of a parade of fleeting images intended for an audience of one. At times, it's an action flick, with a chase scene that seems endless ... until it dissolves and we're falling, falling, falling into ... is it a field of flowers? And who is the gardener waving at us over there? Could it be our old high-school English teacher? No, it's Jon Stewart. He wants us to sit on the couch right next to him. Are those TV cameras? And what happened to our clothes? (Kantrowitz & Springen, 2004, p. 41)

Two years later, *U.S. News and World Report* used exactly the same headline and offered the same type of fairy-tale lead-in for a special story on dreams:

> Strange images appear from long-forgotten memories. Or out of nowhere: You're roller-skating on water; your mother flashes by on a trapeze; your father is in labor; a friend dead for years sits down at the dinner table. (Szegedy-Maszak, 2006, p. 55)

The popular idea that dreams are mostly strange and other worldly is reinforced by well-known Freudian claims that they are full of disguised impulses and arcane symbolism. Bizarreness is also a dominant theme in one of the most publicly visible dream theories to emerge from the discovery of REM sleep in the 1950s, the activation-synthesis theory advocated by J. Allan Hobson and his coworkers (e.g., Hobson, 2002; Hobson, Pace-Schott, & Stickgold, 2000a, 2000b). For them, however, bizarreness is not due to disguise or symbolism but is simply the reaction of an ill-prepared forebrain to allegedly random activation that arises periodically from the brain stem due to the onset of REM sleep.

Although Freudians and activation-synthesis theorists are at opposite poles when it comes to the degree of meaning and sophisticated thinking said to present in dreams, they both believe the dreaming brain is in a highly emotional and psychotic state—schizophrenia for the Freudians (Solms & Turnbull, 2002) and delirium for the activation-synthesis theorists, an organic brain disease that is characterized by disorientation, illogical cognition, distracted attention, unstable emotion, and dull intellectual functions (Hobson, 2002, p. 23; Kahn & Hobson, 2005a, p. 436). However, activation-synthesis theory then allows for the possibility that the forebrain can draw on thought patterns and memories developed in the waking state to impose at least some degree of coherence on these unexpected stimuli, which means that dreams can provide psychological information about the dreamer. All in all, however, dreaming is said to be "cognitive trash" (Hobson, 2002, p. 23).

But are dreams really as bizarre and emotional as they are made out to be by the mass media and rival dream theorists? And could future research adjudicate the disagreements between the Freudians and activation-synthesis theorists about the degree to which bizarreness is the product of figurative thinking or simply the result of cognitive defects? Drawing on a wide range of studies in both laboratory and nonlaboratory settings, this chapter shows that dreams are far more coherent, patterned, and thoughtful than is suggested by the usual image. Instead, they are by and large a realistic simulation of waking life. At the same time, this chapter shows that there are aspects of dream content that are unusual and perhaps nonsensical. But it then cautions that any claims about the bizarreness of dreams must be made on the basis of comparisons with relaxed waking thought because it, too, is subject to sudden shifts in topics, the intrusion of irrelevant thoughts and memories, and other "bizarre" features that are often taken for granted (for example, Klinger, 1999; Klinger & Cox, 1987–1988).

With the predominantly realistic nature of most dreams established, this chapter goes on to suggest ways to resolve arguments about the nature of bizarreness in dreams. Specifically, it argues that studies of the unusual elements embedded in lengthy individual dream journals provide the best possible context for finding any plausible figurative meanings that may be produced by the dreaming mind based on "resemblances" (that is, shared "properties") between people, activities, or objects. Elements that still do not make any sense after the careful study of a dream journal can plausibly be chalked up to cognitive breakdowns that reveal the limits of coherent thinking in the dreaming state.

To accomplish its goals, the chapter begins with an overview of major studies of dream content collected through awakenings in sleep laboratories, which have the advantage of being immediately recalled in a controlled setting. These studies reveal that dreams are overwhelmingly about everyday settings, people, activities, and events, with only a relatively small amount of bizarreness. The chapter then proceeds to studies that compare dreams collected in the laboratory and at home from the same participants, which show that there are only minor differences between dreams in the two settings. Then, the chapter turns to large samples of dream reports collected in a systematic fashion from students in university settings. These studies add to the picture by uncovering patterns in dream content based on gender and cross-national comparisons. They also provide normative figures on the degree to which settings are distorted, characters change from one person to another, and feelings of confusion and surprise are experienced.

To provide greater depth to the analysis, the chapter then moves to a consideration of the results from detailed analyses of lengthy dream journals kept by a variety of individuals for their own separate reasons. These studies reveal the consistency of specific dream elements (for example, characters, types of social interactions, and themes) over months, years, and decades, which supports the idea that dreams are coherent and meaningful. Studies of dream journals also contribute to the evidence that dreams are usually not bizarre by showing that many aspects of dream content are continuous with waking conceptions and concerns, with "concerns" defined in a general way that covers wishes, interests, worries, and fears. Moreover, and most importantly in terms of whether unusual elements in dreams have figurative meaning or are just the result of cognitive glitches, the information available to date suggests that some unusual elements in a dream series probably have figurative meaning, but that many others do not. This divided verdict sets the stage for future research projects that go beyond the old dichotomies.

DREAM CONTENT FROM LABORATORY AWAKENINGS

Although there is clear evidence that nonrapid eye movement (NREM) dreams can be similar in content to rapid eye movement (REM) dreams (Antrobus, 1983; Foulkes, 1962; Foulkes & Schmidt, 1983; Herman,

Ellman, & Roffwarg, 1978; Kamiya, 1961; Rechtschaffen, Verdone, & Wheaton, 1963), especially late in the sleep period (Antrobus, Kondo, & Reinsel, 1995; Cicogna, Natale, Occhionero, & Bosinelli, 1998; Fosse, Stickgold, & Hobson, 2004, p. 302), REM dream reports are usually longer, more frequent, and more vivid. This section will therefore focus on the content of dreams reported from REM awakenings, first in adults, then in children and adolescents.

The most comprehensive study of adult REM dream content in the sleep laboratory is based on 635 dream reports collected "for a variety of experimental purposes" in a series of investigations over a period of seven years between 1960 and 1967 (Snyder, 1970, p. 127; Snyder, Karacan, Tharp, & Scott, 1968) The 58 young adult men and women who participated in these studies were awakened on 250 nights in two different laboratories, one at the National Institute of Mental Health in Bethesda, the other at the Downstate Medical Center in Brooklyn. Owing to the varying purposes of the original investigations, some participants were simply asked to report anything they remembered upon awakening. Others were questioned in detail about what they recalled, a procedure that tended to produce longer dream reports. Still others, 20 male students taking part in an investigation of the sequence of dream emotions, were questioned at each awakening for details about any emotional accompaniments of the dream.

The investigators defined a dream report by specifying that "the subject's words must clearly convey an experience of complex and organized perceptual imagery," which also must have "undergone some temporal process or change" (Snyder, 1970, p. 129). They thereby excluded the isolated visual images, fragmented auditory recall, and thoughts that are also part of the more general category of sleep mentation. Based on this definition, 75% of the awakenings led to dream recall. The reports were divided into short (less than 150 words), medium (150–300 words), and long (over 300 words) sets as a control for length.

Although there were some small differences because of word length, the overall finding was that "dreaming consciousness" is "a remarkably faithful replica of waking life" (Snyder, 1970, p. 133). For example, 38 percent of the settings were familiar to the dreamers, and another 43 percent were similar to places they knew (the remaining 19 percent of reports, most of them of short length, did not mention a setting). Of the identified settings, only 5 percent were "exotic," in the sense of highly unusual or out of the ordinary, and less than 1 percent were "fantastic," in the sense of unrealistic (Snyder, 1970, p. 134). Ninety-five percent of the dreams contained at least one other character in addition to the dreamer. The most frequent activity was talking, which appeared in 86 percent of the medium-length reports and 100 percent of the long reports. By contrast, "active exertion" (for example, running, playing a sport, fighting) occurred in only 15–20 percent. Using a conservative standard to guard against imputing any emotions to the dreamers, specific emotions were judged to be present in only 30–35 percent of the reports, with unpleasant emotions outnumbering pleasant ones by two to one. Anxiety and anger were the most frequent types of emotions; erotic feelings occurred in only 8 of the 635 reports (1.3 percent) (Snyder, 1970. p. 141).

The investigators made a series of ratings for coherence (does the narrative hold together as a story), dramatic quality (are the events outside the ordinary gamut of waking life), credibility (are the events conceivable, even if unlikely), and bizarreness (are any events "outside the conceivable expectations of waking life"). They found that 60–80 percent of dream reports were highly coherent on a three-point scale compared with less than 5 percent that were rated as low on coherence. Three-fourths had a "nil" or "low" degree of drama on a four-point scale, and less than 10 percent were high on drama. Fully 65 percent of the dream reports were rated as highly credible, and another 25 percent as of medium credibility; about 8 percent were rated as low on credibility and 2 percent as having no credibility. In keeping with the findings on credibility, the dreams were rated as having a low degree of bizarreness. Focusing here on the longest reports because they were more frequently rated as bizarre, 50 percent were rated as having no bizarreness, 30 percent as having a low degree, 8 percent as having a medium degree, and 2 percent as having a high degree of bizarreness (Snyder, 1970, p. 145–146).

The researchers also made a search for "typical" dreams, which are defined by certain common themes that many people report they have experienced in response to questionnaires. The themes in most typical dreams readily fit into the characterization of dreams as "bizarre," such as appearing partially dressed or naked in public (with feelings of great embarrassment), suddenly losing teeth, flying under one's own power, or falling through space. At the same time, other typical dream themes are more realistic, such as failing an examination or finding money. The investigators discovered that the more bizarre types of typical dreams were not very frequent in their sample. For example, only ten mentioned any degree of nudity, none of which included any embarrassment. The loss of teeth occurred in three dreams, while flying and falling made one appearance each (Snyder, 1970, p. 148). Even the more realistic types of typical dreams were rare: eleven dreams related to examinations, none of which involved failure, and one dream included the finding of money.

Based on their wide range of findings, the authors conclude that adult dreams are very different from what is commonly believed. They characterize a prototypical REM dream report as a "clear, coherent, and detailed account of a realistic situation involving the dreamer and other people caught up in very ordinary activities and preoccupations, and usually talking about them" (Snyder, 1970, p. 148). Overall, they believe that as many as "90% would have been considered credible descriptions of everyday experience" (Snyder et al., 1968, p. 375).

BIZARRENESS IN LABORATORY DREAM REPORTS

The unexpected lack of highly unusual dream content in REM reports was investigated in more detail in a study of sixteen young adult women who spent two consecutive nights each in the lab and answered questions about the familiarity and likelihood of specific dream elements after an average of four REM awakenings per night (Dorus, Dorus, & Rechtschaffen, 1971). First, the contents of dreams were categorized as (1) physical surroundings (settings and objects), (2) characters (humans, animals, and creatures), (3) activities (physical, expressive, verbal, and cognitive), or (4) social interactions (aggressive, friendly, and sexual). Next, each type of element was placed in one of six categories for types of "novelty." Three of these categories ranged from the exact replication of the dreamers' reality to large but plausible differences from their waking experience; the other three categories ranged from previously unexperienced but realistic elements to elements that were fantastic or improbable.

The investigators concluded that their results "emphasize the rarity of the bizarre in dreams" because major distortions of actual waking experiences reach a high of only 16.7 percent of all the activities and social interactions and a high of 6.2 percent and 7.8 percent for all characters and physical surroundings (Dorus et al., 1971, p. 367). The figures for the most improbable category of event never experienced by the dreamer in waking life were 4.9 percent of all physical surroundings, 1.3 percent of all characters, and 6.8 percent of all activities and social interactions. When they carried out global ratings of each dream for overall novelty, the investigators found that 25.8 percent showed large but plausible differences from previous waking experiences and that 8.9 percent were highly improbable by waking standards.

As one part of a comprehensive laboratory investigation of dream content in Switzerland, based on 500 REM dream reports from forty-four participants (twenty-six women, eighteen men) who spent 161 nights in the laboratory, Strauch and Meier (1996) examined a subsample of 117 dreams with a variety of bizarreness scales. They report that they "collected only very few dreams in which coherent thought and experience were entirely lacking, which remained totally unintelligible, or were even seemingly disturbed"

(Strauch & Meier, 1996, p. 103). They found that unusual dream content, ranging from mild violations of social or cultural standards to improbable-to-eccentric actions by characters, were more than twice as frequent as bizarreness in dream structure, such as sudden appearances or disappearances or sudden scene changes. There were no bizarre elements of any kind in 23.9 percent of the reports and only one bizarre element in another 39.3 percent.

Rather clearly, then, there is some bizarreness in adult dreams, but far less than might be expected based on the claims by the mass media, Freudians, and activation-synthesis theorists.

EMOTIONS IN LABORATORY DREAMS

The issue of emotionality in dreams initially addressed in the Bethesda/Brooklyn study was investigated in great depth in the sleep lab in three different studies. In the first, seventeen young adults (nine women, eight men) were questioned in detail after each awakening as to the presence of emotions and the appropriateness of the emotion to the content over two nonconsecutive nights, with a mean of six REM awakenings per participant (Foulkes, Sullivan, Kerr, & Brown, 1988). Drawing on ratings by both participants and naïve judges, it was concluded that about 70 percent of the dream reports had at least some affect, a much higher figure than in the Bethesda/Brooklyn study, but one that is supported in the later studies of REM reports to be discussed in the next two paragraphs. The type of emotion, or lack thereof, was appropriate to the dream situation in 60 percent of the dreams. However, there was no emotion in 17 percent of the cases where there would have been some in a similar waking situation, and the presence of dream emotion in 3.2 percent where there would have been none in waking life. The investigators concluded that emotions are generally appropriate in dreams, with the major anomaly being the absence of emotion when it would have been present in waking life.

In a Swiss study by Strauch and Meier (1996) that was discussed in the previous subsection, participants were asked after each awakening how they felt during the dream and how intense their feelings were. Based on all 500 REM dream reports, they found that 26.4 percent of the dream reports had no emotions, 23.4 percent had general mood states, and 50.2 percent had specific emotions. Overall, a variety of negative emotions appeared twice as often as positive ones, with the intensity of the emotions in a middle range, that is, rarely extremely mild or extremely intense. By and large, the participants "registered the same emotional reactions that they would have had while awake and facing a similar situation," but some dreams lacked the emotional involvement that would have been part of the same experience in waking life (Strauch & Meier, 1996, p. 95). Based on the significant number of dreams without emotions in them, they concluded "the interesting observation that many dreams did not cause emotional reactions stands in contrast to a conception that emotions are crucial to the dream experience" (Strauch & Meier, 1996, p. 95).

A third study that focused exclusively on the issue of emotions reported findings similar to those in the first two studies. Using REM reports from nine Norwegian participants (seven women, two men) whose sleep stages were monitored in their homes with a portable polysomonographic machine, it was discovered that 26 percent of the reports had no emotional elements, which is almost exactly the same as the findings in the two laboratory studies just cited (Fosse, Stickgold, & Hobson, 2001). Moreover, emotion was rated as "low" in 18 percent and "medium" in 28 percent of the remaining dreams in this study, leaving only 28 percent of the dream reports in this study with "high" emotional content.

The finding in these three studies that emotions are absent from about one-fourth of all REM dream reports, and that sometimes there are no emotions where they would have been present in waking life, does not support the general claims about emotionality in dreams by Freudians and activation-synthesis theorists; nor does the distribution of emotional intensity fit with their assumptions.

LABORATORY STUDIES OF CHILDREN'S DREAMS

The findings from REM awakenings with children and young adolescents reveal their dreams to be even less bizarre and emotional than those of adults, as first shown in longitudinal laboratory study of children between the ages of 3 and 15, supplemented by a cross-sectional laboratory replication a few years later with children between the ages of 5 and 8 (Foulkes, 1982; Foulkes, Hollifield, Sullivan, Bradley, & Terry, 1990). A 5-year longitudinal laboratory study of Swiss children ages 9–15 replicated these findings and added new insights as well (Strauch, 2003, 2005).

The original longitudinal study involved two groups of children who slept in the laboratory every other year for nine nonconsecutive nights over a 5-year period. The first group was between 3 and 4 years of age when the study started. The second group was between 9 and 10. The study began with a total of 30 children in the two groups; six boys ages 11 to 12 were added at the start of the third year, and seven girls ages 7 to 8 were added at the start of the fifth year. In all, 46 children were studied—26 for all five years, 34 for at least three years, and 43 for at least one complete year. The investigator made 2,711 awakenings over the 5-year period.

The first unexpected finding was the low amount of recall from REM periods in the 3- to 5-year-olds (only 27 percent of the REM awakenings yielded any recall that could reasonably be called a dream), along with the static, bland, and underdeveloped content of the few reports that were obtained. The reports became more "dreamlike" (in terms of characters, themes, and actions) in the 5- to 7-year-olds, but it was not until the children were 11 to 13 years old that their dreams began to resemble those of adult laboratory participants in frequency, length, emotions, and overall structure, or began to show any relationship to personality (Foulkes, 1982, p. 217).

The cross-sectional replication study focused on 10 boys and 10 girls within one month of their fifth, sixth, seventh, and eighth birthdays because the most dramatic changes in the longitudinal study seemed to occur during this age period. These 80 children were awakened 10 times each over a period of three nonconsecutive nights for a total of 800 awakenings. All of the main original findings were supported. The median rate of reporting was only 20 percent for all age groups. The imagery in the dreams was more static than dynamic until age seven, and the child's "self" character did not tend to take an active role in the dreams until age eight (Foulkes et al., 1990). There were very few aggressive interactions, negative emotions, misfortunes, or failures; friendly interactions were few in number as well (Domhoff, 1996, p. 94).

The longitudinal study of Swiss children between the ages of nine and fifteen involved twelve boys and twelve girls who slept in the laboratory for three nonconsecutive nights every other year and provided a total of 551 REM reports. The results were generally similar to those for preadolescents and adolescents in the American longitudinal study. In addition, rating scales for self-involvement, the inclusion of speech, and the inventiveness of the dream structure showed increases over time, supporting Foulkes's (1982, 1999) conclusion that there are subtle changes in dreaming cognition in adolescence. Only 13–14 percent of the dreams were accompanied by emotions or feelings of well-being in the first year of the study. The figures were 15 percent for boys and 25 percent for girls by age 13–15, which is well less than half of what was found with adults in the same laboratory setting (Strauch, 2005, p. 161, Table 4). In terms of content, most of the dreams concerned a variety of everyday situations, such as playing sports (20 percent), moving from one place to another (20 percent), being around home (20 percent), and being involved in interesting activities—not classroom work—at school (10 percent). However, 10 percent were adventure stories that included unlikely encounters with robbers, ghosts, or movie heroes.

The dreams were also rated on a scale that ranged from the realistic to the inventive to the unrealistic. "Inventive" was defined as the combination of familiar waking experiences in an unusual, creative manner. "Unrealistic" elements, which were also called "bizarre" or "unlikely," were defined by a lack of any relation to the waking world. In terms of these categories, 39–41 percent of the dream reports were realistic at all three age levels, which was essentially the same as the 37 percent of realistic dream reports found with the young adult control group. Inventive dream reports rose from 29 percent to 44 percent over the 5-year period, just below the 50 percent level for the control group. Unrealistic/bizarre dreams declined from 31 percent to 15 percent, with the latter figure similar to the 13 percent of unrealistic dream reports for the young adult group (Strauch, 2005, p. 162, Figure 2). Several of the unrealistic dream elements occurred within the context of otherwise everyday situations, such as when a soccer game was being playing with balls of many different colors. But others were completely unrealistic, as when an 11-year-old boy reported from the third REM period that rats were riding on birds in the underground sewer system (Strauch, 2005, p. 162).

In summary, the most comprehensive and detailed descriptive laboratory studies of REM reports from both children and adults provide strong evidence that dreaming is far less bizarre than is generally claimed. However, it might be argued that REM dream reports are not a good sample of dream life, which is what Hobson and his coworkers (2000b) have done in downplaying the results of laboratory dream studies in general. It, therefore, is necessary to look at studies comparing laboratory and home dreams before turning to the findings from the many thousands of dream reports collected outside the laboratory setting.

LABORATORY AND HOME DREAM COMPARISONS

There are several plausible reasons why REM dream reports might be different from those collected via morning recall in a home setting. They include the possible inhibitory effect of the laboratory setting, differences in the method of reporting in the two settings (spoken versus written), and selective recall at home (forgetting small details or highlighting emotionally salient and bizarre elements). However, despite early claims to the contrary (Domhoff & Kamiya, 1964), several later studies of laboratory and home dreams from the same participants demonstrate that there are not many differences in favor of home dreams, even when there are no controls for the possibility of selective memory for more emotional and bizarre dreams at home (Domhoff & Schneider, 1999; Hall, 1966; Heynick & deJong, 1985; Hunt, Ogilvie, Belicki, Belicki, & Atalick, 1982; Strauch & Meier, 1996; Zepelin, 1972). Furthermore, most of these differences disappear when the proper controls are introduced (Foulkes, 1979; Weisz & Foulkes, 1970). The one regular difference between the two types of reports seems to be in the realm of hostile and aggressive dream elements, which occur more frequently in the home dream reports of young adults in three different studies (Domhoff & Kamiya, 1964; Domhoff & Schneider, 1999; Weisz & Foulkes, 1970).

These general conclusions are demonstrated in a reanalysis of the large and detailed comparison of lab and home reports by Hall (1966), based on transcribed laboratory reports and written home reports. Using the corrections for dream length based on percentages and rates that are built into the Hall and Van de Castle (1966) content indicators for twenty-one categories of dream content, the reanalysis found there were only four statistically significant differences between 120 home dreams and 272 lab dreams from eight young adult males who recalled at least thirty-four lab dreams and fifteen home dreams. The percentage of characters that were animals was higher in the home dreams, as were three aggression indicators (Domhoff & Schneider, 1999). Most notably in terms of bizarreness, there were no differences in this study in the percentage of dreams with at least one bizarre element using an "unrealistic elements" scale that has categories for (1) unusual activities, (2) unusual occurrences, (3) distorted objects or arrangements of objects, and (4) metamorphoses of the dreamer, other characters, or objects (Domhoff, 1996, p. 278; Hall, 1966, p. 40). Overall, only 10.4 percent of the 815 dreams had at least one unrealistic element. This result was later replicated in a Canadian laboratory (Hunt et al., 1982).

The higher frequency of aggression in home dream reports in the reanalysis of Hall's study supports the concern that there is some selective recall in everyday dream reports, but it is noteworthy that 44 percent of the dreams did not contain any form of aggression, whether physical or nonphysical, and 72 percent were without any physical aggression. Moreover, aggressive interactions, many of which simply involve hostile thoughts, criticisms, and rejections, are not what Freudians and activation-synthesis theorists have in mind when they characterize dream content as bizarre. It, therefore, seems reasonable to use the results of content studies of home-reported dreams as a further guide to the general nature of dream content.

FINDINGS FROM OUTSIDE THE LABORATORY SETTING

As might be expected from the results of the laboratory versus home comparisons, studies of large samples of dream content collected from young college-educated adults outside the laboratory show many similarities with the laboratory results when the same or comparable content categories are employed.

The general flavor of these findings can be seen in a study of German college students that used 246 reports from ninety-eight women and ninety-five reports from thirty-seven men that were collected in the mid-1990s (Domhoff, Meyer-Gomes, & Schredl, 2005–2006). They were coded for at least one instance of several simple categories developed in order to determine the degree to which the dreams involve people and activities from everyday life. There were four categories for familiar characters: (1) parents or siblings; (2) spouses, boyfriends, or girlfriends; (3) other family members; and (4) friends. There were five categories for commonplace leisure activities: (1) traveling or vacationing; (2) watching or playing sports; (3) going to parties, cafes, or bars; (4) watching entertainers or shows; and (5) shopping. There also was a single category for involvement in work, school, or politics. The everyday nature of most of these dreams is seen in the fact that 75.2 percent of the women's dreams and 62.1 percent of the men's have at least one instance of one of the four categories of familiar characters. Similarly, 42.3 percent of the women's dreams and 27.4 percent of the men's have at least one instance from one of the five leisure-time categories. The routine matters of work, school, or politics appear in 20.3 percent of the women's dreams and 29.5 percent of the men's dreams. Overall, only 12.6 percent of the women's dreams and 20.0 percent of the men's have no instance of any of the above categories. Compared to women, the men's dreams are less likely to have familiar characters and familiar leisure time activities and are more likely to have instances of school/work/politics. However, the important point for purposes of this chapter is that only a minority of dreams from either gender involves unknown characters or activities that are out of the ordinary.

The most systematic research on large samples of dreams from college students has been performed using the Hall and Van de Castle (1966) coding system, which has 10 general categories that cover everything from characters to types of activities to emotions to such descriptive elements as intensity, size, and temperature. Since the results with this coding system are fairly well known and readily accessible, they can be presented in relatively brief compass here, with a focus on how they relate to the issues of coherence, bizarreness, and emotionality in dreams (Domhoff, 1996).

First, Hall and Van de Castle's (1966) normative study, based on 500 dreams from 100 predominantly white middle-class women and 500 dreams from 100 men of the same demographic at two universities in Cleveland between 1949 and 1951, uncovered gender similarities and differences that are similar to gender similarities and differences in waking life; this is evidence for the patterned nature of dream content. For instance, there is a higher percentage of physical aggressions in men's dreams and a higher percentage of rejections and exclusions in women's dreams, which parallels the waking finding that boys engage in more physical aggression than girls and that girls are more likely to engage in "social aggression"—exclusion, rejection, and criticism (Underwood, 2003).

At the same time, the normative results also reveal that dreams are not a perfect simulation of everyday life. For example, 7 percent of the familiar settings in men's dreams and 14 percent of the familiar settings in women's dreams are in some way different from the way they actually are in waking life, and almost 2 percent of the characters are dead, imaginary, or turn into another character for both men and women. It is also noteworthy that about one-third of all dream reports contain "misfortunes" that range from being lost to illness to the death of a loved one, and that the negative emotions of sadness, anger, confusion, and apprehension, when taken as a whole, greatly outnumber the expression of happiness. More generally, when the number of dreams with at least one aggression, misfortune, failure, or negative emotion is totaled, 80 percent of men's dreams and 77 percent of women's have at least one of these negative elements. On the other hand, only 53 percent of dreams for both men and women have at least one of several positive elements, such as friendly interactions, good fortune, success, and happiness. Results such as these show that dreams are not a complete replica of waking life.

The discovery that 11.6 percent of the men's dreams and 13.4 percent of the women's dreams contain at least one instance of confusion, surprise, puzzlement, or uncertainty is of special interest for the purposes of this chapter because this feeling is "generally produced either through confrontation with some unexpected event or else through inability to choose between available alternatives" (Hall & Van de Castle, 1966, p. 112). The following example from the male norms shows that the feeling of confusion might be a useful marker in analyzing bizarreness in dreams:

> I was at a birthday party, and present were, as I remember, my girlfriend, my brother, and my sister-in-law. They sang "Happy Birthday" to me. There was a huge, decorated birthday cake in the center of the table. Every time I counted the candles on the cake they increased in number. Amazed at this, I was told that when one reaches 21, the rest of his life passes quickly, and I shouldn't be surprised at this at all. Even in the dream this did not make sense to me but worried me intensely.

The normative gender findings were replicated for men and women at the University of Richmond in 1981, for women at the University of California, Berkeley, in 1985, for women at Salem College in the late 1980s, and for women at the University of California, Santa Cruz, in the early

1990s (Domhoff, 1996; Dudley & Swank, 1990; Hall, Domhoff, Blick, & Weesner, 1982; Tonay, 1990/1991). Generally speaking, then, there is reason to believe that there was little or no change in the dream life of American college students over a 45-year period, which speaks to the regularity of dream content.

The results with American college students also are broadly similar to what has been reported in investigations of young Canadian, Dutch, Swiss, and German college-educated adults, although there are fewer physical aggressions in the dreams of the Dutch and Swiss samples (Lortie-Lussier, Simond, Rinfret, & De Koninck, 1992; Rinfret, Lortie-Lussier, & de Koninck, 1991; Schredl, Petra, Bishop, Golitz, & Buschtons, 2003; Waterman, Dejong, & Magdelijns, 1988). Dream content is also more similar than different for college students in two large industrialized societies outside of Europe and North America—India and Japan (Bose, 1983; Prasad, 1982; Yamanaka, Morita, & Matsumoto, 1982). These and other findings with dreams from other cultures, including small indigenous cultures, add a cross-cultural component to the claim that dreams have a patterned nature, with a tendency to focus on personal concerns (Domhoff, 1996, Chapter 6).

Typical dreams have been studied in large samples outside the laboratory, where they turn out to be as rare as they are in the laboratory. An analysis of 983 dream reports from two-week journals provided by 126 students at the University of California, Santa Cruz, revealed that virtually none of ten typical dreams occurred more than a few times. For example, there were only five flying dreams in the two-week sample, 0.5 percent of the total, which is of special interest because activation-synthesis theorists believe that flying is prevalent in dreams because the vestibular system is reactivated during REM sleep (Hobson & McCarley, 1977). The figures for several other typical dreams were even lower. Two people dreamed of finding money, two became lost, two were taking an examination, one lost his teeth, and one fell (Domhoff, 1996, p. 198). A study based on 1,910 dream reports from students at the University of North Carolina, Chapel Hill, reported a similar low figure for flying dreams; seventeen participants reported twenty-two flying dreams, 1.2 percent of the total dream report sample (Barrett, 1991).

EMOTIONS IN HOME-REPORTED DREAMS

People tend to attribute many more emotions to their home dreams than they do when they are awakened in the laboratory and asked about the emotions they experienced during the dream. They also find more emotions than do blind judges when they are asked to rate their dream reports line-by-line, after the reports are written out. In these studies, the possible emotions that might appear are listed in separate columns that are to be marked if they are deemed appropriate (Kahn & Hobson, 2002; Kahn, Pace-Schott, & Hobson, 2002; Merritt, Stickgold, Pace-Schott, Williams, & Hobson, 1994). However, based on the laboratory finding that only about 70–75 percent of dream reports have any emotion in them, it is an open question in need of further study as to whether or not this greater amount of emotions in self-ratings of home dream reports is an actual finding or the result of two confounding factors: the demand characteristics of such a rating task and the waking-life assumption that certain emotions would logically be present in many of the situations experienced in the dream. These questions may be especially important where the dreams and ratings were obtained as part of "a graded class exercise," even though students were told that they could obtain dreams from the instructor if they did not remember their dreams (Kahn & Hobson, 2002; Kahn et al., 2002, p. 35).

THINKING IN HOME-REPORTED DREAMS

In addition to the talking, laughing, and smiling that goes on in many dreams, all of which imply that the characters in dreams are thinking, there is also evidence of thinking in a more goal-directed sense, as evidenced by such terms as "contemplate," "decide," "ponder," and "think about:" 13.8 percent of the men's dreams and 21.0 percent of the women's dreams in the Hall and Van de Castle (1966) normative sample contain at least one such thinking element. The figure would be higher if "transient mental activities" such as remembering, forgetting, recognizing, wishing, and feeling sorry were included (Hall & Van de Castle, 1966, p. 90). When talking, expressive behaviors like laughing and crying, and goal-directed thinking are combined, a total of 67.2 percent of the men's dreams and 74.3 percent of the women's dreams have at least one of these three elements.

There is further evidence for the presence of appropriate thinking in dreams when the dreamers themselves go back through their dreams in a line-by-line fashion (Kahn & Hobson, 2005a, 2005b). These studies show that the dreamers are often aware of how they feel toward other characters and how the characters feel about them, which suggests that the ability to understand that others have thoughts and feelings ("theory of mind") remains intact during dreaming (Kahn & Hobson, 2005b). Although these results may overstate the degree of thinking and feeling that is going on during dreaming, because of the same potential demand characteristics and after-the-fact reasoning that raise questions about similar studies asking participants to judge their own emotions in dreams, they do show that dreams can be as thoughtful and subtle as waking thought.

BIZARRENESS IN HOME-REPORTED DREAMS

As noted earlier, less than 10 percent of both REM and home dreams have bizarre elements when the focus is on highly unusual or clearly impossible events (Dorus et al., 1971; Hall, 1966; Snyder, 1970). However, when mildly unusual contents and "features" like sudden scene changes, unusual juxtapositions of images, uncertainties, confusion, and small distortions are added to the picture, the figure rises to between 40 and 60 percent in home-reported dreams (for example, Revonsuo & Salmivalli, 1995; Rittenhouse, Stickgold, & Hobson, 1994).

Abrupt scene changes are the most frequent of these bizarre features, occurring in 34 percent of 200 dreams in one study (Rittenhouse et al., 1994). However, not all studies agree that there are frequent discontinuities within dream reports. In a detailed study of this issue, Foulkes and Schmidt (1983) divided REM dream reports into a series of "temporal units," defined by the appearance of a new activity in the dream, such as the sequence of "coming out of school/opening the gate/children saying goodbye to each other/walking down the street." They found that only one in eight temporal transitions was accompanied by a discontinuity in both setting and characters. They argue that the relatively small discontinuities in dreams are consistent with, and probably necessary for, the considerable degree of narrative and thematic development that is found in most REM reports.

Whatever the exact number of abrupt scene changes and other unusual features within dreams, it is not obvious that these and other unusual events in dreams are inherently bizarre if they are compared to either the stories people are familiar with in waking life or with their waking thought flow. That is, bizarre dream events that could not happen in reality do occur in many of the stories, fairy tales, and videos that everyone experiences from preschool onwards. Metamorphoses and blended characters, for instance, are standard features of imaginative productions. So, too, are animals that talk and sudden changes in settings.

Even everyday waking thought has more of the features that Freudians and activation-synthesis theorists see as unique to dreams. For example, in a study comparing REM reports to waking streams of thought from the same participants sitting in a darkened room, it was found that there were more abrupt scene changes in the waking sample than in the REM reports (Reinsel, Antrobus, & Wollman, 1992). In everyday thought sampling with large numbers of people by means of pagers, about a third of all thoughts are judged by participants as "spontaneous," meaning that they just popped into their minds (Klinger, 1999; Klinger & Cox, 1987–1988). Furthermore,

21 percent of the thoughts analyzed in these studies have aspects that are physically impossible, and many thoughts are judged as disconnected. Importantly, there are also wide individual differences in how much thinking is said to be deliberate or spontaneous. For two-thirds of the participants, the majority of their thoughts are deliberate and intentional, but the majority of their thoughts are spontaneous for the other one-third. In judging the bizarreness of dreams in the future, the proper baseline, therefore, must be the same person's waking thought patterns, as randomly sampled by means of a pager (compare Bednar, 2000, p. 909; Chapman & Underwood, 2000, p. 917).

The most likely difference between dreaming and waking thought concerns the lack of awareness for the unusualness of some events in dreams. In one of the earlier-cited studies of thinking in dreams, the activation-synthesis theorists Kahn and Hobson (2005a, p. 437) conclude that thinking is much like it is in waking, that is, there is "more or less normal cognition," which is quite a concession on their part. But they also stress that the participants in their study mention, when going over the home dream reports they write down, that they sometimes did things in the dreams they would judge as unlikely in their waking life. The authors believe this is evidence for the lack of "metacognition" in dreams, that is, for the absence of an understanding that the person is in bed and "hallucinating." This is in fact a distinctive feature of the dream state, sometimes called the "single-mindedness" of dreams (Rechtschaffen, 1978, 1997). Whether this lack of metacognition is evidence for the psychotic nature of the dreaming state is a question that deserves further examination by dream researchers.

FINDINGS WITH INDIVIDUAL DREAM JOURNALS

Within the context of the many well-established group findings highlighted in previous sections, blind analyses of dream journals kept by individuals for their own reasons—whether personal, intellectual, or artistic—are of great value in assessing the nature of dream content. They have standing as a form of personal document long recognized in psychology as possessing the potential to provide new insights (Allport, 1942; Baldwin, 1942). They are valued as "nonreactive" measures that have not been influenced by the purposes of the investigators who later analyze them. Put another way, they are devoid of the demand characteristics that confound in many types of psychological research, including dream research. The findings with nonreactive archival data such as dream journals are considered most persuasive when they lead to the same conclusion even though the various journals have different types of potential biases because of the differing motivations and purposes of the journal keepers (Webb, Campbell, Schwartz, Sechrest, & Grove, 1981).

CONSISTENCY IN LENGTHY DREAM JOURNALS

Studies of several different dream journals first proved their usefulness for scientific purposes by revealing an unexpected consistency in dream content that stretches from the late teens to old age. Such consistency is further evidence for the coherence and regularity of dream content. People's dream lives vary from day to day and week to week, but consistency in both themes and Hall/Van de Castle coding categories manifests itself through comparisons of hundreds of dream reports and with time spans of months and years (Domhoff, 1996, Chapter 7). The short-term variation in dream content, when combined with the fact that most recalled dreams are soon forgotten, may contribute to the belief that dream contents are unsystematic and bizarre.

The thematic consistency of dreams can be seen in a dream journal kept out of personal interest by an adult woman over a period of 50 years between 1912 and 1962. The themes in the first 600 of her dream reports, some of which might be called unusual or bizarre if not seen in the context of the whole series, remained quite constant. She was eating, preparing to eat, preparing a meal, buying or seeing food, watching someone eat, or mentioning she is hungry in 21 percent of her dreams. The loss of an object, usually her purse, occurred in 17 percent of her dreams. She was in a small or disorderly room, or her room was being invaded by others, in 10 percent of the dreams, and another 10 percent involved the dreamer and her mother. She was trying to go to the toilet in 8 percent, usually being interrupted in the process, and she was late, concerned about being late, or missing a bus or train in 6 percent. These six themes accounted for at least part of the content in almost 75 percent of her dreams. The main exception to this consistency was a decline in the percentage of characters who were identified as men, dropping from 53 percent in the first half of the series to 39 percent when she was in her seventies, living in a women's retirement home and having fewer contacts with men (Domhoff, 1996, pp. 150, 206).

Consistency within an even longer series of dreams can be demonstrated using the statistical tools available on www.dreambank.net, a dream archive that contains over 16,000 dreams in English and 6,000 in German (Schneider & Domhoff, 1999). The Barb Sanders series contains 4,253 dreams over a 20-year period. When the 3,115 dreams Ms. Sanders wrote down before giving her dream journal to dream researchers were compared with the

1,138 she recalled after being aware her dreams would be studied, it was found that at least one of the thirteen main people in her life (parents, ex-husband, three siblings, three children, granddaughter, and three best women friends) appeared in 33.6 percent of the dreams in the first set and in 35.1 percent of the second set. Her interest in theatrical productions as a writer, actor, and producer appeared in 4.9 percent of the dreams in the first set and in 5.2 percent of the dreams in the second set. Using long word strings for each of the five emotions that are coded for in the Hall and Van de Castle coding system, the percentages for the two sets were very similar for emotions in general and for specific categories; the only slight difference was an increase from 15.6 percent to 20.2 percent for dreams with at least one term for happiness (Domhoff & Schneider, 2004).

Three separate studies of discontinuous dream series show that the consistency revealed in continuous dream journals is not the result of practice effects. One was based on dreams provided by the same women when they were young and middle-aged (Lortie-Lussier, Cote, & Vachon, 2000), one compared the dreams of a young man at ages seventeen, twenty-one, and twenty-four (Schneider & Domhoff, 1995), and one compared the dreams from a woman when she was in her twenties and in her sixties (Domhoff, 1996, p. 146).

THE CONTINUITY OF DREAM CONTENT WITH WAKING CONCERNS

Blind analyses of dream journals also show that much dream content is continuous with the dreamers' waking conceptions and concerns, which is further evidence for the coherence and regularity of dreams. The most direct continuities involve the main people in a dreamer's life and the nature of the social interactions with them. There also is good continuity for many of the dreamer's main interests and activities (Domhoff, 1996, Chapter 8). However, this general finding has to be qualified in one important way: the continuity is not with day-to-day events, but with general concerns. Three studies that tried to match detailed waking reports of daily concerns with dream reports (two based on REM awakenings, one based on morning recall at home) found that blind judges could not reliably match records of daily concerns or events with dream content. The content of the dreams often revolved around daily life, such as family, friends, and school, but if the actual events of the day were incorporated in any specific way, it was not understandable to independent raters (Roussy, 2000; Roussy et al., 1996; Roussy et al., 2000). This finding is consistent with studies showing low levels of episodic memory in dreams (Baylor & Cavallero, 2001; Fosse, Fosse, Hobson, & Stickgold, 2003).

The most complete study of a lengthy dream journal is based on the first 3,118 dream reports in the Barb Sanders series discussed in the previous subsection for its evidence of consistency (Domhoff, 2003, pp. 111–133). A blind analysis of social interactions with family members and friends showed that the dream enactments were continuous with her waking thoughts and concerns in terms of the frequency of their appearance and the balance of aggressive and friendly interactions with them. For example, the continuing anger and turmoil the dreamer felt in relation to her ex-husband were expressed in the dreams through repeated negative interactions with him over the first 15 years of the series, many of which dramatized their past waking conflicts. However, there was a significant (but not complete) change in the balance of aggressive and friendly interactions in her dreams at about the time when, according to both the dreamer and her friends, she could think or talk about him in waking life without becoming upset.

To take an example at the other extreme, her dreams over a two-year period involving a man for whom she developed a great infatuation contained at the outset numerous portrayals of sexual interactions. Later on they presented a picture of betrayal and rejection by him. In reality, she had never had anything but a friendly social relationship with this person, who was several years younger, and according to her friends, had no romantic interest in her. This example demonstrates very clearly that continuity is sometimes with waking fantasy, but not waking behavior. She imagined a love affair, and then she imagined that he had rejected her for another woman, but she knew better in waking life.

UNUSUAL ELEMENTS IN LONG DREAM SERIES

However, not all the elements in dreams are continuous with waking conceptions and concerns, and some are highly unusual. It is these anomalous aspects of dream content that may be the products of either figurative thinking or impaired cognitive functioning. Looked at from the perspective of recent thinking on metaphors, some dreams may have the form of proverbs or parables, which can be understood only by extracting generic information from specific stories. Such dreams may rely on "resemblance" metaphors, which depend upon the perception of the common aspects—or "properties"—in two representational schemas (Grady, 1999; Grady, Oakley, & Coulson, 1999). Although the potential number of figurative meanings in any given dream is potentially limitless because so many aspects of the content can be construed as sharing at least some kinds of properties, the likely meanings are greatly constrained by the information that is provided in other dreams in the person's journal. Likely meanings then can be checked by presenting inferences to the dreamer and/or people knowledgeable about the dreamer for confirmation, emendation, or rejection.

Early work by Hall (1953) demonstrated how these constraints could work to produce plausible figurative meanings based on blind analyses of dream series. To take his best example, a young woman had an especially striking dream in which she was searching for her wedding gown because she and her husband were to be married again on their first wedding anniversary. However, she was very disappointed to find the gown was dirty and torn. With tears in her eyes, she put the gown under her arm and went to the church, only to have her husband ask why she had brought the gown. She wrote at the end of her dream report that she was "confused and bewildered and felt strange and alone," which are potential markers of metaphoric bizarreness in dreams (Hall, 1953, p. 179).

Looking at the dream from a figurative point of view, Hall hypothesized that the state of the dress might express her conception of her marriage. That is, the dream may be a conceptual blend based upon a metonymy, with the torn gown standing for an unhappy marriage (Gibbs, 1999). To test this hypothesis, Hall looked to see whether there were other dreams in the series that might suggest the marriage was in difficulty, and there were several: (1) the stone from her engagement ring was missing; (2) her husband had tuberculosis; (3) one of her women friends was going through a divorce; and (4) a friend who was about to be married received a lot of useless bric-a-brac for wedding presents. If the Hall and Van de Castle system had been available when this analysis was made, the case could have been improved by comparing the dreamer's aggressions-per-character ratio with her husband to the same ratio with other adult males. If it were higher with her husband than with other adult males, and if there were a lower rate of friendly interactions as well, then the metaphoric hypothesis would have been supported by means of a nonmetaphoric content analysis. It also would have been useful to ask the dreamer to respond to this inference, but this was not possible because the sample of college students from which this series was drawn used code numbers to report their dreams.

In the Barb Sanders series, where inferences could be checked with the dreamer after the blind analysis was completed, several appearances of cats that were underfed, lost, or deformed do not reflect any waking concerns in regard to her great affection for cats. This discontinuity suggests that this unusual repeated element might be metaphoric in nature, reflecting her painful physical ailments or perhaps her concern for forlorn people (in four other dreams, she refers to lost and lonely men as "stray kittens") (Domhoff, 2003, p. 128). There were also composite characters in her dreams, that is, a blending of two people, that make sense, such as a person who was a composite of the two men she had loved the most in her life, one when she was in high school, the other when she was in her forties. In addition, there were metamorphoses that had plausibility as expressions of issues in the dream narrative, but most of them did not make any figurative sense within the context of the given dream or the series as a whole. If such elements cannot be argued to have figurative meaning even with a deep knowledge of a large number of dreams and considerable information about the dreamer, then by a process of elimination it seems plausible to attribute them to confabulation or some other cognitive breakdown.

DISCUSSION AND CONCLUSION

Taken as a whole, the overall results from laboratory and home studies do not provide evidence for the characterization of dream content as highly emotional, bizarre, and similar in structure and content to schizophrenia or delirium. Contrary to Freud's (1900/1999) claim that the "manifest" content of the dream is rendered confusing and incomprehensible by the efforts of the dream-work, and to Hobson's (2002, p. 23) assertion that dreams are "cognitive trash," dreams are for the most part reasonable simulations of waking life that contain occasional unusual features in the form of distorted settings and objects, highly unusual characters, inexplicable activities, strange images and metamorphoses, and sudden scene shifts (Dorus et al., 1971; Foulkes, 1985; Snyder, 1970).

At the same time, the results of detailed studies of unusual elements in the Barb Sanders series suggest that some of them may well be expressions of figurative thinking, as the Freudians would expect, but that others are more likely due to cognitive defects in the dreaming state, just as activation-synthesis theorists would insist. The conclusion that some unusual elements probably have no figurative meaning is reinforced by the finding that there are more bizarre features in dream mentation at sleep onset, when a transition from waking to a brief dreaming state occurs (Foulkes & Vogel, 1965; Vogel, 1991). In sleep-onset dream reports, there are far more instances of partial images, superimpositions of unrelated images, and completely unrealistic content (Foulkes, 1999, p. 135). Generally speaking, then, if dreaming is viewed as a cognitive achievement of great complexity, it is plausible that the pervasive system of figurative thinking available in waking life may sometimes be operative, but it is equally plausible that some conceptual operations could go wrong, especially in transitional states within sleep or at times of stress or physical illness for the dreamer.

Based on the overall findings presented in this chapter, future studies of the degree to which dreams are psychologically meaningful or bizarre would benefit by starting with the idea that dreams dramatize conceptions and concerns, and that they are generally consistent over time and continuous with waking thoughts. Then the deviations and discrepancies from consistency and continuity could be used to add nuance to the picture. In particular, unusual features and elements in some of the dreams in a dream series should be studied more closely to see whether they have plausible figurative meanings within the constraints provided by the many realistic simulations within the series. If such an analysis fails to find figurative meaning for various types of unusual elements, then the unusual features and elements could be studied to see whether they share common features that can be attributed to one or another type of cognitive defect during dreaming.

REFERENCES

Allport, G. (1942). *The use of personal documents in psychological science*. New York: Social Science Research Council.

Antrobus, J. (1983). REM and NREM sleep reports: Comparisons of word frequencies by cognitive classes. *Psychophysiology, 20*, 562–568.

Antrobus, J., Kondo, T., & Reinsel, R. (1995). Dreaming in the late morning: Summation of REM and diurnal cortical activation. *Consciousness & Cognition, 4*, 275–299.

Baldwin, A. (1942). Personal structure analysis: A statistical method for investigating the single personality. *Journal of Abnormal & Social Psychology, 37*, 163–183.

Barrett, D. (1991). Flying dreams and lucidity: An empirical test of their relationship. *Dreaming, 1*, 129–134.

Baylor, G., & Cavallero, C. (2001). Memory sources associated with REM and NREM dream reports throughout the night: A new look at the data. *Sleep, 24*, 165–170.

Bednar, J. A. (2000). Internally-generated activity, non-episodic memory, and emotional salience in sleep. *Behavioral & Brain Sciences, 23*, 908–909.

Bose, V. S. (1983). *Dream content transformations: An empirical study of Freud's secondary revision hypothesis*. Unpublished manuscript, Andhra University, Andhra, India.

Chapman, P., & Underwood, G. (2000). Mental states during dreaming and daydreaming: Some methodological loopholes. *Behavioral & Brain Sciences, 23*, 917–918.

Cicogna, P., Natale, V., Occhionero, M., & Bosinelli, M. (1998). A comparison of mental activity during sleep onset and morning awakening. *Sleep, 21*, 462–470.

Domhoff, G. W. (1996). *Finding meaning in dreams: A quantitative approach*. New York: Plenum.

Domhoff, G. W. (2003). *The scientific study of dreams: Neural networks, cognitive development, and content analysis*. Washington, DC: American Psychological Association.

Domhoff, G. W., & Kamiya, J. (1964). Problems in dream content study with objective indicators: I. A comparison of home and laboratory dream reports. *Archives of General Psychiatry, 11*, 519–524.

Domhoff, G. W., Meyer-Gomes, K., & Schredl, M. (2005–2006). Dreams as the expression of conceptions and concerns: A comparison of German and American college students. *Imagination, Cognition & Personality, 25*, 269–282.

Domhoff, G. W., & Schneider, A. (1999). Much ado about very little: The small effect sizes when home and laboratory collected dreams are compared. *Dreaming, 9,* 139–151.

Domhoff, G. W., & Schneider, A. (2004, May). *Studying dream content using the search engine and dream archive on dreambank.net.* Paper presented at the meeting of the American Psychological Society, Chicago, Illinois.

Dorus, E., Dorus, W., & Rechtschaffen, A. (1971). The incidence of novelty in dreams. *Archives of General Psychiatry, 25,* 364–368.

Dudley, L., & Swank, M. (1990). A comparison of the dreams of college women in 1950 and 1990. *ASD Newsletter, 7,* 3.

Fosse, M., Fosse, R., Hobson, J. A., & Stickgold, R. (2003). Dreaming and episodic memory: A functional dissociation? *Journal of Cognitive Neuroscience, 15,* 1–9.

Fosse, R., Stickgold, R., & Hobson, J. A. (2001). The mind in REM sleep: Reports of emotional experience. *Sleep, 24,* 947–955.

Fosse, R., Stickgold, R., & Hobson, J. A. (2004). Thinking and hallucinating: Reciprocal changes in sleep. *Psychophysiology, 41,* 298–305.

Foulkes, D. (1962). Dream reports from different states of sleep. *Journal of Abnormal & Social Psychology, 65,* 14–25.

Foulkes, D. (1979). Home and laboratory dreams: Four empirical studies & a conceptual reevaluation. *Sleep, 2,* 233–251.

Foulkes, D. (1982). *Children's dreams.* New York: Wiley.

Foulkes, D. (1985). *Dreaming: A cognitive-psychological analysis.* Hillsdale, NJ: Erlbaum.

Foulkes, D. (1999). *Children's dreaming and the development of consciousness.* Cambridge, MA: Harvard University Press.

Foulkes, D., Hollifield, M., Sullivan, B., Bradley, L., & Terry, R. (1990). REM dreaming and cognitive skills at ages 5–8: A cross-sectional study. *International Journal of Behavioral Development, 13,* 447–465.

Foulkes, D., & Schmidt, M. (1983). Temporal sequence and unit comparison composition in dream reports from different stages of sleep. *Sleep, 6,* 265–280.

Foulkes, D., Sullivan, B., Kerr, N., & Brown, L. (1988). Appropriateness of dream feelings to dreamed situations. *Cognition & Emotion, 2,* 29–39.

Foulkes, D., & Vogel, G. (1965). Mental activity at sleep onset. *Journal of Abnormal Psychology, 70,* 231–243.

Freud, S. (1999). *The interpretation of dreams* (J. Crick, Trans.). London: Oxford University Press. (Original work published 1900)

Gibbs, R. (1999). Speaking and thinking with metonymy. In K. Panther & G. Radden (Eds.), *Metonymy in language and thought* (pp. 61–75). Philadelphia, PA: Benjamins.

Grady, J. (1999). A typology of motivation for conceptual metaphor: Correlation vs. resemblance. In R. Gibbs & G. Steen (Eds.), *Metaphor in cognitive linguistics* (pp. 79–100). Philadelphia, PA: Benjamins.

Grady, J., Oakley, T., & Coulson, S. (1999). Blending and metaphor. In R. Gibbs & G. Steen (Eds.), *Metaphor in cognitive linguistics* (pp. 101–124). Philadelphia, PA: Benjamins.

Hall, C. (1953). A cognitive theory of dream symbols. *Journal of General Psychology, 48,* 169–186.

Hall, C. (1966). *Studies of dreams collected in the laboratory and at home.* Santa Cruz, CA: Institute of Dream Research.

Hall, C., Domhoff, G. W., Blick, K., & Weesner, K. (1982). The dreams of college men and women in 1950 & 1980: A comparison of dream contents and sex differences. *Sleep, 5*, 188–194.

Hall, C., & Van de Castle, R. (1966). *The content analysis of dreams*. New York: Appleton-Century-Crofts.

Herman, J., Ellman, S., & Roffwarg, H. (1978). The problem of NREM dream recall reexamined. In A. Arkin, J. Antrobus, & S. Ellman (Eds.), *The mind in sleep: Psychology and psychophysiology* (pp. 59–62). Hillsdale, NJ: Erlbaum.

Heynick, F., & deJong, M. (1985). Dreams elicited by the telephone: A comparative content analysis. In W. Koella, E. Ruther, & H. Schulz (Eds.), *Sleep '84* (pp. 341–343). New York: Gustav Fischer Verlag.

Hobson, J. A. (2002). *Dreaming: An introduction to the science of sleep*. New York: Oxford University Press.

Hobson, J. A., & McCarley, R. (1977). The brain as a dream state generator: An activation-synthesis hypothesis of the dream process. *American Journal of Psychiatry, 134*, 1335–1348.

Hobson, J. A., Pace-Schott, E. F., & Stickgold, R. (2000a). Dream science 2000: A response to commentaries on dreaming and the brain. *Behavioral & Brain Sciences, 23*, 1019–1034.

Hobson, J. A., Pace-Schott, E. F., & Stickgold, R. (2000b). Dreaming and the brain: Toward a cognitive neuroscience of conscious states. *Behavioral & Brain Sciences, 23*, 793–842.

Hunt, H., Ogilvie, R., Belicki, K., Belicki, D., & Atalick, E. (1982). Forms of dreaming. *Perceptual & Motor Skills, 54*, 559–633.

Kahn, D., & Hobson, J. A. (2002). Stereotypic gender-based emotions are not detectable in dream reports. *Dreaming, 12*, 209–222.

Kahn, D., & Hobson, J. A. (2005a). State-dependent thinking: A comparison of waking and dreaming thought. *Consciousness & Cognition, 14*, 429–438.

Kahn, D., & Hobson, J. A. (2005b). Theory of mind in dreaming: Awareness of feelings and thoughts of others in dreams. *Dreaming, 15*, 48–57.

Kahn, D., Pace-Schott, E., & Hobson, J. A. (2002). Emotion and cognition: Feeling and character identification in dreaming. *Consciousness & Cognition, 11*, 34–50.

Kamiya, J. (1961). Behavioral, subjective, and physiological aspects of drowsiness and sleep. In D. W. Fiske & S. R. Maddi (Eds.), *Functions of varied experience* (pp. 145–174). Homewood, IL: Dorsey.

Kantrowitz, B., & Springen, K. (2004, August 9). What dreams are made of. *Newsweek*, 41–47.

Klinger, E. (1999). Thought flow: Properties and mechanisms underlying shifts in content. In J. Singer & P. Salovey (Eds.), *At play in the fields of consciousness* (pp. 29–50). Hillsdale, NJ: Erlbaum.

Klinger, E., & Cox, W. (1987–1988). Dimensions of thought flow in everyday life. *Imagination, Cognition, and Personality, 7*, 105–128.

Lortie-Lussier, M., Cote, L., & Vachon, J. (2000). The consistency and continuity hypotheses revisited through the dreams of women at two periods of their lives. *Dreaming, 10*, 67–76.

Lortie-Lussier, M., Simond, S., Rinfret, N., & De Koninck, J. (1992). Beyond sex differences: Family and occupational roles' impact on women's and men's dreams. *Sex Roles, 26*, 79–96.

Merritt, J., Stickgold, R., Pace-Schott, E., Williams, J., & Hobson, J. (1994). Emotion profiles in the dreams of men and women. *Consciousness & Cognition, 3*, 46–60.

Prasad, B. (1982). Content analysis of dreams of Indian and American college students: A cultural comparison. *Journal of Indian Psychology, 4*, 54–64.

Rechtschaffen, A. (1978). The single-mindedness and isolation of dreams. *Sleep, 1*, 97–109.

Rechtschaffen, A. (1997). Postscript, 1995: The single-mindedness and isolation of dreams. In M. Myslobodsky (Ed.), *The mythomanias: The nature of deception and self-deception* (pp. 219–223). Mahwah, NJ: Erlbaum.

Rechtschaffen, A., Verdone, P., & Wheaton, J. (1963). Reports of mental activity during sleep. *Canadian Psychiatric Association Journal, 8*, 409–414.

Reinsel, R., Antrobus, J., & Wollman, M. (1992). Bizarreness in dreams and waking fantasy. In J. Antrobus & M. Bertini (Eds.), *The neuropsychology of sleep and dreaming* (pp. 157–184). Hillsdale, NJ: Erlbaum.

Revonsuo, A., & Salmivalli, C. (1995). A content analysis of bizarre elements in dreams. *Dreaming, 5*, 169–187.

Rinfret, N., Lortie-Lussier, M., & de Koninck, J. (1991). The dreams of professional mothers and female students: An exploration of social roles and age impact. *Dreaming, 1*, 179–191.

Rittenhouse, C., Stickgold, R., & Hobson, J. (1994). Constraint on the transformation of characters, objects, and settings in dream reports. *Consciousness & Cognition, 3*, 100–113.

Roussy, F. (2000). Testing the notion of continuity between waking experience and REM dream content. *Dissertation Abstracts International: Section B, 61*(2-B), 1106.

Roussy, F., Brunette, M., Mercier, P., Gonthier, I., Grenier, J., Sirois-Berliss, et al. (2000). Daily events and dream content: Unsuccessful matching attempts. *Dreaming, 10*(2), 77–83.

Roussy, F., Camir, C., Foulkes, D., De Koninck, J., Loftis, M., & Kerr, N. (1996). Does early-night REM dream content reliably reflect presleep state of mind? *Dreaming, 6*, 121–130.

Schneider, A., & Domhoff, G. W. (1995). The quantitative study of dreams. Retrieved January 15, 2007 from http://www.dreamresearch.net.

Schneider, A., & Domhoff, G. W. (1999). DreamBank. Retrieved January 15, 2007 from www.dreambank.net.

Schredl, M., Petra, C., Bishop, A., Golitz, E., & Buschtons, D. (2003). Content analysis of German students' dreams: Comparison to American findings. *Dreaming, 13*, 237–243.

Snyder, F. (1970). The phenomenology of dreaming. In L. Madow & L. Snow (Eds.), *The psychodynamic implications of the physiological studies on dreams* (pp. 124–151). Springfield, IL: Thomas.

Snyder, F., Karacan, I., Tharp, V., & Scott, J. (1968). Phenomenology of REM dreaming. *Psychophysiology, 4*, 375.

Solms, M., & Turnbull, O. (2002). *The brain and the inner world.* New York: Other Press.

Strauch, I. (2003). *Träume im Übergang von der Kindheit ins Jugendalter. Ergebnisse einer Langzeitstudie* [Dreams from childhood to adolescence]. Bern: Huber.

Strauch, I. (2005). REM dreaming in the transition from late childhood to adolescence: A longitudinal study. *Dreaming, 15*, 155–169.

Strauch, I., & Meier, B. (1996). *In search of dreams: Results of experimental dream research*. Albany, NY: State University of New York Press.

Szegedy-Maszak, M. (2006, May 15). What dreams are made of. *U.S. News & World Report*, 55–64.

Tonay, V. (1990/1991). California women and their dreams: A historical and subcultural comparison of dream content. *Imagination, Cognition, & Personality, 10*, 83–97.

Underwood, M. (2003). *Social aggression among girls*. New York: Guilford.

Vogel, G. (1991). Sleep-onset mentation. In S. Ellman & J. Antrobus (Eds.), *The mind in sleep: Psychology & psychophysiology* (2nd ed., pp. 125–136). New York: Wiley & Sons.

Waterman, D., Dejong, M., & Magdelijns, R. (1988). Gender, sex role orientation and dream content. In W. Koella, W. Obai, H. Schaltz, & P. Visser (Eds.), *Sleep '86* (pp. 385–387). New York: Gustav Fischer Verlag.

Webb, E., Campbell, D., Schwartz, R., Sechrest, L., & Grove, J. (1981). *Nonreactive measures in the social sciences* (2nd ed.). Chicago: Rand McNally.

Weisz, R., & Foulkes, D. (1970). Home and laboratory dreams collected under uniform sampling conditions. *Psychophysiology, 6*, 588–596.

Yamanaka, T., Morita, Y., & Matsumoto, J. (1982). Analysis of the dream contents in college students by REM-awakening technique. *Folia Psychiatrica et Neurologica Japonica, 36*, 33–52.

Zepelin, H. (1972, June). *Comparison of dreams recalled in the laboratory and at home*. Paper presented at the Association for the Psychophysiological Study of Sleep, Chicago, Illinois.

Two

Gender Differences in Dreaming

Michael Schredl

INTRODUCTION

Gender differences have been of interest and a topic of heated debates, both for the public and for psychologists as well—see, for example, the special issue of the *American Psychologist* (Buss, 1995; Eagly, 1995; Hyde & Plant, 1995; Marecek, 1995). It is not surprising, therefore, that gender differences in dream recall and dream content have been studied quite extensively. Although several marked differences regarding the dreams of men and women have been found, empirically sound studies aimed at explaining these differences by eliciting the corresponding waking-life data are scarce.

DREAM RECALL

Despite the assumption that dreaming is present during the whole sleep period, everyday dream recall is variable (Schredl, 1999b). On one extreme, there are persons who can remember their dreams almost every morning and, at the other end of the spectrum, some persons state that they do not dream at all. Even within one person, phases with increased or impoverished dream recall occur.

The majority of the studies investigating the gender differences in dream recall are based on questionnaire data, even if there are other sound approaches for measuring dream recall (such as a dream diary or laboratory awakenings). As a retrospective approach, the presentation of a dream frequency scale within a questionnaire has the advantage that the dependent variable (everyday dream recall) is not biased by the measurement; however, problems in remembering the number of mornings with dream recall or the number of dreams per night over the last few weeks might affect the results. By using dream diaries that should be completed by the participants directly upon awakening, recall errors are minimized. On the other hand, several studies have demonstrated that dream recall frequency will increase if the person is focusing on dreams (for comparison, Schredl, 2002a), that is, the variable that should be elicited is markedly affected by the measuring procedure.

For awakenings in a sleep laboratory, large-scaled studies are lacking because of the high expense incurred in carrying out such studies, a fact that does not allow a generalization of lab findings to be made with respect to gender differences. Furthermore, the lab technique has an even more marked effect on dream recall (everyday dream recall is correlated with lab dream recall but is much lower than lab dream recall; for comparison, Schredl, 1999b), and researchers often selected highly motivated subjects for such lab studies in order to maximize the probability of obtaining dream reports upon awakening.

Despite the methodological pros and cons of each measurement technique, the three different methods of eliciting dream recall frequency show moderate-to-high intercorrlations (for example, between the dream recall frequency scale [questionnaire] and dream diary: $r = .557$, $p < .0001$, $N = 285$; Schredl, 2002a). Also, both the questionnaire scales (Schredl, 2004a) as well as the dream diary approaches (Schredl & Fulda, 2005) have high reliability indices.

In Table 2.1, the relevant studies regarding gender differences in dream recall frequency are depicted.

For almost all small to medium studies, effect sizes for the gender differences have been found; for example women recall their dreams more often than men. Only the Austrian study (Stepansky et al., 1998) did not find a gender difference. The other two representative studies (Borbely, 1984; Schredl & Piel, 2003) found small but significant effects, so the only negative finding is difficult to explain. When dream recall frequency was measured with dream diaries, significant gender differences were also reported ($d = 0.16$; $N = 285$; Schredl, 2002a; $d = 0.48$, $N = 444$; Schredl, 2004b); women recorded more dreams than men.

Nielsen, Laberge, Tremblay, Frank, and Montplaisir (1999) reported a marked gender difference in dream recall in adolescents (13 years); for younger children, most findings (for example, Foulkes, 1982; Keßels, 2004) indicated no differences in dream recall between girls and boys. The database for gender differences in children, however, is very small, and large-scaled

TABLE 2.1
Gender Differences in Dream Recall

Authors	Sample Size	Age Range	Effect Size
Heerwagen (1889)	406	Adults	0.53
Wynaendts-Francken (1907)	300	Adults	0.44
Middleton (1942)	277	Students	0.38
Giambra (1979)	1200	17–93 years	0.28
Borbely (1984)	1000	>16 years	0.15[a]
Gruber (1988)	1468	Mean: 19.8 years	0.35
Pagel, Vann & Altomare (1995)	265	Adults	0.34
Giambra, Jung & Grodsky (1996)	2328	17–77 years	0.26
Stepansky et al. (1998)	1000	14–69 years	0.00
Nielsen et al. (1999)	600	13 years	0.50
	600	16 years	0.55
Schredl (2000)	762	18–65 years	0.47
Schredl (2002b)	941	18–93 years	0.33
Schredl & Piel (2003)	5946	>18 years	0.25

[a]Possible underestimation of the effect size because only 2 of 5 categories have been published in the article.

questionnaire surveys are necessary to generalize these findings and to estimate the age that might mark the beginning of gender differences in dream recall.

In view of the stable findings regarding gender differences in dream recall frequency, the question arises as to what variables might explain this difference. Because dream recall frequency is associated with a large variety of factors (for example, personality dimensions like openness to experience, creativity, sleep behavior, and interest in dreams; for an overview, see Schredl & Montasser, 1996/1997), it seem plausible to study variables that themselves show marked gender differences and to investigate whether gender differences in these variables might explain the gender difference in dream recall.

Gender differences have been reported for two variables that are associated with dream recall frequency (for comparison, Schredl, 1999b): sleep quality including the frequency of nocturnal awakenings (for example, Schredl, Schenck, Görtelmeyer, & Heuser, 1998), and interest in dreams/positive attitude toward dreams (Domino, 1982; Schredl, 2004b; Schredl, Nürnberg & Weiler, 1996; $d = 0.64$, $N = 444$). Whereas sleep variables like subjective sleep quality and frequent nocturnal awakenings did not affect the gender difference in dream recall, it vanished if the "engagement in dreams" variable was statistically controlled (Schredl, 2000); for example, the gender difference regarding the frequency with which the person is thinking about her/his dreams ($d = 0.71$; $N = 722$) explained the gender difference in dream recall. This seems plausible since the deliberate focusing on dreams increases dream recall frequency in most people (for example, Cory, Orniston, Simmel, & Dainoff, 1975). It is also possible, however, that a heightened dream recall stimulates interest in dreams (by thinking about the recalled dreams) and leads to a positive attitude towards dreams, so that a causal explanation of the gender difference in dream recall frequency by the "interest" variable is not possible. Other variables like emotional intensity of the dream, emotional tone of the dream, and the time of getting up in the morning did not affect the gender difference in dream recall tested by partialling out these variables and, therefore, are not very promising candidates (Schredl, 2002/2003).

To summarize, there is a solid database showing that women report recalling their dreams more often than men. Up until now, the "engagement in dreams" factor was the only empirically identified factor that had a significant effect on the gender difference in dream recall frequency. More detailed studies in children might shed light on the possibility that gender-specific socialization might determine the gender differences in dream recall in adults.

DREAM CONTENT

The findings presented in this section are based on the methodology of dream content analysis. An extensive description can be found in Schredl (1999a). Because the knowledge of the basics of this method is necessary for interpreting the findings, the methodology of dream content analysis is briefly reviewed. One or more external judges code the dream reports that have been ordered randomly along predefined scales, for example, bizarreness or occurrence of aggression. The judges do not know the gender of the dreamer (for a more detailed description see the section *Gender Differences in Dreams: A Matching Study* in this chapter). One of the advantages of dream content analysis is its satisfactory reliability. If the dream material is coded by different judges, the interrater agreement is often quite good (for comparison, Domhoff, 1996). For some scales, however, it is necessary to train the judges to obtain high reliability indices (Schredl, Burchart, & Grabatin, 2004).

The major problem of dream content analysis is its validity. Schredl and Doll (1998) and Schredl and Erlacher (2003) have demonstrated that external judges underestimated the occurrence of dream emotions as well as bizarre dream elements in comparison with the data reported by the dreamer. These findings are based on the fact that dream reports as the basic unit of analysis in dream content analysis are more or less accurate

TABLE 2.2
Gender Differences in Dream Content

Variable	Men (N = 500), %	Women (N = 500), %
Settings ("outdoor"/"indoor" + "outdoor")	52	39
Proportion of male dream characters	67	48
Proportion of strangers	55	42
Physical aggression/total aggression	50	34
Sexuality	11.6	3.6
Objects[a]		
Household objects	8.1	10.5
Weapons	3.0	0.8
Clothing	5.7	10.2
Explicitly mentioned emotions per dream	0.48	0.70
Number of dream persons per dream	2.2	2.7

Source: Hall & Van de Castle, 1966.
[a]Total number of objects for men (N = 2422) and for women (N = 2659).

descriptions of the dream experience itself. Nevertheless, most content analytic scales showed obvious face validity, for example, for measuring the
occurrence of aggression (for comparison, Schredl, 1999a).

The first dream content analysis of a large sample of dream reports
(N = 1000) that were collected in the years 1948 to 1952 was published
by Hall and Van de Castle (1966). They included five dreams of each of
100 male and 100 female students. The most relevant results are depicted
in Table 2.2.

In men's dreams, outdoor settings are present more often than in wom-
en's dreams. In addition, a higher proportion of male dream characters and
unknown characters and more physical aggression, weapons, and sexuality
were found in men's dreams. In women's dreams, more dream persons,
explicitly mentioned dream emotions, household objects, and clothing
occurred within the dreams.

Several follow-up studies (Domhoff, 1996; Schredl, Sahin, & Schäfer,
1998; Hall, Domhoff, Blick, & Weesher, 1982; Schredl, Cinic, Bishop,
Gölitz, & Buschtöns, 2003) confirmed many of the differences reported by
Hall and Van de Castle (1966). Quite consistent were the difference regarding the proportion of male dream characters, sexuality, and physical aggression (see Table 2.3). The dreams of Sigmund Freud himself (N = 28),
which he published, contained 72 percent male dream characters, a figure
that is typical for males (Hall, 1984).

The results concerning dream emotions have not been confirmed. When
the self-ratings of the dreamers were analyzed, no differences between men

TABLE 2.3
Gender Differences in Dream Content

Variable	Women ($N = 177$)	Men ($N = 69$)	Effect Size	Statistical Test
Dream length	84.9 ± 57.4	91.8 ± 77.8	0.10	$t = 0.7; p = .5068$
Bizarreness	2.47 ± 0.82	2.58 ± 0.86	0.11	$z = 0.8; p = .4284$
Emotional intensity	2.14 ± 1.42	1.91 ± 1.25	−0.14	$z = -1.0; p = .3280$
Proportion of male characters	0.50 ± 0.42	0.66 ± 0.36	0.33	$t = 2.3; p = .0101$
Verbal interactions	59.3	55.1	−0.08	$\chi^2 = 1.4; p = .243$
Physical interactions	11.9	13.0	0.03	$\chi^2 = 0.1; p = .800$
Sexuality	3.4	8.7	0.23	$\chi^2 = 3.0; p = .042$
Physical aggression	5.1	15.9	0.36	$\chi^2 = 7.8; p = .003$

Source: Schredl, Sahin, & Schäfer, 1998.

and women were observed (Schredl, Sahin, & Schäfer, 1998). This might be explained by the restricted validity of measuring dream emotions by external judges (see previous discussion). Similarly, general dream characteristics like dream length (number of words per report), bizarreness, and occurrence of verbal and physical interactions seem not to differ between women and men (see Table 2.3 and the overview in: Schredl, Sahin, & Schäfer, 1998).

Interestingly, the gender differences in dream content are quite stable over time despite the changes that have occurred in society (women's liberation, for example).

About 30 years after their initial study (Hall & Van de Castle, 1966) the authors were able to demonstrate (Hall, Domhoff, Blick, & Weesner, 1982) that most of the gender differences, such as more physical aggression in men and differences in the proportion of male dream characters, were still present. Similarly, a recent study (Schredl et al., 2003) replicated the gender differences found in the 1950s. For so-called typical dream themes, gender differences also remained stable from 1958 to 2002 (Griffith, Miyagi, & Tago, 1958; Nielsen et al., 2003; Schredl et al., 2004). Schredl and Piel (2005) investigated the time course of two gender differences (work-related dreams and dreams of deceased persons) over the time span from 1956 to 2000 (four representative cross-sectional studies, overall $N = 5946$). Although there was an overall increase of work-related dream topics in general over the years, the gender difference in which men reported work-related dreams more often remained stable over the study period. Women reported dreams of deceased persons more often in all four studies.

Another interesting gender difference relates to the gender of dream aggressors in bad dreams of children and adolescents (see Table 2.4).

TABLE 2.4
Human Aggressors in Dreams

Aggressors	Total ($N = 111$), %	Boys ($N = 35$), %	Girls ($N = 76$), %
Male stranger	49.7	51.4	48.7
Female stranger	3.6	0.0	5.3
Male (familiar)	27.8	31.4	26.2
Female (familiar)	18.9	17.2	19.8

Source: Schredl & Pallmer, 1998.

For both genders, girls and boys, strange male characters are the dream aggressors that occur most often, whereas women comprise only about 20 percent of the aggressors (Schredl & Pallmer, 1998). Although specific correlation analyses have not been carried out, the parallel with the fact that the majority of violent crimes in our society are committed by men (Brannon, 1996) seems interesting and plausible.

Interestingly, most gender differences that were reported for adults were also found in children and adolescents. Solely in very young children (3 to 5 years), no gender differences in dream content were detected (Foulkes, 1982); the dream reports in this age group have been very brief. In older age groups, boys dreamt more often about male characters (Foulkes, 1982; Hall & Domhoff, 1963a; reanalysis in Domhoff, 1996; Strauch, 2004; Strauch & Lederbogen, 1999;) and physical aggression (Hall & Domhoff, 1963b; Avila-White, Schneider & Domhoff, 1999) than did girls, although Saline (1999) and Strauch (2004) did not find a higher percentage of physical aggression in boys' dreams. Several studies (Beaudet, 1990; Garfield, 1984; Schredl & Pallmer, 1998) reported that boys dream more often about monsters and wild, large animals than do girls. Strauch (2004), studying 24 children in a longitudinal design over 4 years (mean ages of 10 to 14 years), found that boys were delayed in the development of dream contents, such as frequency of interaction of the dream ego with other dream persons and frequency of talking within the dream, which are characteristic for adults. Strauch (2004) hypothesized that this reflects gender differences in developmental issues in waking life. However, the database for children's dreams is still very small (Foulkes, 1982; Strauch, 2004), so that further research linking the gender differences in dream content to gender-specific socialization is needed to corroborate the findings reported above.

To summarize, stable gender differences in dream content have been reported over the years. However, most of the findings—with few exceptions (Schredl & Piel, 2005; Winget, Kramer, & Whitman, 1972)—are based on dreams stemming from students, so that more representative studies are necessary in order to generalize the gender differences found so far.

GENDER DIFFERENCES IN DREAMS: A MATCHING STUDY

This section will investigate whether it is possible to judge the gender of the dreamer solely on reading one dream report (cf. Schredl, Schwenger & Dehe, 2004). In clinical practice, this question often arises.

Whereas a considerably large number of content analytic studies comparing different groups with each other (for example, patients versus controls) have been published (Domhoff, 1996; Schredl, 1999a; Winget & Kramer, 1979;), matching studies that investigate the predictive value of dreams have been rarely carried out. Roussy et al. (1996, 2000), for example, instructed blind judges to match presleep thought reports with corresponding dream reports. Overall, in most cases, this task was not accomplished at a rate better than chance, in contrast to the original study of Rados and Cartwright (1982). For one matching task, however, the findings were significant: The judges were presented one dream report and six descriptions of daily events of different persons (Roussy et al., 2000). On average, 1.4 pairs (24 percent) were matched correctly.

Kramer, Hlasny, Jacobs, and Roth (1976) gave judges the dream series ($N = 15$ dreams) of five healthy persons and the dream series ($N = 13$ dreams) of five schizophrenic patients. The task was to group the randomly ordered dreams according to the respective dreamer. For the healthy controls, the success rate was high (78.7 percent; $p < .0001$), whereas the correct matching was lower for patients (48.5 percent; $p < .01$). This study illustrates that persons judging blindly are able to find similarities in dreams and, thus, can bring together the dreams of one person better than chance. A task including the question whether a specific dream was provided by a schizophrenic patient or a healthy person, however, was not carried out in this study.

In another matching study, DeDonato, Belicki, and Cuddy (1996) presented twenty-eight dream reports to seventy-five judges. These dreams consisted of the fourteen worst nightmares of women who had been sexually abused during childhood and the fourteen worst nightmares of age-matched controls. The authors emphasized that explicit sexual content that would allow an easy identification was scarcely present in these dreams. The matching was correct, on average, in 69.4 percent of the cases (chance probability: 50 percent), a highly significant finding. This figure does not permit a good interpretation to be made in single cases (high rates of false-positives and false-negatives), however.

The present study focused on gender differences, that is, the judges were asked to predict the dreamer's gender from of a randomly sorted list of dream reports. This characteristic was selected because fairly consistent differences between women's dreams and men's dreams have been reported in the literature (see the section *Dream Content* in this chapter). Whereas for variables such as dream length, bizarreness, emotional tone, and intensity the findings are inhomogeneous (Schredl, Sahin, & Schäfer, 1998), women's dreams included indoor settings (Hall & Van de Castle, 1966) and interpersonal problems (Schredl, 2001) more often than men's dreams, and men more often dreamed about physical aggression ($d = 0.36$, largest effect size in the study of Schredl, Sahin, & Schäfer, 1998) and sexuality (Hall et al., 1982). In addition, men's dreams more often included men, whereas the gender distribution of dream characters was balanced in women's dreams (Hall, 1984). It was hypothesized that persons judging blindly are able to match gender better than chance and that they are more confident in their correct decisions than in their incorrect ones.

Method

Measurement Instruments

The two judges received forms to record their decision (male or female). In addition, the judges were asked to estimate their subjective confidence in this decision on a four-point scale ($0 = very low confidence$, $1 = low confidence$, $2 = moderate confidence$, $3 = high confidence$).

Procedure

The first author selected dream reports from the material of several studies (Schredl, 1991; Schredl, Ciric, Bishop, Gölitz, & Büschtons, 2003; Schredl & Hofmann, 2003; Schredl, Schäfer, Hofmann, & Jacob, 1999). In the course of these studies, the participants kept a dream diary over a two-week period and recorded their dreams on a maximum of five mornings. All the dreams of one morning (if more than one dream was reported) have been used as an analysis unit.

For each participant, a dream report fulfilling the criteria that it consisted of 30 to 300 words was selected randomly. In 26 of 200 cases (18 female dreams, 8 male dreams), the dream first selected was not included in the analysis because of explicit gender-specific content, for example, penis, wearing a bridal dress, disguised as Queen Elizabeth, serving the country ("Zivildienst"), painted toenails, and so on. In these cases, another dream of the person was selected randomly. A total of 73 of 200 dreams were altered linguistically to avoid matching based on formal criteria; for example, boy or girl friend was altered into boy/girl friend (he/she, his/her etc.). The dream reports were ordered randomly.

First, the judges were provided with several studies on gender differences in dream content (Hall, 1984; Hall & Domhoff, 1963a; Hall et al., 1982; Schredl & Jacob, 1998; Schredl, Loßnitzer, & Vetter, 1998; Schredl & Pallmer, 1998; Schredl, Sahin, & Schäfer, 1998; Winget, Kramer, & Whitman, 1972). After a training period that included the independent scoring of 20 dreams stemming from other sources and a discussion of the disagreements, each of the two judges rated all 200 dream reports independently with regard to the gender of the dreamer and their subjective confidence in their decisions. Statistical analyses were carried out with the SAS 8.2 software package for Windows.

Participants

One hundred dream reports from male dreamers and the same number of dream reports from female dreamers were included in this study. With very few exceptions, the sample population consisted of psychology students. Each dream report stemmed from a different person. The mean age of the male group (24.2 ± 5.2 years) was slightly higher than that of the female group (22.6 ± 3.0 years; $t = 2.7$; $p = .0081$). Mean dream length also differed between the sexes (125.8 ± 67.8 [women] versus 103.4 ± 55.7 [men]; $t = 2.6$; $p = .0114$). The two judges were female and also psychology students.

Results

Matching Task

The exact agreement between the two judges amounted to 73.5 percent. Judge 1 matched 64.0 percent of the dreams correctly ($d = 0.28$; $\chi^2 = 15.7$; df = 1; $p < .0001$) and Judge 2 matched 64.5 percent of the dreams correctly ($d = 0.29$; $\chi^2 = 16.8$; df = 1; $p < .0001$).

Whereas dream length ($r = .265$; $p = .0002$) and age ($r = -.163$; $p = .0207$) affected the correct decisions of Judge 1, these two variables were not associated with the judgments of Judge 2 (dream length: $r = .083$, $p = .2426$; $r = -.093$, $p = .1914$).

Altering the dream report linguistically to ensure gender neutrality was necessary more often for women's dreams than for men's dreams (46 women's dreams versus 27 men's dreams; $\chi^2 = 7.8$; df = 1; $p = .0053$). These alterations, however, did not affect the decisions of the two judges (Judge 1: 39.8 percent [correct] versus 30.6 percent [incorrect], $\chi^2 = 1.7$, df = .1903; Judge 2: 35.7 percent [correct] versus 38.3 percent [incorrect], $\chi^2 = 0.1$, df = 1, $p = .7391$; the figures are the percentages of altered dreams in the

TABLE 2.5
Confidence Ratings of the Matching Task

		Correct (N)	Incorrect (N)	Effect Size, d	t Test[a] t	p
All dreams	Judge 1	1.74 ± 0.59 (128)	1.53 ± 0.67 (72)	0.32	2.3	.0126
	Judge 2	1.72 ± 1.05 (129)	1.30 ± 1.05 (71)	0.40	2.7	.0034
Male dreams	Judge 1	1.68 ± 0.59 (63)	1.65 ± 0.59 (37)	0.05	0.3	.3910
	Judge 2	1.57 ± 1.10 (64)	1.42 ± 1.02 (36)	0.14	0.7	.2359
Female	Judge 1	1.80 ± 0.67 (65)	1.40 ± 0.74 (35)	0.57	2.8	.0035
dreams	Judge 2	1.86 ± 1.00 (65)	1.17 ± 1.07 (35)	0.67	3.2	.0009

[a]One-tailed statistical tests.

group of correctly versus incorrectly matched dreams). Similarly, more women's dreams ($N = 18$) had to be excluded from the analysis than men's dreams ($N = 8$, $\chi^2 = 3.8$, df $= 1$, $p = .0499$; see *Procedure* section).

Confidence Ratings

Both Judge 1 and Judge 2 rated their confidence in their correct judgments as being higher than in the incorrect ones (see Table 2.1). If the confidence ratings were analyzed for women's dreams and men's dreams separately, an interesting result emerged: Both judges were more confident in their matching of women's dreams correctly in contrast to their confidence in their matching of men's dreams (see Table 2.5).

Discussion

The study demonstrated that an above-chance matching of the dreamer's gender based on a single dream is possible. The effect size (small to medium according to Cohen, 1988) was comparable to that of content analytic studies (Schredl, Sahin, & Schäfer, 1998). The percentage of correct matching is also comparable with the findings of DeDonato, Belicki, and Cuddy (1996) regarding nightmares of sexually abused women (69.9 percent correct judgments). However, if one takes into consideration that merely matching by chance yields 50 percent correct judgments, it seems clear that a reliable matching is only possible for a limited number of dream reports, that is, in a single case, the rate of false-positives and false-negatives will be very high (see *Dream Example* section).

A factor that might contribute to the accuracy of the matching is the amount of the dream material that was included. Kramer, Roth, and Cisco (1976), for example, did not obtain significant results regarding the matching of the time order using single dreams, but—presenting the judges all the rapid eye movement (REM) dreams from one night—the pairs first versus twentieth night and third versus eighteenth night could be matched at a rate better than chance. Similarly, Roussy et al. (1996) did not obtain successful matching for relatively short REM dreams stemming from the first REM period of the night, but for the longer diary dreams the judges were able to match these reports with corresponding descriptions of the day before at a rate above chance (between-subjects design; Roussy et al., 2000). Regarding this influencing factor, it will be promising to carry out a matching study with one, two, three, or more dream reports per person in order to determine how the accuracy of the judgment is affected by the amount of dream material that is provided.

Another factor needs to be considered. The present dream sample was obtained from students, that is, female and male students share the same environment, lectures, classes, studying similar subjects at home, and so on. It might be hypothesized that gender differences in dream reports of persons with a wider age range (including working persons, housewives, men, and so on) are more pronounced, and the matching regarding the gender of the dreamer would be much easier.

With regard to potential mediating variables, such as dream length, dreamer's age, and linguistic alteration of the dream report, it may be concluded quite safely that their influences on the present findings are rather small because they did not play a role in the judgments of Judge 2 (only for Judge 1), and the findings of the two judges are similar in every respect.

For the confidence ratings, the expected result was obtained: the confidence ratings have been significantly higher for the correct decisions than for the incorrectly matched dreams. This can be interpreted as saying that some dreams can be matched relatively easily, whereas other dreams are difficult to judge with respect to the dreamer's gender. The findings regarding the differences in the confidence rating for men's and women's dreams separately are very interesting. This might be explained in two ways. First, because the judges of the present study were female, it seems plausible that women are more confident about matching women's dreams. A similar study with female and male judges will shed light on this hypothesis.

Second, women's dreams were often discarded in the selection process and subsequently altered linguistically more often, that is, these dreams included more direct references to the dreamer's gender. Although the linguistic alternations did not affect the accuracy of the judgment, it might be possible that women's dreams are more characteristic of women than men's dreams are of men. In order to investigate what kind of characteristics these might be, qualitative studies have to be carried out, eliciting the judges' decision rules in addition to the matching decision and confidence rating. If such characteristics can be identified, content analytic studies comparing women's and men's dreams along specifically constructed content scales should complement the qualitative findings.

To summarize, the judges were able to match the dreamer's gender based on a single dream report better than chance. The rate of correct decisions, however, was not extremely high, so a reliable matching for a single case is often not possible (see also *Dream Examples*). It must be concluded that even for simple characteristics of the dreamer, more dream material is necessary to make a valid prediction.

DREAM EXAMPLES

Dream Example 1

A recurring sequence of driving a car from my apartment to the apartment of my friend, always being in a traffic jam and smoking one cigarette after the other and listening to flower power music (radio). I never arrived.

Dream Example 2

I was just opening the door to the apartment of my parents. When I entered, an unpleasant feeling came up. I knew that my parents were not present but imagined that people are in the apartment lying in wait for me. I dared to move further into the entrance hall cautiously and looked briefly into the living room which was illuminated with a strange dark red light. In addition, the balcony door was open and the wind blew the curtains into the room. I didn't muster up the courage to go into the other rooms but ran from the apartment and called the police from a neighbor.

Both dream examples are taken from the study of Schredl, Schwenger, and Dehe (2004). Both judges were very confident that the first dream example was reported by a man, but this was not the case. The second dream was classified by both judges as being a female dream, but again they were both wrong; the dream was reported by a man. The selected examples show clearly that it can be very difficult to classify a single dream in a correct way. Usually one would need more dream material to draw conclusions about the dreamer.

EXPLAINING GENDER DIFFERENCES IN DREAM CONTENT

Based on the consistent findings regarding several gender differences, the question arises how these gender differences in dream content can be explained. The continuity hypothesis states that dreams reflect waking-life and is broadly supported by empirical evidence (for an overview, see Schredl, 2003a). The continuity hypothesis predicts that corresponding gender differences in waking life parallels the reported gender differences in dream content. Metaanalyses for sexuality (Oliver & Hyde, 1993) and physical aggression (Eagly, 1987) clearly indicate gender differences similar to the reported differences in dreams do occur in waking life; men, for example, more often reported about engaging in sexual fantasies and about physical aggression during waking. The higher figures for empathy in women operationalized as a personality dimension ($d = -0.97$; Feingold, 1994) might hint at an increased emotional involvement in interpersonal relationships and possibly explain the heightened occurrence of dreams of deceased persons in women (Schredl & Piel, 2005).

Whereas Hall (1984) speculated about the Oedipus complex as one possible explanation for the preponderance of male dream characters in men's dreams (in contrast to the equal amount of men and women in women's dreams), Schredl and Jacob (1998) were able to demonstrate that the ratio of male to female dream characters depended on the dreamer's environment. The male dreamer recorded one hundred dreams while being in a men-dominated environment (studying electrical engineering; 95 percent of the students are male) and one hundred dreams while being in a female-dominated environment (studying psychology; 80 percent of the students are female). In the first period, 63 percent of the dream characters were male, whereas the dreams in the second period contained 51 percent male dream characters (a significant difference). For a sample of thirty-five female students, Schredl, Loßnitzer, and Vetter (1998) found that the amount of time spent with men and women during the day, especially on weekends, directly correlated with the gender ratio of the dream characters (social activities and dreams were recorded over a two-week period). In a similar way, it was very interesting to compare the gender ratio of dream characters in singles and persons with stable partnerships (Schredl, 2001). Whereas the expected difference (61 percent men in men's dreams and 48 percent men in women's dreams) was replicated for singles, the difference was not present in the sample of persons with stable partnerships (49 percent men in men's dreams and 62 percent men in women's dreams). This was simply explained by the fact that both sexes often dreamed about their partner (a person of the opposite sex). Similar, Lortie-Lussier, Simond, Rinfret, and de Koninck (1992) demonstrated that working women's dreams showed more similarities with the "male" dream pattern than those of housewives.

To summarize, these studies clearly indicate that gender differences in dream content are reflecting gender differences in waking life, thus providing further support for the continuity hypothesis of dreaming.

CONCLUSION

Women recall dreams more often than men. A factor that might explain this difference is the positive attitude towards dreams in women. Up until now, it was not clear whether this factor was a causal explanation or whether gender specific socialization contributed to the gender difference in dream recall. Similarly, stable gender differences in dream content have been reported: men dream more often about physical aggression, sexuality and work, whereas women dream more often about persons and clothing. These differences reflect differences between the sexes in waking life and, thus, are in accordance with the continuity hypothesis of dreaming. Further studies that elicit dream reports as well as measures of waking life (personality, waking-life experiences, concerns, thoughts, and so on) and relate these variables in a direct way are necessary to clarify whether all gender differences in dream content are reflections of waking-life differences. Especially interesting will be longitudinal studies in larger samples of children that will study the critical age at which gender differences in dream recall and dream content are developing.

REFERENCES

Avila-White, D., Schneider, A., & Domhoff, G. W. (1999). The most recent dreams of 12–13 year-old boys and girls: A methodological contribution to the study of dream content in teenagers. *Dreaming, 9*, 163–171.

Beaudet, D. (1990). *Encountering the monster: Pathways in children's dreams*. New York: Continuum.

Brannon, L. (1996). *Gender: Psychological perspectives*. Boston, MA: Allyn and Bacon.

Borbely, A. (1984). Schlafgewohnheiten, schlafqualität und schlafmittelkonsum der schweizer bevölkerung: Ergebnisse einer repräsentativumfrage [Sleep habits, sleep quality, and sleeping pill consumption in Switzerland: Results of a representative survey]. *Schweizerische Ärztezeitung, 65*, 1606–1613.

Buss, D. M. (1995). Psychological sex differences: Origins through sexual selection. *American Psychologist, 50*, 164–166.

Cohen, J. (1988). Statistical power analysis for the behavioral sciences. Hillsdale, NJ: Lawrence Erlbaum.

Cory, T. L., Orniston, D. W., Simmel, E., & Dainoff, M. (1975). Predicting the frequency of dream recall. *Journal of Abnormal Psychology, 84*, 261–266.

DeDonato, A., Belicki, K., & Cuddy, M. (1996). Rater's abilities to identify individuals reporting sexual abuse from nightmare content. *Dreaming, 6*, 33–41.

Domhoff, G. W. (1996). Finding meaning in dreams: A quantitative approach. New York: Plenum Press.

Domino, G. (1982). Attitudes toward dreams, sex differences and creativity. *Journal of Creative Behavior, 16*, 112–122.

Eagly, A. H. (1987). Sex differences in social behavior: A social-role interpretation. Hillsdale, NJ: Lawrence Erlbaum.

Eagly, A. H. (1995). The science and politics of comparing women and men. *American Psychologist, 50,* 145–155.

Feingold, A. (1994). Gender differences in personality: A meta-analysis. *Psychological Bulletin, 116,* 429–456.

Foulkes, D. (1982). *Children's dreams: Longitudinal studies.* New York: John Wiley and Sons.

Garfield, P. L. (1984). *Your child's dreams.* New York: Ballentine.

Giambra, L. M. (1979). Sex differences in daydreaming and related mental activity from the late teens to the early nineties. *International Journal of Aging and Human Development, 10,* 1–34.

Giambra, L. M., Jung, R. E., & Grodsky, A. (1996). Age changes in dream recall in adulthood. *Dreaming, 6,* 17–31.

Griffith, R. M., Miyagi, O., & Tago, A. (1958). The universality of typical dreams: Japanese vs. Americans. *American Anthropologist, 60,* 1173–1179.

Gruber, R. E. (1988). Dreaming style and waking personality. Unpublished doctoral dissertation. University of Cincinnati.

Hall, C. S. (1984). "A ubiquitous sex difference in dreams" revisited. *Journal of Personality and Social Psychology, 46,* 1109–1117.

Hall, C. S., & Domhoff, B. J. (1963a). A ubiquitous sex difference in dreams. *Journal of Abnormal and Social Psychology, 66,* 278–280.

Hall, C. S., & Domhoff, B. J. (1963b). Aggression in dreams. *International Journal of Social Psychiatry, 9,* 259–267.

Hall, C. S., Domhoff, G. W., Blick, K. A., & Weesner, K. E. (1982). The dreams of college men and women in 1959 and 1980: A comparison of dream contents and sex differences. *Sleep, 5,* 188–194.

Hall, C. S., & Van de Castle, R. L. (1966). *The content analysis of dreams.* New York: Appleton-Century-Crofts.

Heerwagen, F. (1889). Statistische untersuchungen über träume und schlaf [Statistical studies on dreams and sleep]. *Philosophische Studien, 5,* 301–320.

Hyde, J. S., & Plant, E. A. (1995). Magnitude of psychological gender differences: Another side to the story. *American Psychologist, 50,* 159–161.

Keßels, T. (2004). Angstträume bei neun- bis elfjährigen Kindern [Anxiety dreams in nine- to eleven-year-old children]. *Praxis der Kinderpsychologie und Kinderpsychiatrie, 53,* 19–38.

Kramer, M., Hlasny, R., Jacobs, G., & Roth, T. (1976). Do dreams have meaning? An empirical inquiry. *American Journal of Psychiatry, 133,* 778–781.

Kramer, M., Roth, T., & Cisco, J. (1976). The meaningfulness of dreams. *Sleep Research, 5,* 118.

Lortie-Lussier, M., Simond, S., Rinfret, N., & de Koninck, J. (1992). Beyond sex differences: Family and occupational roles' impact on women's and men's dreams. *Sex Roles, 26,* 79–96.

Marecek, J. (1995). Gender, politics, and psychology's ways of knowing. *American Psychologist, 50,* 162–163.

Middleton, W. C. (1942). The frequency with which a group of unselected college students experiences colored dreaming and colored hearing. *Journal of General Psychology, 27,* 221–229.

Nielsen, T. A., Laberge, L., Tremblay, R., Frank, V., & Montplaisir, J. (1999). Prevalence of bad dream recall in 13 and 16 year olds: A longitudinal study. *Sleep Supplement, 22,* S178.

Nielsen, T. A., Zadra, A. L., Simard, V., Saucier, S., Stenstrom, P., Smith, C., et al. (2003). The typical dreams of Canadian university students. *Dreaming, 13,* 211–235.

Oliver, M. B., & Hyde, J. S. (1993). Gender differences in sexuality: A meta-analysis. *Psychological Bulletin, 114,* 29–51.

Pagel, J. F., Vann, B. H., & Altomare, C. A. (1995). Reported association of stress and dreaming: Community background levels and changes with disaster (hurricane Iniki). *Dreaming, 5,* 43–55.

Rados, R., & Cartwright, R. D. (1982). Where do dreams come from? A comparison of presleep and REM sleep thematic content. *Journal of Abnormal Psychology, 91,* 433–436.

Roussy, F., Brunette, M., Merier, P., Gonthier, I., Grenier, J., Sirois-Berliss, et al. (2000). Daily events and dream content: Unsuccessful matching attempts. *Dreaming, 10,* 77–83.

Roussy, F., Camirand, C., Foulkes, D., De Koninck, J., Loftis, M., & Kerr, N. H. (1996). Does early-night REM dream content reliably reflect presleep state of mind? *Dreaming, 6,* 121–130.

Saline, S. (1999). The most recent dreams of children ages 8–11. *Dreaming, 9,* 173–181.

Schredl, M. (1991). *Traumerinnerungshäufigkeit und trauminhalt bei schlafgestörten, psychiatrischen patienten und gesunden* [Dream recall and dream content in patients with sleep disorders, psychiatric patients, and healthy controls]. Universität Mannheim: Unveröffentlichte diplomarbeit.

Schredl, M. (1999a). *Die nächtliche traumwelt: Einführung in die psychologische traumforschung* [The nocturnal dream world: Introduction into psychological dream research]. Stuttgart: Kohlhammer.

Schredl, M. (1999b). Dream recall, research, clinical implications and future directions. *Sleep and Hypnosis, 1,* 99–108.

Schredl, M. (2000). Gender differences in dream recall. *Journal of Mental Imagery, 24,* 169–176.

Schredl, M. (2001). Dreams of singles: Effects of waking-life social contacts on dream content. *Personality and Individual Differences, 31,* 269–275.

Schredl, M. (2002a). Questionnaires and diaries as research instruments in dream research: Methodological issues. *Dreaming, 12,* 17–26.

Schredl, M. (2002b). Messung der traumerinnerung: Skala und daten gesunder personen [Measuring dream recall frequency: Seven-point rating scale and data of healthy persons]. *Somnologie, 6,* 34–38.

Schredl, M. (2002/2003). Factors influencing the gender difference in dream recall frequency. *Imagination, Cognition and Personality, 22,* 33–39.

Schredl, M. (2003). Continuity between waking and dreaming: A proposal for a mathematical model. *Sleep and Hypnosis, 5,* 38–52.

Schredl, M. (2004a). Reliability and stability of a dream recall frequency scale. *Perceptual and Motor Skills, 98,* 1422–1426.

Schredl, M. (2004b). Traumerinnerung: Modelle und empirische untersuchungen [Dream recall: Models and empirical studies]. Marburg: Tectum. Schredl, M., & Doll, E. (1998). Emotions in diary dreams. *Consciousness and Cognition, 7,* 634–646.

Schredl, M., Burchert, N., & Grabatin, Y. (2004). The effect of training on interrater reliability in dream content analysis. *Sleep and Hypnosis, 6,* 139–144.

Schredl, M., Ciric, P., Bishop, A., Gölitz, E., & Buschtöns, D. (2003). Content analysis of German students' dreams: Comparison to American findings. *Dreaming, 13,* 237–243.

Schredl, M., & Erlacher, D. (2003). The problem of dream content analysis validity as shown by a bizarreness scale. *Sleep and Hypnosis, 5,* 129–135.

Schredl, M., & Fulda, S. (2005). Reliability and stability of dream recall frequency. *Dreaming, 15,* 240–244.

Schredl, M., & Hofmann, F. (2003). Continuity between waking activities and dream activities. *Consciousness and Cognition, 12,* 298–308.

Schredl, M., & Jacob, S. (1998). Ratio of male and female characters in a dream series. *Perceptual and Motor Skills, 86,* 198–200.

Schredl, M., Loßnitzer, T., & Vetter, S. (1998). Is the ratio of male and female dream characters related to the waking-life pattern of social contacts? *Perceptual and Motor Skills, 87,* 513–514.

Schredl, M., & Montasser, A. (1996/1997). Dream recall: State or trait variable? Part I: Model, theories, methodology and trait factors and Part II: State factors, investigations and final conclusions. *Imagination, Cognition and Personality, 16,* 181–210, 239–261.

Schredl, M., Nürnberg, C., & Weiler, S. (1996). Dream recall, attitude toward dreams, and personality. *Personality and Individual Differences, 20,* 613–618.

Schredl, M, & Pallmer, R. (1998). Geschlechtsunterschiede in angstträumen von schüler-Innen. *Praxis der Kinderpsychologie und Kinderpsychiatrie* [Gender differences in anxiety dreams of school-aged children]. *47,* 463–476.

Schredl, M., & Piel, E. (2003). Gender differences in dream recall frequency: Data from four representative German samples. *Personality and Individual Differences, 35,* 1185–1189.

Schredl, M., & Piel, E. (2005). Gender differences in dreaming: Are they stable over time? *Personality and Individual Differences, 39,* 309–316.

Schredl, M., Sahin, V., & Schäfer, G. (1998). Gender differences in dreams: Do they reflect gender differences in waking-life? *Personality and Individual Differences, 25,* 433–442.

Schredl, M., Schäfer, G., Hofmann, F., & Jacob, S. (1999). Dream content and personality: Thick vs. thin boundaries. *Dreaming, 9,* 257–263.

Schredl, M., Schenck, W., Görtelmeyer, R., & Heuser, I. (1998). Einflußfaktoren auf die schlafqualität bei gesunden [Influencing factors on sleep quality in healthy persons]. *Somnologie, 2,* 99–103.

Schredl, M., Schwenger, C., & Dehe, A. (2004). Gender differences in dreams: A matching study. *Counseling and Clinical Psychology Journal, 1,* 61–67.

Stepansky, R., Holzinger, B., Schmeiser-Rieder, A., Saletu, B., Kunze, M., & Zeitlhofer, J. (1998). Austrian dream behavior: Results of a representative population survey. *Dreaming, 8,* 23–30.

Strauch, I. (2004). Träume im übergang von der kindheit ins jugendalter: Ergebnisse einer langzeitstudie [Dreams in the transition from childhood to adolescence: Results of a longitudinal study]. Bern: Hans Huber.

Strauch, I., & Lederbogen, S. (1999). The home dreams and waking fantasies of boys and girls ages 9 and 15: A longitudinal study. *Dreaming, 9*, 153–161.

Winget, C., & Kramer, M. (1979). *Dimensions of dreams.* Gainesville, FL: University of Florida Press.

Winget, C., Kramer, M., & Whitman, R. M. (1972). Dreams and demography. *Canadian Psychiatric Association Journal, 17*, 203–208.

Wynaendts-Francken, C. J. (1907). Träume bei männern und frauen. [Dreams of men and women]. *Neurologisches Centralblatt, 26*, 941.

Three

Dreaming as Non-Executive Orienting: A Conceptual Framework for Consciousness during Sleep

Roar Fosse and G. William Domhoff

INTRODUCTION

Research over the past thirty-five years has led to a set of systematic descriptive findings on dream content and on dreaming as a cognitive process that can be used as a starting point in the difficult process of developing a new conceptual framework for neurocognitive models of dreaming. These new dream findings come from sleep laboratory awakenings, ambulatory home studies using portable electroencephalograms (EEGs), neuropsychological studies of brain-injured patients, and functional neuroimaging studies that compare waking with nonrapid eye movement (NREM) and rapid eye movement (REM) sleep. During roughly the same time period, many discoveries in neurophysiology have led to a better understanding of the brain basis for such important waking capacities as arousal, attention, orienting, decision-making, memory, emotions, and even consciousness itself. The new neurophysiological findings and ideas come from a wide range of studies, often using animal models.

In this chapter, we attempt to synthesize the separate literatures on dreams and waking neurophysiology, an attempt that seems plausible to us because of the many parallels between dreaming and waking cognition that have been discovered by cognitively oriented dream researchers (Antrobus, 1978, 2000; Domhoff, 2003; Foulkes, 1985). We proceed on the assumption that specific findings on dreams can serve as both a guide and a constraint in examining the literature on waking neurophysiology for clues about what waking processes might be involved in dreaming. To anticipate our conclusions, we argue that dreaming is a perceptual-attentive, emotional process during sleep, with characteristics similar to that of orienting behavior during waking, but with the noteworthy absence of contributions from core processes of executive thought.

We begin with a brief review of the main dream findings that need to be encompassed within neurocognitive models. Then, we turn to an overview of the functioning of the waking brain, with a special emphasis on those parts and systems of the brain that contribute to neurocognitive processes relevant for dreaming. We then describe the changes that occur in neurocognitive functions over the wake-sleep cycle. We argue that it is the differential patterns of reactivation during sleep that explain both the similarities and the differences between dreaming and waking cognition.

We think the following findings need to be explained by neurocognitive models. We begin with insights based on studies of the waking brain and then explain dreaming on the basis of the complex and still not yet fully understood patterns of deactivation and differential reactivation that characterize sleep onset, NREM sleep, and REM sleep. First, dreaming is present during sleep-onset, but in a more brief, fragmented, and incoherent form than in NREM or REM sleep (Fosse, Stickgold, & Hobson, 2001a; Foulkes & Vogel, 1965; Vogel, 1991). Second, dreams can occur in NREM, especially late in the sleep period, that are very similar in structure and content to dreams reported from REM awakenings, but REM provides the platform for the most frequent and vivid dream reports (for example, Antrobus, Kondo, & Reinsel, 1995; Cicogna, Natale, Occhionero, & Bosinelli, 1998; Fosse, Stickgold, & Hobson, 2004; McNamara, McLaren, Smith, Brown, & Stickgold, 2005). Third, longitudinal and cross-sectional studies in which young children ages 3–15 were awakened in the sleep laboratory suggest that dreaming is a gradual cognitive achievement based on the development of a variety of cognitive skills, especially the ability to create mental imagery; dreaming may not be adult-like until ages 9–10 (Foulkes, 1982, 1999; Strauch, 2005).

Fourth, neuropsychological studies of brain-injured patients suggest that damage to large swaths of the outer cortex, including the dorsolateral prefrontal cortex, sensori-motor cortex, and primary visual cortex, do not affect dreaming. On the other hand, injuries to other areas of the brain can lead to changes in dream imagery or to the loss of dreaming (Kerr & Foulkes, 1981; Kerr, Foulkes, & Jurkovic, 1978; Solms, 1997). These findings imply a relatively specific "neural network for dreaming." Fifth, the notion that dreaming is subsumed by relatively specific cortical regions is supported by findings from neuroimaging studies (using brain reactivation patterns during REM periods as a proxy for dreaming) that point to the same regions as the neuropsychological studies (for example, Braun et al., 1997; Maquet, 2000). Sixth, and finally, content analyses of dreams collected in sleep laboratories suggest that most dreams are coherent, reasonable, and focused on everyday life, although they may sometimes contain unusual perceptual qualities, settings that seem familiar but somehow different, or highly unusual scenarios (Dorus, Dorus, & Rechtschaffen, 1971; Snyder, 1970).

The discussion that follows does not attempt to encompass each of these six specific points in a detailed way. In particular, we do not address the developmental aspects of dreaming at this time, nor do we focus in detail on dream content. Nonetheless, we think that the discussion that follows is consistent with the findings on all six of these general types of findings.

Our framework for considering dreaming draws on a *biological rhythm* (or *brain state*) *approach to cognition*. That is, we identify and describe the overall characteristics and changes in psychological and biological function within and between the basic states of the brain-mind (brainmind) system. We include the higher order aspects of neurocognitive functions, as well as the basic regulatory processes of deeper brain regions that modify neurocognitive functions during waking states and regulate the overall behavioral/conscious state of the system. We seek to integrate evidence from various levels of analysis of the biological, neurocognitive, and psychological properties of brainmind function, including levels that approach the issue of consciousness, such as oscillatory brain dynamics. Ideally, this approach allows us to study the covariation in psychology and biology around the clock.

Because this chapter is primarily intended for readers with a focus on dreaming, we attempt to present our model with the necessary minimum of detail on neurophysiology. We often draw on the current consensus on contested issues where there indeed remain doubts or rival interpretations. A more detailed analysis of the neurophysiological issues we overview here will be presented in a more specialized and technical version of this chapter, which is available upon request from the first author.

THE WAKING BRAIN

In the waking state, neurocognitive functions are generally available to allow for alert cognitive-emotional activity and flexible interaction with the environment and researchers from many fields have extensively studied them. The detailed knowledge of neural behavior that now exists for cognition and consciousness during waking provides a solid empirical basis for considering the changes that take place during sleep and dreaming. We, therefore, begin with the alert waking brain.

Neurocognitive functions are characterized by four key features: (1) their spatial distribution over subcortical and cortical regions, (2) pathways of interconnections with other systems, (3) chemical modulation by arousal systems, and (4) oscillatory neural firing dynamics. General aspects of these features are noted in the next section for neurocognitive functions of particular relevance for dreaming, including executive thinking, perception/attention, emotion, and orienting behavior. Since consciousness is a central feature of dreaming, we put weight on neural and psychological processes that may be associated with subjective experience.

Regionally Distributed Neurocognitive Functions

Neurocognitive functions are constituted by networks of neural assemblies that typically are distributed along the brain axis, ranging from the brain stem to the cerebral cortex. For higher cognitive functions, deeper brain regions have basic roles, such as arousal and neurochemical modulation, whereas the cerebral cortex has more complex, integrative, and governing roles. During the use of a neurocognitive capacity, the network system functions in highly specific ways with respect to the speed, pattern, and synchronization of neural activity.

Among sensory and perceptual systems, visual perception is the most important for us because of the highly visual nature of dreaming. It also can serve as a prototype of what is likely to be the pattern for the other sensory/perceptual systems. As is well known, the visual system innervates the inner eye, responding to light and color in a manner that sends waves of neural impulses from the retina to core brain regions such as the thalamus. From the thalamus, visual stimuli propagate further to the primary visual cortex and to visual association regions in the posterior cortex. In doing so, they follow two major trajectories of long-projection cells called the magnocellular and parvocellular pathways, which interact and develop in their complexity along their cross-regional pathways.

The visual system is also of relevance to our model because of its close association with mechanisms of attention, especially processes of shifting and reorienting attention. Orienting responses to external events are triggered by visual, auditory, tactile, and other sensory stimuli with novelty values. They induce processes of attention shifts at several levels of the brain in which ongoing information processing is interrupted and the brain adjusts to perceive and treat information about potentially important external events. The orienting response facilitates (attends) the thalamus to enhanced processing of further perceptual information. From the thalamus and the basal forebrain, which is activated in parallel during detection of novelties, an alerting message of attention is sent upwards to an array of cortical regions, thereby facilitating these regions in the processing of the novel perceptual information. These processes reflect a basic shift in brain function where the brain both prunes perceptive systems and utilizes acquired knowledge to form its focus in the most efficient direction.

Processes of reorienting attention integrate with processes of executive cognition at several levels of the brain. The executive cognitive system has its most advanced components of integration and control in the prefrontal and parietal cerebral cortex. This executive cognitive system includes executive attention areas in the anterior cingulate of the medial prefrontal cortex, working memory areas for perception and thought in the lateral prefrontal cortex, and regions around the posterior cingulate region in the mediodorsal parietal cortex that have monitoring capabilities for perceptual events in the environment. This executive cognitive system integrates abilities to focus attention, sustain information, be attentive to change, and provide people with an experience of agency. Its activity is also strongly associated with consciousness of the reflective type, with a deactivation or disfacilitation being associated with reductions and loss of self-consciousness, reflective thought, and insight.

In addition to being a part of the executive cognitive system, areas in and around the anterior cingulate region in the medial prefrontal cortex participate in emotion. Together with ventral and orbitofrontal regions along the midline of the prefrontal cortex, the anterior cingulate area controls and integrates emotion with cognition, memory, perception, and behavior. The prefrontal cortical emotion regions interact with subcortical emotion regions in the amygdala and associated basal forebrain, midbrain, and brain stem. Emotional influence includes reward and alarm emotions, with the amygdala being involved in both types because of its connectivity with neurochemically specific emotion regulation regions, such as the noradrenergic locus coeruleus of the brain stem and dopamine neurons of the mesolimbic reward system.

Several other systems of the brain contribute to adaptive behavior, such as systems for motor control and memory. Aspects of these systems that are particularly relevant for dreaming are noted throughout the chapter.

Functional Neural Assemblies and Networks

The functioning of the brain below the global level is not easily explained in terms of a few general principles. However, the architecture of the brain, and studies of its function, suggest that neurocognitive functions have local building blocks in which two classes of neurons are crucial and where functionality is established through the active, reciprocal interaction between these neuronal classes. These major building blocks of *functional neural assemblies* are (1) small interneurons that produce gamma-immunobutyric acid (GABA), and (2) larger, often powerful neurons with long axons (which we will call "long-projection neurons") that typically produce glutamate (Yuste, 2005). Interneurons and long-projection neurons come in a variety of shapes and fashions. The long-projection cells can be further differentiated into glutamatergic projection neurons (for example, corticospinal, thalamo-cortical, cortico-cortical neurons) and chemically specific neuromodulatory brain stem neurons that project to and modify the midbrain and forebrain.

Both interneurons and long-projection neurons in functional assemblies can be viewed as having specialized roles. Long-projection cells typically convey neural traffic and information over both local and distant areas of the brain, together constituting highways and expressways of information processing. Networks of local interneurons, in contrast, sculpt the activities in cortical circuits through feedforward and feedback inhibition, and both prevent runaway excitation and mold signal conduction paths. They also have regulatory effects on functional assemblies and neurocognitive networks. In addition, GABA interneurons exhibit processes of "self-control" or intrinsic modulation as a consequence of their own activity, indicating that they perhaps represent a "brainy" category of neurons in the brain (Bacci, Huguenard, & Prince, 2003, 2004).

Neurochemical Modulation of Arousal and Neurocognition

Neurons and neurochemical processes within the reticular core of the brain stem and in the midbrain, hypothalamus, and basal forebrain are basic prerequisites for adaptive, alert activity in waking. These regions contain nuclei of arousal neurons with axons that innervate and modulate the entire brain, including the cerebral cortex. Among the central arousal systems of the pons, caudal midbrain, and basal forebrain are those that produce and transmit acetylcholine, serotonin, noradrenalin, and dopamine. We outline general effects of these arousal systems, all of which play key roles in the behavior of the brain during waking and dreaming.

Activity in the cholinergic neurons in the brain stem is a crucial prerequisite for the waking state as such, for consciousness more generally, and for sensitive processing of external and internal information (Steriade & McCarley, 2005). Cholinergic arousal neurons often accelerate the firing behavior of projection neurons and interneurons that they target, although cholinergic modulation also has inhibitory effects through intermediary actions on GABA interneurons. An acceleration of the firing rate of cholinergic arousal neurons in the brain stem leads to activation of the thalamus, and through the connectivity of the thalamus, to a further activation of perceptual and cognitive systems subserved by complex reciprocal thalamocortical networks. Together with associated activity in the basal forebrain, this thalamic activation is akin to turning on the light in the cerebral cortex, allowing consciousness to emerge through the establishment of active and ready states of neural network functions. This point is very important to our framework because, as we will explain more fully later, the thalamus shuts down very quickly at sleep onset and remains deactivated during the deeper states of NREM. It then is partially reactivated in Stage 2 NREM and fully reactivated, in cholinergic terms, in REM, which we think may be an important clue as to why there can be dreaming in Stage 2 NREM and REM.

Within the waking state, a responsive cholinergic brain stem and basal forebrain are necessary for crucial adaptive functions such as the orienting response and the startle response to novel events, associated respectively with approach and avoidance behavior. Both orienting and startle responses are characterized by a basis in an integrated activation of the brain stem and forebrain, in turn facilitated by a reflexive engagement of the cholinergic brain stem, which emits spikes of high frequency waves that activate neural networks of attention shifts in the forebrain.

The two novelty responses are differentiated by their pattern of coengagement with other neurocognitive systems and by their association with sympathetic activity (for example, when startling to sudden noise) versus parasympathetic activity (orienting to stimulation change). Environmental novelties that have pleasant connotations tend to be conceived in a reward-oriented manner by the brain, where orienting to the novelty may occur with a pleasure and excitement that is fueled by the mesolimbic dopamine systems. During startle and alarm responses, cholinergic engagement of the orienting system is accompanied by engagement of progressive alarm-like neural networks. Full alarm responses are characterized by a strong noradrenergic drive of the locus coeruleus, which alerts the brain and prepares the organism for fight or flight. The locus coeruleus region is interconnected with behavioral, somatic, and cognitive processes of fear and alarmed attention and is well equipped to orchestrate neurobehavioral commands in response to threatening affairs.

Noradrenergic neurons in the locus coeruleus generally contribute to both emotion and cognition, which is markedly indicated by the central role of noradrenaline in both executive cognition (focused attention) and anxiety and fear. Together with orexine and histamine, which are produced in the hypothalamus, noradrenaline is necessary to sustain an alert waking state. Dysfunction in these processes leads to unstable state boundaries where sleep and waking processes become mixed, such as in narcolepsy.

Serotonergic activity in the raphe nuclei in the brain stem is crucial for most neurocognitive functions in waking. The serotonergic raphe system has strong projections to an array of neurocognitive functions, including executive thought, emotion, and perception. Reduced serotonin activity is associated with symptoms such as impaired cognitive flexibility and long-term memory, as well as with depression, but it is also notably associated with an improvement in focused attention (Schmitt, Wingen, Ramaekers, Evers, & Riedel, 2006). Main targets for serotonergic release are interneurons within local neural assemblies, but serotonin also affects other neurons, having complex effects on brain behavior.

The neurotransmitter dopamine plays a key role in processes of positive emotions of reward and pleasure, as well as in processes of focused attention, cognition, and thought, in addition to motor function. High activity in the mesocorticolimbic dopamine system, ranging from the ventral tegmental area of the brain stem to the medial prefrontal cortex, is a typical companion to reward and approach behavior and is intricately involved in the rewarding effects of many recreational drugs. The role of dopamine in cognition is effectuated through connections of the mesocorticolimbic system with forebrain regions of cognition, such as the frontoparietal executive cognitive system. It is indicated by the dysfunction of memory and attention seen in schizophrenia, where disruption of thought is believed to result from altered dopamine function, which in turn leads to hallucinations (Lennox, Park, Medley, Morris, & Jones, 2000).

Oscillatory Brain Dynamics

Evidence from neuroscience and cognitive neuroscience suggests that the functional properties of the brain intricately depend on oscillatory firing dynamics of neurons and neural networks (Basar, 2006; Llinas, Ribrary, Contreras, & Pedroarena, 1998; Varela, Lachaux, Rodgriguez, & Martinene, 2001). It now appears that the dynamics of any neurocognitive function are in large part executed by neural behavior that leads to oscillatory rhythms (Basar, Basar-Eroglu, Karakas, & Schurmann, 2001; Steriade, 2006). Based on this evidence, it is likely that the changes in cognition and consciousness from waking to sleep can be described in terms of changes in the dynamics of the oscillatory activity of neural networks (Cantero & Atienza, 2005; Llinas et al., 1998; Steriade, 2006).

The functions of cognition and consciousness depend on inherent capacities of neurons and networks to fire in certain oscillatory patterns, most notably the low-frequency ranges of slow (0.5–1 Hz), delta (1–3 Hz), theta (7–12 Hz), and spindles (12–15 Hz), and the high-frequency ranges of beta (20–30 Hz) and gamma (30–60 Hz) (for example, Basar, 2006; Steriade, 2006). These frequency ranges, although at times categorized differently, represent the basic, natural rest and activity states of various types of networks. In cortico-thalamo-cortical networks, which are basic for all neurocognitive functions, cells that have high-frequency behavior as a natural property are found particularly in the cortex, where they are prominent in layers 2–6 of the cortical mantle. In addition, the cortex initiates spindle activity, although in this rhythm a major orchestrating role is played by the reticular nucleus of the thalamus that modifies cortical activity through spindle oscillatory behavior (Steriade, 2006).

Functional beta and gamma waves occur nested within (or superimposed on) slower-traveling, low-frequency waves during alert cognitive activity (for example, Basar, 2006). Without the presence of simultaneous low-frequency waves, gamma waves tend to stay local, requiring the low-frequency oscillations to extend over functional networks. Alert cognition depends on the specific carrying of nested waveforms over relatively distant regions, with disruption in this binding associated with neurological disorders and loss of consciousness. Thus, alert neuropsychological function is characterized by intertwined low- and high-frequency waves that traverse neural networks. In addition, these waves oscillate back and forth through the networks in a reentrant manner, creating an ultrasynchrony or sypersynchrony in the brain.

SLEEP ONSET

The sleep-onset period appears to offer a transition "window" lasting from several seconds to a few minutes in which dreamlike mentation is experienced. The sleep-onset period is associated with the occurrence of brief hallucinations and small dreams that may have visual and auditory qualities similar to those that occur in REM (Foulkes & Vogel, 1965). However, as we noted in the introduction, sleep-onset dreams are usually briefer, less intense, and most interesting of all for our purposes, less coherent than REM dreams. In addition to the occurrence of dreams, sleep onset is associated with changes in the quality of thinking, including a loss of focused attention, an increased tendency to associate, and a decreasing prevalence of directed thoughts (Fosse et al., 2001a; Vogel, 1991). Emotional content has not been rigorously studied at sleep onset, but sleep onset dreaming appears normally to be associated with relatively mundane emotional experience.

The circadian rhythmicity of waking and sleeping in mammals has its molecular basis in the suprachiasmatic nucleus and other processes of the hypothalamus and in homeostatic and molecular processes throughout the brain. The suprachiasmatic nucleus and hypothalamus become entrained by light stimulation of the eye, which modifies internal clocks to convey circadian rhythmicity to structures that control physiological processes such as sleep.

The appearance of dreamlike mentation at sleep onset appears concomitant with and probably because of a staged process of biological changes within the brain. Driven by homeostatic processes, endogenous somnogens, and chrono-biological mechanisms (endogenous clocks), the brain enters sleep when GABAergic interneurons in the clustered ventrolateral preoptic area of the hypothalamus increase their activity level. Sending axons to the brain stem, these preoptic interneurons cause an inhibition of the brain-stem arousal nuclei that produce noradrenaline, serotonin, and acethylcholine (Steriade, Timofeev, & Grenier, 2001). In effect, this deprives the forebrain of neuro-chemicals that are necessary to sustain an alert, attentive state. Changes are seen in parallel in the cerebral cortex at sleep onset, where low-frequency, slow waveforms develop over increasingly large volumes of brain tissue.

Throughout the sleep-onset period, there is a gradual reduction in firing activity in a network of cholinergic cell groups in networks ranging from the brain stem to the basal forebrain. This network includes pontine neurons that later reactivate the thalamus in REM (Steriade, 2000). This reduced pontine cholinergic activity dramatically changes the operating mode of key brain structures, especially the thalamus, which is the relay station for sensory input that at the same time shapes attentive brain states. When cholinergic modulation is withdrawn by the brain stem at sleep onset, intrathalamic processes leave control to GABA interneurons in the thalamic reticular sheet, which in turn responds with an extensive expression of synchronized spindle wave oscillations. In this process, the thalamus literally becomes insensitive to external stimulation that might arrive along primary sensory pathways at this time. In addition to not conveying stimuli any further downstream, the spin-dle oscillations of the thalamic reticular nucleus, which is wrapped around the lateral thalami as a sheet, contribute to locking most neurocognitive func-tions of the brain into sleep (Steriade, 2006). Thus, sleep results from the massive synchronization of thalamo-cortico-thalamic and cortico-thalamo-cortical networks into spatially synchronized spindle oscillations, synchron-ized further by slow oscillations (0.5 Hz) that develop across the cortex and that are initiated in anterior frontal cortical regions (Steriade & McCarley, 2005).

As a result, during the sleep-onset period and into sleep, most of the brain enters a mode in which (1) neural firing activity is characterized by a pattern of synchronized spindle and slow wave activities, consisting of pro-longed periods of hyperpolarization with cessation of firing accompanied by common burst-firing during depolarization phases, (2) individual neurons and small networks that operate in a highly specific, information-dependent manner in waking enter a globally synchronized pattern of low-frequency oscillations, and (3) a gradual loss of the trajectory-specific ultrasynchrony of the cognizing waking brain occurs, where networks are traversed by continuous, nested low- and high-frequency oscillatory firing dynamics.

According to current brain network theories arising from studies of the intricate web of the brain (Varela et al., 2001), the neurobiological changes of sleep onset should knock out neurocognitive functions and associated consciousness altogether. That is, the spindle waveforms that occur within the brain at sleep onset are similar to the spindle oscillations of neural networks following administration of anesthetic drugs (for example, Cote, Epps, & Campbell, 2000; Pivik, Joncas, & Busby, 1999). This is consistent with the reductions seen in reflective and sensory awareness, attention, and reflective thought over the sleep-onset period.

As can be seen, then, the main characteristics of the transition to sleep are not sufficient to account for the appearance of hallucinatory dream images at sleep onset. Various solutions to this problem have been suggested, including the intrusion of REM sleep processes and remnants of activation in perceptual systems (for example, Nielsen, 2000). However, to our knowledge no neural substrate or network has been demonstrated that remains activated following sleep onset and that is likely to support hallucinations. To approach this issue, we adopt a "retrospective" perspective, first asking how dreaming can be sustained during some periods of NREM sleep, then backtracking to sleep onset for a reconsideration.

NON-REM SLEEP

NREM occupies about 80 percent of human sleep and is, according to neurophysiological studies in animals and positron emission tomography (PET) studies in humans, characterized by a relatively low global brain activation level. According to the PET studies, a general characteristic of NREM is a low blood flow in core structures of the brain (deactivation) that include the brain stem, thalamus, and basal forebrain. The low activation level in slow wave sleep also includes the cerebral cortex, which is massively deactivated because of internal processes and interactions with deactivated subcortical regions in the basal forebrain, thalamus, and brain stem. Brain activity in NREM is thus dominated by synchronized slow, delta, and spindle wave firing patterns that traverse all important neurocognitive networks, but that are not a part of ultradynamic nested oscillations, with an essential lack of coherent gamma oscillations occurring synchronized along specific paths across brain regions. This low-frequency, global synchronization and gamma interruption is consistent with the low levels of dreaming and generally bland nature of mentation found in NREM sleep as a whole.

However, there is a factor that differentiates light (Stage/State 2) from deep (Stages 3 and 4) NREM sleep: a higher activation level of the midbrain reticular formation and the thalamus. PET studies in humans, as well as neurophysiological recordings in animals, indicate that this difference is particularly related to a higher activity level in cholinergic neurons in the pons, which also leads to a disruption of all-neuron type slow wave oscillations (Kajimura et al., 1999; Steriade et al., 2001). It is this partial reactivation of basic components of arousal systems, we hypothesize, that sets the stage for dreaming in Stage 2 sleep.

Based on the cortical EEG characteristics of Stage 2 sleep, which is dominated by massively synchronized spindle wave patterns in the absence of coherent gamma oscillations, it appears paradoxical that periods of hallucinatory dreaming take place. Dreaming would be expected to require nested oscillatory activation within cortical processes, in addition to a reactivation of subcortical arousal and modification regions. To resolve this problem, we think it is useful to investigate whether there are regions in the forebrain and cerebral cortex that are relatively devoid of spindle, slow, and delta wave neural activity in Stage 2 NREM. Such regions could be viewed as candidates to support dreaming in this state.

In cats, synchronized spindle bursting of neurons has been found to be absent from anterior regions of the thalamus in Stage 2 and from cortical areas receiving projections from these thalamic regions (Mulle, Steriade, & Deschenes, 1985). Although it was previously thought that spindles dominated neural activity in all regions of the thalamus during Stage 2, the demonstrated absence of spindles in the anterior nuclei is consistent with anatomical evidence in cats that the reticular thalamus, the pacemaker of spindle rhythms, lacks synaptic connections with the anterior nuclei. Anterior thalamic nuclei also belong to specific and different networks from most other thalamic regions, being a part of a limbic loop that includes the hippocampus, posterior hypothalamus, and allocortical areas (Pare, Steriade, Deschenes, & Oakson, 1987).

In human epileptics, intracranial EEG measures of spindle oscillations have indicated a near absence of these anesthetic waves in areas of the temporal lobe (in the healthy hemisphere), and they are only marginally present in the orbitofrontal cortex in Stage 2 sleep (Nakabayashi et al., 2001; Uchida, Hirai, Nakabayashi, Maehara, & Shimizu, 1999). These cortical regions have an intricate connectivity with the network associated with the anterior thalamus; they are cortical components of an extended limbic loop of emotional-mnemonic processing.

The regions indicated to be spindle-free in these studies of Stage 2 include networks that 80 years ago were suggested to be a core brain system of emotion (Papez, 1995). These indications of a possible regional reactivation pattern in Stage 2 may suggest the existence of neural processes that support dreaming in this state.

Several studies have indicated that as the night progresses, mental activity within NREM Stage 2 approximates the characteristics of REM dreaming, becoming more hallucinatory and less thought-like over the night (Antrobus et al., 1995; Wamsley et al., in press). The dreams in Stage 2 sleep late in the night are similar to and difficult to distinguish from REM dreams. In an internal pilot study at the Neurophysiology Laboratory at Harvard Medical Schoo,l founded by J. Allan Hobson, none of ten expert judges was able to correctly sort a mixed sample of twenty early-night REM and late-night Stage 2 NREM dreams above a chance level, using any criteria they wanted. If it is the case that Stage 2 dreaming becomes like REM dreaming late in the night, we would expect future functional neuroimaging studies to reveal general changes within Stage 2 toward morning awakenings, such as a further engagement of the extended limbic system.

SLEEP ONSET RECONSIDERED

Based on the discussion of Stage 2 dreaming, a natural hypothesis for sleep-onset hallucinations is a sustained activation of anterior thalamic nuclei and associated limbic circuits. This network could remain moderately activated because of remaining activity in the cholinergic brain stem, which would prune the network toward gamma activity. Since it is still receptive to external changes and alarming internal affairs, we speculate that this network would support perceptual hallucinations to the extent that it includes functional high-frequency oscillations in unimodal perceptual association regions of the cortex.

REM SLEEP

In contrast to NREM sleep, REM sleep is characterized by specific regional activation of the forebrain and by a differentiated engagement of neurochemically specific arousal processes deep in the brain.

Neurochemical Activation and Modulation

According to animal studies, REM is triggered by a network of structures that include GABA interneurons in the hypothalamic ventrolateral preopic region (VLPO) region. The activity of the VLPO interneurons follows ultradian and circadian rhythms, and at ultradian time points for REM sleep, the interneurons increase their activity level, which leads to the release of inhibitory signals to the aminergic arousal systems in the brain stem (Hobson, McCarley, & Wyzinski, 1975; Lu, Sherman, Devor, & Saper, 2006). These inhibitory signals lock up with a flip-flop switch along the reticular core of the brain stem, together leading to the triggering of REM sleep. In this process, the shutdown of serotonergic neurons in the dorsal raphe nucleus at the entry to REM sleep leads to the release of cholinergic neurons in the pons (Lu, Greco, Shiromani, & Saper, 2000; Lu et al., 2006; Pace-Schott & Hobson, 2002).

The activation waves transmitted from the brain stem reoccur particularly potently in the thalamus and in cortical components of the visual system, but they are also seen in limbic and paralimbic structures (such as the amygdala and ventromedial prefrontal cortex) and in integrative brain regions (such as the hippocampus and unimodal cortical association regions of audition and vision).

After the tonic activation process has established REM sleep, a second network of cholinergic arousal neurons starts to fire in bursts of gamma waves in REM. These firing bursts consist of repetitive volleys of firing streaks that traverse the occulomotor system in particular, facilitating the occular muscles to move the eyes in the saccadic fashion of REM. At the same time, the activations of the occulomotor and cholinergic arousals system have many meeting points up through the brain, reflecting the fact that both systems are intricately coupled during processes such as attention, orienting, and startle.

The activity of the noradrenaline-producing locus coeruleus in the brain stem is generally low during sleep, and this arousal nucleus terminates its firing activity almost completely during REM. We hypothesize that this is likely to have marked effects upon both executive cognition and emotion, because the noradrenergic projection system is a key process in focused attention and alarm emotions. The effect of the noradrenaline blockade is likely to include a decline in the ability to sustain attention over time and a tendency to not engage in alarm behavior and fear emotions.

Serotonergic arousal neurons of the dorsal raphe nuclei terminate their firing activity during REM, whereas serotonergic activity within the brain in total reaches a minimum at this time. Serotonergic axons tend to innervate GABA interneurons throughout the brain, such as in the prefrontal cortex, and a drop in serotonin activity in REM would be likely to demodulate interneurons, modify the activity of functional assemblies, and have effects such as the loss of executive cognitive capabilities. Given the concomitant high level of basic cholinergic activation in REM, this may lead to functional shifts in neural assemblies, resulting in a condition that is differ-ent from both the low-frequency spatial synchronization of NREM and alert waking thought.

In contrast to serotonin and noradrenaline, the activity level of dopami-nergic projection neurons appears to regain a high-firing frequency during REM compared to NREM, where dopaminergic activity is low (Lena et al., 2005). Because dopamine is a key neurotransmitter of the reward emotions of pleasure and approach, the high activity level of these neurons in REM indicates that the emotional tendency of the brain is shifted away from alarm and fear and toward reward and approach in this state. In understand-ing the further role of brain state settings on dream emotions, the more pre-cise behavior of the mesocorticolimbic dopamine system is of particular interest. Of relevance to this point, GABA interneurons in the ventral teg-mental area of the brain stem, which is the seat of numerous long-projecting dopamine neurons, are highly active in REM (Lee, Steffensen, & Heneriksen, 2001). Since these interneurons are likely to have modulatory effects upon dopaminergic activity, a question of particular interest would be their exact behavior during dreaming.

Regional Activation

PET studies in humans have demonstrated regional activation patterns in REM that are consistent with the networks of neurons found to be acti-vated in neurophysiological and cellular studies of animals. This activation pattern can be grouped into three specific regionally distributed networks.

First, a network corresponding to the core of the tonic, cholinergically based arousal systems is activated, including the mesopontine tegmentum, thalamus, and basal forebrain (Braun et al., 1997). Studies of cats show that the cholinergic mesopontine tegmentum neurons that activate the brain in REM are the same nuclei that respond to novel stimuli during orienting responses in the waking state (Morrison, 1979).

Animal studies show that the most prominent thalamic activation that is part of this first state takes place in the visual nuclei of the lateral geniculate region. The lateral geniculate region is arranged in nuclear layers that in the waking state receive visual stimuli along the optic tract from long-projection neurons that code for specific aspects of the visual scenario that is detected by the eye. The lateral geniculate region and other thalamic nuclei use powerful long-projection neurons to convey their messages further down-stream to sensory, associative perceptive, attentional, emotional, and mne-monic regions of the forebrain. Animal studies have shown that the further activation of the thalamus in REM is regionally and functionally specific, with an array of thalamic nuclei becoming engaged by the pontine waves of this state. To the extent that the visual system contributes to dream construction, the lateral geniculate region, and more generally the thalamus, may be a core factor, in particular since the primary visual cortex appears to be offline, making it relevant to find out what inherent and evoked tendencies the thalamus expresses at this time (Braun et al., 1998).

An additional aspect of the first stage of brain activation in human REM is that the basal forebrain lights up in human PET studies. Being itself largely cholinergic, the basal forebrain may contribute to an array of processes of REM dreaming, since cholinergic activity is greater in the basal forebrain in this state than in waking and NREM (Vazquez & Baghdoyan, 2001). Basic processes that the basal forebrain contributes to are attention shifts, where specific nuclei of cholinergic neurons project to perceptual attention regions in the posterior cortex; control of motor behavior; and reward and approach behaviors associated with their interaction with the mesocorticolimbic dopamine systems (Gallagher, 2000; Reid et al., 1998). Indeed, the effect of cholinergic activation upon the cortex is basically orchestrated by the basal forebrain, suggesting that the basal forebrain contributes with its processes to dreaming.

A second network that is reactivated according to PET studies of human REM is a "limbic" loop that encompasses nuclei with strong tendencies toward emotional and mnemonic processing. This limbic loop includes the anterior thalamus, hippocampus, amygdala, regions of the basal forebrain, parahippocampal and entorhinal cortex, and medial orbitofrontal and anterior cingulate regions in the prefrontal cortex. Included in this loop are the limbic and extralimbic regions indicated to be partially activated in Stage 2 NREM.

With respect to emotion, this loop is centered in the amygdala. The contributions of the amygdala to dreaming may be particularly profound, given that its central nuclei have strong modifying effects upon the pontine cholinergic arousal system through massive projections to these pontine transmission regions. The amygdala appears to respond to its activation by modifying the firing properties of the entire network that is online, presumably according to its inherent emotional tendencies and learning history. Notably, this possibility is consistent with the idea of a similar role of the amygdala in navigating and orienting during waking (Wright et al., 2003).

The activation of the hippocampus formation and surrounding temporal cortex in REM may be a crucial component for the facilitation of dreaming. The hippocampus is a highly integrative region within the temporal lobes that binds together widespread processes of the brain and supports spatial and contextual integration in memory function, attention, behavior, and experience. Animal and human studies have shown that the hippocampus enters an active state of firing within the theta frequency range in REM in a manner that is otherwise seen during orienting behavior in waking (Bodizs et al., 2001; Buzsaki, 2002; Cantero et al., 2003). The hippocampus region has nearby generators of theta waves (in the septum), but hippocampal theta waves are also triggered by waves generated by the pontine brain stem that activate the brain in REM. This in-facing of the hippocampus formation in the overall network activity would be likely to provide an integrated dynamic between processes of emotion, memory, and orienting that could shape the brain further toward supersynchronous dynamics consistent with REM dreaming.

A third network activated in human REM encompasses "classical" perceptual regions in the occipital and temporal cortices. Receiving activation input from the two formerly described networks, these regions include unimodal association areas for visual and auditory processing, but notably not primary visual cortex (Braun et al., 1997, 1998; Maquet, 2000; Maquet et al., 1996, 1997; Nofzinger, Mintun, Wiseman, Kupfer, & Moore, 1997). These areas coincide with regions found to be active in animal REM, exhibit high-frequency firing patterns in the gamma frequency range in animals as well as in humans, and are likely to be key components in cortical contributions to dream hallucinations.

PET studies in humans have found that some brain areas are deactivated in REM; in particular, the dorsolateral prefrontal cortex and the medial posterior parietal cortex (Braun et al., 1998). These deactivations occur in key regions of the executive cognitive system, with the deactivation of the dorsolateral PFC being consistent with the low level of reflective awareness, directed thought, and voluntary control over mentation apparent in mentation reports from REM (Rechtschaffen, 1978, 1997). Likewise, the deactivation of the posterior component of the executive cognitive system around the precuneus region in the medial posterioparietal cortex suggests that monitoring and surveillance capacities for perceptual events are reduced in REM. There is, however, one notable exception from the general deactivation of the executive cognitive system; the medial frontal component, which includes the anterior cingulate region, is reactivated in this state. This reactivation of the main executive attention region is likely to be associated with emotion and orienting processes and with activity in the amygdala (Maquet, 2000). Through its connections with the basal forebrain, the amygdala is likely to contribute to the activation of emotion regions in the orbitofrontal and medial prefrontal cortex, such as the anterior cingulate. Thus, we suspect that the executive components remaining active in REM would primarily be of an emotional and orientational nature.

DREAMING AS NONEXECUTIVE ORIENTING

As we noted in the introduction and have now demonstrated with the best available evidence, we think dreaming is a perceptual-attentive, emotional process during sleep, with characteristics similar to those of orienting behavior during waking, but with the noteworthy absence of contributions from core processes of executive thought.

The similarities between dreaming and orienting behavior include an array of aspects ranging from heart rate changes to cortical function; the evidence for this conclusion is derived from different lines of research into sleep that are summarized in Table 3.1. This notion that dreaming is related to orienting functions is in keeping with similar suggestions made throughout the last 40 years (for example, Johnson, 2005; Koukkou & Lehman, 1983; Kuiken, Busink, Dukewich, & Gendlin, 1996; Nielsen, Kuiken & McGregor, 1989; Soh, Morita & Sei, 1992; Taylor, Moldofsky, & Furedy, 1985).

TABLE 3.1
The Brain during Orienting Responses and REM Sleep; Hypothesis of Similarities

Functions and Processes	Orienting in Wake	REM Sleep
Eyes	Rapid sharp movements	Rapid sharp movements
Ears	Activated by P-waves	Activated by P-waves
Breathing	Irregular	Irregular
Heart rate	Deceleration	Deceleration (during pontine bursts)
Muscle activity	Contractions	Contractions
Alarm system	Off (but available[a])	Off
Reward system	On	On
Pontine/midbrain tegmentum	Gamma firing (P-waves)	Gamma firing (P-waves)
Thalamus	P-waves in LGN/thalamus	P-waves in LGN/thalamus
Hippocampus	P-waves and theta waves	P-waves and theta waves
Amygdala	P-waves, modifies network	P-waves, modifies network
Basal forebrain	Cholinergically active	Cholinergically active
Unimodal association regions, cortex	Activated by attention processes (P-waves)	Activated by attention processes (P-waves)
Executive cognitive system	Dampened	Off
Serotonergic modulation	Reduced	Off
Functional neural assemblies	Tilted toward novelties	Tilted toward novelties
Oscillatory dynamics	Nested ultra-synchronous oscillations	Nested ultra-synchronous oscillations?

Note: These statements are interpretations based on the available evidence from sleep research and associated disciplines.
[a]If alarm system turns on, the orienting response evolves to startle and responses associated with an array of changes different from those depicted here.

The functional morphology of the REM state indicates that the brain may not only be in a mode of brief orienting at this time, but in a state of enduring orienting activity more similar to that of exploration and navigation in waking within which novel events occur. Because of the dysfunction of executive thought, we predict that this exploratory REM cognition will be demonstrated to lack crucial aspects of the sharpness and alert attentiveness of waking navigation.

In spite of this general tendency, the activation of the anterior cingulate region, which is involved in focused attention in the waking state, indicates that an attending tendency is a marked characteristic of the brain during REM. In particular, since working memory processes and perceptual surveillance functions are disfacilitated while orienting systems and attention shift processes are engaged, the mind in REM could be characterized by brief periods of focus before reorienting occurs toward new and perhaps associated objects of attention. When maintained over time, this state could lead to the rapid occurrence of successive integrated foci of neural network processing, we suspect, that contribute to the experience of dream consciousness.

From a chronobiological perspective, the neural network that supports dreaming seems to stand in an opposite, orthogonal relationship to the neural network that supports executive thinking. Reciprocal, orthogonal changes in these two domains of cognition have been seen from wake to sleep and over the NREM-REM cycles of the night (Fosse et al., 2004). The role of the orienting system in dreaming suggests that the functional reciprocity in cognitive function may have its natural concomitant in waking situations of reorienting attention toward novel stimuli. During sudden orienting shifts toward novel happenings in waking, brain and behavior are characterized by a maximization of the efficiency in processing of the novel information, accompanied by an interruption of executive cognitive activity for a brief period of time. In waking, this obviously does not lead to hallucinations and is usually followed by a return to executive control for dealing with the novelty. REM sleep may represent an extreme pole on a dimension defined by executive cognition-orienting cognition, where orienting occurs relatively exclusively and in a continuous manner over time.

Because thinking, but not hallucinating, is a basic property of waking function, one question is whether a decline in thought processes in waking would lead to hallucinations in this state. Research on schizophrenia has provided a view on this question, because hallucinating in this disorder is thought to arise from a dysfunction of executive memory regions in the lateral prefrontal cortex (Goldman-Rakic, 1994). These deficits are assumed to follow a more primary dopaminergic but perhaps also serotonergic dysfunction, which alters the activities of interneurons and long-projection cells in local functional assemblies. The consequence of the symptoms of neuromodulatory function is thought to be that neural assemblies and cognitive functions shift away from ongoing foci and redirect toward novel information, akin to a loss of focus accompanied by reorienting (Winterer & Weinberger, 2004). This is similar to the neuronal network mechanisms we suggest to underlie dreaming. Further comparisons of chronobiological cognitive and conscious processes of dreaming in psychiatric patients and other people may shed light on these issues.

The orthogonal relationship between two categories of neurocognitive systems and tendencies, that is, those of executive cognition and orienting attention, could prove to be a phenomenon that is relevant in a relatively general sense during waking. Representing a basic evolutionary adaptation, we hypothesize that the orienting system may be a generalized tool of the brain that is intricately involved in many cognitive processes, such as memory access and recall. Parts of this system have also been shown to be engaged during resting and cognitively relaxed states of waking thought. Functional neuroimaging studies have focused on the neurocognitive activation profile of these relaxed states, often called the "baseline resting state" (Gusnard & Raichle, 2001). Although the baseline resting state is inherently heterogeneous, it has characteristic brain activation patterns that suggest it lies between alert executive waking cognition and REM sleep. The baseline state in particular seems to include activation of mediofrontal and medioparietal cortical regions that belong to the executive cognitive system, in addition to ventromedial prefrontal regions and the temporoparietal junction on the right side of the brain. These latter two regions appear to be activated during both REM sleep and orienting responses (Gusnard & Raichle, 2001).

This mix of executive cognitive activation and REM-like/orienting activation is consistent with the notion of the baseline state as a condition of reduced cognitive control combined with enhanced thought flow and imagery. Indeed, we suspect thought to be colored by interactions between these systems more generally, even in a competing manner, as with challenging situations where associations should be avoided. In this case, it has been demonstrated to be almost impossible to avoid mind wandering and imagistic thought, even under the most challenging cognitive situations (for example, Klinger, 1999; Klinger & Cox, 1987–1988).

Behavioral preparedness is a central feature of orienting behavior, occurring during active or passively alert behavioral states. REM sleep is characterized consistently by activation of primary regions of behavioral systems, including the vestibular nucleus of the pontine brainstem and the basal ganglia. REM could thus retain core brain characteristics of orienting behavior, suggesting that the concept of dreaming as "nonexecutive orienting" could provide a pathway for further investigations into the dreaming mind.

During orienting responses in waking, attention shifts are typically triggered by auditory stimuli, in addition to visual, nociceptive, and tactile stimuli with novelty values. For REM sleep, the cholinergic neurons in the midbrain tegmentum that activate the forebrain are known to be triggered by even deeper-lying generator neurons in the brain stem. These generator neurons include auditory neurons, which generally become activated by auditory stimulation in all basic behavioral states. Further suggesting a role of auditory systems in REM, high-frequency gamma firing activity traverses auditory pathways of the ear in this state as in waking orienting. Future studies of this activity are needed to better understand the role of auditory systems in dreaming.

Dream Consciousness

Dream consciousness is shaped by the neurobiology of the dreaming brain but still has properties with remarkable resemblance to those of active waking function. This resemblance is particularly striking for visual consciousness given the experience of vivid and integrated visual scenarios in dreams. More generally, dreaming provides reasonably integrated scenarios of social perception and action, suggesting a high degree of similarity between neurocognitive function and comparable experiences in waking (Domhoff, 2003). The first exception from adequate neurocognitive function in dreaming is, of course, the biological decoupling of executive thought, meaning that this capacity contributes much less to focusing and tracking in dreaming than in waking. But there is another exception that has not been relevant until this point: the notable lack of episodic memories in dreaming.

Memories of actual events experienced in an integrated situational fashion, which are readily recalled in waking life, are rarely present in dreams (Baylor & Cavallero, 2001; Fosse, Fosse, Hobson, & Stickgold, 2003). Dreamers have access to information on who they are, who their friends are, their feelings about the main people in their lives, and what their main interests and concerns are, but they do not know where they are (in bed), what they did the day before, or where they were two weeks ago. Although the state of dreaming does retain several memory capabilities, it does not easily support the integration of memory components, such as places, persons, objects, and actions, into an integrated phenomenology that is faithful to the dreamer's experiential background and current situation. Instead, the landscape of dreams reflects the gluing together of different but perhaps associated memory pieces into novel combinations, giving rise to familiar albeit changed subjective scenarios and actions.

In view of our conceptual framework, which highlights executive cognitive disfacilitation and emotional-perceptual activation, dreams may portray emotional tendencies of the dreamer (in feelings, actions, and so on) that are informative about waking conceptions and emotional predispositions. This is also suggested from longitudinal studies of dreaming based on diary dreams from the same person over periods of years, where it is apparent that dreams portray concerns about people and emotional matters that are consistent with their concerns, wishes, and worries in waking life (Domhoff, 2003). The expression of such emotional matters in dreams may be facilitated by the orientational state of the brain, within which the self-in-the-dream may be expressed in a somewhat basic and uncensored way. Because emotion may play a role in the developmental of (perceptual) dream scenarios, the scenarios that are experienced may not be coincidental but rather (emotionally) personalized ones, as has been indicated also by laboratory studies (Hoelscher, Klinger, & Barta, 1981).

Although the dreaming brain tends to process information in an emotionally positive (versus fearful) way, we hasten to add that the mnemonic tendencies expressed by the activated neurons may not be constrained by this tendency. That is, we hypothesize that the overall emotional settings of the brain have a strong effect upon the way that information is processed, but not so much upon the emotional nature of the memories that are engaged by the traveling dynamic oscillations in the networks that are online. Instead, we suggest that all types of emotional memories inherent in the activated neurobiology may be engaged and expressed during dreaming.

No consensus has been reached on the distribution of emotions during REM dreaming. In addition, only limited data exist on the relationship between emotions in waking and dreaming, where experiential data are strongly needed. However, Foulkes and his coworkers (1988) noted that a difference between waking and dreaming is that emotions are at times suspiciously lacking in situations where emotions would have been found during waking. A hyporeactivity of emotional recognition and consciousness could be a feature of REM that is associated with the disfacilitation of executive cognitive processes, leaving executive emotion to dull itself and with minimal support from working memory and perceptual surveillance processes. Thus, we suggest that although basic emotion systems are among the driving circuitry of dreaming, there is a combination of lowered consciousness for the experience of emotion and a drive away from excited emotion existing in parallel, which dulls down emotions of the self, allowing other brain processes to become salient in the shaping of dream consciousness.

Consistent with these predictions, in representative samples of REM dreams, emotions of anxiety and fear are more often absent than present (up to 90 percent absent for REM dreams) and are significantly less intense than other emotions when they occur (Fosse, Stickgold, & Hobson, 2001b; Strauch & Meier, 1996). At the same time, the same studies show that sexual engagement and feelings of eroticism and love are also rare in dreams, indicating that the most alarmed and exciting states of conscious experience are not typically entered during dreaming. Instead, we suggest that the higher degrees of excitement, anxiety, and self-reflective awareness seen in the dreams of people with sleep and anxiety disorders occur when biological or psychological processes lead to instabilities in state-controlling systems that affect the aminergic/cholinergic balance of brain stem function. Such imbalances could facilitate alarm emotion, alarmed attention, perceptual attention, and a sustained focus, and thus make it possible for the dreamer to obtain a subjective, phenomenological distance from dream percepts. Such changes have been indicated in narcoleptic REM, where dreaming is more reflective and anxious and where the aminergic-cholinergic balance, and thus the sleep-wake balance, is altered compared to normal REM (Fosse, Stickgold, & Hobson, 2002).

Although anxiety dreams seem to be more readily recalled than other dreams, we don't think the relative absence of anxiety dreams in representatively sampled REM dreams means that processes of anxiety and fear are not relevant to dreaming. To the contrary, we argue that it is precisely alarm-producing situations in waking life that most efficiently modify the orienting network that is activated in REM, conveyed through alarm-induced releases of noradrenaline and cortisol upon amygdalo-hippocampal networks, which have been shown to lead to synaptic modifications in processes such as place cells in the CA1 in the hippocampus. Thus, we suspect that fear-evoking events will impact dream processes through affecting basic regions of the orienting system, modifying the expression of this system during dreaming to extents that signify the seriousness of the event to the dreamer.

OSCILLATORY DYNAMICS OF DREAM CONSCIOUSNESS

Spatially synchronized gamma waves, which have been shown to be necessary for cognition and consciousness, are seen in REM sleep, as well as in states of active information processing in waking. Although the gamma waves in REM are synchronized over large networks, interruptions of gamma continuity are seen within some functions, such as across the executive cognitive system, in this state (Cantero, Atienza, Madsen, & Stickgold, 2004; Perez-Garci, Del-Rio-Portilla, Guevara, Arce, & Corsi-Cabrera, 2001).

To search for a nested synchronous context for the gamma waves in REM, which should be needed to support consciousness according to studies of waking thought, studies of the hippocampal formation may be informative.

Gamma waves, as well as theta waves, are a fundamental neurophysiologic feature of the hippocampus formation during spatial orienting in waking as well as in animal REM sleep. Cantero and his colleagues (2004) recently demonstrated that theta waves occur also in human REM, then in a briefer fashion with the theta bouts having a duration of about one second. This pattern of theta is, however, reminiscent of the theta activity seen during cognitive tasks in waking humans, where approximately 1- to 2-second theta bursts are seen that are time-locked to the cognitive task (Rizzuto et al., 2003). Furthermore, according to animal studies, in REM, as during orienting, the activation waves of the pontine brain stem interlock with the hippocampal theta activity, leading to a synchronization of the two systems (Karashima, Nakamura et al., 2002; Karashima, Nakao, Katayama, & Honnda, 2005).

There is also evidence that delta waves (1.5–3 Hz) are present in the hippocampus in human REM and occur in a synchronized fashion that last throughout REM periods (Bodizs et al., 2001). Similarly, in waking, both theta and delta oscillations have been found in the hippocampus formation in people subject to a virtual orienting task (playing a taxi-driver) (Ekstrom et al., 2005). This presence of various oscillatory types could suggest the presence also of functionally nested oscillations of low and high frequencies in the hippocampus during dreaming and REM, similar to those seen in this region during orienting and exploration in waking.

To explain the coherence of the visual scenarios of dreams and of integrated dream consciousness, the concept of self-organizing processes is often evoked. In keeping with this concept, we think the coherence of visual and perceptual scenarios in dreams reflects the nested ultrasynchronous behavior of neural networks that are engaged. Within this context, we speculate that an increasing specificity and power in the pattern of dynamic oscillations would focus the brain's attention en route to conscious experience. Then, existing traveling oscillatory patterns would be shaped by the inherent, mnemonic properties of the orienting and activated substrate. We hypothesize that a strong tendency of neurons toward expressions of inherency leads to a further shaping of the dynamic oscillations of the dreaming networks, making them self-organize into narrow but spatially extended and coherent corridors of attention that become crowned with conscious experience.

CONCLUSION

The study of dreaming may help reveal the intricate properties of neural behavior that are associated with consciousness, because the contrasts between consciousness and biological function in these two states now can be compared using increasingly sophisticated instruments and methods for both biological and psychological function. Such endeavors could help explicate the complexity of neural dynamics that is also necessary to address the hard problem of consciousness—the enigma of the exact processes and components of oscillatory neurons that have the capacity of subjective experience (Chalmers, 1996).

Although we have focused on biological and neurocognitive processes, we recognize that the development of specific dream content within the setting of the dreaming brain depends strongly on the psychological processes of the dreamer. Given the theory of mind-brain unity that we espouse, psychological processes are likely to be embedded in and a part of the neurobiological processes of emotion, perception, memory, and thought that we have sought to describe. We think that studies of the psychological properties of dreaming can start out with the particular activation and modification patterns of neurocognitive processing in REM and Stage 2 NREM and can then combine this with psychological and psychosocial investigations to arrive at integrated psychobiosocial models of dreaming.

Whatever the fate of the specific perspective we have presented in this chapter, we hope we have shown that the many solid findings generated by dream researchers inside and outside the sleep laboratory in the past several decades can be combined with more recent findings by neurocognitivists and other neuroscientists to project a plausible conceptual framework for future neurocognitive models of dreaming.

ACKNOWLEDGMENT

Roar Fosse thanks Anne Kari Dersyd for valuable input to this chapter.

REFERENCES

Antrobus, J. (1978). Dreaming as cognition. In A. Arkin, J. Antrobus, & S. Ellman (Eds.), *The mind in sleep: Psychology and psychophysiology* (pp. 569–581). Hillsdale, NJ: Lawrence Erlbaum Associates.

Antrobus, J. (2000). Theories of dreaming. In M. Kryger, T. Roth, & W. Dement (Eds.), *Principles and practices of sleep medicine* (3rd ed., pp. 472–481). Philadelphia, PA: Saunders.

Antrobus, J., Kondo, T., & Reinsel, R. (1995). Dreaming in the late morning: Summation of REM and diurnal cortical activation. *Consciousness & Cognition, 4*, 275–299.

Bacci, A., Huguenard, J. R., & Prince, D. A. (2003). Functional autaptic neurotransmission in fastspiking interneurons: A novel form of feedback inhibition in the neocortex. *Journal of Neuroscience, 23*, 859–866.

Bacci, A., Huguenard, J. R., & Prince, D. A. (2004). Long-lasting self-inhibition of neocortical interneurons mediated by endocannabinoids. *Nature, 431*, 312–316.

Basar, E. (2006). The theory of the whole-brain-work. *International Journal of Psychophysiology, 60,* 133–138.

Basar, E., Basar-Eroglu, C., Karakas, S., & Schurmanna, M. (2001). Gamma, alpha, delta, and theta oscillations govern cognitive processes. *International Journal of Psychophysiology, 39,* 241–248.

Baylor, G., & Cavallero, C. (2001). Memory sources associated with REM and NREM dream reports throughout the night: A new look at the data. *Sleep, 24,* 165–170.

Bodizs, R., Kantor, S., Szabo, G., Szucs, A., Eross, L., & Halasz, P. (2001). Rhythmic hippocampal slow wave oscillations characterizes REM sleep in humans. *Hippocampus, 11,* 747–753.

Braun, A., Balkin, T., Wesensten, N., Carson, R., Varga, M., Baldwin, P., et al. (1997). Regional cerebral blood flow throughout the sleep-wake cycle: An (H2O)-O-15 PET study. *Brain, 120,* 1173–1197.

Braun, A., Balkin, T., Wesensten, N., Gwadry, F., Carson, R., & Varga, M. (1998). Dissociated pattern of activity in visual cortices and their projections during human rapid eye movement sleep. *Science, 279,* 91–95.

Buzsaki, G. (2002). Theta oscillations in the hippocampus. *Neuron, 33,* 325–334.

Cantero, J. L., & Atienza, M. (2005). The role of neural synchronization in the emergence of cognition across the wake-sleep cycle. *Reviews in the Neuroscience, 16,* 69–83.

Cantero, J. L., Atienza, M., Madsen, J. R., & Stickgold, R. (2004). Gamma EEG dynamics in neocortex and hippocampus during human wakefulness and sleep. *NeuroImage, 22,* 1271–1280.

Cantero, J. L., Atienza, M., Stickgold, R., Kahana, M. J., Madsen, J. R., & Kocsis, B. (2003), Sleep-dependent oscillations in the human hippocampus and neocortex. *Journal of Neuroscience, 23,* 10897–10903.

Chalmers, D. (1996). *The conscious mind: In search of a fundamental theory.* New York: Oxford University Press.

Cicogna, P., Natale, V., Occhionero, M., & Bosinelli, M. (1998). A comparison of mental activity during sleep onset and morning awakening. *Sleep, 21,* 462–470.

Cote, K. A., Epps, T. M., & Campbell, K. B. (2000). The role of the spindle in human information processing of high-intensity stimuli during sleep. *Journal of Sleep Research, 9,* 19–26.

Domhoff, G. W. (2003). *The scientific study of dreams: Neural networks, cognitive development, and content analysis.* Washington, DC: American Psychological Association.

Dorus, E., Dorus, W., & Rechtschaffen, A. (1971). The incidence of novelty in dreams. *Archives of General Psychiatry, 25,* 364–368.

Ekstrom, A. D., Caplan, J. B., Ho, E., Shattuck, K., Fried, I., & Kahana, M. J. (2005). Hippocampal theta wave activity during virtual navigation. *Hippocampus, 15,* 881–889.

Fosse, M., Fosse, R., Hobson, J. A., & Stickgold, R. (2003). Dreaming and episodic memory: A functional dissociation? *Journal of Cognitive Neuroscience, 15,* 1–9.

Fosse, R., Stickgold, R., & Hobson, J. A. (2001a). Brain-mind states: Reciprocal variation in thoughts and hallucinations. *Psychological Science, 12,* 30–36.

Fosse, R., Stickgold, R., & Hobson, J. A. (2001b). The mind in REM sleep: Reports of emotional experience. *Sleep, 24,* 947–955.

Fosse, R., Stickgold, R., & Hobson, J. A. (2002). Emotional experience during rapid-eye-movement sleep in narcolepsy. *Sleep, 25*, 724–732.

Fosse, R., Stickgold, R., & Hobson, J. A. (2004). Thinking and hallucinating: Reciprocal changes in sleep. *Psychophysiology, 41*, 298–305.

Foulkes, D. (1982). *Children's dreams.* New York: Wiley.

Foulkes, D. (1985). *Dreaming: A cognitive-psychological analysis.* Hillsdale, NJ: Lawrence Erlbaum Associates.

Foulkes, D. (1999). *Children's dreaming and the development of consciousness.* Cambridge, MA: Harvard University Press.

Foulkes, D., Sullivan, B., Kerr, N., & Brown, L. (1988). Appropriateness of dream feelings to dreamed situations. *Cognition & Emotion, 2*, 29–39.

Foulkes, D., & Vogel, G. (1965). Mental activity at sleep onset. *Journal of Abnormal Psychology, 70*, 231–243.

Gallagher, M. (2000). The amygdala and associative learning. In J. P. Appleton (Ed.), *The amygdale: A functional analysis* (pp. 311–330). New York: Oxford University Press.

Goldman-Rakic, P. S. (1994). Working memory dysfunction in schizophrenia. *Journal of Neuropsychiatry & Clinical Neuroscience, 6*, 348–357.

Gusnard, D. A., & Raichle, M. E. (2001). Searching for a baseline: Functional imaging and the resting human brain. *Nature Reviews Neuroscience, 2*, 685–694.

Hobson, J. A., McCarley, R., & Wyzinski, P. (1975). Sleep cycle oscillation: Reciprocal discharge by two brainstem neuronal groups. *Science, 189*, 55–58.

Hoelscher, T., Klinger, E., & Barta, S. (1981). Incorporation of concern- and nonconcern-related verbal stimuli into dream content. *Journal of Abnormal Psychology, 90*, 88–91.

Johnson, J. D. (2005). REM sleep and the development of context memory. *Medical Hypotheses, 64*, 499–504.

Kajimura, N., Uchiyama, M., Takayama, Y., Uchida, S., Uema, T., Kato, M., et al. (1999). Activity of midbrain reticular formation and neocortex during the progression of human non-rapid eye movement sleep. *Journal of Neuroscience Research, 19*, 10065–10073.

Kerr, N., & Foulkes, D. (1981). Right hemispheric mediation of dream visualization: A case study. *Cortex, 17*, 603–610.

Kerr, N. H., Foulkes, D., & Jurkovic, G. J. (1978). Reported absence of visual dream imagery in a normally sighted subject with Turner's syndrome. *Journal of Mental Imagery, 2*, 247–264.

Karashima, A., Nakamura, K., Sato, N., Nakao, M., Katayama, N., & Yamamoto, M. (2002). Phase-locking of spontaneous and elicited ponto-geniculo-occipital waves is associated with acceleration of hippocampal theta waves during rapid eye movement sleep in cats. *Brain Research, 958*, 347–358.

Karashima, A., Nakao, M., Katayama, N., & Honnda, K. (2005). Instantaneous acceleration and amplification of hippocampal theta wave coincident with phasic pontine activities during REM sleep. *Brain Research, 1051*, 50–56.

Klinger, E. (1999). Thought flow: Properties and mechanisms underlying shifts in content. In J. Singer & P. Salovey (Eds.), *At play in the fields of consciousness* (pp. 29–50). Hillsdale, NJ: Lawrence Erlbaum Associates.

Klinger, E., & Cox, W. (1987–1988). Dimensions of thought flow in everyday life. *Imagination, Cognition & Personality, 7*, 105–128.

Koukkou, M., & Lehmann, D. (1983). Dreaming: The functional state-shift hypothesis. A neuropsychophysiological model. *British Journal of Psychiatry, 142*, 221–231.

Kuiken, D., Businek, R., Dukewich, T. L., & Gendlin, E. T. (1996). Individual differences in orienting activity mediate feeling realization in dreams: II. Evidence from concurrent reports of movement inhibition. *Dreaming, 6*, 251–264.

Lee, R. S., Steffensen, S. C., Henriksen, S. J. (2001). Discharge profiles of ventral tegmental area GABA neurons during movement, anesthesia, and the sleep-wake cycle. *Journal of Neuroscience, 21*, 1757–1766.

Lena, I., Parrott, S., Deschaux, O., Muffat-Joly, S., Sauvinet, V., Renaud, B., et al. (2005). Variations in extracellular levels of dopamine, noradrenaline, glutamate, and aspartate across the sleep-wake cycle in the medial prefrontal cortex and nucleus accumbens of freely moving rats. *Journal of Neuroscience Research, 81*, 891–899.

Lennox, B. R., Park, S. B.G., Medley, I., Morris, P. G., & Jones, P. B. (2000). The functional anatomy of auditory hallucinations in schizophrenia. *Psychiatry Research, 100*, 13–20.

Llinas, R., Ribary, U., Contreras, D., & Pedroarena, C. (1998). The neuronal basis of consciousness. *Philosophical Transactions of the Royal Society of London, 353*, 1841–1849.

Lu, J., Greco, M. A., Shiromani, P., & Saper, C. B. (2000). Effect of lesions of the ventrolateral preoptic nucleus on NREM and REM sleep. *Journal of Neuroscience, 20*, 3830–3842.

Lu, J., Sherman, D., Devor, M., & Saper, C. B. (2006). A putative flip-flop switch for control of REM sleep. *Nature, 441*, 589–594.

Maquet, P. (2000). Functional neuroimaging of normal human sleep by positron emission tomography. *Journal of Sleep Research, 9*, 207–231.

Maquet, P., Degueldre, C., Delfiore, G., Aerts, J., Peters, J. M., Luxen, A., et al. (1997). Functional neuroanatomy of human slow wave sleep. *Journal of Neuroscience, 17*, 2807–2812.

Maquet, P., Peters, J. M., Aerts, J., Delfiore, G., Dequerldre, C., Luxen, A., et al. (1996). Functional neuroanatomy of human rapid-eye-movement sleep and dreaming. *Nature, 383*, 163–166.

McNamara, P., McLaren, D., Smith, D., Brown, A., & Stickgold, R. (2005). A "Jekyll and Hyde" within: Aggressive versus friendly interactions in REM and NREM dreams. *Psychological Science, 16*, 130–136.

Morrison, A. (1979). Brainstem regulation of behavior during sleep and wakefulness. In J. Sprague & A. Epstein (Eds.), *Progress in psychobiology and physiological psychology* (Vol. 8, pp. 91–131). New York: Academic Press.

Mulle, C., Steriade, M., & Deschenes, M. (1985). Absence of spindle oscillations in the cat anterior thalamic nuclei. *Brain Research, 13*, 169–171.

Nakabayashi, T., Uchida, S., Maehara, T., Hirai, N., Nakamura, M., Arakaki, H., et al. (2001). Absence of sleep spindles in human medial and basal temporal lobes. *Psychiatry & Clinical Neurosciences, 55*, 57–65.

Nielsen, T. A. (2000). A review of mentation in REM and NREM sleep: "Covert" REM sleep as a possible reconciliation of two opposing processes. *Behavioral & Brain Sciences, 23*, 851–866.

Nielsen, T. A., Kuiken, D. L., & McGregor, D. L. (1989). Effects of dream reflection on waking affect: Awareness of feelings, Rorschach movement, and facial EMG. *Sleep, 12*, 277–286.

Nofzinger, E., Mintun, M., Wiseman, M., Kupfer, D., & Moore, R. (1997). Forebrain activation in REM sleep: An FDG PET study. *Brain Research, 770*, 192–201.

Pace-Schott, E. F., & Hobson, J. A. (2002). The neurobiology of sleep: Genetics, cellular physiology and subcortical networks. *Nature Reviews Neuroscience, 3*, 591–605.

Papez, J.W. (1995) A proposed mechanism of emotion. 1937. *Journal of Neuropsychiatry & Clinical Neuroscience, 7*, 103–112.

Pare, D., Steriade, M., Deschenes, M., & Oakson, G. (1987). Physiological characteristics of anterior thalamic nuclei, a group devoid of inputs from reticular thalamic nucleus. *Journal of Neurophysiology, 57*, 1669–1685.

Perez-Garci, E., Del-Rio-Portilla, Y., Guevara, M. A., Arce, C., & Corsi-Cabrera, M. (2001). Paradoxical sleep is characterized by uncoupled gamma activity between frontal and perceptual cortical regions. *Sleep, 24*, 118–126.

Pivik, R. T., Joncas, S., & Busby, K. A. (1999). Sleep spindles and arousal: The effects of age and sensory stimulation. *Sleep Research Online, 2*, 89–100.

Rechtschaffen, A. (1978). The single-mindedness and isolation of dreams. *Sleep, 1*, 97–109.

Rechtschaffen, A. (1997). The single-mindedness and isolation of dreams. In M. Myslobodsky (Ed.), *The mythomanias: The nature of deception and self-deception* (pp. 219–223). Mahwah, NJ: Lawrence Erlbaum Associates.

Reid, M., Nishino, S., Tafti, M., Siegel, J., Dement, W., & Mignot, E. (1998). Neuropharmacological characterization of basal forebrain cholinergic stimulated cataplexy in narcoleptic canines. *Experimental Neurology, 151*, 89–104.

Rizzuto, D. S., Madsen, J. R., Bromfield, E., Schulze-Bonhage, A., Seelig, D., Sschenbrenner-Scheibe, R., et al. (2003). Reset of human neocortical oscillations during a working memory task. *Proceedings of the National Academy of Sciences of the United States of America, 100*, 7931–7936.

Schmitt, J. A., Wingen, M., Ramaekers, J. G., Evers, E. A., & Riedel, W. J. (2006). Serotonin and human cognitive performance. *Current Pharmaceutical Design, 12*, 2473–2486.

Soh, K., Morita, Y., & Sei, H. (1992). Relationship between eye movements and oneiric behavior in cats. *Physiology & Behavior, 52*, 553–558.

Solms, M. (1997). *The neuropsychology of dreams: A clinico-anatomical study*. Hillsdale, NJ: Lawrence Erlbaum Associates.

Steriade M. (2000). Corticothalamic resonance, states of vigilance and mentation. *Neuroscience, 101*, 243–276.

Steriade, M. (2006). Grouping of brain rhythms in corticothalamic systems. *Neuroscience, 137*, 1087–1106.

Steriade, M., & McCarley, R. W. (2005). *Brain control of wakefulness and sleep*. New York: Springer.

Steriade, M., Timofeev, I., & Grenier, F. (2001). Natural waking and sleep states: A view from inside cortical neurons. *Journal of Neurophysiology, 85*, 1969–1985.

Snyder, F. (1970). The phenomenology of dreaming. In L. Madow & L. Snow (Eds.), *The psychodynamic implications of the physiological studies on dreams* (pp. 124–151). Springfield, IL: Thomas.

Strauch, I. (2005). REM dreaming in the transition from late childhood to adolescence: A longitudinal study. *Dreaming, 15*, 155–169.

Strauch, I., & Meier, B. (1996). *In search of dreams: Results of experimental dream research*. Albany, NY: State University of New York Press.

Taylor, W. B., Moldofsky, H., & Furedy, J. J. (1985). Heart rate deceleration in REM sleep: An orienting reaction interpretation. *Psychophysiology, 22*, 110–115.

Uchida, S., Hirai, N., Nakabayashi, T., Maehara, T., & Shimizu, H. (1999). Sleep spindle in human orbitofrontal cortex. *Sleep Research Abstract*, S96.

Varela, F., Lachaux, J. P., Rodriguez, E., & Martinerie, J. (2001). The brainweb: Phase synchronization and large-scale integration. *Nature Reviews Neuroscience, 2*, 229–239.

Vazquez, J., & Baghdoyan, H. P. (2001). Basal forebrain acetylcholine release during REM sleep is significantly greater than during waking. *American Journal of Physiological, Regulatory, Integrative, & Comparative Physiology, 280*, 598–601.

Vogel, G. (1991). Sleep-onset mentation. In S. Ellman & J. Antrobus (Eds.), *The mind in sleep: Psychology and psychophysiology* (2nd ed., pp. 125–136). New York: Wiley & Sons.

Wamsley, E. J., Hirota, Y., Tucker, M. A., Smith, M. R., Doan, T., & Antrobus, J. S. (in press). Circadian and ultradian influences on dreaming: A dual rhythm model. *Brain Research Bulletin*.

Winterer, G., & Weinberger, D. (2004). Genes, dopamine and cortical signal-to-noise ratio in schizophrenia. *Trends in Neurosciences, 27*, 683–690.

Wright, C. I., Martis, B., Schwartz, C. E., Shin, L. M., Fischer, H., McMullin, K., et al. (2003). Novelty responses and differential effects of order in the amygdala, substantia innominata, and inferior temporal cortex. *NeuroImage, 18*, 660–669.

Yuste, R. (2005). Origin and classification of neocortical interneurons. *Neuron, 48*, 591–604.

Four

Dream Recall:
Models and Empirical Data

Michael Schredl

INTRODUCTION

Since the discovery of rapid eye movement (REM) sleep (Aserinsky & Kleitman, 1953), it is well documented that every person spends on average about 20 percent of total sleep time every night in a REM stage. If the sleeper is awakened from REM sleep, dream recall rates are very high: 80 to 90 percent of the awakenings yield some kind of dream report (for comparison, Nielsen, 2000). Even after nonrapid eye movement (NREM) awakenings (Stage 2 or slow wave sleep), some mental content has been reported quite often (Foulkes, 1962; Wittmann, Palmy & Schredl, 2004). Some researchers advocate the hypothesis that the mind never sleeps, that is, dreaming of some kind is present during the entire sleep process. Despite the consistency of the physiological processes, the variability of dream recall in the home setting is considerably large. Some persons almost never recall any dream, whereas others can relate a detailed description of their nightly experiences almost every morning.

Dream recall in the present overview is defined as follows: "Successful dream recall is present if a person is able to recollect—after waking up—some mental content which occurred during sleep."

A definite verification that recollections have really occurred during sleep is impossible—not even in the sleep laboratory. But considerable evidence has been published (Schredl, 1999; Strauch & Meier, 2004) that shows dreams remembered upon awakening are experienced during sleep, for example, dream reports were collected that include external stimuli that were applied during REM sleep prior to the awakening. The sleep stage that occurs before waking up can only be determined in the sleep lab or with ambulatory monitoring units (Hobson & Stickgold, 1995). In the home setting, research must rely on the subjective experience of the dreamer. The so-called "white dreaming" (De Gennaro & Violani, 1990) or contentless reports (Cohen, 1972b) are not included in this definition. These are incidents in which the dreamer has the impression of having dreamt but is not able to recall any content.

On average, students recall one to two dreams per week at home (for example, Belicki, 1986; Schredl, 2002a). In representative samples of the general population, dream recall frequency is slightly lower, but about 68 percent recall at least one dream per month (Stepansky, Holzinger, Schmeiser-Rieder, Saletu, Kunze, & Zeitlnofer, 1998).

In the present chapter, models and research findings that try to explain interindividual differences in dream recall frequency (DRF) between subjects, as well as intraindividual fluctuations within one subject, will be presented.

The *influencing factors* can be divided into two groups: trait factors and state factors (Schredl & Montasser, 1996/1997). Trait factors are characteristics that are quite stable over time, such as personality dimensions, cognitive functioning (for example, visual memory), and creativity. Sociodemographic variables, such as age and gender, and the habitual sleep duration can also be classified as trait factors. On the other hand, state factors are short-term acting variables, such as nocturnal awakenings, presleep mood, or major life events. The distinction between state and trait factors, however, cannot always be made in an exclusive way. It is, for example, possible that the habitual sleep duration (long sleepers versus short sleepers) affects dream recall frequency, and the sleep duration changes from night to night of one person have an effect on dream recall, too. Therefore, some factors will be discussed in both sections.

First, the models of dream recall that have been published in the literature will be outlined in the section *Models of Dream Recall*. For each approach, the applicability for explaining state and trait factors will be emphasized. In order to evaluate the empirical data adequately, measurement methods and methodological issues associated with measuring dream recall frequency (for example, reliability) will be discussed (*Measuring Dream Recall Frequency*), because these factors can affect the results of the studies presented in the section *Factors Affecting DRF* in various ways. The last section of *Factors Affecting DRF* comprises the attempt to sort out and bring together the most important influencing factors for which solid evidence was established by the research activities in this field. In the light of these findings, the theories will be evaluated and future directions for researchers will be outlined.

MODELS OF DREAM RECALL

In Table 4.1, the six models of dream recall that have been formulated in the literature are depicted chronologically. These models are based on different paradigms; some are more psychological, whereas others emphasize physiological processes. In order to evaluate the empirical data that will be reviewed in the next sections, two kinds of hypotheses will be derived for each model: one group aims at trait factors, the other at state factors.

Freud's (1900) model of dream generation might be—in a very simplified way—described in the following way. A latent dream thought emerging from the unconscious and often expressing unacceptable drives or wishes is altered so it can pass censorship. This product is the manifest dream, that is, the dream recalled by the dreamer. If the unconscious wishes are not concealed sufficiently, Freud assumed that the dream as a whole would be repressed in order to avoid conscious awareness of these issues. This hypothesis, however, cannot be tested empirically because repressed dreams cannot be elicited and compared to recalled dreams to look for differences in dream content. Despite this limitation, several studies have tried to test the repression hypothesis by using indirect approaches. Research has shown that presleep films can affect dream content (Schredl, 1999). An erotic film presented in the evening might generate dreams that might be an object for repression, and, therefore, dream recall should decrease. This approach is, of course, more complex because other factors have to be taken into account; for example, the question of whether repression of sexual content occurs in all subjects in a similar fashion, that is, interindividual differences regarding repression. This effect on dream recall can subsumed as a state factor. Another approach that targeted at the

TABLE 4.1
Models of Dream Recall

Approach

- Repression hypothesis (Freud, 1900)
- Lifestyle hypothesis (Schonbar, 1965)
- Interference hypothesis (Cohen & Wolfe, 1973)
- Salience hypothesis (Cohen & MacNeilage, 1974)
- Arousal-Retrieval model (Koulack & Goodenough, 1976)
- State-shift model (Koukkou & Lehmann, 1983)

trait aspect investigated the relationship between dream recall in general and repression conceptualized as a personality dimension or coping style. Persons who try to avoid confrontation, introspection, and anxiety (repressors) should recall—according to the repression hypothesis—their dreams less often than so-called sensitizers.

The *life-style hypothesis* of Schonbar (1965) says that persons who are open to inner experiences; are more field-independent, introverted, and creative; and have an internal locus of control, divergent thinking style, and imagination recall their dreams more often. Dream recall is seen as part of a lifestyle. On the other hand, persons who recall their dreams rarely should be extroverted, have an external locus of control, and not be very open to inner experiences. Therefore, the lifestyle hypothesis encompasses Freud's repression hypothesis, if one conceptualizes repression as a personality trait. The hypothesis focuses on the trait factors influencing dream recall, but state factors may also be of importance; for example, a person could dream more in creative periods than in noncreative periods.

The *interference hypothesis* (Cohen & Wolfe, 1973) was derived from classical memory theory. This hypothesis states that recall is difficult or impossible if interferences between the experience and the time of recall are in effect. Applied to the process of dream recall, this can be formulated in this way: The fewer interferences (external noises, internal distractions like thoughts about the upcoming day) that are active in the time span between awakening and recording and telling or mentally rehearsing the dream, the greater the chance of recalling the dream experience. This approach stresses the influence of state factors that may affect the person upon awakening. The model, however, may also explain the effect of trait aspects; for example, field-independent persons show low distractibility by external stimuli and, therefore, should be better dream recallers.

A similar theory is the *salience hypothesis* (Cohen & MacNeilage, 1974), which was also derived from classical memory theory. The more salient (impressive, vivid, and so on) the incident (dream) is, the better is the recall of this incident (dream) will be later. This hypothesis is contrary to the repression hypothesis, which states that instinct-driven (often intense) dreams tend to be repressed and are not recalled. Similar difficulties, however, emerge when it comes to empirically testing the salience hypothesis because it is not possible—in contrast to the experiments of classical memory theory—to measure the salience of the original experience (dream experience); the waking mind and the researcher only have access to the recalled dream. However, the fact that dreams are influenced by waking-life experience may be also helpful in this context. A negative presleep mood, for example, after a frustrating day may yield to more negatively toned dreams and, therefore, to better dream recall. Another example for this relationship is nightmares, which are often easily recalled years later because of their emotional intensity. Giora (1973) suggested another approach for investigating the relationship between emotional arousal and dream recall. In the sleep laboratory, the physiological arousal (respiratory parameters, heart rate, electrodermal activity) during REM sleep can be measured. Because heightened autonomic arousal is related to more intense emotions in the waking state, it can be assumed that the chance of reporting a dream is higher after awakenings from REM periods with high physiological arousal than from REM periods that exhibit low activation. The findings regarding the relationship between emotional intensity of the recalled dream and physiological parameters, however, are not homogeneous (see Schredl, 2000). Similar to the interference hypothesis, the salience hypothesis mainly explains the effect of state factors. But, it seems equally plausible that trait factors are also related to dream recall in terms of the salience hypothesis. It could be that high dream recallers show heightened autonomic activity during REM sleep in general, or some persons are strongly absorbed by waking-life events as well as dreams and, therefore, have more intense emotional reactions to the stimuli/dreams; as a result, these persons recall their dreams more easily.

The *arousal-retrieval model* of Koulack and Goodenough (1976) hypothesizes that two steps are necessary for recalling a dream. For the first step, a certain amount of cortical arousal is necessary in order to transfer the information (in this case, the dream content) from short-term memory into long-term memory. Basic support for this assumption was provided by learning experiments that were carried out with "sleeping" participants (for example, see Koukkou & Lehmann, 1968). Information will only be stored (and later recalled) if the brain is activated (alpha waves = relaxed waking state), because learning of complex material during sleep is not possible (Aarons, 1976). In terms of dream recall, a period of wakefulness must follow the dream experience so that the person can recall the dream. This would explain why dreams that occur during the first part of the night are rarely recalled, whereas the last dreams before the awakening in the morning are much more likely to be accessible (Schonbar, 1961). Once the dream is stored in long-term memory, the second step of the model, the process of retrieval, is important. The salience hypothesis, as well as the interference hypothesis, can be integrated as factors that might affect the retrieval of the information. The more salient the dream experience and the less interference that occurs during the retrieval process, the higher is the probability of recalling the dream. Even the repression hypothesis was integrated into the model, that is, very intense emotions might also result in a smaller chance of recalling the dream. In addition, the model predicts that cues that are related to the dream content can facilitate dream recall. Similar to salience and interference hypotheses, the effects of state factors are stressed, such as frequency of nocturnal awakenings. With respect to trait factors, one might assume that persons with good visual memory are also high dream recallers.

For Koukkou and Lehmann (1980, 1983) who formulated the *functional state-shift model* of dream recall, the following assumptions are basic to their model. They divided cognitive activation of the brain into different functional states with their associated memory storages. Whereas higher functional states have difficult access to "lower" memory storage, the flow of information in the reverse direction is unimpeded. This explains why waking-life elements are reflected in dreams (REM sleep is a functional state that is lower in activation than the waking state), but waking consciousness has limited access to the contents of the REM sleep periods. For the dream recall process (transfer of material of the functional state of REM or NREM sleep to the waking state), it was hypothesized that the closeness (in terms of overall brain activation) of these two functional states is of importance. For example, the more activated the REM or NREM sleep before awakening is, the better is the chance of recalling a dream. This model stresses the role of state factors—the difference between the functional states prior and after awakening—in the recall process, but trait factors may be of importance as well. There might be persons with a generally heightened cognitive activation in REM sleep or persons with a higher permeability between different functional states (the concept of thin boundaries; Hartmann, 1991) and an associated high dream recall.

The six theories just presented will be evaluated in the view of the empirical findings in the section *Evaluation of the Models and Future Directions in DRF Research.*

MEASURING DREAM RECALL FREQUENCY (DRF)

The studies summarized in the next section utilized different methods for measuring DRF. The advantages and disadvantages of these methods and the intercorrelations between these measures will be discussed briefly. In addition, several methodological issues that may affect the measurement of DRF are addressed.

Measurement Methods

Three measurement methods are widely used in DRF research (see Table 4.2). The simplest approach is the presentation of a scale within a *questionnaire*. The participants are asked, for example, to estimate their DRF over

TABLE 4.2
Measuring Dream Recall Frequency (DRF)

Measurement Methods

- Questionnaires
- Dream diaries
- Awakenings in the sleep laboratory

the last few months or to state whether they recalled a dream last night or not. For the rating scales, two different formats are usually chosen: scales with relative categories, ("Have you been able to recall your dreams recently?" Never, rarely, seldom, often, very often [Görtelmeyer, 1986]) and scales that include absolute categories (see Table 4.3).

Although the correlation between these two kinds of measures (items using relative categories versus items with absolute categories) is sufficient ($r = .647$, $N = 444$; Schredl, 2004), items using categories with exact frequencies are preferable because the estimation of what is meant by rarely, seldom, often, and so on, may vary considerably from person to person. This might be the reason for the lower retest reliability in these scales (see the section *Methodological Issues in Measuring DRF*). The advantage of this retrospective measure is that dream recall is not affected by the measurement, thus, the "natural" DRF of everyday life can be elicited. The major shortcoming of this approach is the possible bias caused by imperfect memory. How exactly can one state how often dreams were recalled in the mornings upon awakening during the last week or over the last months? This may be a real problem for persons who do not focus on their dreams.

The second approach requires participants to keep a *dream diary*. Either they should state each morning on a checklist whether they have dreamt or not, or they should, for content analytic studies, record the dream(s) of the

TABLE 4.3
Rating Scale Measuring DRF

How often have you recalled your dreams
recently (several months)?

- almost every morning
- several times a week
- about once a week
- two or three times a month
- about once a month
- less than once a month
- never

Source: Schredl, 2002a.

previous night as completely as possible. Applying this method, the bias due to incorrect recall of previous mornings is minimized. Dream recall, however, is affected by participation in a diary study. Cohen (1969), for example, reported a threefold increase in DRF, and Schredl (1991) found a significant increase from 3.6 dreams per fourteen days (questionnaire) to 5.3 dreams per fourteen days (dream diary). Another problem that also plays a role in laboratory awakenings is the possibility that dreams are not always recalled immediately upon awakening but also during the day, for example, stimulated by cues connected with the dream content. This issue has rarely been studied; Domhoff (1969) has observed that around one-quarter of dreams are remembered during the day. Botman and Crovitz (1989–1990) have demonstrated that the presentation of cues stimulates DRF in comparison to the free dream recall condition. Similarly, some dreams were newly recalled under hypnosis (Stross & Shevrin, 1967).

In general, the correlation coefficients between DRF measured by questionnaires and DRF (dream diary) are of moderate size ($r = .597$, $N = 86$, Belcher, Bone & Montgomery, 1972; $r = .69$, $N = 338$, Cohen, 1979; $r = .568$, $N = 63$, Schredl, 1991; $r = .49$, $N = 106$; Bernstein & Belicki, 1995–1996, $r = .52$, $N = 336$, Hill, Diemer & Heaton, 1997; $r = .557$, $N = 285$, Schredl, 2002b; $r = .562$, $N = 444$, Schredl, Wittmann, Ciric, & Götz, 2003; $r = 52$, $N = 82$, Beaulieu-Prost & Zadra, 2005). Whereas Beaulieu-Prost and Zadra (2005) assumed that persons, especially persons with low interest in dreams, underestimate their DRF retrospectively, Redfering and Keller (1974), Cory, Orniston, Simmel, & Dainoff (1975), and Schredl (2002b) demonstrated that keeping a diary has differential effects on high and low dream recallers. A marked increase can be observed in low dream recallers, whereas no effect or even a decrease was found in high dream recallers. This would explain the medium size of the intercorrelation between questionnaire and diary measures. The hypothesis that dream diaries can measure "true" DRF (Beaulieu-Prost & Zadra, 2005) by minimizing errors resulting from incomplete memory seems implausible, since research has shown that various interventions aside from keeping a dream diary, such as simple encouragement (Halliday, 1992; Redfering & Keller, 1974), filling out a dream questionnaire (Schredl, Brenner & Faul, 2002), and starting psychotherapy (Myers & Solomon, 1989; Schredl, Bohusch, Kahl, Mader, & Somesan, 2000) can increase DRF considerably.

Awakening in a sleep laboratory is the most expensive method for measuring dream recall. The average recall rate for young adults ranges from 80 to 90 percent if the sleeper is awakened out of REM sleep (Dement & Kleitman, 1957). The clear disadvantages of this method are the marked influence on the participants by the unfamiliar setting, the electrodes, the interview by the experimenter, and so on, and—due to the expenditure—the small sample sizes. This method can not measure everyday DRF, and the expenditure of this approach seldom allows the carrying out of correlational studies (for example, including personality measures) because sample sizes of 50 and above would be necessary. The clear advantage of this method is the opportunity of measuring physiological parameters such as electroencephalogram (EEG), respiratory indices, heart rate, and skin resistance, both during sleep and during the awakening process. In addition, interferences that might occur during the awakening process can be minimized in the laboratory. DRF measured by awakenings in the sleep laboratory is related to home dream recall. For high dream recallers (more than three dreams per week), Goodenough, Shapiro, Holden, and Steinschriber (1959) obtained a recall rate of 93 percent for REM awakenings, whereas in only 46 percent of the REM awakenings were low dream recallers (less than once a month) able to report a dream. Meier Faber (1988) who investigated a sample of low dream recallers stressed the fact that some persons of her sample became high dream recallers in the laboratory (about 90 percent dream recall rate), whereas others hardly ever recalled dreams after being awakened out of REM sleep.

Aside from these three often-used methods, several other approaches have been applied in practice. Heynick and de Jong (1985) awakened their participants who slept at home via telephone during the last 2 $1/2$ hours of their sleep and obtained a recall rate of 49 percent. Cohen (1969) found a strong relationship ($r = .54$) between this method and DRF measured by dream diaries. A more recent approach is the utilization of portable recorders (Stickgold, Pace-Schott, & Hobson, 1994). These devices offer the opportunity to measure dream recall in a home setting and allow for additional recording of physiological parameters during sleep in order to determine the sleep stage before awakening.

To summarize, the different measurement methods show medium to high intercorrelations thus, the selection of a specific measurement method should not have too strong effects on the results of a particular study. It should, however, be kept in mind that the different approaches measure different kinds of DRF. Whereas questionnaire scales elicit everyday or home DRF and, therefore, are suitable for investigating the relationship with personality dimensions, the diary method and awakenings in the sleep laboratory are more appropriate for measuring intraindividual fluctuations and factors underlying this variation.

Methodological Issues in Measuring DRF

Several methodological issues that are of importance in measuring DRF are addressed in this section (see Table 4.4).

TABLE 4.4
Methodological Issues in Measuring DRF

Factors

- Reliability of DRF measures
- Variability of DRF
- Experimenter effects
- Re-remembering dreams already reported
- Sample characteristics
- Cognitive development (childhood)

Cohen (1969) reported a *retest reliability* of $r = .906$ ($N = 23$; retest interval: 4 weeks) for a four-point scale including absolute categories (see *Measurement Methods,* above). A scale with relative categories (never, rarely, sometimes, and often) was used by Bernstein and Belicki (1995–1996); its reliability was much lower ($r = .59$; $N = 106$; retest interval: two to three months). The seven-point scale presented in Table 4.3 also has a relatively high retest reliability ($r = .85$; $N = 198$; retest interval: 55 days; Schredl, 2004). The high reliability coefficients of the scales using absolute categories like "once a week" indicate that researchers should use this format.

Regarding the measurement of DRF with a two-week dream diary, Bernstein and Belicki (1995–1996) reported a retest reliability of $r = .67$ ($N = 106$; retest interval: two to three months). Cohen (1969) used a checklist to elicit dream recall over a period of thirty days. The sum score of the first part (fifteen days) correlated more highly with the sum score of the second part ($r = .92$; $N = 23$) than the sum score of the even and odd items ($r = .65$; $N = 23$). This finding and the much lower correlation of a three-day diary score compared with a 25-day diary score with DRF measured by questionnaire before the study ($r = .37$ versus $r = .69$; $N = 339$; Cohen, 1979) indicate that the day-to-day variability is very large. Schredl and Fulda (2005a) analyzed dream diary data to determine the length of the time interval needed to obtain sufficient reliability coefficients. For seven days, the internal consistency was $r = .677$. With increasing measurement intervals, the reliability coefficient increased (14 days: $r = .818$; 21 days: $r = .876$; and 28 days: $r = .904$; all $N = 196$). That is, a two-week diary would normally have sufficient reliability (cutoff: $r = .80$) for measuring DRF. For four-week intervals (DRF was elicited via weekly telephone interviews), Schredl, Funkhouswer, Cornu, Hirsbrunner, and Bahro (2001) showed high retest reliability for a six-month period (averaged correlation: $r = .764$; $N = 21$).

The problem of *the variability of dream recall* that plays a role in studies of the relationship between DRF and trait factors was addressed by Belicki and Bowers (1982) and Belicki (1986) in a different way. The correlation coefficients between DRF and personality measures were considerably larger for participants who reported a stable DRF over the last six months than for the total sample that included persons with strong DRF fluctuations from week to week.

Experimenter effects on dream recall have rarely been investigated. Herman (1971) has found that both the expectations of the participants and the expectations of the experimenter can affect DRF as measured in the sleep laboratory. In the high expectancy conditions, dreams were recalled more often. Similarly, other studies (Halliday, 1992; Redfering & Keller, 1974) have demonstrated how sensitive DRF is to comments of the experimenter; simple encouraging comments produced a marked increase in DRF. Even the completion of a short dream questionnaire yielded a higher DRF after four weeks (Schredl, Brenner, & Faul, 2002).

Some research groups (for example, Baekeland & Lasky, 1968; Cipolli, Bolzani, Cornoldi, De Beni, & Fagioli, 1993; Meier, Ruef, Ziegler, & Hall, 1968; Montangero, Tihon-Ivanyi, & Saint-Hilaire, 2003) have investigated the *morning recall* of dreams that were already reported in the night after awakenings from REM sleep. The findings are quite homogenous and support classical memory theory. Often the last dream (recency effect) and the most intense dream of the night (salience effect) are recalled in the morning. One must, however, keep in mind that these studies did not measure dream recall per se but the recall of material that was previously reported, and it remains unclear whether these findings are related to the dream recall process itself, that is, the transfer of material experienced during sleep to waking consciousness. Trinder, Wills, Barker, Vassar, and Van de Castle (1972) asked their participants to read the dream reports of another person after being awakened from REM sleep and obtained results similar to those of studies investigating the recall of the participants' own dreams.

As in psychological research in general, the *selection of the sample* (gender, age, socioeconomic status, and education) can bias the results of DRF studies. The models and hypotheses presented in this chapter should be valid for all persons and, therefore, it should make no difference whether students or, for example, elderly persons, are investigated. However, several studies (Bone, 1968; Lester & Nowicki, 1989; Spanos, Stam, Radtke, & Nightingale, 1980) have demonstrated that the composition of the sample has an effect on the relationship between DRF and other variables. They found different correlation coefficients for the relationship between influencing factors and DRF for men and women. Schredl, Bozzer, and Morlock (1997) reported that in their sample, DRF was related to the occurrence of stressors in women, whereas dream recall was associated with sleep quality in men. There have been no attempts to integrate such differences into a theoretical model. The age distribution of the sample also seems to be of importance. Whereas Waterman (1991) and Schredl, Schröder, and Löw (1996) have demonstrated a strong relationship between visual memory and DRF in elderly persons (45 to 93 years of age), the findings for young adults are inhomogeneous (Schredl & Montasser, 1996/1997). This may be partly explained by the variance of these variables; although the differences regarding visual memory are not very large in young samples, the range in elderly persons was marked (for example, see Schredl, Schröder, & Löw, 1996).

Another research area that should be addressed briefly is the relationship between *cognitive development* and dream recall. Foulkes (1982) reported the following DRF values for REM awakenings in different age groups: 15 percent (three to four years), 31 percent (five to six years), 43 percent (seven to eight years), 79 percent (nine to ten years), 79 percent (eleven to twelve years), and 73 percent (thirteen to fourteen years). This increase of dream recall related to the cognitive development in children is not explained by any of the DRF models.

FACTORS AFFECTING DRF

Up until now, a considerable number of studies that investigated the relationship between trait and/or state factors and DRF have been carried out. In order to give a general idea of these findings, examples of studies in different areas will be presented. A more thorough overview can be found in Schredl and Montasser (1996/1997). The presentation follows the distinction between trait and state factors. An additional section is dedicated to studies with integrative approaches, for example, studying the relationship between cognitive factors (visual memory), sleep variables (frequency of nocturnal awakenings), creativity, personality dimensions, and DRF in one sample. The findings will be summarized in the section *Most Important Factors*.

Trait Factors

A large variety of trait factors and their relationships to DRF have been investigated; the most important factors are listed in Table 4.5.

In several large-scaled studies (Borbely, 1984; Giambra, Jung, & Grodsky, 1996; Pagel, Vann, & Altomare, 1995; Schredl, 2002a; Schredl & Piel, 2003; Wyneandts-Francken, 1907) with sample sizes ranging from 265 to 2328, *gender* was related to DRF; on average, women tended to recall their dreams more often than men (effect size about $d = 0.3$). The survey of Giambra, Jung, and Grodsky (1996) revealed that gender differences were

TABLE 4.5
Trait Factors and DRF

Factors
Sociodemographic variables
Gender, age, socioeconomic status
Genetic factors
Personality factors
Repression, neuroticism, trait anxiety, introversion, locus of control,
hypnotic ability, absorption, "thin" boundaries
Cognitive factors
Intelligence, memory, fantasy, creativity
Sleep behavior/physiological parameters
Attitude towards dreams

more pronounced in the 25- to 55-year age range, whereas for younger persons as well as elderly persons, DRF does not differ substantially between men and women. A recent representative study (Stepansky et al., 1998) reported no gender difference in DRF; the questionnaire items measuring dream recall, however, included broad answer categories, and the results were not differentiated between age groups.

Large-scaled surveys (Giambra, Jung, & Grodsky, 1996; Schredl & Piel, 2003; Stepansky et al., 1998; Taub, 1972) have shown that DRF decreases with *age*. In contrast, Borbely (1984) found a heightened DRF in the 60- to 74-year age group compared with that of young adults (15 to 19 years of age). Factors that may underlie this decrease in DRF have not yet been investigated. According to the study by Giambra, Jung, and Grodsky (1996), the major decrease in DRF occurred between the ages of 22 to 50 years, thus the physiological aging process (for example, decreasing memory capacity) is unlikely to explain the age-related decline in DRF. Over a time span of 6 to 8 years (longitudinal design), Giambra, Jung, and Grodsky (1996) obtained only a small decrease in DRF. Within a retrospective design (Schredl, Schröder, & Löw, 1996), participants (55 to 93 years of age) were asked to estimate their DRF in young adulthood. For 60 percent of the sample, DRF did not change over the life span, whereas 23 percent reported higher DRF in young adulthood, and 17 percent had a higher DRF in old age. The decrease in DRF reported in cross-sectional studies may be explained by cohort effects (generation effects); attitude towards dreams today may differ from that of previous time periods. The negative attitude (in German "Träume sind Schäume" [Dreams are nonsense]) that was encountered in the study of Schredl, Schröder, and Löw (1996) might quite often explain the lower DRF in elder persons. Other causes such as beginning a professional life, child rearing, and so on that might explain the decrease in DRF after about 25 years of age (see Giambra, Jung, & Grodsky, 1996) have not been systematically investigated. The interviews carried out by Schredl, Schröder, and Löw (1996) showed that some men tend to recall their dreams more often after retirement.

Regarding the influence of *socioeconomic status*, two studies (Stepansky et al., 1998; Vandewiele, 1981) were published. Both found a heightened DRF in persons with higher socioeconomic status and with larger income. The factors that might explain these findings, however, were not investigated.

Only two studies (Cohen, 1973; Gedda & Brenci, 1979) including monozygotic and dizygotic twins investigated a possible *genetic influence* on dream recall. Their findings, however, did not support the hypothesis of a genetic effect. Cohen (1973) reported a concordance in DRF for persons who live together independent of their kind of kinship. A significant correlation between children's DRF and their mothers' was reported by Schredl and Sartorius (Ev. Korrelation Mutter/Kind-DRF).

The most often-investigated personality trait in relation to dream recall is *repression*. Tart (1962) measured the sensitizer versus repressor dimension by a subscale of the Minnesota Multiphasic Personality Inventory (MMPI; German version: Krohne, 1973). Sensitizers pay more attention to inner processes and describe their fears more openly. The correlation between this dimension and DRF was, as expected, $r = -.25$ ($p < .05$, $N = 45$; Tart, 1962). Subsequent studies, however, did not yield a homogeneous picture; the majority of research findings did not reveal a substantial relationship between this or similar personality dimensions and DRF (Bone, Nelson, & McAllister, 1970; Cohen & Wolfe, 1973; Robbins & Tanck, 1970; Stickel & Hall, 1963, 1971; Tonay, 1993). On the contrary, the studies of Schwartz, Kramer, Palmer, & Roth (1973) and Punamäki (1997) yielded a reversed relationship. Similarly, for other personality dimensions such as *neuroticism, trait anxiety, extroversion, introspection,* and *internal locus of control,* the findings are not homogeneous (for comparison, Schredl & Montasser, 1996/1997). Whereas some studies (anxiety: Nguyen, Picchioni, & Hicks, 2001; insecure attachment style: McNamara, Andresen, Zbororowski, & Duffy, 2001) reported positive results, most investigations revealed no substantial relationships to these personality dimensions or parameters of mental health (for example, see Hill, Diemer & Heaton, 1997; Schredl & Doll, 2001; Schredl, 2004; Spanos et al., 1980).

Three investigations that applied the sixteen personality factors (a personality inventory; German version: Schneewind, Schröder, & Catell, 1983) found that *sensitivity* was heightened in high dream recallers (Hill, 1974; Schredl, 1995a; Study 1; Schredl, Nürnberg, & Weiler, 1996). High spontaneity, high enthusiasm, and low norm orientation was reported in two of the studies (Schredl, 1995a, Study 1; Schredl, Nürnberg, & Weiler, 1996). These findings match the research on the "thick versus thin boundaries" personality construct (Hartmann, 1991). Hartmann (1984) carried out studies with adult nightmare sufferers. He characterized this sample as being sensitive, easily hurt, creative, and nonconventional and as having intense, conflict-laden interpersonal relationships and unusual sensual experiences. This was summarized as the notion of *"thin boundaries"* by Hartmann (1991). The sum score of the 138-item questionnaire correlated markedly with DRF ($r = .40$; Hartmann, 1991). Subsequent studies (Cowen & Lewin, 1995; Schredl, Kleinferchner, & Gell, 1996; Schredl, Schäfer, Hofmann, & Jacobs, 1999a; Schredl & Engelhardt, 2001) replicated this relationship. Findings regarding the *"hypnotic ability"* (for example, see Belicki & Bowers, 1982) and absorption (Schredl, Jochum & Sougenet, 1997; Spanos et al., 1980) dimensions have also been unequivocal. These dimensions as well as the boundary construct (Hartmann, 1991) show high correlations with the openness to experience factor of the Big Five Personality model (McCrae, 1994). Hill, Diemer, and Heaton (1997) reported a small correlation between openness to experience and DRF ($r = .23$; $p < .01$; $N = 336$). Whereas Schredl (2002c) was not able to replicate this finding ($r = -.090$ not significant; $N = 108$), subsequent studies found a small but significant relationship between openness to experience and DRF ($r = .16$, $p < .001$, $N = 671$, Blagrove, Button, & Bradshaw, 2003; $r = .22$, $p < .01$, $N = 193$, Watson, 2003; $r = .134$, $p < .01$, $N = 444$, Schredl, 2004). The alexithymia construct (affective deficits, lack of introspection) seems to reflect the other end of the openness dimension and was inversely related to DRF in several studies (De Gennaro, Ferrera, Cristiani, Curcio, Martiradonna, & Bertini, 2003; Lumly & Borydlo, 2000; Parker, Bauermann, & Smith, 2000; Nielsen, Oullet, Warnes, Cartier, Malo, & Montplaisir, 1997). One study (Curcio, Enuncio, Loparco, Fratello, Ferrara, & De Gennaro, 2004), however, was not able to replicate this relationship.

General *intelligence* was not related to DRF (for example, Hill, 1974). Verbal intelligence also did not correlate substantially with DRF (Tonay, 1993). the specific ability to handle complex visual stimuli in different tasks, for example, detecting a figure within a complex environment, was related solely to DRF (e.g., Kramer, 1978). More promising are the studies regarding *visual memory*; persons with high scores tend to recall their dreams more often (Cory, Orniston, Simmel, & Dainoff, 1975; Schredl, Frauscher, & Shendi, 1995; Schredl, Schröder, & Löw, 1996; Waterman, 1991). Other kinds of memory such as verbal memory and short-term memory were rarely connected to DRF (Blagrove & Akehurst, 2000; Cohen, 1971). Three studies (Robbins & Tanck, 1978; Schredl, Morlock, & Bozzer, 1996; Sehulster,

1981) demonstrated that memory for personal experiences (for example, childhood memories) was correlated with heightened DRF. When dream reports were utilized as material for the memory task, no differences between high dream recallers and low dream recallers were found (Barber, 1969). Both groups, however, were able to remember the dreams of high dream recallers, which were more structured and drive-laden better than dreams of low dream recallers. *Visual imagination*, a pronounced *fantasy life*, and the frequency of *daydreaming* correlated with DRF (Giambra, 1979; Hiscock & Cohen, 1973; Levin, Fireman, & Rackley, 2003; Martinetti, 1989; Moffitt, Hoffmann & Galloway, 1990; Okada, Matsuoka, & Hatakeyama, 2000; Starker & Hasenfeld, 1976; Tonay, 1993; Watson, 2003). Likewise, the findings regarding *creativity* were clearcut: creative persons recall their dreams more often than noncreative persons (Belicki, 1986; Chivers & Blagrove, 1999), especially art students and persons who paint in their leisure time (Schechter, Schmeidler, & Staal, 1965; Schredl, 1995b).

Since long sleepers (8 to 10 hours sleep duration) have more REM sleep than short sleepers (Cartwright, 1978), it can be hypothesized that long sleepers recall their dreams more often because their chance of waking up from REM sleep (associated with higher recall rates, Hobson & Stickgold, 1994) is higher. Positive (Bartnicki, 1997; Cohen, 1972a; Hicks, Lucero, & Mistry, 1991) and negative (Blagrove et al., 2003; Cory et al., 1975; Sexton-Radek, Trenholm, Westergaard, & Paul, 1992; Taub, 1972) findings have been often reported, thus, it must be concluded that the effect of habitual *sleep duration* on DRF is small. On the other hand, marked results were reported for the frequency of nocturnal awakenings and low *sleep quality*; persons who awaken often during the night and sleep more poorly trend to recall dreams more often (Borbely, 1984; Cory et al., 1975; Halliday, 1988; Schredl, Schäfer, Weber, & Heuser, 1998). The studies regarding *EEG parameters* during the REM period before awakening and the waking state upon awakening yielded contradictory results (Moffitt, Hoffmann, Wells, Armitage, Pirgeau, & Shearer, 1982; Pivik, Bylsma, Busty, & Sawyer, 1982; Wittmann, Palmy, & Schredl, 2004), although recent studies (Germain, Nielsen, Khadaverd, Bessette, Faucher, & Raymond, 1999; Rochlen, Hoffmann, & Armitage, 1998) demonstrated small effects of a heightened cortical arousal in the beta-frequency range (16–32 Hz) during the REM period before the awakening on dream recall. Similarly complex are the findings regarding hemispheric dominance (Antrobus, 1987); interestingly, Bertini and Violani (1984) found a reduced dominance of the right hemisphere during REM sleep in high dream recallers compared to low dream recallers. The left hemisphere (language areas in right-handed persons) is essential for the transfer of the dream experience into the waking state.

The last factor that might be considered a trait factor is the person's *attitude toward dreams* or interest in dreams. This variable is strongly related to DRF (Bartnicki, 1997; Cernovsky, 1984; Herman & Shows, 1984; Robbins & Tanck, 1988; Violani, Ippoliti, Doricchi, & De Gennaro, 1990; Schredl, Nürnberg, & Weiler, 1996; $r = .41$, Hill, Diemer, & Heaton, 1997; $r = .56$, Schredl & Doll, 2001). Schredl, Wittmann, Ciric, and Götz (2003) pointed out that the scales measuring interest in dreams are confounded with DRF because the items (for example, the item "Have you ever speculated about the possible meaning of one of your dreams?" Hill, Diemer & Heaton, 1997, adopted from Robbins & Tanck, 1988) also follow a format measuring frequency. Using scales without references to frequency, the correlation coefficients between DRF and positive attitude towards dreams/interest in dreams are much smaller ($r = .161$, $N = 56$, Schredl, Brenner, & Faul, 2002; $r = .14$, $N = 173$, Wolcott & Strapp, 2002; $r = .169$, $N = 444$, Schredl et al., 2003). What the causality in this relation looks like is still an open question. On the one hand, the interest in dreams may affect DRF by the person's use of techniques to increase dream recall (for example, keeping a diary) and, on the other hand, interest in dreams might be increased because of the person's curiosity about the meaning of her/his dreams.

To summarize, whereas general personality dimensions like repression and extraversion do not seem to be related to DRF, factors associated with openness to experience like absorption, thin boundaries, creativity, daydreaming, and imagination often showed significant correlations with DRF.

State Factors

The most important state factors are listed in Table 4.6. These findings deal mainly with intraindividual fluctuations of DRF, that is, those factors that affect DRF over the course of time within a person. Many studies also

TABLE 4.6
State Factors and DRF

Factors

- Previous day, stressors
- Therapy
- Sleep duration/nocturnal awakenings
- Activation during sleep
- Interferences during awakening
- Mental disorders
- Drugs
- The occurrence of brain lesions

utilize comparisons between different samples, for example., depressed patients versus healthy controls, to estimate the effect of a mental disorder (which can be conceptualized as state factor) on DRF.

To measure the effects of the *previous day's* experiences on DRF, several studies utilized experimental manipulation; participants were shown a stressful film or an erotic film one evening and a neutral film on another evening (control condition). The basic idea is that film material will be incorporated into the dream and trigger defense mechanisms so that DRF will be reduced. Cartwright, Bernick, Borowitz, and Kling (1969) presented an erotic film to young men and found a reduced DRF that night. Similarly conducted studies, however, could not replicate this finding (Foulkes & Rechtschaffen, 1964; Foulkes, Belvedere, & Brubaker, 1971). In a setting that is closer to everyday dream recall, Cohen (1974) investigated whether negatively toned presleep mood results in heightened dream recall the following morning. The underlying assumption was the salience hypothesis: the negative experienced waking-life experiences of the previous day, reflected in the negatively toned presleep mood, should lead to more intense dreams that are more easily recalled. Cohen's (1974) results confirm this hypothesis. Students reported more dreams in the pre-examination week compared to the postexamination week, indicating stress has an effect DRF. Schredl (1995a; Study 6) also showed that salient events that occurred during the previous day enhanced DRF. In these studies, dream diaries were utilized that were completed by the participants before sleep and upon awakening. An event such as *"participating in a dream study"* often leads to a marked increase in DRF (Halliday, 1992; Redfering & Keller, 1974). Similar increases were reported at the beginning of psychoanalytic or psychotherapeutic treatments (Myers & Solomon, 1989; Schredl, Bohusch, Kahl, Mader, & Somesan, 2000; Schredl, Kronenberg, Nonell, & Heuser, 2002), in which dreams often play an important role. *Meditation* and *autogenic training* were also found to stimulate dream recall (Reed, 1978; Schredl & Doll, 1997). Intense stressors, such as loss of a spouse, are accompanied by reduced DRF (for example, Arkin, Battin, Gerber, & Wiener, 1976), whereas daily hassles are related to heightened DRF (Pagel, Vann, & Altomare, 1995). A diary study (Armitage, 1992) showed that women tend to recall their dreams more often in stressful periods, whereas men reacted to stress with a reduction in dream recall. This finding underlines the fact that many questions are not resolved (compare the effect of sample characteristics on results of DRF studies).

In diary studies (for example, Schredl, 1995a, Study 5) and in an experimental study (Taub, 1970) in which the participants were allowed to sleep 8 hours and 11 hours, *sleep duration* was related to intraindividual variation in DRF in the expected way: long sleep duration was followed by heightened dream recall, whereas short sleep duration reduced dream recall. The former study, however, demonstrated this effect only for low dream recallers. Similarly, the frequency of *nocturnal awakenings* measured on a day-to-day basis by a dream diary is associated with an enhanced probability for recalling a dream (Schredl, 1995a) and, thus, concords with the findings of studies using questionnaires measuring frequency of nocturnal awakenings as a trait factor.

Regarding the relationship between *physiological activity* during REM sleep (as a measure for emotional involvement) and DRF, the findings of Shapiro, Goodenough, Biederman, and Sleser (1964) and Goodenough, Witkin, Lewis, Koulack, and Cohen (1974) provide some evidence that salient dreams (with high physiological activity) are more easily recalled. But the findings are inhomogeneous (compare Schredl & Montasser, 1996/1997), especially if EEG measures or REM density were utilized to assess activation levels in REM sleep.

Using a simple but innovative design, Cohen and Wolfe (1973) tested whether *interferences* during or shortly after the awakening process impair dream recall. One group of participants were asked to call the weather forecast upon awakening (duration: two to three minutes), whereas the other group lay quietly in their beds for the same amount of time. As expected, interference impaired dream recall (29 percent versus 54 percent). A diary study (Schredl, 1995a, Study 5) carried out in a naturalistic home setting, however, did not reveal any effect of interferences that occurred between awakening and filling in the dream diary. Abrupt awakenings carried out in a sleep laboratory resulted in reporting a dream more often than gradual awakenings (slowly increasing the loudness level of a tone until complete awakening) (81 percent versus 70 percent; Goodenough, Lewis, Shapiro, Jaret, & Sleser, 1965). Whether interferences play a role in everyday DRF is still an open question (compare Schredl, 1995a).

Regarding *mental disorders*, depressed patients have shown the largest differences in comparison to healthy controls. After laboratory awakenings (23 percent, Riemann, Löw, Schredl, Wiegard, Dippel, & Berger, 1990) as well as after spontaneous awakenings in the morning, dream recall in this patient group is drastically reduced (Riemann et al., 1990; Schredl, 1995c). It remains unclear whether the altered sleep physiology (advanced REM sleep), cognitive impairment associated with severe depression, or specific illness-related factors account for the reduction in DRF. Similarly, patients with dementia (Kramer, Roth, & Trinder, 1975) and persons with brain atrophy (Nathan, Rose-Itkoff, & Lord, 1981) tend to recall their dreams less often.

Several drugs, especially *psychoactive drugs*, affect dream recall. For instance, leva-dopa enhanced dream recall in patients with Parkinson's disease (Massetani et al., 1986), and the same effect was reported for serotonin reuptake inhibitors in depressed patients (Armitage, Rochlen, Fitch, Trivedi, & Rush, 1995) but not in healthy controls (Pace-Schott et al., 2001). A reduction in dream recall was reported to accompany the intake of tricyclic antidepressants (Riemann et al., 1990; Schredl, Schäfer, Weber & Heuser, 1998; Whitman, Pierce, Mass, & Baldridge, 1961). It is plausible that the effects of these drugs on the amount of REM sleep may explain alterations in DRF, but the findings of Armitage et al. (1995) indicate that other factors may play a role as well.

Very instructive for clarifying the relationship between brain activation and dream recall were the investigations of patients with *brain lesions* (overviews: Doricchi & Violani, 1992; Solms, 1997). Brain lesions within the parietal-occipital junction, which is often associated with loss of spatial perception, results in a cessation of dream recall (Solms, 1997). Also, large lesions in the frontal areas can cause complete inability to remember dreams. Interestingly, most patients recovered over a period of one year and began to remember dreams again (Murri, Mancino, Massetani, Canapicchi, Puglioli, & Rossi, 1989; Solms, 1997). These findings clearly indicate that besides the brain stem, which is important for REM sleep regulation, and the visual cortex, other brain areas are important in the process of dreaming.

In addition to diary and questionnaire studies that related DRF to different kinds of variables, it also feasible to ask the participants themselves which factors they attribute to the occurrence of periods with increased or decreased dream recall. The results of one study are presented in Table 4.7.

Stressful events were associated most often with an increase in DRF, whereas dream recall decreased subjectively after physical activity and during calm life periods. Subsequent studies (Herman & Shows, 1984; Schredl,

TABLE 4.7
Subjective Influencing Factors on DRF ($N = 169$)

Category	Increase (%)	Decrease (%)
• Stressful events	20.4	5.8
• Blue mood or upset emotional state	17.0	7.3
• Amount of mental activity	13.7	6.3
• Change in occupational or study schedule	13.1	7.7
• Vacations	6.9	15.9
• Times when everything is going pleasantly	6.4	18.8
• Injury or illness	6.0	5.8
• Amount of exercise or physical activity	5.2	18.9
• Hormonal change	4.0	5.8
• Seasons	2.4	5.3
• Other	4.9	2.4

Source: Cartwright, 1979.

1995a; Study 2) confirmed these findings. One has to be cautious in interpreting these findings because there is a large overlap, that is, some factors such as regular daily schedule were equally often associated with an increase as well as a decrease in DRF (Schredl, 1995a; Study 2).

To summarize, stress, nocturnal awakenings, and focusing on dreams (for example, keeping a dream diary, starting psychotherapy) are the state factors that have been shown to heighten dream recall.

Integrative Approaches

In this section, several studies that investigated mediator effects (for example, variables explaining the gender difference in dream recall) will be presented. In addition, an integrative study that included factors from different areas (visual memory, creativity, attitude towards dreams, personality, and sleep variables) will be described.

Schredl, Nürnberg, and Weiler (1996) tested the hypothesis as to whether a positive attitude toward dreams mediates the relationship between personality dimensions and DRF. This seems plausible because personality dimensions such as openness to experience showed closer correlations to attitude towards dreams than towards DRF itself ($r = .41$ versus $r = .23$, $N = 336$, Hill, Diemer, & Heaton, 1997; $r = .335$ versus $r = .134$, $N = 444$, Schredl, 2004) and, second, that attitude towards dreams is related to DRF (see *Trait Factors* section). The results indicated, however, that regarding the relationship between DRF and personality dimensions, the mediator effect of attitude toward dreams was negligible; only some aspects of dream recall like clarity, and so on, had been affected.

The second study (Schredl, Jochum, & Souguonet, 1997) investigated a possible mediator effect of visual memory in the relationship between absorption and DRF. That is, persons with high absorption should recall their dreams more often because of their visual memory capacity. This hypothesis was not confirmed: partialling out three measures of visual memory did not reduce the correlation coefficient between absorption and DRF ($r = .408$, $p = .0015$, $N = 51$; after partialling out visual memory variables: $r = .431$, $p = .0011$, $N = 51$).

The next two studies (Schredl, 2000; Schredl 2002/2003) were carried out in order to identify variables that might explain the gender difference in DRF. The study of Schredl (2002/2003) found that the gender difference in DRF ($d = 0.40$; $N = 205$) was affected by nightmare frequency, subjective meaningfulness of dreams, and the frequency of dreams that help to solve a problem. But the gender difference was still significant after partialling out one of these variables. The findings of Schredl (2000) indicated that the variable measuring being concerned with dreams during the day was the most potent in explaining the gender difference in DRF ($d = 0.49$; $N = 722$), whereas sleep variables like subjective sleep quality or frequency of nocturnal awakenings were of minor importance (despite the marked gender differences in these variables: $d = -0.41$ for subjective sleep quality and the relationship of these variables to DRF).

Schredl (1995a; Study 5) divided the participants into high dream recallers (DRF Questionnaire: several times a week, $N = 18$) and the rest group of medium to low dream recallers ($N = 13$). They kept a dream diary over a two-week period. For high dream recallers, interferences between waking up and filling in the diary reduced dream recall, which was not the case for the rest group. For the low to medium recall group, an effect of sleep duration and the number of nocturnal awakenings on dream recall was found. This was not present in the high recall group. The second study (Schredl, 1995a; Study 6) also using a diary approach found that dream recall in the high dream recall group (DRF Questionnaire: often, always, $N = 10$) was correlated negatively with presleep mood and positively with the occurrence of a significant event during the previous day. These relationships were not found for the low recall group ($N = 15$).

The last study (Schredl et al., 2003) included factors from different areas reviewed in the previous sections: visual memory, stress, frequency of nocturnal awakenings, attitude towards dreams, personality dimensions related to the openness to experience factor, and creativity (see Figure 4.1).

FIGURE 4.1
Integrative model of dream recall.

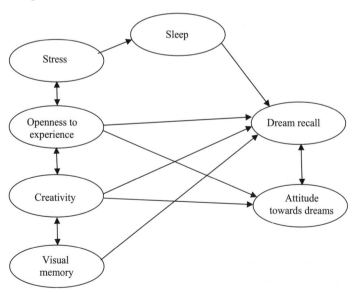

TABLE 4.8
Correlations between the Latent Variables

Scales	Correlation Coefficient		
	r	z	p
DRF—Attitude towards dreams	.158	2.7	.0035
DRF—Sleep	.105	2.0	.0228
DRF—Personality	.165	2.9	.0019
DRF—Creativity	.144	2.2	.0139
DRF—Visual memory	.073	1.2	.1151
Attitude towards dreams—Personality	.464	6.8	.0000
Attitude towards dreams—Creativity	.387	5.1	.0000
Sleep—Stress	.243	4.4	.0000
Stress—Personality	.243	5.3	.0000
Personality—Creativity	.871	9.4	.0000
Creativity—Visual memory	.060	1.0	.1587

Note: Statistical test for rho $= 0$.

The advantage of this integrative approach is that the factors are entered simultaneously into the model so that intercorrelations between the factors and specific pathways (stress leads to nocturnal awakenings, which are associated with higher dream recall) can be modeled. DRF was measured by different questionnaire scales and by a two-week dream diary. The correlations between the latent variables (a structural equation model was computed) and the DRF factor are depicted in Table 4.8.

The model fit was good and—as predicted—the factors showed marked intercorrelations (Schredl et al., 2003). Summing up the squared correlation coefficients revealed that about 8.5 percent of the total variance is explained by the factors included in the model. For example, over 90 percent of the variance is still unexplained. Interestingly, the correlations between creativity, personality, and attitude toward dreams are considerably larger than the corresponding DRF coefficients.

To summarize, although not every study was successful in finding mediator variables, it seems important to conduct research projects that will investigate the relationship between different influencing factors and their relationships to DRF. The integrative model confirmed previous findings (except for visual memory) but also indicated that the correlations between influencing factors and DRF are small.

Most Important Factors

In the previous sections, an overview regarding the research on the effect of influencing factors on dream recall was given. Within this section, the

TABLE 4.9
Most Important Factors That Affect DRF

Factors

- Openness to experience, thin boundaries, absorption
- Fantasy proneness, imagination
- Creativity
- Attitude towards dreams
- Visual memory (threshold model)
- Nocturnal awakenings/low sleep quality
- Stress
- Focusing on dreams

factors for which the empirical evidence indicates a significant effect on DRF in the majority of the studies are listed (see Table 4.9). These are the following trait factors: openness to experience including thin boundaries and absorption, fantasy proneness/imagination, creativity, and attitude toward dreams. For visual memory, the data seems to support a threshold model; for example, the ability to recall a dream is impaired if visual memory is below a certain threshold (see the studies on brain lesion patients and in the elderly) but is not related to the normal range of visual memory (Schredl et al., 2003). The most important state factors are sleep quality, nocturnal awakenings, the occurrence stress, and focusing on dream (like keeping a dream diary).

This list clearly indicates that DRF is determined by several very different factors and that an appropriate model of dream recall should integrate all these variables.

EVALUATION OF THE MODELS AND FUTURE DIRECTIONS IN DRF RESEARCH

On examining the different hypotheses, the *arousal-retrieval model* of Koulack and Goodenough (1976) seems to fit the empirical data best. On the one hand, sleep parameters are of importance in recalling dreams (arousal) and, on the other hand, visual memory might be a distinctive factor for the retrieval capacity. In addition, the *salience hypothesis*, which can be integrated into the second step of the arousal-retrieval model, accounts for the subjectively reported factors affecting dream recall such as stressful events. In addition, the arousal-retrieval model is the only theoretical approach that could explain the latent storage of dreams and the possibility of facilitating retrieval by external cues. The trait aspects such as thin boundaries, absorption, creativity, fantasy life, and attitude toward dreams fits

TABLE 4.10
Topics for Future DRF Research

Topics

- Analyses of moderator/mediator variables
- State versus trait analyses
- Integrative approaches
- Dream detail versus DRF
- Memory and information processing during sleep
- "Carry over" effects: cognitive functioning upon awaking
- "Sleep inertia"

into the framework of the *life-style hypothesis*, but "classical" personality dimensions such as introversion or field independence play a subordinate role. Thus far, the empirical data has not provided clear evidence for the repression hypothesis and the functional state-shift model, so *an integrative model* should focus on the arousal-retrieval model, the salience hypothesis, and the life-style hypothesis in order to explain the variability in dream recall.

In Table 4.10, several topics that seem to be important for promoting the field of dream recall research are listed.

In the earlier section *Integrative Approaches*, several studies investigating *mediator* variables as well as *moderator* variables were been presented. It seems important to carry this research further in order to determine how the various variables affect one another (possible causal pathways) and also to explain the DRF variance. The mediator effect reported by Schredl et al. (2003) regarding the role of nocturnal awakenings in the relationship between stress and DRF serves as an illustrative example; that is, more stress increases the frequency of nocturnal awakenings and, therefore, is associated with heightened dream recall. Interesting moderator effects have been reported by Schredl (1995a): dream recall was associated with different factors depending on whether the persons were high dream recallers or low dream recallers (see the section *Integrative Approaches*). To develop an integrative model, it is necessary to determine the validity of the influencing factor pattern for different groups (see also the findings regarding different patterns in women and men; Schredl, Morlock & Bozzer, 1996).

Schredl and Fulda (2005b) analyzed diary data (kept over 50 days on average) of 196 participants. The correlation between habitual sleep duration and DRF was not significant ($r = .02$), but the averaged correlation coefficients of each participant (correlating day-to-day variation in sleep duration with dream recall [present or not present]) amounted to $r = .13$ ($p < .05$), a small but significant relationship. A mixed-model approach with a logistic regression (random model) was carried out to test the state effect and trait effect simultaneously. As predicted, the between-subjects factor was not significant ($t = 0.5$; $p = .64$), but the within-subject factor was highly significant ($t = 11.2$; $p < .0001$). A difference of one-hour deviation from the person's mean value in sleep duration increases or decreases the probability of recalling a dream about 20 percent. For example, starting from the mean value of about 55 percent (probability of recalling a dream), the reduction or increase will be about 11 percent (20 of 55 percent). Future research can investigate other variables like stress or other sleep variables like nocturnal awakenings to determine whether they explain intraindividual (state) or interindividual (trait) differences.

It seems very promising to conduct *integrative studies*, which include variables from different domains like personality dimensions, cognitive abilities, and so on. To extend the work of Schredl et al. (2003), longitudinal data collection should be included in order to determine the interactions between state and trait factors.

Wolcott and Strapp (2002), for example, stressed the fact that DRF should be differentiated from other aspects related to dream recall (for example, detailed recall) because they assumed that different patterns of influencing factors might emerge. Schredl et al. (2003), for example, reported that a scale measuring various aspects of dream recall (remembering details, remembering childhood dreams, and so on) are more closely related to trait factors like absorption ($r = .419$), thin boundaries ($r = .408$), and openness to experience ($r = .339$) than DRF ($r = .119$, $r = .122$, and $r = .134$, respectively). This clearly indicates that future research should also systematically investigate the influencing factors related to the various different aspects associated with dream recall, in addition to the factors influencing DRF.

Because dream recall is a memory process that involves the "normal" time component (recalling something that has happened earlier) and the "extraordinary" sleep/wake transition (which makes it impossible to transfer the laws of waking short-term memory [compare Baddeley, 1997] directly), some studies looked into memory capacities during sleep. Oltman, Goodenough, Koulack, Maclin, Schroeder, and Flanhagan (1977) presented their participants with one-syllable digits during the whole night (random sequence, every 30 seconds, acoustic presentation). Several times a night, the sleeper was awakened one second after the stimulus presentation and was asked to report what digit they heard. Fifty-nine percent of the stimuli were remembered correctly. A subsequent experiment (Oltman et al., 1977), however, was not able to demonstrate descending recall rates for increasing time intervals (one, five, and ten seconds), which was hypothesized for a normal memory process. Using an event-related potential approach, Atienza, Cantero, and Gomez (2000) were able to show that mismatch negativity for odd stimuli was present for interstimulus intervals of three seconds but not for longer intervals of six or nine seconds (for which effects have been obtained in the waking state). Therefore, it might be concluded that some basic memory processes, maybe associated with the cholinergic neuromodulation, are altered during REM sleep, (Hobson, Pace-Schott, & Stickgold, 2000). Conduit, Crewther, and Coleman (2004) trained their participants to respond to an acoustic signal with specific eye movements. Ninety seconds after the stimulus presentation and the successfully performed eye movements (which was the case in about 50 percent of the cases), the participants were awakened. The person remembered the acoustic signal and the eye movements in 65 percent of the NREM awakenings, whereas in REM sleep all the stimuli were remembered correctly. The individual difference in the recall rates correlated ($r = .72$; $p < .02$) with DRF measured via questionnaire before the lab nights. This finding emphasizes the importance of introducing memory paradigms into DRF research.

Similarly, interindividual differences regarding "carry over" effects (altered cognitive functioning after awakening depending on the sleep stage before waking up; compare Reinsel & Antrobus, 1992) and "sleep inertia" (reduced cognitive abilities shortly after awaking; compare Tassi & Muzet, 2000) should be related to differences in DRF since several studies (Bonnet, 1983; Grosvenor & Lack, 1984; Stones, 1977) showed impaired performance in short-term memory tasks carried out immediately after waking up.

To summarize, despite the large numbers of studies and the evidence supporting—at least partly—the arousal-retrieval model of dream recall (Koulack & Goodenough, 1976), many questions are still not answered, not even asked. It seems important to integrate DRF and memory research in order to arrive at a comprehensive model explaining interindividual and intra-individual differences in dream recall.

REFERENCES

Aarons, L. (1976). Sleep-assisted instruction. *Psychological Bulletin, 83*, 1–40.

Antrobus, J. S. (1987). Cortical hemisphere asymmetry and sleep mentation. *Psychological Review, 94*, 359–368.

Arkin, A. M., Battin, D., Gerber, I., & Wiener, A. (1976). The effects of psychotherapy on the frequency of dreaming and reference to the decreased following bereavement in the aged. *Sleep Research, 5*, 134.

Armitage, R. (1992). Gender differences and the effect of stress on dream recall: A 30-day diary report. *Dreaming, 2*, 137–141.

Armitage, R., Rochlen, A., Fitch, T., Trivedi, M., & Rush, A. J. (1995). Dream recall and major depression: A preliminary report. *Dreaming, 5*, 189–198.

Aserinsky, E., & Kleitman, N. (1953). Regularly occurring periods of eye motility and concomitant phenomena during sleep. *Science, 118*, 273–274.

Atienza, M., Cantero, J. L., & Gomez, C. M. (2000). Decay time of the auditory sensory memory trace during wakefulness and REM. *Psychophysiology, 37*, 485–493.

Baddeley, A. (1997). *Human memory: Theory and practice* (Rev. ed.). Hove, United Kingdom: Psychology Press.

Baekeland, F., & Lasky, R. (1968). The morning recall of rapid eye movement period given earlier in the night. *Journal of Nervous and Mental Disease, 147*, 570–579.

Barber, T.X. (1969). *Hypnosis: A scientific approach.* New York: Van Norstrand Reinhold.

Bartnicki, K. J. (1997). *An exploration of life experiences, personality traits and sleep habits in relation to dream recall and dream content.* Unpublished master's thesis, California State University, Sacramento.

Beaulieu-Prevost, D., & Zadra, A. (2005). Dream recall frequency and attitude towards dreams: A reinterpretation of the relation. *Personality and Individual Differences, 38*, 919–927.

Belcher, M., Bone, R. N., & Montgomery, D. D. (1972). Rigidity and dream recall. *Psychological Report, 30*, 858.

Belicki, K. (1986). Recalling dreams: An examination of daily variation and individual differences. In J. Gackenbach (Ed.), *Sleep and dreams: A sourcebook* (pp. 187–206). New York: Garland.

Belicki, K., & Bowers, P. G. (1982). Consistency in the ability to recall dreams as a moderator in predicting dream recall. *Sleep Research, 11*, 109.

Bernstein, D. M., & Belicki, K. (1995–96). On the psychometric properties of retrospective dream content questionnaires. *Imagination, Cognition and Personality, 15*, 351–364.

Bertini, M., & Violani, C. (1984). Cerebral hemispheres, REM sleep and dream recall. *Research Communications in Psychology, Psychiatry and Behavior, 9*, 3–14.

Blagrove, M., & Akehurst, L. (2000). Personality and dream recall frequency: Further negative findings. *Dreaming, 10*, 139–148.

Blagrove, M. T., Button, L., & Bradshaw, C. (2003). Dream recall frequency is associated with openness to experience but not sleep length. *Sleep Supplement, 26*, A91-A92.

Bone, R. N. (1968). Extraversion, neuroticism and dream recall. *Psychological Reports, 23*, 922.

Bone, R. N., Nelson, A. E., & McAllister, D. S. (1970). Dream recall and repression-sensitization. *Psychological Reports, 27*, 766.

Bonnet, M. H. (1983). Memory for events occurring during arousal from sleep. *Psychophysiology, 20*, 81–87.

Borbely, A. (1984). Schlafgewohnheiten, schlafqualität und schlafmittelkonsum der schweizer bevölkerung: Ergebnisse einer repräsentativumfrage. *Schweizerische Ärztezeitung* [Sleep habits, sleep quality, and sleeping pill consumption in Switzerland: Results of a representative survey]. 1606–1613.

Botman, H. I., & Crovitz, H. F. (1989–1990). Facilitating the reportage of dreams with semantic cues. *Imagination, Cognition and Personality, 9*, 115–129.

Cartwright, R. D. (1978). *A primer on sleep and dreaming*. Reeding, MA: Addison-Wesley.

Cartwright, R. D. (1979). The nature and function of repetitive dreams: A survey and speculation. *Psychiatry, 42*, 131–139.

Cartwright, R. D., Bernick, N., Borowitz, G., & Kling, A. (1969). Effect of an erotic on the sleep and dreams of young men. *Archives of General Psychiatry, 20*, 262–271.

Cernovsky, Z. Z. (1984). Dream recall and attitude toward dreams. *Perceptual and Motor Skills, 58*, 911–914.

Chivers, L., & Blagrove, M. (1999). Nightmare frequency, personality and acute psycho-pathology. *Personality and Individual Differences, 27*, 843–851.

Cipolli, C., Bolzani, R., Cornoldi, C., De Beni, R., & Fagioli, I. (1993). Bizarreness effect in dream recall. *Sleep, 16*, 163–170.

Cohen, D. B. (1969). Frequency of dream recall estimated by three methods and related to defense preference and anxiety. *Journal of Consulting and Clinical Psychology, 33*, 661–667.

Cohen, D. B. (1971). Dream recall and short-term memory. *Perceptual and Motor Skills, 33*, 867–871.

Cohen, D. B. (1972a). Dream recall and total sleep time. *Perceptual and Motor Skills, 34*, 456–458.

Cohen, D. B. (1972b). Failure to recall dream content: Contentless vs dreamless reports. *Perceptual and Motor Skills, 34*, 1000–1002.

Cohen, D. B. (1973). A comparison of genetic and social contributions to dream recall frequency. *Journal of Abnormal Psychology, 82*, 368–371.

Cohen, D. B. (1974). Effect of personality and presleep mood on dream recall. *Journal of Abnormal Psychology, 83*, 151–156.

Cohen, D. B. (1979). Remembering and forgetting dreams. In J. F. Kihlstrom & F. J. Evans (Eds.), *Functional disorders of memory* (pp. 239–274). New York: Wiley.

Cohen, D. B., & MacNeilage, P. F. (1974). A test of the salience hypothesis of dream recall. *Journal of Consulting and Clinical Psychology, 42*, 699–703.

Cohen, D. B., & Wolfe, G. (1973). Dream recall and repression: Evidence for an alternative hypothesis. *Journal of Consulting and Clinical Psychology, 41*, 349–355.

Conduit, R., Crewther, S. G., & Coleman, G. (2004). Poor recall of eye-movement signals from Stage 2 compared to REM sleep: Implications for models of dreaming. *Consciousness and Cognition, 13*, 484–500.

Cory, T. L., Orniston, D. W., Simmel, E., & Dainoff, M. (1975). Predicting the frequency of dream recall. *Journal of Abnormal Psychology, 84*, 261–266.

Cowen, D., & Levin, R. (1995). The use of the Hartmann boundary questionnaire with an adolescent population. *Dreaming, 5*, 105–114.

Curcio, G., Enuncio, F., Loparco, R., Fratello, F., Ferrara, M., & De Gennaro, L. (2004). Dream recall, alexithymia and depression. *Journal of Sleep Research Supplement, 13*, 157.

De Gennaro, L., Ferrera, M., Cristiani, R., Curcio, G., Martiradonna, V., & Bertini, M. (2003). Alexithymia and dream recall upon spontaneous morning awakening. *Psychosomatic Medicine, 65*, 301–306.

De Gennaro, L., & Violani, C. (1990). White dreams: The relationship between the failure in dream recall and degree of hemispheric lateralization. *Association for the Study of Dreams Newsletter, 7*, 7.

Dement, W. C., & Kleitman, N. (1957). The relation of eye movements during sleep to dream activity: An objective method for the study of dreaming. *Journal of Experimental Psychology, 53*, 339–346.

Domhoff, B. (1969). Home dreams versus laboratory dreams: Home dreams are better. In M. Kramer, R. M. Whitman, B. J. Baldridge, & P. H. Ornstein (Eds.), *Dream psychology and the new biology of dreaming* (pp. 199–217). Springfield, IL: Charles C. Thomas.

Doricchi, F., & Violani, C. (1992). Dream recall in brain damaged patients: A contribution to the neuropsychology of dreaming through a review of the literature. In J. S. Antrobus & M. Bertini (Eds.), *The neuropsychology of sleep and dreaming* (pp. 99–140). Hillsdale, NJ: Lawrence Erlbaum.

Foulkes, D. (1962). Dream reports from different stages of sleep. *Journal of Abnormal and Social Psychology, 65*, 14–25.

Foulkes, D. (1982). *Children's dreams: Longitudinal studies.* New York: John Wiley and Sons.

Foulkes, D., Belvedere, E., & Brubaker, T. (1971). Televised violence and dream content. *Television and Social Behavior, 5*, 59–119.

Foulkes, D., & Rechtschaffen, A. (1964). Presleep determinants of dream content. *Perceptual and Motor Skills, 19*, 983–1005.

Freud, S. (1987). *Die Traumdeutung* [The interpretation of dreams]. (1900). Frankfurt: Fischer Taschenbuch.

Gedda, L., & Brenci, G. (1979). Sleep and dream characteristics in twins. *Acta Geneticae Medicae et Gemellologiae, 28*, 237–239.

Germain, A., Nielsen, T. A., Khadaverdi, M., Bessette, P., Faucher, B., & Raymond, I. (1999). Fast frequency EEG correlates of dream recall from REM sleep. *Sleep Supplement, 22*, 131–132.

Giambra, L. M. (1979). Sex differences in daydreaming and related mental activity from the late teens to the early nineties. *International Journal of Aging and Human Development, 10*, 1–34.

Giambra, L. M., Jung, R. E., & Grodsky, A. (1996). Age changes in dream recall in adulthood. *Dreaming, 6*, 17–31.

Giora, Z. (1973). Dream recall: Facts and perspectives. *Comprehensive Psychiatry, 14*, 159–167.

Görtelmeyer, R. (1986). Schlaf-Fragebogen A und B (Sf-A, Sf-B) [Sleep questionnaires A and B (Sf-A, Sf-B)]. In Collegium Internationale Psychiatriae Scalarum (Ed.), *International Skalen für Psychiatrie.* Weinheim: Beltz.

Goodenough, D. R., Lewis, H. B., Shapiro, A., Jaret, L., & Sleser, I. (1965). Dream reporting following abrupt and gradual awakenings from different types of sleep. *Journal of Personality and Social Psychology, 2*, 170–179.

Goodenough, D. R., Shapiro, A., Holden, M., & Steinschriber, L. (1959). A comparison of "dreamers" and "nondreamers." *Journal of Abnormal and Social Psychology, 59*, 295–302.

Goodenough, D. R., Witkin, H. A., Lewis, H. B., Koulack, D., & Cohen, H. (1974). Repression interference and field dependence as factors in dream forgetting. *Journal of Abnormal Psychology, 83*, 32–44.

Grosvenor, A., & Lack, L. C. (1984). The effect of sleep before and after learning on memory. *Sleep, 7*, 155–167.

Halliday, G. (1988). Relationship of spontaneous awakenings to dreams and nightmares. *Association for the Study of Dreams Newsletter, 5*, 4.

Halliday, G. (1992). Effect of encouragement on dream recall. *Dreaming, 2,* 39–44.

Hartmann, E. (1984). *The nightmare: The psychology and biology of terrifying dreams.* New York: Basic Books.

Hartmann, E. (1991). *Boundaries in the mind.* New York: Basic Books.

Herman, J. H. (1971). *Social variables influencing dream recall.* Unpublished doctoral dissertation, Yeshiva University, New York.

Herman, S., & Shows, W. D. (1984). How often do adults recall their dreams? *International Journal of Aging and Human Development, 18,* 243–254.

Heynick, F., & de Jong, M. A. (1985). Dreams elicited by telephone: A comparative content analysis. In W. P. Koella, E. Rüther, & H. Schulz (Eds.), *Sleep 1984* (pp. 341–343). Stuttgart: Gustav Fischer Verlag.

Hicks, R. A., Lucero, K., & Mistry, R. (1991). Dreaming and habitual sleep duration. *Perceptual and Motor Skills, 72,* 1281–1282.

Hill, A. B. (1974). Personality correlates of dream recall. *Journal of Consulting and Clinical Psychology, 42,* 766–773.

Hill, C. E., Diemer, R. A., & Heaton, K. J. (1997). Dream interpretation sessions: Who volunteers, who benefits, and what volunteer clients view as most and least helpful. *Journal of Counseling Psychology, 44,* 53–62.

Hiscock, M., & Cohen, D. B. (1973). Visual imagery and dream recall. *Journal of Research in Personality, 7,* 179–188.

Hobson, J. A., Pace-Schott, E. F., & Stickgold, R. (2000). Dreaming and the brain: Toward a cognitive neuroscience of conscious states. *Behavioral and Brain Sciences, 23,* 793–842.

Hobson, J. A., & Stickgold, R. (1994). Dreaming: A neurocognitive approach. *Consciousness and Cognition, 3,* 1–15.

Hobson, J. A., & Stickgold, R. (1995). The conscious state paradigm: A neurocognitive approach to waking, sleeping, and dreaming. In M. S. Gazzaniga (Ed.), *The cognitive neurosciences* (pp. 1373–1388). Cambridge, MA: MIT Press.

Koukkou, M., & Lehmann, D. (1968). EEG and memory storage in sleep experiments with humans. *Electroencephalography and Clinical Neurophysiology, 25,* 455–462.

Koukkou, M., & Lehmann, D. (1980). Psychophysiologie des träumens und der neurosentherapie: Das zustands-Wechsel-Modell-eine synopsis [Psychophysiology of dreaming and of neurosis therapy. The functional state-shift model: A synopsis]. *Fortschritte der Psychiatrie, Neurologie, 48,* 324–350.

Koukkou, M., & Lehmann, D. (1983). Dreaming: The functional state-shift hypothesis. *British Journal of Psychiatry, 142,* 221–231.

Koulack, D., & Goodenough, D. R. (1976). Dream recall and dream recall failure: An arousal-retrievel model. *Psychological Bulletin, 83,* 975–984.

Kramer, I. I. (1978). Differential dream recall as a function of differential memory for ambiguous material. *Dissertation Abstracts International, 39,* 1014-B.

Kramer, M., Roth, T., & Trinder, J. (1975). Dreams and dementia: A laboratory exploration of dream recall and dream content in chronic brain syndrome patients. *International Journal of Aging and Human Development, 6,* 169–178.

Krohne, H. W. (1973). Untersuchungen mit einer deutschen form der repression-sensitization-skala [Investigations of a German version of the repressor sensitization scale]. *Zeitschrift für Klinische Psychologie, 3/4,* 238–260.

Lester, D., & Nowicki, M. (1989). Remembering dreams and the fear of death: Report of a sex difference. *Perceptual and Motor Skills, 68*, 470.

Levin, R., Fireman, G., & Rackley, C. (2003). Personality and dream recall frequency: Still further negative findings. *Dreaming, 13*, 155–162.

Lumley, M. A., & Bazyldo, R. A. (2000). The relationship of alexithymia characteristics to dreaming. *Journal of Psychosomatic Research, 48*, 561–567.

Martinetti, R. F. (1989). Sex differences in dream recall and components of imaginal life. *Perceptual and Motor Skills, 69*, 643–649.

Massetani, R., Lucchetti, R., Piccini, P., Bianchi, F., Maestrini, M., & Muratorio, A. (1986). Dream recall and dream content in leva-dopa treated Parkinsonian patients. *Research Communications in Psychology, Psychiatry and Behavior, 11*, 65–73.

McCrae, R. R. (1994). Openness to experience: Expanding the boundaries of factor V. *European Journal of Personality, 8*, 251–272.

McNamara, P., Andresen, J., C., J., Zbororowski, M., & Duffy, C. A. (2001). Impact of attachment style on dream recall and dream content: A test of the attachment hypothesis of REM sleep. *Journal of Sleep Research, 10*, 117–127.

Meier, C. A., Ruef, H., Ziegler, A., & Hall, C. S. (1968). Forgetting of dreams in the laboratory. *Perceptual and Motor Skills, 26*, 551–557.

Meier Faber, B. (1988). Psychophysiologische Faktoren der REM-Traumerinnerung [Psychophysiological factors of REM dream recall]. Universität Zürich: Philosophische Fakultät I.

Moffitt, A., Hoffmann, R., & Galloway, S. (1990). Dream recall: Imagination, illusion and tough-mindedness. *Psychiatric Journal of the University of Ottawa, 15*, 66–72.

Moffitt, A., Hoffmann, R., Wells, R., Armitage, R., Pirgeau, R., & Shearer, J. (1982). Individual differences among pre- and post-awakening EEG correlates of dream reports following arousals from different stages of sleep. *Psychiatric Journal of the University of Ottawa, 7*, 111–125.

Montangero, J., Tihon Ivanyi, C., & Saint-Hilaire, Z. de. (2003). Completeness and accuracy of morning reports after a recall cue: Comparison of dream and film reports. *Consciousness and Cognition, 12*, 49–62.

Murri, L., Mancino, M. Massetani, C., Canapicchi, R., Puglioli, M., & Rossi, G. (1989). Effects of acute and chronic brain damage on dreaming. *Research Communications in Psychology, Psychiatry and Behavior, 14*, 121–142.

Myers, W. A., & Solomon, M. (1989). Dream frequency in psychoanalysis and psychoanalytic psychotherapy. *Journal of the American Psychoanalytic Association, 37*, 715–725.

Nathan, R. J., Rose-Itkoff, C., & Lord, G. (1981). Dreams, first memories and brain atrophy in the elderly. *Hillside Journal of Clinical Psychiatry, 3*, 139–148.

Nguyen, T. T., Picchioni, D., & Hicks, R. A. (2001). Correlations between locus of control and aspects of dreaming. *Sleep Supplement, 24*, A180–A181.

Nielsen, T., Oullet, L., Warnes, H., Cartier, A., Malo, J. L., & Montplaisir, J. (1997). Alexithymia and impoverished dream recall in asthmatic patients: Evidence for self-report measures. *Journal of Psychosomatic Research, 42*, 53–59.

Nielsen, T. A. (2000). Covert REM sleep effects on REM mentation: Further methodological considerations and supporting evidence. *Behavioral and Brain Sciences, 23*, 1040–1056.

Okada, H., Matsuoka, K., & Hatakeyama, T. (2000). Dream-recall frequency and waking imagery. *Perceptual and Motor Skills, 91*, 759–766.

Oltman, P. K., Goodenough, D. R., Koulack, D., Maclin, E., Schroeder, H. R., & Flanhagan, M. J. (1977). Short-term memory during stage-2 sleep. *Psychophysiology, 14*, 439–444.

Pace-Schott, E. F., Gersh, T., Silvestri, R., Stickgold, R., Salzman, C., & Hobson, J. A. (2001). SSRI treatment suppresses dream recall frequency but increases subjective dream intensity in normal subjects. *Journal of Sleep Research, 10*, 129–142.

Pagel, J. F., Vann, B. H., & Altomare, C. A. (1995). Reported association of stress and dreaming: Community background levels and changes with disaster (hurricane Iniki). *Dreaming, 5*, 43–55.

Parker, J. D. A., Bauermann, T. A., & Smith, C. T. (2000). Alexithymia and impoverished dream content: Evidence from rapid eye movement sleep awakenings. *Psychosomatic Medicine, 62*, 486–491.

Pivik, R. T., Bylsma, F., Busty, K., & Sawyer, S. (1982). Interhemispheric EEG changes: Relationship to sleep and dreams in gifted adolescents. *Psychiatric Journal of the University of Ottawa, 7*, 56–76.

Punamäki, R. L. (1997). Determinants and mental health effects of dream recall among children living in traumatic conditions. *Dreaming, 7*, 235–263.

Redfering, D. L., & Keller, J. N. (1974). Influence of differential instruction on the frequency of dream recall. *Journal of Clinical Psychology, 30*, 268–271.

Reed, H. (1978). Improved dream recall associated with meditation. *Journal of Clinical Psychology, 39*, 150–156.

Reinsel, R. A., & Antrobus, J. S. (1992). Lateralized task performance after awakening from sleep. In J. S. Antrobus & M. Bertini (Eds.), *The neuropsychology of sleep and dreaming* (pp. 63–85). Hillsdale, NJ: Lawrence Erlbaum.

Riemann, D., Löw, H., Schredl, M., Wiegand, M., Dippel, B., & Berger, M. (1990). Investigations of morning and laboratory dream recall and content in depressive patients during baseline conditions and under antidepressive treatment with trimipramine. *Psychiatric Journal of the University of Ottawa, 15*, 93–99.

Robbins, P. R., & Tanck, R. H. (1970). The repression-sensitization-scale, dreams and dream association. *Journal of Clinical Psychology, 26*, 219–221.

Robbins, P. R., & Tanck, R. H. (1971). MMPI scales and dream recall: A failure to confirm. *Perceptual and Motor Skills, 33*, 473–474.

Robbins, P. R., & Tanck, R. H. (1978). Early memories and dream recall. *Journal of Clinical Psychology, 34*, 729–731.

Robbins, P. R., & Tanck, R. H. (1988). Interest in dreams and dream recall. *Perceptual and Motor Skills, 66*, 291–294.

Rochlen, A., Hoffmann, R., & Armitage, R. (1998). EEG correlates of dream recall in depressed outpatients and healthy controls. *Dreaming, 8*, 109–123.

Schechter, N., Schmeidler, G. R., & Staal, M. (1965). Dream reports and creative tendencies in students of the arts, sciences and engineering. *Journal of Consulting Psychology, 29*, 415–421.

Schneewind, K. A., Schröder, G., & Cattell, R. B. (1983). *Der 16-PF-Persönlichkeits-Faktoren-Test* [The Sixteen Personality Factors Test]. Bern: Hans Huber.

Schonbar, R. A. (1961). Temporal and emotional factors in the selective recall of dreams. *Journal of Consulting Psychology, 25*, 67–73.

Schonbar, R. A. (1965). Differential dream recall frequency as a component of "life style." *Journal of Consulting Psychology, 29,* 468–474.

Schredl, M. (1991). *Traumerinnerungshäufigkeit und trauminhalt bei schlafgestörten, psychiatrischen patienten und gesunden* [Dream recall frequency and dream content in patients with sleep disorders, psychiatric patients, and healthy persons]. Universität Mannheim: Unveröffentlichte diplomarbeit.

Schredl, M. (1995a). Traumerinnerung: Persönlichkeitsdimension oder von situativen Faktoren beeinflußt? *Psychologische Beiträge, 37,* 133–180.

Schredl, M. (1995b). Creativity and dream recall. *Journal of Creative Behavior, 29,* 16–24.

Schredl, M. (1995c). Traumerinnerung bei depressiven Patienten. *Psychotherapie, Psychosomatik und Medizinische Psychologie* [Dream recall: Personality dimension or affected by state factors?], *45,* 414–417.

Schredl, M. (1999). *Die nächtliche Traumwelt: Eine Einführung in die psychologische Traumforschung* [*The nocturnal dream world: Introduction into psychological dream research*]. Stuttgart: Kohlhammer.

Schredl, M. (2000). Gender differences in dream recall. *Journal of Mental Imagery, 24,* 169–176.

Schredl, M. (2002a). Messung der Traumerinnerung: Siebenstufige Skala und Daten gesunder Personen [Measuring dream recall: A seven-point rating scale and data of healthy persons]. *Somnologie, 6,* 34–38.

Schredl, M. (2002b). Questionnaire and diaries as research instruments in dream research: Methodological issues. *Dreaming, 12,* 17–15.

Schredl, M. (2002c). Dream recall and openness to experience: A negative finding. *Personality and Individual Differences, 33,* 1285–1289.

Schredl, M. (2002/2003). Factors influencing the gender difference in dream recall frequency. *Imagination, Cognition and Personality, 22,* 33–39.

Schredl, M. (2004). *Traumerinnerung: Modelle und empirische Untersuchungen* [Dream recall: Models and empirical studies]. Marburg: Tectum.

Schredl, M., Bohusch, C., Kahl, J., Mader, A., & Somesan, A. (2000). The use of dreams in psychotherapy: A survey of psychotherapists in private practice. *Journal of Psychotherapy Practice and Research, 9,* 81–87.

Schredl, M., Bozzer, A., & Morlock, M. (1997). Traumerinnerung und Schlafstörungen [Dream recall and sleep disorders]. *Psychotherapie, Psychosomatik und Medizinische Psychologie, 47,* 108–116.

Schredl, M., Brenner, C., & Faul, C. (2002). Positive attitude toward dreams: Reliability and stability of a ten-item scale. *North American Journal of Psychology, 4,* 343–346.

Schredl, M., & Doll, E. (1997). Autogenic training and dream recall. *Perceptual and Motor Skills, 84,* 1305–1306.

Schredl, M., & Doll, E. (2001). Dream recall, attitude towards dreams, and mental health. *Sleep and Hypnosis, 3,* 135–143.

Schredl, M., & Engelhardt, H. (2001). Dreaming and psychopathology: Dream recall and dream content of psychiatric inpatients. *Sleep and Hypnosis, 3,* 44–54.

Schredl, M., Frauscher, S., & Shendi, A. (1995). Dream recall and visual memory. *Perceptual and Motor Skills, 81,* 256–258.

Schredl, M., & Fulda, S. (2005a). Reliability and stability of dream recall frequency. *Dreaming, 15,* 240–244.

Schredl, M., & Fulda, S. (2005b). Dream recall and sleep duration: State or trait factor. *Perceptual and Motor Skills, 101*, 613–616.

Schredl, M., Funkhouser, A. T, Cornu, C. M., Hirsbrunner, H. P., & Bahro, M. (2001). Reliability in dream research: A methodological note. *Consciousness and Cognition, 10*, 496–502.

Schredl, M., Jochum, S., & Souguenet, S. (1997). Dream recall, visual memory, and absorption in imaginings. *Personality and Individual Differences, 22*, 291–292.

Schredl, M., Kleinferchner, P., & Gell, T. (1996). Dreaming and personality: Thick vs. thin boundaries. *Dreaming, 6*, 219–223.

Schredl, M., Kronenberg, G., Nonell, P., & Heuser, I. (2002). Sleep quality in patients with panic disorder: Relationship to nocturnal panic attacks. *Somnologie, 6*, 149–154.

Schredl, M., & Montasser, A. (1996/1997). Dream recall: State or trait variable? Part I: Model, theories, methodology and trait factors and Part II: State factors, investigations, and final conclusions. *Imagination, Cognition and Personality, 16*, 181–210, 231–261.

Schredl, M., Morlock, M., & Bozzer, A. (1996). Kindheitserinnerungen und Träume Erwachsener [Childhood memories and dreams of adults]. *Zeitschrift für Psychosomatische Medizin und Psychoanalyse, 42*, 25–33.

Schredl, M., Nürnberg, C., & Weiler, S. (1996). Dream recall, attitude toward dreams, and personality. *Personality and Individual Differences, 20*, 613–618.

Schredl, M., & Piel, E. (2003). Gender differences in dream recall frequency: Data from four representative German samples. *Personality and Individual Differences, 35*, 1185–1189.

Schredl, M., Schäfer, G., Hofmann, F., & Jacob, S. (1999a). Dream content and personality: Thick vs. thin boundaries. *Dreaming, 9*, 257–263.

Schredl, M., & Sartorius, H. (2006). Frequency of dream recall by children and their mothers. *Perceptual and Motor Skills, 103*, 657–658.

Schredl, M., Schäfer, G., Weber, B., & Heuser, I. (1998). Dreaming and insomnia: Dream recall and dream content of patients with insomnia. *Journal of Sleep Research, 7*, 191–198.

Schredl, M., Schröder, A., & Löw, H. (1996). Traumerleben von älteren Menschen-Teil 2: Empirische Studie und Diskussion [Dreaming in the elderly: Part two]. *Zeitschrift für Gerontopsychologie und -psychiatrie, 9,* 43–53.

Schredl, M., Wittmann, L., Ciric, P., & Götz, S. (2003). Factors of home dream recall: A structural equation model. *Journal of Sleep Research, 12*, 133–141.

Schwartz, J., Kramer, M., Palmer, T., & Roth, T. (1973). The relationship of personality factors to REM interruption and diary recall of dreams. *Sleep Research, 2*, 113.

Sehulster, J. R. (1981). Structure and pragmatics of a self-theory of memory. *Memory and Cognition, 9*, 263–276.

Sexton-Radek, K., Trenholm, I., Westergaard, D., & Paul, P. (1992). Cognitive styles in dream recollections of unusual sleepers. *Sleep Research, 21*, 133.

Shapiro, A., Goodenough, D. R., Biederman, I., & Sleser, I. (1964). Dream recall and the physiology of sleep. *Journal of Applied Physiology, 19*, 778–783.

Solms, M. (1997). *The neuropsychology of dreams: A clinical-anatomical study.* Mahwah, NJ: Lawrence Erlbaum.

Spanos, N. P., Stam, H. J., Radtke, H. L., & Nightingale, M. E. (1980). Absorption in imaginings, sex-role orientation and the recall of dreams by males and females. *Journal of Personality Assessment, 44*, 227–282.

Starker, S., & Hasenfeld, R. (1976). Daydream styles and sleep disturbance. *Journal of Nervous and Mental Disease, 163*, 391–400.

Stepansky, R., Holzinger, B., Schmeiser-Rieder, A., Saletu, B., Kunze, M., & Zeitlhofer, J. (1998). Austrian dream behavior: Results of a representative population survey. *Dreaming, 8*, 23–30.

Stickel, E. G., & Hall, C. S. (1963). *The relation of reported frequency of dreaming to some personality variables* (Research Report No. 1). Miami, FL: Institute of Dream Research.

Stickgold, R., Pace-Schott, E., & Hobson, J. A. (1994). A new paradigm for dream research: Mentation reports following spontaneous arousal from REM and NREM sleep recorded in a home setting. *Consciousness and Cognition, 3*, 16–29.

Stones, M. J. (1977). Memory performance after arousal from different sleep stages. *British Journal of Psychology, 68*, 177–181.

Strauch, I., & Meier, B. (2004). *Dem Traum auf der Spur: Zugang zur modernen Traumforschung (2. Auflage)* [In search of dreams: Access to modern dream research]. Bern: Hans Huber.

Stross, L., & Shevrin, H. (1967). A comparison of dream recall in wakefulness and hypnosis. *International Journal of Clinical and Experimental Hypnosis, 15*, 63–70.

Tart, C. T. (1962). Frequency of dream recall and some personality measures. *Journal of Consulting Psychology, 26*, 467–470.

Tassi, P., & Muzet, A. (2000). Sleep inertia. *Sleep Medicine Reviews, 4*, 341–353.

Taub, J. M. (1970). Dream recall and content following extended sleep. *Perceptual and Motor Skills, 30*, 987–990.

Taub, J. M. (1972). Dream recall and content in long and short sleepers. *Perceptual and Motor Skills, 35*, 267–270.

Tonay, V. K. (1993). Personality correlates of dream recall: Who remembers? *Dreaming, 3*, 1–8.

Trinder, J., Wills, N., Barker, R., Vassar, C., & Van de Castle, R. (1972). Inhibitory factors as determinants of the recency effect in dream recall. *Sleep Research, 1*, 115.

Vandewiele, M. (1981). Wolof adolescents' dreams. *Journal of Psychology, 109*, 3–10.

Violani, C., Ippoliti, C., Doricchi, F., & De Gennaro, L. (1990). Correlates of individual differences in dream recall. *Sleep Research, 19*, 144.

Waterman, D. (1991). Aging and memory for dreams. *Perceptual and Motor Skills, 73*, 355–365.

Watson, D. (2003). To dream, perchance to remember: Individual differences in dream recall. *Personality and Individual Differences, 34*, 1271–1286.

Whitman, R. M., Pierce, C. M., Mass, J. W., & Baldridge, B. J. (1961). Drugs and dreams II: Imipramine and prochlorperazine. *Comprehensive Psychiatry, 2*, 219–226.

Wittmann, L., Palmy, C. & Schredl, M. (2004). NREM sleep dream recall, dream report length and cortical activation. *Sleep and Hypnosis, 6*, 54–58.

Wolcott, S., & Strapp, C. M. (2002). Dream recall frequency and dream detail as mediated by personality, behavior, and attitude. *Dreaming, 12*, 27–44.

Wynaendts-Francken, C. J. (1907). Träume bei Männern und Frauen [Dreams of men and women]. *Neurologisches Centralblatt, 26*, 941.

Five

Dreaming and Personality

Mark Blagrove

There is a wide range of differences in dream recall between people. Stepansky et al. (1998), in a sample of 1000 Austrians, found that 31 percent report dreaming ten times per month or more, 37 percent report dreaming one to nine times per month, and 32 percent report dreaming less than once per month. There is also, obviously, a wide range of dream content, with some stable differences in types of dream content between people (Domhoff, 1996). The first part of this chapter will summarize research into the personality correlates of the frequency of dreams, including the frequency of particular types of dreams, and the second part will address the personality correlates of dream content.

RELATIONSHIPS BETWEEN PERSONALITY AND FREQUENCY OF RECALLING DREAMS, AND OF RECALLING PARTICULAR TYPES OF DREAMS

This section first lists various personality dimensions that have been studied as potential correlates with dream recall frequency (DRF). Personality correlates of particular types of dreams are also addressed within each personality dimension section (for lucid dreams and nightmares) and after the personality dimension sections (for recurrent and precognitive dreams).

Repression-Sensitization

Up to the early 1970s, according to Cohen (1974a), the most tested hypothesis regarding dream recall was its proposed negative relationship with repression. This hypothesis was derived from the claims by Freud (1900/ 1953) that dreams pass through a censor to achieve representation, with the memory of dreams then being repressed once one woke up. The personality dimension used to study this hypothesis was repression-sensitization, which concerns defense mechanisms involving approach and avoidance responses to threatening stimuli. The sensitizing process involves intellectualization in approaching or controlling the threatening stimulus, whereas repression involves unconscious denial in avoiding the stimulus. However, whereas Williamson, Heckel, and Boblitt (1970) found sensitizers to have significantly higher dream recall than repressors, and Tart (1962) found that high scorers on the Minnesota Multiphasic Personality Inventory (MMPI) repression scale have fewer dreams than low scorers, this relationship was not found by Bone, Nelson, and McAllister (1970) or Handal and Rychlak (1971). In addition, Cohen (1974a) summarized the literature in this field as opposing the link between dream recall and repression-sensitization, although he allowed that repression may occur in some situations.

Robbins and Tanck (1970) similarly found that the Repression-Sensitization (R-S) scale was not a useful predictor of dream recall or dream content, but it did relate to the number and type of associations made in interpreting dreams. The R-S scale was related to the tendency to recognize sexual or aggressive implications in dream incidents. Gerber (1978) also found no relationship between repression-sensitization and dream recall when subjects used a 30-day diary; however, there was an interactive effect of dreams on morning mood. Repressors had a positive morning mood, regardless of whether the ending of their dream was positive or negative, but the morning mood of sensitizers was dependent on the pleasantness/unpleasantness of the dream ending.

Field Independence-Dependence

Related to repression-sensitization is the cognitive style of field independence-dependence, which is the ability to detect stimuli that are embedded within a larger field or context, versus the tendency to be distracted or influenced by the wider field when analyzing its component parts. Schonbar (1965) hypothesized that field-independent (FID) individuals would have higher dream recall than field dependents (FDs) and confirmed this by use of an embedded figures test, in which a small figure embedded in a larger complex figure has to be identified. But, this hypothesis was not confirmed by Montgomery and Bone (1970), using an Identical Figures task (correlations $r = .09$ for males and $r = .02$ for females), nor by Bone, Thomas, and Kinsolving (1972) using a Rod and Frame test and retrospective ($r = -.11$)

and prospective ($r = .03$) dream recall. (Related to field dependence, however, is rigidity, which is a preference for symmetrical, simple, or regular designs: on this, Belcher, Montgomery, and Bone (1972) found that retrospective and prospective dream recall were negatively associated with Breskin Rigidity Test scores in males but not females.)

Goodenough, Witkin, Lewis, Koulack, and Cohen (1974) also found FID and FD subjects did not differ in dream recall following abrupt REM awakening under neutral conditions, but in a stress condition FD participants, but not FID participants, gave more no-content dream reports and fewer content reports than in the no-stress condition. This result favors an interference or attention on waking view of low dream recall. However, this effect of field independence on dream recall does not extend to affecting the content of dreams: Baekeland (1971) found that FD and FID individuals sleeping in the sleep laboratory did not differ in their likelihood of dreaming of the laboratory.

There have been claims, though, that the ability to realize in a dream that one is dreaming (termed lucid dreaming) is related to FID. Gackenbach, Heilman, Boyt, and LaBerge (1985) provided some equivocal empirical support for this, and Patrick and Durndell (2004) reported frequent but not occasional lucid dreamers were more field independent on an Embedded Figures Test. However, Blagrove and Tucker (1994), also using an embedded figures test, found no significant mean group differences between lucid versus nonlucid dreamers. However, Gruber, Steffen, and Vonderhaar (1995), using the 16 PF (a self-report personality measure), compared waking personality traits of individuals who lucid dream at least once or twice per month with infrequent lucid dreamers. Frequent lucid dreamers had higher management and control of cognitive, emotional, and social functioning when awake. Gruber et al. (1995) characterized this personality style as field independence, but in a broader cognitive sense than the more usual perceptual style sense.

Memory

There have been many tests of what is possibly the simplest and most parsimonious hypothesis: that individuals differ in their ability to remember dreams because they differ in some more general memory ability. Cory, Ormiston, Simmel, and Dainoff (1975) tested such a hypothesis: fifty dream recaller and fifty dream nonrecaller undergraduates were given tests of short- and long-term memory, including visual memory, incidental memory, and a personality battery consisting of measures of anxiety, repression-sensitization, and internal-external locus of control. The results found that the memory variables and the individuals' self-reported number of awakenings distinguished between recallers and nonrecallers, whereas personality measures did not.

Cory et al. (1975) concluded that the most important variable in dream recall may be individual differences in memory ability rather than differences in personality. Schredl and Montasser's (1996–1997a) review and the data of Butler and Watson (1985) also support this correlation of visual memory with DRF. However, Cohen (1971a) reports two studies showing no correlation between the amount of dream recall and short-term memory for verbally or visually encoded material, and Blagrove and Akehurst (2000) found no correlation with short- or long-term story narrative recall.

Imagery Salience

Whereas the repression, field independence, and memory studies reviewed so far emphasize individual differences in the ability to recall a dream, the salience hypothesis holds that some individuals have more vivid or striking dreams, and that it is this characteristic of the dream that leads to it being better recalled. Cohen (1974a) summarized the literature up to that time as having no clearly supportive studies for repression as an explanation for differences in dream recall, 50 percent of studies supporting interference on waking, and 80 percent of studies supporting salience as an explanation for differences in dream recall. In addressing differences between people in dream recall, the aim for this hypothesis would be to correlate dream recall with vividness-related characteristics of waking mental imagery or with vividness-related characteristics of dreams. For example, Hiscock and Cohen (1973) found high dream recallers have a generalized capacity for visualization in waking life (including visualizing clear, vivid, and controllable images), which they proposed may contribute to the quality of the dreaming experience and, consequently, to its recallability.

Cohen and MacNeilage (1974) thus proposed that individual differences in dream recall act at the level of dream production, that is, more salient, and hence more memorable dreams are produced by those with high dream recall. They found that verbal reports of the dreams of frequent recallers were more salient than dream reports of low frequency recallers, but with this difference between the groups being greater for nonrapid eye movement (NREM) dreams than rapid eye movement (REM) dreams. Here, salience was calculated as the sum of scores of vividness, bizarreness, emotionality, and activity for each dream report.

Absorption

Absorption refers to how involved one is in an experience, such as watching a film or having a daydream, as opposed to being distractible, indifferent, or detached from the experience. Spanos, Stam, Radtke, and Nightingale (1980) found that absorption was the most important predictor of dream recall in females, although in males the only significant predictor was sex-role orientation contrary to stereotype (that is, femininity). Schredl, Jochum, and Souguenet (1997) tested whether visual memory may function as a mediator variable in the relationship between absorption in imaginings and dream recall frequency. Participants estimated their DRF and completed two visual memory tasks and the Absorption Questionnaire (Tellegen & Atkinson, 1974). Absorption in imaginings was related to DRF, but this was not mediated by visual memory. However, Schredl, Wittmann, Ciric, and Götz (2003) found only a marginal correlation of absorption and DRF ($r = .09$), finding instead that absorption correlated highly with attitude toward dreams ($r = .31$). Levin, Fireman, and Rackley (2003) found also that absorption correlated insignificantly with DRF ($r = .18$), although an earlier study found a higher correlation ($r = .30$; Levin & Young, 2001–2002).

In Levin and Fireman (2001–2002), nightmare prevalence and nightmare distress were associated with higher levels of fantasy proneness, psychological absorption, and a guilty-dysphoric daydreaming style. These results were not due to higher levels of overall dream recall. Belicki and Belicki (1986) also found the frequency of nightmares is positively related to absorption.

Creativity

There has been some support for the association of DRF with creativity. Bone and Corlett (1968) found that frequency of dream recall correlated with a creativity score on the remote associates test, a test in which participants are given three words and must respond with a fourth that is linked with each of the three presented words. However, this correlation was lowered by anxiety, which correlated positively with dream recall but negatively with the remote associates score, and controlling for the effect of anxiety led to an increase in the dream recall-remote associates correlation. Fitch and Armitage (1989) evaluated creative thinking among retrospectively assessed high- and low-frequency dream recallers. Participants completed the Torrance Tests of Creative Thinking (including an original uses task), on which high-frequency dream recallers generated more elaborate and original responses. They were also more fluent in processing picture completion tasks. The authors concluded that there is higher cognitive flexibility and more divergent information processing among high-frequency dream recallers, and that there is a "fundamental cognitive style variation in sleep and in wakefulness."

Schechter, Schmeidler, and Staal (1965) addressed the relationship of dreaming to creativity within different disciplines. They found that the proportion of dream recallers was greater among art students than science students, who had greater recall than engineering students. The art students were also higher on the creativity measure used, but it is not clear whether the difference in dream recall is due to differences in the disciplines studied rather than differences in creativity between the disciplines. A further problem arises in that the measure of creativity used, an independence of judgment self-report questionnaire, is not a standard measure of creativity, unlike the Torrance tests and remotes associates test mentioned above. The dream recallers and nonrecallers did not differ on this independence of judgment test.

Domino (1976a) studied the dream content of creative and noncreative participants; this study will be described further later in this chapter. What is important here is that, in order to obtain the dream reports, participants kept a dream diary for two weeks. The thirty-eight creative students recalled 167 dreams, whereas the thirty-eight noncreative students recalled 152 dreams; only three creative and two control students could recall no dreams during the two weeks. This means that there is a negligible difference in dream recall between the two groups. The importance of this study, and of this result, follows from two advantageous components of its design: first, dream recall was assessed prospectively with the diary, which can be more accurate than a retrospective estimation. Second, assignment to groups was performed by the students' teachers on the basis of students' "originality, adaptiveness to reality, and elaboration of original insight", which may have less of a verbal intelligence confound than the remote associates and original uses tests mentioned above.

Thus, it is not clear whether creativity is associated with higher dream recall. As will be seen later in this chapter, there is good evidence that creative individuals have more bizarre dreams, which could provide an explanation for findings of creative people having higher dream recall, in that their dreams would be more memorable. Support for this explanation is provided by Worthen, Eisenstein, Budwey, and Varnado-Sullivan (2004–2005), who found that bizarre content is recalled better than common content of dreams. However, despite this plausible line of reasoning, there remains the problem that some of the evidence is against a link between creativity and dream recall. Creativity has, however, been associated with frequent lucid dreaming, with creativity either self-assessed on a Creative Personality scale (Blagrove & Hartnell, 2000) or assessed by performance on a creative problem-solving task (Brodsky, Esquerre, & Jackson, 1990–1991). Potential for artistic achievement has also been linked to frequent nightmares (Hartmann, Russ, Oldfield, Sivan, & Cooper, 1987; Hartmann, Russ, van der Kolk, Falke, & Oldfield, 1981), although Chivers and Blagrove (1999) did not find an association between self-assessed creativity and nightmare frequency, and Levin, Galin, and Zywiak (1991) found mixed support for the relationship.

Fantasy Proneness

Similar to creativity is the trait of fantasy proneness. Giesbrecht and Merckelbach (2006) describe this as being profoundly involved with fantasy and daydreaming, including the consequences of daydreaming, and with having vivid childhood memories. Tonay (1993) compared self-rated dream recall frequency with scores on adjustment, anxiety, attitude toward dreams, ego strength, introspectiveness, social introversion, fantasy-proneness, metaphorical scope, repression, and suggestibility. Recall was only significantly related to positive attitude toward dreams (which will be addressed below), and fantasy proneness (that is, fantasy behavior in childhood and frequency of adult fantasy). Giesbrecht and Merckelbach (2006) found that the score on the General Sleep Experiences subscale of the Iowa Sleep Experiences Survey (which assesses dream recall frequency combined with frequency of vivid dreams and other sleep experiences) significantly correlated ($r = .38$) with fantasy proneness, as assessed by the Creative Experiences Questionnaire (Merckelbach, Horselenberg, & Muris, 2001). Also using this scale, Watson (2003) found individuals high in absorption, imagination, and fantasy were particularly likely to remember their dreams and to report other vivid nocturnal experiences. He concluded these results are consistent with a salience model of dream recall and a continuity model of human consciousness.

Levin and Young (2001–2002) found a correlation of $r = .28$ between fantasy proneness and DRF. Levin et al. (2003) had 116 college undergraduates keep a dream log for twenty-one consecutive nights and complete self-report measures assessing fantasy proneness, psychological absorption, and imaginative involvement. The only significant correlate with dream recall was fantasy proneness, but this correlation was of a small magnitude ($r = .19$) and, of the two genders, was only significant for women.

Finally, Levin and Fireman (2001–2002) found nightmare prevalence and nightmare distress were associated with higher levels of fantasy proneness, psychological absorption, and a guilty-dysphoric daydreaming style. These results were not due to higher levels of overall dream recall in individuals high on fantasy proneness and absorption.

Hypnotic Suggestibility

Nadon, Laurence, and Perry (1987) reviewed work showing that hypnotizability is associated with positive relationships to dreaming, such as enjoying dreaming, and obtaining creative ideas from dreams, and that highly hypnotizable individuals are more likely to be influenced by presleep instructions that aim to change dream content. They then present data showing that greater hypnotizability is associated with the score on a dream questionnaire that assesses dream experience and behaviors, such as vividness and satisfaction of dreaming and control of dreaming. In contrast to these results, Belicki and Belicki (1986) found that hypnotizability is also positively related to frequency of nightmares.

Attitude Toward Dreams

Cernovsky (1984) followed suggestions that dream recall is related to interest in dreams and belief in their meaningfulness by devising a 16-item measure of attitudes toward dreams. The measure had three subscales: the person's own attitude toward dreams (for example, "practical everyday life is too important to me to pay any attention to my dreams"), the person's perception of the attitudes of their significant others toward dreams ("the members of my family used to talk about the dreams they had"), and the person's perception of the attitudes of people in general toward dreams ("those who try to discuss their dreams in public will only regret it later"). DRF correlated significantly with the first subscale ($r = .32$) and with the whole 16-item scale ($r = .31$). The attitude toward dreams scale and its subscales did not correlate significantly with incidence of nightmares.

The relationship of ATD and DRF was confirmed by Tonay (1993), but Schredl, Brenner, and Faul (2002) found that the relationship of attitude toward dreams and recall frequency appears not as strong as previously reported when items with direct reference to dream recall are not included in the scale, and Domhoff (1968) had found that attitudes toward dreams, as measured by a semantic differential scale, did not differ between recallers and nonrecallers.

Thus, it may be that people recall more dreams because they have a favorable attitude toward them, in that an unfavorable attitude causes them to not attend to their dreams on waking, and the dreams are hence forgotten. However, the direction of causation may be the other way, with frequent dream recall causing greater appreciation of dreams.

Schredl, Nürnberg, and Weiler (1996) showed that correlations between positive attitude toward dreams and personality dimensions of the Sixteen Personality Factor Questionnaire (16PF) were stronger than similar correlations between DRF and personality. However, Jacka (1991) reported no difference in attitudes to dreams between introverts and extraverts.

Thin and Thick Boundaries

Hartmann (1989) noted that frequent nightmare sufferers have striking personality characteristics that could be called "thin boundaries"; boundariness is the degree of separation of intrapsychic components of the mind. Boundary thinness also correlated positively with frequency of dream recall and with length of sleep. Nightmare sufferers and art students usually scored thin, whereas members of a group of naval officers had thick boundaries. Full details of the Boundary Questionnaire and its design and rationale are described in Hartmann (1991), who reported a correlation of $r = .40$ between thin boundariness and dream recall. He also found that women tended to score thinner than men, and older individuals tended to score thicker than younger individuals; along these lines Levin, Gilmartin, and Lamontanaro (1998–1999) found that visual artists score more thin boundaried than Wall Street brokers.

In Hartmann, Elkin, and Garg (1991), there was a highly significant positive correlation between thinness of boundaries and frequency of dream recall, and the dreams of thin-boundaried individuals were more vivid, more emotional, and had more interaction between characters, compared with dreams of thick-boundaried individuals. These results were supported by Schredl, Kleinferchner, and Gell (1996), and Hartmann, Rosen, and Rand (1998); the latter also showing a trend towards a correlation of thin boundariness with aggressive interaction and nightmare-like dreams. As well as finding that thin boundariness correlates with retrospective ($r = .30$) and prospective ($r = .26$) DRF, Schredl, Schäfer, Hofmann, and Jacob (1999) also found that thin boundaries correlate with level of negative emotions in dreams ($r = .31$), emotional intensity of dreams ($r = .27$), how favorably dreams are regarded (that is, as more meaningful [$r = .29$] and creative [$r = .21$]), and with level of dreamt verbal interaction with others in the dream ($r = .20$). Schredl and Engelhardt (2001) showed that, within a psychiatric inpatient group, boundary questionnaire score correlates with retrospective ($r = .26$) and prospective ($r = .31$) dream recall, with mean word count of dreams ($r = .39$) and with dream bizarreness ($r = .25$). Similarly, in Hartmann et al. (1998), thinness of boundaries was significantly correlated with dream length, vividness, amount of detail, and amount of emotion, and showed a trend towards a correlation with aggressive interaction and nightmare-likeness.

However, it should be noted that that Hartmann et al. (1998) also found that many correlations with dream content became insignificant when the number of words in the dream was partialled out. Hartmann et al. performed this procedure because the number of words in the dream correlated highly with boundariness ($r = .49$). However, as noted later in this chapter, the procedure of partialling out number of words is opposed by some researchers.

Levin et al. (1998–1999) found boundary thinness was positively correlated with dream recall, greater reported dream salience, and increased access to subliminal activation, and Kunzendorf, Hartmann, Cohen, and Cutler (1997) found that, whereas night dreams in general are more bizarre than daydreams, the daydreams of persons with thin boundaries are rated as bizarre as the night dreams of persons with thick boundaries.

Relationships with nightmares have also been found. In Schredl et al. (1996), individuals who reported that they had frequent nightmares or recurrent nightmares during childhood were more thin boundaried than those not reporting this. Also, for adolescents, Cowen and Levin (1995) found that boundary thinness was related to dream recall ($r = .16$), nightmare recall ($r = .16$), and distress due to nightmares.

Funkhouser, Wurmle, Comu, and Bahro (2001) provide interesting additions to the previously discussed studies. Boundariness was assessed at the beginning and end of a 26-week study and showed a very high test-retest correlation ($r = .87$). There was no significant correlation between boundary score and dream recall, but being allowed to tell one's dreams resulted in a small increase in boundary score, that is, in the direction of thinner boundaries, which raises questions as to the directions of causality in the Boundaries-DRF correlations.

Openness to Experience

Watson (2003) found that dream recall was specifically associated with openness but not with the other Big Five traits. However, Schredl (2002a) was unable to demonstrate a relationship between openness and dream recall frequency, and Schredl, Ciric, Götz, and Wittmann (2003) found that although openness to experience and thin boundaries correlate with dream recall frequency, the correlation coefficients are small ($r = .17$ and $.18$, respectively). Schredl, Ciric, and colleagues (2003) found that the correlations of openness and boundariness are much larger with attitude toward dreams, thus they suggested that Schonbar's (1965) "lifestyle" hypothesis should be revised, with attitude toward dreams, and not dream recall frequency, being part of a broader lifestyle of acceptance of inner processes.

Schredl and Erlacher (2004) found lucid dreaming frequency did not correlate with openness to experience but had small correlations with two components of openness to experience ("fantasy" and "ideas") and with three dimensions that are associated with the openness-to-experience factor: thin boundaries, absorption, and imagination. Since these correlations are similar to corresponding correlations with DRF, and therefore the relationships between lucid dreaming frequency and these personality dimensions may be mediated by DRF, it might be concluded that the direct relationship between lucid dreaming frequency and these aspects of personality are rather small. Lucid dreaming frequency was not associated with any of the other Big Five personality factors, thus, theories linking lucid dreaming with introversion or low neuroticism were not supported.

A Problem With Retrospective Dream Questionnaires

As reviewed previously in this chapter, many studies have reported positive correlations between DRF and measures of absorption, psychological boundaries, and attitude toward dreams. Beaulieu-Prévost and Zadra (2007) note, however, that a majority of these studies has relied exclusively on retrospective measures of DRF. They conducted three meta-analyses to evaluate the effect sizes of these three variables (absorption, psychological boundaries, and attitude toward dreams) as correlates of DRF, as operationalized by retrospective questionnaire versus dream logs. Data from twenty-five studies were included in the analyses. For each of the three variables investigated, correlations with retrospective measures of DRF were of greater magnitude than those obtained with daily logs. Absorption and psychological boundaries were not related to diary dream recall, but were related to retrospective dream recall, indicating that they were only related to people's tendency to underestimate or overestimate their DRF retrospectively. A similar point is made by Levin et al. (2003), who found small correlations between prospectively assessed DRF and waking fantasy measures, whereas in an earlier study there were higher correlations with a retrospective assessment of DRF (Levin & Young, 2001–2002). Levin and Young also cautioned that correlations might be inflated by having the retrospective questionnaire completed in the same session as the personality measure.

Social Psychology Correlates

McNamara, Andresen, Clark, Zborowski, and Duffy (2001) found that individuals scoring high on insecure attachment dream more frequently and have more intense dreams than people who are more securely attached. They propose that dreams promote attachment, either by attachment-related themes in dream content, or by the activation of attachment systems by REM sleep, independent of dream content.

Related to McNamara et al.'s hypothesis are the results of Ward, Ward, Randers-Pehrson, and Runion (1973), who asked eighty-eight male and ninety-one female college students to write down their most recent dreams in as much detail as possible. The dreams were subjected to a content analysis to discover possible differences in affiliative imagery between firstborn and later-born participants. As expected, firstborns recalled fewer dreams than later-born participants, presumably because of their more highly socialized personalities. Among males, a theme of "positive interaction" was more frequent in the dreams of firstborns than in those of laterborns, and dreams of firstborns also tended to contain more persons than those of laterborns. No such differences were evident in the dreams of females.

Neuroticism and Extraversion

Tart (1962) found no relationship between dream recall and neuroticism, and Farley, Schmuller, and Fischbach (1971) and Blagrove and Akehurst (2000) found no relationship between dream recall and neuroticism or extraversion. There are, however, some small correlations in some studies: Bone (1968) found that the correlation between extraversion and dream recall was significant for females but not for males, and that the correlation between neuroticism and dream recall was significant for males but not for females. Lang and O'Connor (1984) found frequency and image-intensity of dreams was related to neuroticism scores. Finally, Watson (2001) used the Iowa Sleep Experiences scale that combined dream recall frequency with various dream intensity and content items, such as frequency of flying dreams, of vivid dreams, and of dreams on waking and on going to sleep. Neuroticism had small correlations with such sleep experiences ($r = .24$ and $.28$).

Thus, there is no consensus that extraversion or neuroticism is related to DRF. However, an association between nightmare frequency and neuroticism was found by Berquier and Ashton (1992) and Schredl (2003), although in a regression analysis the latter indicated that neuroticism did not add to the variance explained by state measures. In a sample of young people, Roberts and Lennings (2006) found that neuroticism correlated with trait nightmare distress ($r = .29$) but not with frequency of nightmares, and extraversion correlated with neither. In accord with the latter study, Chivers and Blagrove (1999) found nightmare frequency did not correlate with extraversion or neuroticism.

Locus of Control

As part of an article addressing dream recall correlates with various personality measures that may comprise a lifestyle: of being accepting of one's inner experience, Schonbar (1965) hypothesized that individuals who "experience the control of their destiny to reside within themselves" will have higher dream recall. This hypothesis was confirmed, with high recallers scoring more on the internal dimension on a locus of control questionnaire. However, Blagrove and Akehurst (2000) did not find this association with locus of control. Instead, there is a more robust association with lucid dreaming. Blagrove and Tucker (1994) found that high-frequency lucid dreamers were significantly more internal on Rotter's Internal/External Locus of Control (LOC) scale than were people who frequently recalled ordinary but nonlucid, dreams, and Blagrove and Hartnell (2000) found frequent lucid dreamers had higher scores than nonlucid dreamers on the internal dimension of Levenson's LOC scale, but not on Levenson's LOC powerful others and chance dimensions. These results were replicated by Patrick and Durndell (2004).

Need for Cognition

Blagrove and Akehurst (2000) hypothesized an association between dream recall and Need for Cognition, which is the liking for the activity of thinking and problem-solving; this was not found and may be evidence against an intellectual function of dreaming. Schonbar (1965) had similarly hypothesized that individuals who exhibit curiosity would have higher dream recall, but instead found that high recallers had significantly less "noninterpersonal curiosity," defined as curiosity for the working of things within science and engineering, than did low recallers and found that high and low recallers did not differ on interpersonal curiosity. Frequent lucid dreamers, however, do score significantly higher on Need for Cognition than do nonlucid dreamers (Blagrove & Hartnell, 2000; Patrick & Durndell, 2004).

Cognitive Arousal

Hicks, Fortin, and Brassington (2002) find that cognitive arousability, as measured by the self-report Arousal Predisposition scale, is not related to DRF but is positively related to dream unpleasantness and to frequency of night terrors and fantastic or posttraumatic nightmares.

Depression

In Barrett and Loeffler's study (1992), depressed participants recalled fewer dreams, had significantly shorter dream length, displayed less anger in their dreams, and had fewer characters, especially strangers, in their dreams. A trend for lower dream recall in depressed psychiatric inpatients, and significantly shorter dreams, was also found by Schredl and Engelhardt (2001). Similarly, in Armitage, Rochlen, Fitch, Trivedi, and Rush (1995), dream recall rates were extremely low in depressed patients (<20 percent) and decreased further when antidepressants were used, with the exception of fluoxetine (Prozac), where there was an increase in dream recall. Most dreams were short and bland. Those who responded to antidepressant use did not show changes in dream content, which may reflect a continuing vulnerability to depression. However, in Dow, Kelsoe, and Gillin (1996), dream recall rate and report length did not differ between three groups of veterans, those with posttraumatic stress disorder (PTSD) and major depression, those with depression alone, and those with neither PTSD nor depression.

It is not clear how these findings relate to the sleep of people with depression, who have disturbances of sleep continuity, a reduction of slow wave sleep, decreased REM latency, a prolongation of the first REM period, and increased REM density (Riemann, Berger, & Voderholzer, 2001).

The relationship between depression and dream recall, however, seems to be in the other direction for nonclinical depression. Robbins and Tanck (1988–1989) had undergraduates keep a 10-day diary and found depression tended to be higher preceding nights for which dreams were recalled and described than for nights in which no dreaming was reported. (Interestingly, Robbins and Tanck found even lower depression on nights preceding reports of contentless dreaming [where no content can be recalled, but one is certain that one had been dreaming] than for nights in which there was no memory of dreaming having occurred. They stated this suggests that contentless dreams are not in the middle of a continuum from no dream to recallable dream.) Also using a student sample, Miró and Martínez (2005) found that depressed mood was associated with a higher number of nightmares.

Anxiety and Acute Stress

Connor and Boblitt (1970) found a significant correlation between anxiety and dream recall ($r = .44$), but the review of correlational studies in Blagrove and Haywood (2006) found a median correlation of 0.26 from such studies. In adolescents, Nielsen et al. (2000) found anxiety at ages thirteen and sixteen years was related to presence of disturbing dreams at those ages, and anxiety at thirteen years was predictive of disturbing dreams at sixteen years. Using a more general measure of waking life acute stress, Chivers and Blagrove (1999) found nightmare frequency correlated significantly with General Health Questionnaire score. Also, it should be noted that there is an effect of dreams on waking life: Köthe and Pietrowsky (2001) found that, following a nightmare, participants were significantly more anxious and were of a less stable mental condition compared to nights without nightmares.

MMPI Scales

In accordance with the results reviewed in the last section, Tart (1962) found dream recall correlated positively with MMPI anxiety. However, although Wallach (1963) found four of the 16 MMPI scales are negatively correlated with reports of dream frequency, Robbins and Tanck (1971) and Redfering and Keller (1974) found no significant MMPI differences between high and low reporters, although the latter did find high reporters tended to be more restless and nervous than low reporters.

In contrast to the general lack of MMPI correlates in dream recall, Kales et al. (1980) found that the MMPI shows relatively high levels of psychopathology in people with frequent nightmares, with many showing a "chronic schizoid pattern of adjustment," while not being overly psychotic. Similarly, Berquier and Ashton (1992) found that adult lifelong nightmare sufferers scored significantly higher on eight MMPI clinical scales than did a control group, with the results being interpreted as a reflection of global maladjustment rather than of specific psychotic symptomatology.

Intrapsychic Conflict

Hill (1974) found that frequent dream recallers experience less and infrequent recallers experience more intrapsychic conflict, as assessed by six scales from the 16 PF. Hill stated that this may be related to repression in those with greater disturbance. In contrast, Foulkes, Spear, and Symonds (1966) found that nocturnal dream recall varies positively with waking maladaptive symptomatology, whereas presence of dreamlike imagery at sleep onset (hypnagogic imagery) varied with "waking ego strength" and "adaptive flexibility."

Schizophrenia and Schizotypy

These do not appear to have relationships with frequency of dream recall. However, Hartmann et al. (1981, 1987) found nightmare sufferers may be seen as unusually vulnerable, with a potential for mental illness—especially schizophrenia. Levin (1998) also found that individuals with frequent nightmares demonstrated greater schizotypy than did controls, and in Levin and Raulin (1991) there was a significant positive relationship between nightmare frequency and three (perceptual aberration, intense ambivalence, and somatic symptoms) of four schizotypy measures. The latter relationships appeared to be stronger for females than for males. However, whereas Roberts and Lennings (2006) found the score on Eysenck's scale of psychoticism to be correlated with nightmare frequency ($r = .22$), Chivers and Blagrove (1999) did not find this, and Levin and Fireman (2002) found no evidence for a specific relationship between nightmares and psychosis proneness.

In an assessment of various personality measures Claridge, Clark, and Davis (1997) found the best predictor of trait nightmare distress was Schizotypal Personality, but, using Eysenck's Personality Questionnaire Psychoticism scale, Roberts and Lennings (2006) did not find this.

Dissociation

Watson (2001) used the Iowa Sleep Experiences scale that combined DRF with various dream intensity and content items, such as frequency of flying dreams, of vivid dreams, and of dreams on waking and on going to sleep. Dissociation subscales had moderate correlations with the Sleep Experiences score ($r = .42$ to $.57$), and schizotypy subscales had small to moderate correlations with the Sleep Experiences score ($r = .31$ to $.47$). Watson interprets the results as showing that sleep experiences are related to absorption, imagination, daydreaming, and fantasy, with high dream recall and sleep experience individuals being able to pass more easily between different states of consciousness, as in Hartmann's concept of thin boundaries. Giesbrecht and Merckelbach (2006) similarly found that the score on the General Sleep Experiences subscale of the Iowa Sleep Experiences Survey significantly correlated ($r = .35$) with dissociation, as assessed by the Dissociative Experiences scale.

In Agargün et al. (2003a), a 57 percent prevalence of nightmares was found among patients with dissociative disorder. Also, among patients with dissociative disorder, those with nightmares had a higher rate of self-mutilating behavior, a greater history of attempting suicide during the last year, and comorbidity with borderline personality disorder, than did those without nightmares.

Borderline Personality

Claridge, Davis, Bellhouse, and Kaptein (1998) found that borderline personality score correlates with trait nightmare distress ($r = .42$) and with strength of adult nightmare content ($r = 31$) in a student nonclinical sample.

Alexithymia

This is a deficit in emotional cognition, where people are mostly unaware of their feelings or don't know what they signify, and hence they rarely talk about their emotions or motivations.

Nielsen et al. (1997) examined a carefully screened clinical population, finding that, in men, dream recall was negatively related to alexithymia, whereas in women dream and nightmare recall were positively correlated with neuroticism. Explanations for the results in males are suggested by the work of Tantam, Kalucy, and Brown (1982), who found alexithymia to be associated with a trend toward less REM sleep and a significant lack of involvement in dreams collected under standardized sleep laboratory conditions. A problem, however, remains as to whether any effects of alexithymia on dreaming occur at the level of dream formation or at the point of recall, a problem that will be addressed in the discussion to follow.

Other Traits

Blagrove and Akehurst (2000) found DRF correlates marginally with interrogative suggestibility, indicating that DRF obtained by questionnaire may be subject to demand bias. DRF did not correlate with hypochondriasis or with morningness-eveningness (the tendency to be more alert and to prefer scheduling effortful work in the morning or in the evening).

Personality and Frequency of Specific Types of Dreams

Recurrent or Recurring Dreams

Brown and Donderi (1986) investigated 67 people either with recurrent dreams, or who in the past had recurrent dreams, and nonrecurrent dreamers (aged 18–88 years). They recorded their dreams for 14 days. Recurrent dreamers scored low on psychological well-being (PWB) and reported more anxious, aggressive, and dysphoric dream content. Those who used to have recurrent dreams scored high on PWB and reported more positive dream content. These findings were replicated by Zadra, O'Brien, and Donderi (1997–1998), who also concluded that recurrent dreams occur at times of stress.

Precognitive Dreams

Blackmore (1997) found that believers in the paranormal have a propensity to give affirmative answers to everyday factual questions such as "Do you have a scar on your left knee?" Using this method, Blagrove, French, and Jones (2006) found that the specific paranormal belief in precognitive dreams was also associated with the giving of affirmative answers to everyday factual questions. The authors explained this as showing that individuals who have the cognitive flexibility to see their dreams as connected to future events also have the flexibility to alter the interpretations of the everyday questions so as to be able to answer them affirmatively: this can also be seen as an affirmative bias. There was also evidence that belief in precognitive dreams is associated with deficiencies in reasoning about probability, such as in reasoning about chances of winning the lottery.

Discussion

The previous review shows that most traits that have been proposed as correlates of DRF have been found to have at best only weak relationships with DRF. Schredl, Wittmann, and colleagues (2003) came to a similar conclusion, with the four factors they found to be significantly related to DRF—personality (openness to experience, thin boundaries, absorption), creativity, nocturnal awakenings, and attitude toward dreams—explaining only 8.4 percent of the total variance in DRF. Levin et al. (2003) similarly concluded that DRF is largely independent from stable personality traits and is better understood in terms of expectancy and attitudinal factors.

It may even be that these small relationships are inflated and spurious. As already described, Beaulieu-Prévost and Zadra (in press) showed that two of the strongest personality relationships with retrospective dream recall frequency, boundariness and absorption, become negligible when dream recall is assessed prospectively, and even attitude toward dreams had only a marginal relationship with prospective dream recall. Furthermore, Schredl, Wittmann, and colleagues (2003) found that relationships between personality and dream recall are considerably smaller in studies where many variables are assessed than in studies investigating a single influencing factor and using similar measurement instruments, and so concluded that there may be expectancy effects in studies that assess the correlation of DRF with just one personality variable. One such expectancy effect will be shown to have an effect on reporting of dream content later in this chapter.

Accepting that the correlations between trait measures and DRF are at best small, and may even be inflated, various explanations for these findings of small or negligible correlations will now be discussed.

Possible Explanations for the Generally Small or Negligible Personality Trait—DRF Correlations

(1) *There may be problems in the validity of retrospective or prospective questionnaires in assessing DRF.* For example, Beaulieu-Prévost and Zadra

(2005a) found retrospective estimations of DRF to be inaccurate when compared to diary measures, and that individuals with a negative attitude toward dreams were more likely to underestimate their dream recall retrospectively in comparison to their dream recall when assessed with a diary. Also, Schredl (2004) found that responses to a seven-point DRF question were affected by whether the participants' focus was directed explicitly toward dreaming, or not directed, such as by presenting the scale within a general sleep questionnaire. There may also be problems with prospective assessment by diaries in that participants may become fatigued about keeping the diary, be stimulated by the diary to have more dreams, or expect that they should be reporting more dreams (Halliday, 1992; Schredl, 2002b). The claim here would be that "real" DRF has a higher correlation with some of the personality measures than does DRF as measured retrospectively or prospectively. The problems, however, with this argument, are first, there may not be any other way of obtaining a DRF measure, even if there was such a hypothesized purer DRF, and second, the supposed problems with retrospective and prospective measures as just described may be inflating the personality-DRF correlations, which would, if properly measured, be far smaller.

A third argument against this view is that many correlations of trait measures with frequency of nightmares have been found to be of moderate size, using retrospective and prospective assessments, which indicates that these measures do not intrinsically have high error variance with consequent small or unreliable correlations with trait variables.

(2) *It may be that it is our measurements of traits that are unreliable, and that better assessment of traits would result in larger correlations with dream recall frequency.* Greater aggregation of data across occasions and situations may be needed, as suggested by Mischel (1983). On this point, Epstein and O'Brian (1985) show that the common $r = .30$ ceiling for correlations between personality and behavior can be exceeded by aggregating measurements. Thus, it may be that various behavioral measures need to be combined to produce a better correlate. For example, Blagrove and Akehurst (2000) suggest that frequency of visits to art galleries could be included in a creativity measure before its use as a correlate. The issue of a greater aggregation of data would also apply to the measures of dream recall; for example, a four-week log may provide a better measure than a two-week log.

(3) *The prediction of DRF from a specific trait may only apply to some people.* For example, Cohen (1979) warned that a trait may only be predictive if that trait is a central dimension of that person's personality and is also a significant capacity of that person.

(4) *It may be that state factors are the main factors in affecting dream recall.* Such state factors may be, for example, nocturnal awakening or focusing on dreams in the morning, as argued by Schredl and Montasser (1996–1997b).

Another state factor is described by Cohen (1974b), who found a small within-subjects effect of dream recall was more likely following negative pre-sleep mood, with this effect being greater for infrequent dream recallers. Cohen suggests this effect could be mediated by increased dream salience, which is increased by negative presleep mood. This finding was confirmed and extended by Cohen (1974c). His extension of those findings leads to the following possibility.

(5) *Cohen (1974c) points out that the interaction of traits with state factors (such as pre-sleep stress or mood) may be a better predictor of dream recall than trait or state factors alone.* In this study he found that, of eighty-one college women who served as participants, infrequent (but not frequent) dream recallers were more likely to recall dreams when their presleep self-confidence was at its lowest than when it was at its highest. Similarly, in Cohen and Cox (1975), the negative presleep condition was associated with a higher percent-age of participants with dream recall at the end of the night, and this was especially marked for infrequent dream recallers. (Incidentally, these results contradict the repression hypothesis of dream recall.)

Schredl (2003) compared in a regression the relative size of trait and state factors in predicting nightmare recall, finding that the traits neuroticism and boundariness do not add to the variance in nightmare frequency explained by state factors. But the point made in this section is a different one, that an interaction may be occurring between state and trait factors, such that, for example, a particular presleep mood only has an effect on dream recall for people with a certain range of scores on a particular trait. Such interac-tion studies have been very rare in the investigation of dreaming. One of the rare examples of this is Cohen (1971b), who found that "relatively high anx-iety was related to significantly lower frequency of dream recall in groups marked by intellectualization and abnegation."

Cohen (1979, p. 239) thus warns about dismissing relationships between personality and dreaming because of not taking care with various methodo-logical points, such as the interaction with state factors. He also distin-guishes whether one is measuring a habitual and possibly unimportant behavior, as against a distinctive and rare maximal capacity (for example, in aggression), which may be more predictive of dream characteristics.

(6) *It may be that the results of small or negligible relationships between personality and dream recall are valid, and that dream recall is determined more by physiology than by personality.* Farley et al. (1971), having found that extraversion and neuroticism did not predict DRF, hypothesized that physi-ological arousal during dreaming predicts recall. Similarly, Webb and Kersey (1967) hypothesized that individual differences in likelihood of waking from REM sleep may account for differences in habitual recall.

Blagrove and Akehurst (2000) list various studies that find electroencephalogram (EEG) frequencies related to dream recall. For example, Rochlen, Hoffmann, and Armitage (1998) assessed the sleep EEG for depressed and control participants for successful dream recall and no recall. Increased high-frequency beta incidence in the right hemisphere and amplitude in both hemispheres during sleep were associated with dream recall in both groups. Post-awakening EEG did not relate to success or failure of dream recall in either group. To these may be added Takeuchi et al.'s (1999) prediction of dream recall by EEG activity in sleep onset REM periods, part of the basis for the relationships between dream properties, such as emotionality, activity, and impression, and EEG power spectral values (Takeuchi, Ogilvie, Ferrelli, Murphy, & Belicki, 2001).

(7) *The dichotomous measure of a dream being either present or absent on a night, whether such dichotomous instances are summed retrospectively or prospectively, may be an inappropriate measure of amount of dream recall or amount of dream production.* There may be better or alternate measures. The following are examples:

(a) Dream length. An advantage of diaries is that they can provide a measure of dream report word length: such a measure could be used to alter the criterion of what is counted as an instance of dream recall. It could also provide an alternate measure of amount of dreaming, as proposed by Waterman (1991), who showed that dream length can have higher correlations with trait variables than does the dichotomous measure.

(b) Dream detail, defined as the individual ratings of vividness or detailed content of dreams. This measure was proposed by Wolcott and Strapp (2002), who found DRF and dream detail had different patterns of association in relation to behaviors, attitude, and personality. DRF was associated with the frequency of experiencing emotionally disturbing dreams and trying to interpret dreams, whereas detail of dreams was associated with positive attitude toward dreaming and type B personality (defined as being relaxed, uncompetitive, and inclined to self-analysis).

It may thus be that measures of dream length or detail are needed in addition to dream frequency, because individuals may interpret dream frequency on the basis of such content criteria. For example, Watson (2001) used the Iowa Sleep Experiences scale, which combines DRF with various dream intensity and content items, and obtained impressive correlations with personality measures. An emphasis on frequency of vivid types of dreams resulted in findings that these vivid dreams are related to handedness (Hicks, Bautista, & Hicks, 1999; McNamara, Clark, & Hartmann, 1998), and supports the use of Spadafora and Hunt's (1990) dream scale, which assesses frequency of types of dreams, such as vivid or lucid dreams.

Do the Individual Difference Variables Act at Dream Production or Recall?

There is evidence that individuals have their own style of dream reporting: Stickgold, Malia, Fosse, Propper, and Hobson (2001) found that the length in words of REM dream reports correlated significantly with length of NREM reports ($r = .70$), sleep onset reports ($r = .74$), and wake reports of what was happening in the last fifteen minutes before the report ($r = .40$). It may thus be that correlations with individual difference variables operate at this recall level.

Cohen and MacNeilage (1974), however, reviewed work showing that high- and low-frequency recallers do not differ on variables that might be expected to affect recall, such as short- or long-term memory. They thus proposed that individual differences in dream recall act at the level of dream production; that is, those with high recall produce more salient, and hence more memorable, dreams. However, and this problem recurs with many individual difference correlates of DRF, they rightly conclude that it is difficult to separate generation and recall aspects of dream reports, and hence it may be difficult to ascertain whether an individual difference variable that correlates with dream recall acts at the level of dream production, or of recall, or at both levels.

There are some findings, however, that fit best with the claim that it is characteristics of the dream itself that differs between people. Cohen (1974d) reviewed early work showing that sleep physiological events that correlate with increased dream salience also correlate with dream recallability. To give an example of this type of argument, Goodenough (1991) reviewed work showing that high dream recall was associated with REM periods with high eye-movement density, and Goodenough, Witkin, Koulack, and Cohen (1975) showed that eye-movement activity was greater for high-affect dream reports, which this theory would claim to be salient, and hence memorable.

However, even if dream production is a different mechanism from dream recall, for after all, they are different activities separated in time, there is the methodological problem that a measure of ability to form vivid images may itself be confounded by one's ability to recall the image whose vividness is being measured. One series of studies, though, that may have successfully excluded the recall confound, is described in Foulkes (1999). Here, in children, level of dream recall was related to spatial reasoning as assessed by the block design task. Foulkes claimed that the abilities assessed by the spatial reasoning task were clearly concerned with dream formation rather than with the interpersonal matters of dream recall and telling. Similarly, an association between score on block design and recall of REM dreams of adults in the sleep laboratory was found by Butler and Watson (1985), to which the same argument can be applied.

However, it remains unclear for the other correlational studies at which of the levels of dreaming, whether it is at the formation and having the dream, or at encoding into memory and then recalling the dream, that individual difference variables are acting. It is a standard procedure within memory research to differentiate whether a variable that affects memory acts at the point of encoding or at retrieval. Thus, it is at first tempting to think that analogous double dissociation studies could be performed to distinguish variables that act at dream production from those that act at dream recall, or even at dream re-recall at a later time or date. Certainly, many experiments on dreams have addressed experimental variables that act at production or at recall. For example, having people delay writing down their dreams lessens the amount recalled (Goodenough, 1991). But the problem with individual difference variables is that in almost all cases, an argument can be made for how they could act at dream production, and how they could also act at dream recall. For example, creative people might dream more, or they might dream just as much as noncreative people, but be better at recalling those dreams. Even the Repression-Sensitization dimension, hypothesized to act at recall, could be argued to have an effect on dream production through diminishing or enhancing the recruitment of source memories and emotions for the dream, with these differences in recruitment causing the dream to be respectively vague or memorable. Given that it is unclear whether at the point of recall, the short-term memory of the dream is then being consolidated into long-term memory, or whether it is being retrieved from long-term memory, even assessing how individual difference variables act at the point of recall is problematic.

In favor, however, of the view that some people may produce more dreams than others was the finding by Dement and Kleitman (1957) that people differ in their ability to recall dreams when woken in the sleep laboratory. However, it could still be argued that, although these differences between people occur in a situation where one is suddenly woken and asked to report a dream, there may still be a memory effect operating. This argument follows from the results of Conduit, Crewther, and Coleman (2004). During Stage 2 and REM sleep, Conduit et al. (2004) presented an auditory tone below the waking threshold to which participants had been instructed to respond with an eye movement. Soon after the signal and response, if the person remained asleep, they were woken up (with control awakenings when no signal and/or no response had occurred). Compared to the REM sleep condition, in the Stage 2 condition, participants were less able to judge correctly whether they had responded to the tone. Stage 2 sleep thus has a memory recall deficit in comparison to REM sleep. Conduit et al. concluded that the low level of dream recall from Stage 2 sleep may be due to deficiencies in recall, rather than because dreams are produced at a lower level in Stage 2 sleep than in REM sleep. It is arguable that a similar, albeit milder, level of this recall deficiency is present in REM sleep (after all, recall of REM dreams can be difficult), and that this level of recall deficiency differs between individuals and affects home recall of dreams, as well as recall after sudden awakenings in the sleep laboratory.

Implications of the Findings of Correlates of Dream Recall Frequency for Theories of Dream Formation

It may be that all the individual difference variables found previously to correlate with dream recall are acting at the level of dream recall rather than dream production. This data would then be useful for knowing how dreams are remembered and reported and passed on to others, but does not provide information on how they are produced. It may be that the work of Foulkes (1999), just cited, is the only correlational study to date in a normal population that gives information about dream production pointing to the use of spatial information at this level. There is also the correlational work of Solms (1997) in individuals with brain lesions, showing cessation of dreaming after lesions of particular cortical areas, but this again illustrates the importance of showing that it is dream production rather than recall that is being affected. The failure to find memory deficiencies when awake in some of the brain-lesioned patients has been used to argue against there being a deficit in dream recall, and in favor of there being a deficit in dream production.

Implications of the Variation in Dream Recall for the Evolution of Dreaming

There is speculation about the function of dreaming, ranging from a function being denied (Blagrove, 2000; Domhoff, 2003; Flanagan, 2000), to dreaming protecting sleep (Freud, 1900/1953), to dreams processing emotional and other memories (Hartmann, 1998; Nielsen, Kuiken, Alain, Stenstrom, & Powell, 2004; Stickgold, Hobson, Fosse, & Fosse, 2001). Partly dependent on the investigation of those speculations are arguments about how dreaming evolved. Here there are two options: one is that the ability to dream was selected for in evolution because it is itself useful, the other is that dreaming is a by-product of the evolution of some other faculty, such as waking life imagination. The first part of this chapter is relevant to these questions in two ways:

(a) The variability between people in dream recall may be explained by differing intensities of dream content, different abilities at recall, and possibly by people having differing amounts of dreaming from other people. According to Pagel (2003), for example, in a sample of sleep laboratory clients, 6.5 percent reported never dreaming when assessed by questionnaire, and 0.4 percent reported no recall when assessed by interview and sleep laboratory awakenings. Never recalling a dream, and the related characteristic of never dreaming, are thus quite rare. The important point to be raised here is that such wide variation of dream recall or of dreaming between people does not mean that dreaming is inconsequential and that evolution is not selecting for this ability. Nettle (2006) gives many examples from animal behavior and human personality to show that there can be a variation of a characteristic in a population, and that whereas in some circumstances evolution selects only one part of that variation to survive, for other characteristics that variation itself can be adaptive. So, for example, Nettle describes how there may be two mating strategies coexisting in a population, or there may be a variation in a personality trait, such as agreeableness, or extraversion, which may continue to exist because different levels of it have their own benefits and costs. Time spent dreaming, and confusion with reality on waking, may be costs of dreaming, but there may be benefits to dreaming, with individuals differing as to the costs and benefits of dreaming to them.

(b) It may point to what the specific benefits of dreaming are, or alternatively, point to what has evolved, with dreaming as its epiphenomenal by-product. Here, the largest correlates seem to be creativity and openness to experience. Nettle (2006) describes the benefits of openness that would cause it to be selected for in evolution: that this divergent cognitive style "seeks novelty and complexity, and makes associations or mappings between apparently disparate domains." But although this appears to be an "unalloyed good," a variation in the population remains because its "fitness payoffs" are counteracted by its associated openness to psychosis, as well as likelihood of depression and delusion, and associated reduced reproductive success.

There is thus an argument that dreaming has evolved in association with an openness trait that acts creatively for a greater connectedness of memories. Unfortunately, the question remains of whether dreaming is an essential component of this function, a useful but not necessary part of it, or an epiphenomenon of it. And a further possibility remains, that dreaming has resulted from selection for something other than these personality traits, and that these traits are only relevant to dream recall and not to dream production.

Conclusion

Although some personality traits do have associations with the occurrence of particular types of dreams, such as nightmares and lucid dreams, decades of research has shown only weak relationships between psychometrically assessed personality traits and the frequency of dream recall.

PERSONALITY AND DREAM CONTENT

This section of the chapter assesses whether psychometric personality traits, examples of which were reviewed above, are related to dream content.

To hypothesize such relationships between waking traits and dream content trait-like aspects of dream content that are stable over time are required. Much evidence for this is cited in Chapter 7 of Domhoff's (1996) book *Finding Meaning in Dreams: A Quantitative Approach.* The studies cited there involved dreams being collected in the laboratory, at home over a period of weeks, or in personal dream diaries that an individual kept, often over many years. Domhoff summarized this work as showing "amazing consistency" in dreaming of "types of characters, social interactions, objects, and activities," and the dream content as being "relatively free of major changes in life circumstances."

Domhoff (1996) also provided considerable evidence for correspondences between dreams and waking life, such that there are differences between individuals (such as famous writers) in these dream characteristics, and differences between groups, such as cross-cultural or gender differences. This follows the work of Calvin Hall: Hall (1947) had thirty dream cycles of college students analyzed by several judges, showing consistent agreement with their postulated conflicts. Hall's (1953) book, *The Meaning of Dreams,* looked at 10,000 dreams of people of all ages and professions. The thesis investigated that dreams are the embodiment of the person's whole personality, dealing with inner problems that the person is facing. As in Freud, however, the symbolism of dreams is purely personal. In a posthumous article, Hall (1991) discusses the status of dreams in the cognitive and diagnostic provinces of psychology. The manifest dream is claimed to be a source of information about the dreamer, and it is argued that dreams can be a valuable tool for psychologists because they express, directly and explicitly, what is on the dreamer's mind, his or her preoccupations, conflicts, anxieties, wishes, and conceptions of him or herself and the world.

Claims That Dreams May in Some Cases Predict Future Behavior

There has also been evidence of predictive abilities of dream content. Illustrative of this is the finding of Hajek and Belcher (1991) that, in abstinent former smokers, dreaming of smoking was predictive of relapse. Regarding work on traits, as concerns us here, Cartwright and Wood (1993) examined masochistic dreaming, defined as present if a dream has any of ten listed characteristics, including a negative representation of the self. Twenty-five women and twenty-one men undergoing divorce had dreams collected in the sleep laboratory. Women masochistic dreamers (fifteen of the participants) had significantly higher scores on a scale of negative aspects of traditional feminine gender-role identity than did men or women without such dreams. Importantly, the women with masochistic dreams showed less improvement at follow-up and had more need for emotional support. Similarly, in a study of men and women undergoing divorce, Cartwright (1991) found that those who were depressed and incorporated the ex-spouse into their dreams at the time of breaking up were less depressed at follow-up than were those who did not incorporate their spouse into their dreams.

There is, therefore, evidence for connections between waking life and dream content, and for dream content sometimes being predictive of waking behavior. However, given this meaningfulness of dreams, the focus of this chapter is on the narrower issue of whether there are relationships between standard psychometric personality tests and dream content. We will now proceed to the evaluation of this stronger claim.

Further Evidence of Relationships Between Waking Life and Dream Content

In addition to the work of Domhoff, and the work of Hall before him, there is other evidence that differences between people when awake are reflected in dream content. De Koninck and Koulack (1975) had subjects in the sleep lab watch a stressful film before going to sleep and again in the morning. Participants who exhibited more emotionality at the second presentation of the film tended to be those who had more incorporations of film elements in their dreams. Lortie-Lussier, Schwab, and De Koninck (1985) asked fifteen employed mothers and fifteen nonemployed mothers to report dreams collected over a period of three weeks and to complete a Personality Inventory. The two groups could be statistically differentiated on the basis of several dream content scales: employed mothers experienced more unpleasant emotions, more male characters, and less residential dream settings than did the nonemployed mothers. The authors concluded that as the trend toward carrying the dual role of wage earner and homemaker is expanding, the gender differences typically observed in dream content may decrease. A final example is Foulkes, Larson, Swanson, and Rardin (1969): dreams collected during periods of REM sleep were compared for healthy and emotionally disturbed adolescents. Their dreams were generally directly related to their waking lives, but personality pathology was associated with more vivid and unrealistic dreaming.

Dream Content and Psychometrically Assessed Personality Traits

There are also findings of relationships between psychometrically assessed personality with dream content. Evans and Singer (1994–1995) scored dream reports for intimacy motivation. These scores were positively related to self-reported nurturance in waking life and negatively related to dominance in waking life. Similarly, Domino (1976b) obtained three dream reports from each of sixty-two male students. These reports were rated by five judges on fifteen personality dimensions, such as achievement, deference, affiliation, and aggression. These dream dimensions were then compared with scores on the same dimensions as measured by the Edwards Personal Preference Schedule (EPPS) and the Adjective Check List (ACL). Six of the fifteen EPPS scales and ten of the fifteen ACL scales correlated significantly with their appropriate dream rating scales. Also, Rim (1986, 1988) found that coping styles in dreams (such as detachment, seeking support, and various others) were correlated with the use of the same coping styles when awake. As a final example, Bruni, Lo Reto, Recine, Ottaviano, and Guidetti (1999) had children aged 9–13 years consider their recent or emotional dreams and complete the Dream Content Questionnaire for Children. Various correlations were found, for example, between neuroticism and negative dream emotions $(r = .34)$ and between extraversion and sexual interactions in the dream $(r = .24)$.

Problems With the Study of Relationships Between Personality Traits and Dream Content

Although there have been some findings of mapping psychometrically measured personality traits to dream content, such findings are not common, and there have been the following problems in this field.

1. Many studies do not find relationships between waking life personality measures and dream content. Howarth (1962) failed to reveal an association between either extroversion or neuroticism and dream content. Woods, Cole, and Ferrandez (1977) found no significant correlations between three dimensions of emotional style and two dream content variables. In Volpe and Levin (1998), dream reports were analyzed for attributional style in making causal inferences. These scores were found not to correlate with a waking measure of attributional style. Most importantly, however, whereas the internal/external, stable/unstable, and

global/specific dimensions of waking attributional style did correlate with level of depression in waking life, this level of depression did not correlate with attributional style during dreams.

This lack of relationship between waking personality and dream content can be compared to a similar lack of relationship between dream content and chronic physiological medical condition. MacFarlane and Wilson (2006) examined the influence of specific chronic sleep disorders (obstructive sleep apnea, where the person repeatedly stops breathing during the night; narcolepsy; an EEG arousal disorder during sleep; or periodic leg movements during sleep) on dream content. A significant proportion of patients who complain of excessive perspiration dream about perspiring, and significant proportions of those who report difficulty breathing while awake dream about feelings of choking and suffocation. In addition, recurring dreams and dreams of paralysis were significantly more prominent in patients with narcolepsy. However, patients with sleep apnea did not dream of choking/feelings of suffocation with greater frequency than patients without apnea. These findings suggest that chronic physiological conditions have an inconsistent influence on dream content items.

2. Where significant relationships are claimed, the dream content is often not a simple depiction or reflection of the waking trait. Robbins, Tanck, and Houshi (1985) found waking life anxiety level was related to symbolic sexual dream content. Coolidge and Bracken (1984) found people with recurring teeth-loss dreams were significantly more anxious *and* depressed, and less satisfied with their lives, compared to people who dream of flying. Cann and Donderi (1986) found introverts recalled more everyday dreams, and high neuroticism scorers recalled fewer archetypal dreams. These researchers provided justifications for these hypotheses. The point here, however, is that these are indirect relationships, and if many such indirect relationships are investigated, there is a potential for type 2 errors, that is, with a large number of relationships possible in a study some will be found to be significant just by chance.

It should be remarked, however, in justification of investigating such indirect relationships, that correspondences between waking life variables and dream content can be quite tangential. For example, there is a greater vividness of dreams, but not greater violent content, after seeing a violent film (Foulkes & Rechtschaffen, 1964), and greater intensity of the central image of a dream, but no significant change towards more negative emotions pictured after abuse (Hartmann, Zborowski, Rosen, & Grace, 2001) and after 9/11 (Hartmann & Basile, 2003). There can even be paradoxical effects, such that it is repressed rather than consciously acknowledged thoughts that are preferentially incorporated into dreams (Wegner, Wenzlaff, & Kozak, 2004).

3. Where relationships are found between dream content and waking traits, the significant findings may be due to response biases. This is especially possible when a retrospective account of one's dreams is made at the same time as personality tests are completed. Bernstein and Belicki (1995–1996) had subjects fill out a

Hall and Van de Castle's (1966) Dream Content Questionnaire, which assesses frequency of various dream contents, such as fortune, aggression, and social interactions. They also kept a 14-day dream diary on two separate occasions, in addition to completing personality trait inventories. The dream diary content was found to be inconsistent over time and was unrelated to any of the ten personality traits assessed, whereas the Dream Content Questionnaire did show relationships with seven of the personality traits (for example, openness and absorption both correlated with dream bizarreness [$r = .38$ and $.34$, respectively], and extraversion correlated with number of dream characters [$r = .27$]). Bernstein and Belicki suggested that dream diaries might reflect state concerns, that is, concerns of the preceding day, whereas the retrospective content questionnaire tapped more enduring dispositions. Of course, there is a third possibility, which they go on to note, that self-concept may influence responses to retrospective dream questionnaires, which are thus an inaccurate measure of actual dream content, but which result in spuriously enhanced correlations with trait variables that are also related to each individual's self-concept.

A similar point was made by Bernstein and Roberts (1995). They found significant correlations between personality as assessed by the Five Factor Model and items of the Dream Content Questionnaire; for example, agreeable subjects reported more dream characters ($r = .30$), subjects who were open to experience reported more unfamiliar dream characters ($r = .34$), and extraverts reported more dreams set at night ($r = .34$). (However, a hypothesized correlation between extraversion and number of dream characters was not found [$r = .11$].) The authors acknowledged that because a retrospective questionnaire was used to assess dream content, items may have been answered according to subjects' self-concept. This may have inflated the correlations between dream content measures and waking traits, notwithstanding the fact that dream contents for this sample were consistent with past norms obtained from dream diary reports and lab reports.

A direct test of this hypothesized problem with retrospective assessment was made by Beaulieu-Prévost and Zadra, (2005b). They showed that (a) when memories of past dreams are readily available (that is, when DRF is high), people's beliefs about their general dream content are closely related to their actual dream experiences as measured by a dream diary, and (b) when such memories are not easily available (that is, when DRF is low), people's beliefs about their dream content are influenced by their current emotional state.

4. Some of the significant results involve a comparison of psychiatric patient groups with controls, rather than groups differing on a trait measure but within a normal population. There are many examples of the dreams of psychiatric patients differing from those of nonpatients. Cohen's (1979) review showed that, in general, people with schizophrenia have dreams with more strangers, more aggression directed at themselves, and more bizarreness, than do people without schizophrenia. Hauri (1976) found that patients who had been fully remitted from serious

reactive depression showed more masochism in their dreams and more hostility in the dream environment than did healthy controls. Remitted patients also dreamed more about the past than did controls. This suggests that some personality traits are chronically disturbed and do not improve when patients remit from reactive depression.

Firth, Blouin, Natarajan, and Blouin (1986) found that both suicidal and violent depressed patients had more death content and destructive violence in their dreams than did depressed patients who were not violent or suicidal. Agargün and Cartwright (2003) examined the relationship between the emotional quality of dreams, REM sleep variables, and suicidal tendency in depressed individuals. For most of the people in this study, as in healthy subjects, there was an increase in the dreamlike quality of REM dream reports across the nights; however, a reduction in the dreamlike quality of the REM content reports between the first and second halves of the night was found to be associated with suicidal tendency. The authors argued that this indicated that these subjects fail to self-regulate mood and integrate affect into long-term memory networks during sleep.

Guralnik, Levin, and Schmeidler (1999) compared dreams of patients with a personality disorder with normative data on dream content from Hall and Van de Castle (1966). The personality-disordered group had more estrangement in their dreams, fewer interactions, and more emotionality. In their interactions, they demonstrated a lower ratio of aggressive interactions yet a higher tendency to view themselves as the aggressors.

Schredl and Engelhardt (2001) found within a group of depressed patients that level of depression correlated with presence of death dreams and with dream negative emotional tone. They also found a relationship between psychotic symptoms and dream bizarreness. However, they made the important point that the environmental setting for patients is different from that of healthy controls and is thus a confounding variable in many of these studies.

5. An example of a problem within a widely cited trait-dream content relationship, that between creativity and dream imaginativeness/bizarreness. Schechter et al. (1965) investigated the relationship between creativity and dream bizarreness by taking students from three disciplines (art, science, and engineering), assessing the imaginativeness of their dreams, and assessing their creativity with a self-report independence of judgment test. They found that within each of these groups, creativity only correlated with dream imaginativeness for the students in the art group. Also, the art students were higher on the creativity measure used and had more imaginative dreams than the science and engineering students, but this difference in dream imaginativeness could just be due to differences in the disciplines studied rather than due to creativity differences between the disciplines.

Sylvia, Clark, and Monroe (1978) used various creativity tests (for example, Remote Associates, Brick uses) to obtain two groups of university students that were extremely high or extremely low in creativity. REM dream reports were then obtained in the sleep laboratory. Blind judges were able to discriminate successfully between dream reports from the two groups, in that content for the creative group was significantly more novel and unique, and their report lengths, measured in total number of words, were longer. Furthermore, Domino (1976a) found that the dreams of a high creative group (as defined by teachers' ratings) had more primary process thinking (for example, were more bizarre, with more improbable or impossible events) in dream reports collected over eleven nights than did a low creative group. Both groups also had significant correlations ($r = .29$ for creative group and .43 for the noncreative group) between primary process thinking in dreams and a creativity score based on the Remote Associates and Alternate Uses tests.

However, these results do not show conclusively that creative people really have more bizarre dreams because, as concluded by Domino (1976a), the creative participants may instead just be better able to report or tolerate less logical dream content. This possibility is supported by the results of Wood, Sebba, and Domino (1989–1990), who noted that many creativity tests might just be assessing language fluency. They found that partialling out verbal ability or partialling out length of dream report resulted in the correlation between creativity and dream bizarreness becoming insignificant. This can be interpreted as dream bizarreness being larger for participants who are so verbally skilled that they can provide a longer report of their dream, which therefore has more chance of having bizarreness included in it. So, the result of Auld, Goldenberg, and Weiss (1968), that bizarre-like primary process thinking is highly correlated ($r = .6$) with the average length of subjects' dreams, can be interpreted as showing that producing a longer dream report results in more bizarreness being present. Significant creativity-dream bizarreness correlations are thus due to a confound of verbal fluency/intelligence.

However, Hunt, Ruzycki-Hunt, Pariak, and Belicki (1993) conducted three studies to critique this view that dream bizarreness is an artifact of dream report length and that correlations of bizarreness with measures of waking imagination are an artifact of report length and verbal fluency/intelligence. In Study I they showed that describing a bizarre pictorial stimulus entails the use of more words than a mundane stimulus, so it is more plausible to conclude that bizarreness results in a longer dream, rather than the other way around. Their Study II distinguished words describing or consequent upon bizarreness from words describing mundane parts of the dream, to show that controlling for total report length is an invalid procedure, in that a larger number of words is needed to describe bizarre content. In

Study III, they showed that measures of nonverbal imaginativeness are much stronger in predicting bizarreness, and both report length measures (bizarre and mundane content), than was a measure of verbal ability. They conclude that controlling for report length may be a methodological error that falsely dilutes a defining dimension of dreaming, namely, its bizarreness.

According to Hunt et al. (1993), therefore, creative or imaginative people really do have more bizarre dreams. The point of this section, however, is to show the care that is needed in assessing the meaning of a waking trait-dream content relationship, in that some attempt is needed to distinguish dream content from the recall of dream content.

Discussion

The main conclusion from the previous review is that there is mixed evidence for waking-life psychometrically assessed personality traits being associated with dream content variables. Domhoff (1996, Chapter 8) also reviews studies on the relationship between dream content and personality. Although he cites some relationships, such as in dream themes of tension in those who have greater hostility when awake, he points out that the studies generally have low sample sizes, no mention of effect sizes, lack of replication studies, and, above all, have so many waking and dream variables that multiple comparisons are occurring. He concludes that because of the "meager findings" with personality tests, "dream content may not be about 'personality' in the usual sense of the term." Instead, dream content may provide us with different information about people than most personality tests do because dream content reveals conceptions and concerns of the dreamer.

While accepting Domhoff's conclusions, two further considerations will now be detailed.

1. *There may be interactions of state and trait factors.* In Cohen (1974c), the lowest self-confidence rating during a five-day recording period was associated with unpleasant dream affect, and the highest self-confidence rating was associated with pleasant dream affect; however, this result was only true for a subset of the participants in the study, those habitually low in self-confidence and high on "sensitization." Thus, it may be that some traits only affect dream content in combination with another factor, in this case presleep mood. Because the personality trait is related to dream content only under certain circumstances, a study that relied on simple correlations between trait and content would not discern these relationships. The following is another example of a study in which relationships between waking variables and dream content were only present for a subset of participants. In Goodenough et al. (1975), a stressful film increased dream anxiety and

REM-period breathing irregularity, but only for those subjects who showed irregular breathing as a response to the film in the waking state. A further possibility is that compensatory or continuous relationships between waking variables and dream content may have an interactive effect with neuroticism (Cohen, 1977; Cohen & Cox, 1975; Samson & de Koninck, 1986).

Of course, however, it may be that state factors are found to have a greater influence than trait factors. Schredl and Jacob (1998) tested the influence of state factors on the gender ratios of dream characters reported by a 23-year-old male. The study investigated whether a typical "male environment" (studying engineering) would be accompanied by a preponderance of male dream characters, whereas a "female environment" (studying psychology) would result in a balanced ratio of male and female dream characters. Data came from a dream diary kept by the participant while he was studying engineering and then, three years later, when he was studying psychology. There was a preponderance of male characters in the participant's dreams when he was in a male environment but not when he was in a female environment. These results support the continuity hypothesis of dreaming and stress the importance of situational factors rather than personality factors in the explanation of the gender ratio of dream characters.

2. *Claims that dreams may in some cases be a better measure of personality traits.* There was work performed some years ago on whether dreams may have advantages in the assessment of personality over standard measures of personality. Gordon (1953) suggested that some, but not all, differences in content between a subject's dreams and their Thematic Apperception Test (TAT) stories could be explained by assuming a greater concern with, consciously or unconsciously, defending and enhancing an idealized concept of the self in the TAT stories. This means that the subject attempts in the TAT stories to keep the central character of his/her projections from expressing any material that is clearly inconsistent with his/her concept of self or that violates cultural sanctions. It may be that dreams do not exhibit this censoring, and that the generally small correlations reviewed above are due to a deficiency in the waking assessment measure rather than with the dream measure. Similarly, Robbins and Tanck (1978) used the Dream Incident Technique (DIT) as a psychometric method that uses dream associations as its basic data, with the rationale that the scales of the DIT provide information about unresolved problems on a level below that of full conscious awareness.

Conclusion

There is much evidence that dreams incorporate the concerns of the individual, such as is seen in the work of Domhoff and Hall, and also in that, for example, waking concerns can be matched by independent judges with dream content (Nikles, Brecht, Klinger, & Bursell, 1998). However, this review has shown that there have been mixed results in the search for personality traits being incorporated into dreams. This could be because a trait may only be predictive of dream content if that trait is important to that person's overall personality (Cohen, 1979). For such individuals, there may then be correspondences at an idiographic level between the psychometric personality trait and dream content, but the inclusion in a nomothetic correlational study of individuals for whom the trait is not important may result in the diluting and diminishing of any trait-dream content relationship.

REFERENCES

Agargün, M. Y., & Cartwright, R. (2003). REM sleep, dream variables and suicidality in depressed patients. *Psychiatry Research, 119,* 33–39.

Agargün, M. Y., Kara, H., Ozer, O. A., Selvi, Y., Kiran, U., & Ozer, B. (2003a). Clinical importance of nightmare disorder in patients with dissociative disorders. *Psychiatry and Clinical Neurosciences, 57,* 575–579.

Armitage, R., Rochlen, A., Fitch, T., Trivedi, M., & Rush, A. J. (1995). Dream recall and major depression: A preliminary report. *Dreaming, 5,* 189–198.

Auld, F., Goldenberg, G. M., & Weiss, J. V. (1968). Measurement of primary-process thinking in dream reports. *Journal of Personality & Social Psychology, 8,* 418–426.

Baekeland, F. (1971). Effects of presleep procedures and cognitive style on dream content. *Perceptual & Motor Skills, 32,* 63–69.

Barrett, D., & Loeffler, M. (1992). Comparison of dream content of depressed vs. nondepressed dreamers. *Psychological Reports, 70,* 403–406.

Beaulieu-Prévost, D., & Zadra, A. (in press). Absorption, psychological boundaries and attitude towards dreams as correlates of dream recall: Two decades of research seen through a meta-analysis. *Journal of Sleep Research.*

Beaulieu-Prévost, D., & Zadra, A. (2005a). Dream recall frequency and attitude towards dreams: A reinterpretation of the relation. *Personality and Individual Differences, 38,* 919–927.

Beaulieu-Prévost, D., & Zadra, A. (2005b). How dream recall frequency shapes people's beliefs about the content of their dreams. *North American Journal of Psychology, 7,* 253–264.

Belcher, M. M., Montgomery, D. D., & Bone, R. N. (1972). Rigidity and dream recall. *Psychological Reports, 30,* 858.

Belicki, K., & Belicki, D. (1986). Predisposition for nightmares: A study of hypnotic ability, vividness of imagery, and absorption. *Journal of Clinical Psychology, 42,* 714–718.

Bernstein, D. M., & Belicki, K. (1995–1996). On the psychometric properties of retrospective dream content questionnaires. *Imagination, Cognition & Personality, 15,* 351–364.

Bernstein, D. M., & Roberts, B. (1995). Assessing dreams through self-report question-naires: Relations with past research and personality. *Dreaming, 5,* 13–27.

Berquier, A., & Ashton, R. (1992). Characteristics of the frequent nightmare sufferer. *Journal of Abnormal Psychology, 101,* 246–250.

Blackmore, S. J. (1997). Probability misjudgement and belief in the paranormal: A news-paper survey. *British Journal of Psychology, 88,* 683–689.

Blagrove, M. (2000). Dreams have meaning but no function. *Behavioral & Brain Sci-ences, 23,* 910–911.

Blagrove, M., & Akehurst, L. (2000). Personality and dream recall frequency: Further negative findings. *Dreaming, 10,* 139–148.

Blagrove, M., French, C. C., & Jones, G. (2006). Probabilistic reasoning: Affirmative bias and belief in precognitive dreams. *Applied Cognitive Psychology, 20,* 65–83.

Blagrove, M., & Hartnell, S. J. (2000). Lucid dreaming: Associations with internal locus of control, need for cognition and creativity. *Personality & Individual Differences, 28,* 41–47.

Blagrove, M., & Haywood, S. (2006). Evaluating the awakening criterion in the defini-tion of nightmares: How certain are people in judging whether a nightmare woke them up? *Journal of Sleep Research, 15,* 117–124.

Blagrove, M., & Tucker, M. (1994). Individual differences in locus of control and the reporting of lucid dreaming. *Personality and Individual Differences, 16,* 981–984.

Bone, R. N. (1968). Extroversion, neuroticism and dream recall. *Psychological Reports, 23,* 922.

Bone, R. N., & Corlett, F. (1968). Brief report: Frequency of dream recall, creativity, and a control for anxiety. *Psychological Reports, 22,* 1355–1356.

Bone, R. N, Nelson, A. E., & McAllister, D. S. (1970). Dream recall and repression-sensitization. *Psychological Reports, 27,* 766.

Bone, R. N, Thomas, T. A., & Kinsolving, D. L. (1972). Relationship of rod-and-frame scores to dream recall. *Psychological Reports, 30,* 58.

Brodsky, S. L., Esquerre, J., & Jackson, R. R. (1990–1991). Dream consciousness in problem solving. *Imagination, Cognition and Personality, 10,* 353–360.

Brown, R. J., & Donderi, D. C. (1986). Dream content and self-reported well-being among recurrent dreamers, past-recurrent dreamers, and nonrecurrent dreamers. *Jour-nal of Personality and Social Psychology, 50,* 612–623.

Bruni, O., Lo Reto, F., Recine, A., Ottaviano, S., & Guidetti, V. (1999). Development and validation of a dream content questionnaire for school age children. *Sleep and Hypnosis, 1,* 41–46.

Butler, S. F., & Watson, R. (1985). Individual differences in memory for dreams: The role of cognitive skills. *Perceptual & Motor Skills, 61,* 823–828.

Cann, D. R., & Donderi, D. C. (1986). Jungian personality typology and the recall of every-day and archetypal dreams. *Journal of Personality and Social Psychology, 50,* 1021–1030.

Cartwright, R. D. (1991). Dreams that work: The relation of dream incorporation to adaptation to stressful events. *Dreaming, 1,* 3–9.

Cartwright, R. D., & Wood, E. (1993). The contribution of dream masochism to the sex ratio difference in major depression. *Psychiatry Research, 46,* 165–173.

Cernovsky, Z. Z. (1984). Dream recall and attitude toward dreams. *Perceptual and Motor Skills, 58,* 911–914.

Chivers, L., & Blagrove, M. (1999). Nightmare frequency, personality and acute psychopathology. *Personality and Individual Differences, 27,* 843–851.

Claridge, G., Clark, K., & Davis, C. (1997). Nightmares, dreams, and schizotypy. *British Journal of Clinical Psychology, 36,* 377–386.

Claridge, G., Davis, C., Bellhouse, M., & Kaptein, S. (1998). Borderline personality, nightmares, and adverse life events in the risk for eating disorders. *Personality and Individual Differences, 25,* 339–351.

Cohen, D. B. (1971a). Dream recall and short-term memory. *Perceptual & Motor Skills, 33,* 867–871.

Cohen, D. B. (1971b). Current research on the frequency of dream recall: Erratum. *Psychological Bulletin, 76,* 382.

Cohen, D. B. (1974a). Toward a theory of dream recall. *Psychological Bulletin, 81,* 138–154.

Cohen, D. B. (1974b). Presleep mood and dream recall. *Journal of Abnormal Psychology, 83,* 45–51.

Cohen, D. B. (1974c). Effect of personality and presleep mood on dream recall. *Journal of Abnormal Psychology, 83,* 151–156.

Cohen, D. B. (1974d). A test of the salience hypothesis of dream recall. *Journal of Consulting & Clinical Psychology, 42,* 699–703.

Cohen, D. B. (1977). Neuroticism and dreaming sleep: A case for interactionism in personality research. *British Journal of Social and Clinical Psychology, 16,* 153–163.

Cohen, D. B. (1979). *Sleep and dreaming: Origins, nature and functions.* Oxford: Pergamon Press.

Cohen, D. B., & Cox, C. (1975). Neuroticism in the sleep laboratory: Implications for representational and adaptive properties of dreaming. *Journal of Abnormal Psychology, 84,* 91–108.

Cohen, D. B., & MacNeilage, P. F. (1974). A test of the salience hypothesis of dream recall. *Journal of Consulting and Clinical Psychology, 42,* 699–703.

Conduit, R. Crewther, S. G., & Coleman, G. (2004). Poor recall of eye-movement signals from Stage 2 compared to REM sleep: Implications for models of dreaming. *Consciousness and Cognition, 13,* 484–500.

Connor, G. N., & Boblitt, W. E. (1970). Reported frequency of dream recall as a function of intelligence and various personality test factors. *Journal of Clinical Psychology, 26,* 438–439.

Coolidge, F. L., & Bracken, D. D. (1984). The loss of teeth in dreams: An empirical investigation. *Psychological Reports, 54,* 931–935.

Cory, T. L., Ormiston, D. W., Simmel, E., & Dainoff, M. (1975). Predicting the frequency of dream recall. *Journal of Abnormal Psychology, 84,* 261–266.

Cowen, D., & Levin, R. (1995). The use of the Hartmann boundary questionnaire with an adolescent population. *Dreaming, 5,* 105–114.

De Koninck, J. M., & Koulack, D. (1975). Dream content and adaptation to a stressful situation. *Journal of Abnormal Psychology, 84,* 250–260.

Dement, W. C., & Kleitman, N. (1957). The relation of eye movements during sleep to dream activity: An objective method for the study of dreaming. *Journal of Experimental Psychology, 53,* 339–346.

Domhoff, B. (1968). An unsuccessful search for further correlates of everyday dream recall. *Psychophysiology, 4,* 386.

Domhoff, G. W. (1996). *Finding meaning in dreams: A quantitative approach.* New York: Plenum Press.

Domhoff, G. W. (2003). *The scientific study of dreams: Neural networks, cognitive development, and content analysis.* Washington, DC: APA Press.

Domino, G. (1976a). Primary process thinking in dream reports as related to creative achievement. *Journal of Consulting and Clinical Psychology, 44,* 929–932.

Domino, G. (1976b). Compensatory aspects of dreams: An empirical test of Jung's theory. *Journal of Personality and Social Psychology, 34,* 658–662.

Dow, B. M., Kelsoe, J. R., & Gillin, C. (1996). Sleep and dreams in Vietnam PTSD and depression. *Biological Psychiatry, 39,* 42–50.

Epstein, S., & O'Brian, E. J. (1985). The person-situation debate in historical and current perspective. *Psychological Bulletin, 98,* 513–537.

Evans, K. K., & Singer, J. A. (1994–1995). Studying intimacy through dream narratives: The relationship of dreams to self-report and projective measures of personality. *Imagination, Cognition and Personality, 14,* 211–226.

Farley, F. H., Schmuller, J., & Fischbach, T. J. (1971). Dream recall and individual differences. *Perceptual & Motor Skills, 33,* 379–384.

Firth, S. T., Blouin, J., Natarajan, C., & Blouin, A. (1986). A comparison of the manifest content in dreams of suicidal, depressed and violent patients. *Canadian Journal of Psychiatry, 31,* 48–53.

Fitch, T., & Armitage, R. (1989). Variations in cognitive style among high and low frequency dream recallers. *Personality & Individual Differences, 10,* 869–875.

Flanagan, O. (2000). *Dreaming souls: Sleep, dreams, and the evolution of the conscious mind.* New York: Oxford University Press.

Foulkes, D. (1999). *Children's dreaming and the development of consciousness.* Cambridge: Harvard University Press.

Foulkes, D., Larson, J. D., Swanson, E. M., & Rardin, M. (1969). Two studies of childhood dreaming. *American Journal of Orthopsychiatry, 39,* 627–643.

Foulkes, D. & Rechtschaffen, A. (1964). Presleep determinants of dream content: Effects of two films. *Perceptual and Motor Skills, 19,* 983–1005.

Foulkes, D., Spear, P. S., & Symonds, J. D. (1966). Individual differences in mental activity at sleep onset. *Journal of Abnormal Psychology, 71,* 280–286.

Freud, S. (1953). The interpretation of dreams. In J. Strachey (Ed. and Trans.), *The standard edition* (Vols. 4 and 5). London: Hogarth Press. (Original work published 1900)

Funkhouser, A. T., Wurmle, O., Comu, C. M., & Bahro, M. (2001). Boundary questionnaire results in the mentally healthy elderly. *Dreaming, 11,* 83–88.

Gackenbach, J., Heilman, N., Boyt, S., & LaBerge, S. (1985). The relationship between field independence and lucid dreaming ability. *Journal of Mental Imagery, 9,* 9–20.

Gerber, G. L. (1978). Coping effectiveness and dreams as a function of personality and dream recall. *Journal of Clinical Psychology, 34,* 526–532.

Giesbrecht, T., & Merckelbach, H. (2006). Dreaming to reduce fantasy? Fantasy proneness, dissociation, and subjective sleep experiences. *Personality and Individual Differences, 41,* 697–706.

Goodenough, D. R. (1991). Dream recall: History and current status of the field. In S. J. Ellman & J. S. Antrobus (Eds.), *The mind in sleep* (2nd ed., Chapter 4, pp. 143–171). New York: Wiley and Sons.

Goodenough, D. R., Witkin, H. A., Koulack, D., & Cohen, H. (1975). The effects of stress films on dream affect and on respiration and eye-movement activity during rapid-eye-movement sleep. *Psychophysiology, 12,* 313–320.

Goodenough, D. R., Witkin, H. A., Lewis, H. B., Koulack, D., & Cohen, H. (1974). Repression interference and field dependence as factors in dream forgetting. *Journal of Abnormal Psychology, 83,* 32–44.

Gordon, H. L. (1953). A comparative study of dreams and responses to the Thematic Apperception Test: A need-press analysis. *Journal of Personality, 22,* 234–253.

Gruber, R. E., Steffen, J. J., & Vonderhaar, S. P. (1995). Lucid dreaming, waking personality and cognitive development. *Dreaming, 5,* 1–12.

Guralnik, O., Levin, R., & Schmeidler, J. (1999). Dreams of personality disordered subjects. *Journal of Nervous & Mental Disease, 187,* 40–46.

Hajek, P., & Belcher, M. (1991). Dream of absent-minded transgression: An empirical study of a cognitive withdrawal symptom. *Journal of Abnormal Psychology, 100,* 487–491.

Hall, C. S. (1947). Diagnosing personality by the analysis of dreams. *Journal of Abnormal and Social Psychology, 42,* 68–79.

Hall, C. S. (1953). *The meaning of dreams.* Oxford, England: Harper.

Hall, C. S. (1991). The two provinces of dreams. *Dreaming, 1,* 91–93.

Hall, C. S., & Van de Castle, R. I. (1966). *The content analysis of dreams.* New York: Appleton-Century-Crofts.

Halliday, G. (1992). Effects of encouragement on dream recall. *Dreaming, 2,* 39–44.

Handal, P. J., & Rychlak, J. F. (1971). Curvilinearity between dream content and death anxiety and the relationship of death anxiety to repression-sensitization. *Journal of Abnormal Psychology, 77,* 11–16.

Hartmann, E. (1989). Boundaries of dreams, boundaries of dreamers: Thin and thick boundaries as a new personality measure. *Psychiatric Journal of the University of Ottawa, 14,* 557–560.

Hartmann, E. (1991). *Boundaries in the mind: A new psychology of personality.* New York: Basic Books.

Hartmann, E. (1998). *Dreams and nightmares: The new theory of the origin and meaning of dreams.* New York: Plenum.

Hartmann, E., & Basile, R. (2003). Dream imagery becomes more intense after 9/11/01. *Dreaming, 13,* 61–66.

Hartmann, E., Elkin, R., & Garg, M. (1991). Personality and dreaming: The dreams of people with very thick and very thin boundaries. *Dreaming, 1,* 311–324.

Hartmann, E., Rosen, R., & Rand, W. (1998). Personality and dreaming: Boundary structure and dream content. *Dreaming, 8,* 31–39.

Hartmann, E., Russ, D., Oldfield, M., Sivan, L., & Cooper, S. (1987). Who has nightmares? The personality of the lifelong nightmares sufferer. *Archives of General Psychiatry, 44,* 49–56.

Hartmann, E., Russ, D., van der Kolk, R., Falke, R., & Oldfield, M. (1981). A preliminary study of the personality of the nightmare sufferer: Relationship to schizophrenia and creativity? *American Journal of Psychiatry, 138,* 794–797.

Hartmann, E., Zborowski, M., Rosen, R., & Grace, N. (2001). Contextualizing images in dreams: More intense after abuse and trauma. *Dreaming, 11,* 115–126.

Hauri, P. (1976). Dreams in patients remitted from reactive depression. *Journal of Abnormal Psychology, 85,* 1–10.

Hicks, R. A., Bautista, J., & Hicks, G. J. (1999). Handedness and the vividness of dreams. *Dreaming, 9,* 265–269.

Hicks, R. A., Fortin, E., & Brassington, G. S. (2002). Arousability and dreaming. *Dreaming, 12,* 135–139.

Hill, A. B. (1974). Personality correlates of dream recall. *Journal of Consulting & Clinical Psychology, 42,* 766–773.

Hiscock, M., & Cohen, D. B (1973). Visual imagery and dream recall. *Journal of Research in Personality, 7,* 179–188.

Howarth, E. (1962). Extroversion and dream symbolism: An empirical study. *Psychological Reports, 10,* 211–214.

Hunt, H., Ruzycki-Hunt, K., Pariak, D., & Belicki, K. (1993). The relationship between dream bizarreness and imagination: Artifact or essence? *Dreaming, 3,* 179–199.

Jacka, B. (1991). Personality variables and attitudes toward dream experiences. *Journal of Psychology: Interdisciplinary & Applied, 125,* 27–31.

Kales, A., Soldates, C., Caldwell, A., Charney, D., Kales, J., Markel, D., et al. (1980). Nightmares: Clinical characteristics and personality patterns. *American Journal of Psychiatry, 137,* 1197–1201.

Köthe, M., & Pietrowsky, R. (2001). Behavioral effects of nightmares and their correlations to personality patterns. *Dreaming, 11,* 43–52.

Kunzendorf, R. G., Hartmann, E., Cohen, R., & Cutler, J. (1997). Bizarreness of the dreams and day-dreams reported by individuals with thin and thick boundaries. *Dreaming, 7,* 265–271.

Lang, R. J., & O'Connor, K. P. (1984). Personality, dream content and dream coping style. *Personality and Individual Differences, 5,* 211–219.

Levin, R. (1998). Nightmares and schizotypy. *Psychiatry, 61,* 206–216.

Levin, R., & Fireman, G. (2001–2002). The relation of fantasy proneness, psychological absorption, and imaginative involvement to nightmare prevalence and nightmare distress. *Imagination, Cognition and Personality, 21,* 111–129.

Levin, R., & Fireman, G. (2002). Nightmare prevalence, nightmare distress, and self-reported psychological disturbance. *Sleep, 25,* 205–212.

Levin, R., Fireman, G., & Rackley, C. (2003). Personality and dream recall frequency: Still further negative findings. *Dreaming, 13,* 155–162.

Levin, R., Galin, J., & Zywiak, B. (1991). Nightmares, boundaries, and creativity. *Dreaming, 1,* 63–73.

Levin, R., Gilmartin, L., & Lamontanaro, L. (1998–1999). Cognitive style and perception: The relationship of boundary thinness to visual-spatial processing in dreaming and waking thought. *Imagination, Cognition & Personality, 18,* 25–41.

Levin, R., & Raulin, M. L. (1991). Preliminary evidence for the proposed relationship between frequent nightmares and schizotypal symptomatology. *Journal of Personality Disorders, 5,* 8–14.

Levin, R., & Young, H. (2001–2002). The relation of waking fantasy to dreaming. *Imagination, Cognition and Personality, 21,* 201–219.

Lortie-Lussier, M., Schwab, C., & De Koninck, J. (1985). Working mothers versus homemakers: Do dreams reflect the changing roles of women? *Sex Roles, 12,* 1009–1021.

MacFarlane, J. G., & Wilson, T. L. (2006). A relationship between nightmare content and somatic stimuli in a sleep-disordered population: A preliminary study. *Dreaming, 16,* 53–59.

McNamara, P., Andresen, J., Clark, J., Zborowski, M., & Duffy, C. A. (2001). Impact of attachment styles on dream recall and dream content: A test of the attachment hypothesis of REM sleep. *Journal of Sleep Research, 10,* 117–127.

McNamara, P., Clark, J., & Hartmann, E. (1998). Handedness and dream content. *Dreaming, 8,* 15–22.

Merckelbach, H., Horselenberg, R., & Muris, P. (2001). The Creative Experiences Questionnaire (CEQ): A brief self-report measure of fantasy proneness. *Personality and Individual Differences, 31,* 987–995.

Miró, E., & Martínez, M. P. (2005). Affective and personality characteristics in function of nightmare prevalence, nightmare distress, and interference due to nightmares. *Dreaming, 15,* 89–105.

Mischel, W. (1983). Alternatives in the pursuit of the predictability and consistency of persons: Stable data that yields unstable interpretations. *Journal of Personality, 51,* 578–604.

Montgomery, D. D., & Bone, R. N. (1970). Dream recall and cognitive style. *Perceptual and Motor Skills, 31,* 386.

Nadon, R., Laurence, J. R., & Perry, C. (1987). Multiple predictors of hypnotic susceptibility. *Journal of Personality and Social Psychology, 53,* 948–960.

Nettle, D. (2006). The evolution of personality variation in humans and other animals. *American Psychologist, 61,* 622–631.

Nielsen, T. A., Kuiken, D., Alain, G., Stenstrom, P., & Powell, R. A. (2004). Immediate and delayed incorporations of events into dreams: Further replication and implications for dream function. *Journal of Sleep Research, 13,* 327–336.

Nielsen, T. A., Laberge, L., Paquet, J., Tremblay, R. E., Vitaro, F., & Montplaisir, J. (2000). Development of disturbing dreams during adolescence and their relation to anxiety symptoms. *Sleep, 23,* 727–736.

Nielsen, T. A., Ouellet, L., Warnes, H., Cartier, A., Malo J. L., & Montplaisir, J. (1997). Alexithymia and impoverished dream recall in asthmatic patients: Evidence from self-report measures. *Journal of Psychosomatic Research, 42,* 53–59.

Nikles, C. D., II, Brecht, D. L., Klinger, E., & Bursell, A. L. (1998). The effects of current-concern- and nonconcern-related waking suggestions on nocturnal dream content. *Journal of Personality and Social Psychology, 75,* 242–255.

Pagel, J. F. (2003). Non-dreamers. *Sleep Medicine, 4,* 235–241.

Patrick, A., & Durndell, A. (2004). Lucid dreaming and personality: A replication. *Dreaming, 14,* 234–239.

Redfering, D. L., & Keller, J. (1974). Comparison between dream reporters and low reporters as measured by MMPI. *Social Behavior and Personality, 2,* 201–203.

Riemann, D., Berger, M., & Voderholzer, U. (2001). Sleep and depression: Results from psychobiological studies: An overview. *Biological Psychology, 57,* 67–103.

Rim, Y. (1986). Dream content and daytime coping styles. *Personality and Individual Differences, 7,* 259–261.

Rim, Y. (1988). Comparing coping styles: Awake and asleep. *Personality and Individual Differences, 9,* 165–170.

Robbins, P. R., & Tanck, R. H. (1970). The Repression-Sensitization Scale, dreams, and dream associations. *Journal of Clinical Psychology, 26,* 219–221.

Robbins, P. R., & Tanck, R. H. (1971). MMPI scales and dream recall: A failure to confirm. *Perceptual & Motor Skills, 33,* 473–474.

Robbins, P. R., & Tanck, R. H. (1978). The Dream Incident Technique as a measure of unresolved problems. *Journal of Personality Assessment, 42,* 583–591.

Robbins, P. R., & Tanck, R. H. (1988–1989). Depressed mood, dream recall and contentless dreams. *Imagination, Cognition and Personality, 8,* 165–174.

Robbins, P. R., Tanck, R. H., & Houshi, F. (1985). Anxiety and dream symbolism. *Journal of Personality, 53,* 17–22.

Roberts, J., & Lennings, C. J. (2006). Personality, psychopathology and nightmares in young people. *Personality and Individual Differences, 41,* 733–744.

Rochlen, A., Hoffmann, R., & Armitage, R. (1998). EEG correlates of dream recall in depressed outpatients and healthy controls. *Dreaming, 8,* 109–123.

Samson, H., & de Koninck, J. (1986). Continuity or compensation between waking and dreaming: An exploration using the Eysenck Personality Inventory. *Psychological Reports, 58,* 871–874.

Schechter, N., Schmeidler, G. R., & Staal, M. (1965). Dream reports and creative tendencies in students of the arts, sciences and engineering. *Journal of Consulting Psychology, 29,* 415–421.

Schonbar, R. A. (1965). Differential dream recall frequency as a component of "life style." *Journal of Consulting Psychology, 29,* 468–474.

Schredl, M. (2002a). Dream recall frequency and openness to experience: A negative finding. *Personality & Individual Differences, 33,* 1285–1289.

Schredl, M. (2002b). Questionnaires and diaries as research instruments in dream research: Methodological issues. *Dreaming, 12,* 17–26.

Schredl, M. (2003). Effects of state and trait factors on nightmare frequency. *European Archives of Psychiatry & Clinical Neuroscience, 253,* 241–247.

Schredl, M. (2004). Reliability and stability of a Dream Recall Frequency Scale. *Perceptual and Motor Skills, 98,* 1422–1426.

Schredl, M., Brenner, C., & Faul, C. (2002). Positive attitude toward dreams: Reliability and stability of a ten-item scale. *North American Journal of Psychology, 4,* 343–346.

Schredl, M., Ciric, P., Götz, S., & Wittmann, L. (2003). Dream recall frequency, attitude towards dreams and openness to experience. *Dreaming, 13,* 145–153.

Schredl, M., & Engelhardt, H. (2001). Dreaming and psychopathology: Dream recall and dream content of psychiatric inpatients. *Sleep and Hypnosis, 3,* 44–54.

Schredl, M., & Erlacher, D. (2004). Lucid dreaming frequency and personality. *Personality and Individual Differences, 37,* 1463–1473.

Schredl, M., & Jacob, S. (1998). Ratio of male and female characters in dream series. *Perceptual & Motor Skills, 86,* 198–200.

Schredl, M., Jochum, S., & Souguenet, S. (1997). Dream recall, visual memory, and absorption in imaginings. *Personality and Individual Differences, 22,* 291–292.

Schredl, M., Kleinferchner, P., & Gell, T. (1996). Dreaming and personality: Thick vs. thin boundaries. *Dreaming, 6,* 219–223.

Schredl, M., & Montasser, A. (1996–1997a). Dream recall: State or trait variable? Part I: Model, theories, methodology and trait factors. *Imagination, Cognition and Personality, 16,* 181–210.

Schredl, M., & Montasser, A. (1996–1997b). Dream recall: State or trait variable? Part II. State factors, investigations, and final conclusions. *Imagination, Cognition and Personality, 16,* 231–261.

Schredl, M., Nürnberg, C., & Weiler, S. (1996). Dream recall, attitude toward dreams, and personality. *Personality and Individual Differences, 20,* 613–618.

Schredl, M., Schäfer, G., Hofmann, F., & Jacob, S. (1999). Dream content and personality: Thick vs. thin boundaries. *Dreaming, 9,* 257–263.

Schredl, M., Wittmann, L., Ciric, P., & Götz, S. (2003). Factors of home dream recall: A structural equation model. *Journal of Sleep Research, 12,* 133–141.

Solms, M. (1997). *The neuropsychology of dreams.* Mahwah, NJ: Lawrence Erlbaum Associates.

Spadafora, A., & Hunt, H. T. (1990). The multiplicity of dreams: Cognitive affective correlates of lucid, archetypal and nightmare dreaming. *Perceptual & Motor Skills, 71,* 627–644.

Spanos, N. P., Stam, H. J., Radtke, H. L., & Nightingale, M. E. (1980). Absorption in imaginings, sex-role orientation, and the recall of dreams by males and females. *Journal of Personality Assessment, 44,* 277–282.

Stepansky, R., Holzinger, B., Schmeiser-Rieder, A., Saletu, B., Kunze, M., & Zeitlhofer, J. (1998). Austrian dream behavior: Results of a representative population survey. *Dreaming, 8,* 23–30.

Stickgold, R., Hobson, J. A., Fosse, R., & Fosse, M. (2001). Sleep, learning, and dreams: Off-line memory reprocessing. *Science, 294,* 1052–1057.

Stickgold, R., Malia, A., Fosse, R., Propper, R., & Hobson, J. A. (2001). Brain-mind states: I. Longitudinal field study of sleep/wake factors influencing mentation report length. *Sleep, 24,* 171–179.

Sylvia, W., Clark, P. M., & Monroe, L. J. (1978). Dream reports of subjects high and low in creative ability. *Journal of General Psychology, 99,* 205–211.

Takeuchi, T., Ferrelli, A. V., Murphy, T., Wrong, A., Veenhof, W., Lazic, S., et al. (1999). Should we dismiss the hypothesis "REM sleep is necessary to produce dreams"? Prediction of dream recall by EEG activity in sleep onset REM periods elicited in normal sleepers. *Sleep, 22,* S130–S131.

Takeuchi, T., Ogilvie, R. D., Ferrelli, A. V., Murphy, T. I., & Belicki, K. (2001). The Dream Property Scale: An exploratory English version. *Consciousness & Cognition, 10,* 341–355.

Tantam, D., Kalucy, R., & Brown, D. G. (1982). Sleep, scratching and dreams in eczema: A new approach to alexithymia. *Psychotherapy & Psychosomatics, 37,* 26–35.

Tart, C. T. (1962). Frequency of dream recall and some personality measures. *Journal of Consulting Psychology, 26,* 467–470.

Tellegen, A., & Atkinson, G. (1974). Openness to absorbing and self-altering experiences ("absorption"), a trait related to hypnotic susceptibility. *Journal of Abnormal Psychology, 83,* 268–277.

Tonay, V. K. (1993). Personality correlates of dream recall: Who remembers? *Dreaming, 3,* 1–8.

Volpe, N., & Levin, R. (1998). Attributional style, dreaming and depression. *Personality and Individual Differences, 25,* 1051–1061.

Wallach, M. S. (1963). Dream report and some psychological concomitants. *Journal of Consulting Psychology, 27,* 549.

Ward, C. D., Ward, K. M., Randers-Pehrson, S. B., & Runion, L. (1973). Birth order and dreams. *Journal of Social Psychology, 90,* 155–156.

Waterman, D. (1991). Aging and memory for dreams. *Perceptual and Motor Skills, 73,* 355–365.

Watson, D. (2001). Dissociations of the night: Individual differences in sleep-related experiences and their relation to dissociation and schizotypy. *Journal of Abnormal Psychology, 110,* 526–535.

Watson, D. (2003). To dream, perchance to remember: Individual differences in dream recall. *Personality & Individual Differences, 34,* 1271–1286.

Webb, W. B., & Kersey, J. (1967). Recall of dreams and the probability of stage 1-REM sleep. *Perceptual and Motor Skills, 24,* 627–630.

Wegner, D. M., Wenzlaff, R. M., & Kozak, M. (2004). Dream rebound: The return of suppressed thoughts in dreams. *Psychological Science, 15,* 232–236.

Williamson, R. W., Heckel, R. V., & Boblitt, W. E. (1970). Reported frequency of dream recall as related to repression-sensitization and intelligence. *Journal of Clinical Psychology, 26,* 300–301.

Wolcott, S., & Strapp, C. M. (2002). Dream recall frequency and dream detail as mediated by personality, behavior, and attitude. *Dreaming, 12,* 27–44.

Wood, J. M., Sebba, D., & Domino, G. (1989–1990). Do creative people have more bizarre dreams? A reconsideration. *Imagination, Cognition and Personality, 9,* 3–16.

Woods, D. J., Cole, S., & Ferrandez, G. (1977). Dream reports and the test of emotional styles: A convergent-discriminant validity study. *Journal of Clinical Psychology, 33,* 1021–1022.

Worthen, J. B., Eisenstein, S. A., Budwey, S. C., & Varnado-Sullivan, P. (2004–2005). Tests of structural hypotheses in free recall of bizarre and common dream reports: Implications for sleep research. *Imagination, Cognition and Personality, 24,* 315–330.

Zadra, A. L., O'Brien, S. A., & Donderi, D. C. (1997–1998). Dream content, dream recurrence and well-being: A replication with a younger sample. *Imagination, Cognition and Personality, 17,* 293–311.

Six

Dreams and Psychotherapy

Clara E. Hill and Patricia Spangler

We begin this chapter with a brief history of dreams in psychotherapy. We then review the empirical evidence about the occurrence of dream work[1] in ongoing therapy, the outcome of dream work, predictors of who benefits from dream work, and the process of dream work, and predictors of who benefits from dream work. Finally, we discuss new areas of interest related to dream work in psychotherapy.

HISTORY OF DREAMS AND PSYCHOTHERAPY

For millennia, humans have recognized and cultivated the healing potential of dreams (Van de Castle, 1994). Ancient civilizations—Mesopotamian, Hebrew, Egyptian, Chinese, Greek—developed complex rituals around dreams toward the end of improving physical and spiritual well-being. The ancient Greeks, for example, had temples designed for incubating and interpreting dreams. They went through elaborate rituals to prepare themselves and then spent the night in the temples awaiting healing dreams, which were expected to offer direction for further treatment or new glimpses of reality. Dreams were shared the next morning with specially designated priests or other dreamers staying at the temple.

Dream Theories for Individual Therapy

The early psychoanalysts, too, recognized the power and utility of dreams. They strongly advocated working with dreams in therapy as a way of uncovering conscious and unconscious conflicts. Perhaps the best-known book about dreams is Sigmund Freud's *The Interpretation of Dreams* (1900/1953), in which he suggested that dreams occur primarily for the fulfillment of primitive, infantile wishes. These wishes, he posited, are not acceptable to our conscious minds and are thus repressed during waking life. Freud believed that we are unable to censor thoughts as much during sleep as when awake. Because of the absence of a conscious censor these wishes come out in our dreams, usually in distorted form. Dreams, then, according to Freud, are an ideal therapeutic device, indeed the "royal road," for examining unconscious processes. Freud's most powerful tool for working with dreams was free association, in which the dreamer is asked to say whatever comes to mind, with as much honesty as possible. Through associations, the dreamer is thought to come to the origins of the conflicts embedded in the dream. Freud would listen to the dream and the related associations and then suggest an interpretation of the dream using his knowledge of the dreamer and of the symbolic meanings of dreams.

In contrast to Freud, Carl Jung (1964, 1974) viewed dreams as more of a normal, creative expression of the unconscious mind. His view was that dreams serve a compensatory function, such that they express issues not expressed during waking life. Thus, he believed that dreams are a key to uniting the conscious and unconscious by helping dreamers become aware of hidden feelings. Dream interpretation is one of the main treatment methods in Jungian therapy, although Jung did not codify procedures for dream work. Rather, Jung suggested working with dreams in whatever way seemed most useful for the dreamer. He often used associations, enacting dreams through artistic expressions, and interpreting dreams in terms of archetypes and myths.

Another influential early theorist was Alfred Adler (1936, 1938, 1958). Adler conceptualized personality as a unitary construct and thus believed that the conscious and unconscious minds are the same and that the individual's waking personality is the same in dreams. Adler believed that dreams are an expression of the conscious mind and function to preserve the unity of one's personality. Adler viewed dreams as a means for the person to get reassurance, security, and protection against damage to self-worth. Of central importance to Adler was the emotion roused by the dream, which he believed enables the individual to find resolutions that are in keeping with the dreamer's style of life. He also thought that dreams are a way of rehearsing for future activities and thus have a problem-solving function. Unfortunately, Adler provided no clear guidelines for working with dreams in therapy.

Spanning the time gap between the early analytic theorists and current thinkers, a number of theorists might be grouped together under the rubric of existential, phenomenological, humanistic, and experiential theories.

These theorists generally suggest that reimmersion into the experience of the dream is crucial. Phenomenologists believe that dreams reflect conscious experiences and can be examined just as one would examine any other experience in waking life (Boss, 1958, 1963; Craig & Walsh, 1993). Relatedly, Gestalt therapists such as Fritz Perls (1969) and Erving and Miriam Polster (1973) focused on the here and now and encouraged dreamers to consider each part or image of the dream as part of themselves; their view is that these parts need to be integrated for the person to become whole. In addition, Eugene Gendlin (1986) and Alvin Mahrer (1990) articulated experiential approaches for helping dreamers re-experience the feelings in their dreams.

Also arising during the mid half of the twentieth century was Aaron Beck's theory of cognitive patterns in dreams (1971). Beck posited that dreams are consistent with an individual's waking thoughts and that cognitive patterns do influence dreams. While acknowledging that dreams have many functions and the dreamer does not necessarily gain knowledge from every dream, Beck held that certain types of dreams can help clarify an individual's problem. Dreams that Beck called "pathognomonic" (p. 31) were notable for the way they dramatized an individual's view of self and the world. He believed that without external stimuli the dreamer reaches a state of arousal in which his or her automatic thought patterns exert the maximum possible influence on the individual's thinking and are reflected in the thematic content of the dream. Beck further suggested that the patterns present in dreams affect waking behavior and emotion, of which the individual may or may not be aware. For Beck, one function of dreams is to bring automatic, unrealistic thought patterns to the dreamer's awareness. In this way, dreams can be used in therapy to enable the client[2] to gain awareness of distorted thinking, which can then be addressed in a fully conscious way using cognitive behavioral techniques.

Since 1980 there has been a wave of new interest in dreams, and a number of new models have been proposed. Among these are several that derive from the psychoanalytic tradition (Fosshage, 1983, 1987; Garma, 1987; Glucksman, 1988; Glucksman & Warner, 1987; Lippman, 2000; Natterson, 1980, 1993; Schwartz, 1990). The major break from the earlier Freudian tradition is that these theorists now propose, more in line with recent research, that the manifest content of dreams reflects waking life rather than distortions from the unconscious. Contemporary Jungian authors (Beebe, 1993; Bonime, 1987; Bosnak, 1988; Johnson, 1986) have stayed relatively close to the original Jungian theory but have provided more explicit guidelines for how to work with dreams in therapy. Contemporary Adlerians (Bird, 2005; Lombardi & Elcock, 1997) have also provided more explicit guidelines for implementing Adler's theory, including a rejection of fixed symbolism in favor of an understanding of dream metaphors as a means of constructing one's own private logic, a focus on providing encouragement and positive interpretations, and the idea that the interpreter should serve as a collaborator rather than an expert. In this model, the therapist's role is to facilitate the dreamer's understanding of a dream and use this new knowledge to gain insight about the events in his or her life, always being aware of and respecting the client's individuality.

Several models for using dreams in cognitive therapy have recently emerged. Arthur Freeman and Beverly White (2004) outlined a method for using dreams as homework in cognitive-behavioral therapy (CBT). In this cognitive model, the dream is an idiosyncratic dramatization of the dreamer's view of self and the world. Fifteen assumptions are given regarding CBT dream work, including that emotional responses to dreams are similar to the dreamer's responses to waking situations, dream content and images are amenable to the same cognitive restructuring as are automatic thoughts, the dream is the product and the responsibility of the dreamer, and specific language and images are important.

Also from the cognitive school of thought is Barry Krakow's (2004) use of imagery rehearsal therapy for posttraumatic nightmares. Clients select a nightmare and decide how they would change it. These changes are then rehearsed during the session by activating the client's imagery system. Krakow posits that this technique jumpstarts the client's dormant healing system so that it has an affect on other nightmares as well as the targeted dream.

A number of integrative approaches have also appeared recently. Gayle Delaney (1991, 1993), Ann Faraday (1972, 1974), and Lillie Weiss (1986, 1999) have developed models that incorporate elements of Gestalt and Jungian theories, relate dreams closely to waking life problems, are clear and easy to understand, and have been widely disseminated to the lay public.

Finally, Clara Hill (1996, 2004) developed a cognitive-experiential dream model that integrates many of the components of previous models. Assumptions underlying the model are that dreams are a continuation of waking thought without input from the external world; the meaning of dreams is personal (so one cannot use standard symbols or dream dictionaries); working with dreams requires a collaborative process between the therapist and client; dreams are a useful tool for helping people understand more about themselves; dreams involve cognitive, emotional, and behavioral components; and therapists need to have expertise in using the basic helping skills before they can be effective in applying the dream model. The Hill dream model integrates experiential, psychoanalytic, Gestalt, and behavioral approaches to dream work through the use of a three-stage model (exploration, insight, action). In the exploration stage, the therapist helps the client sequentially explore a few dream images in great depth by going through four steps for each image (description, re-experiencing, association, and waking life triggers). Once they have thoroughly explored the dream, the therapist works with the client to co-construct the meaning of the dream, focusing on the experience itself, waking life, or inner dynamics (parts of self, conflicts from childhood, spiritual-existential). Once some idea of the meaning of the dream has been co-constructed, therapists work with clients to help them decide what they might like to do differently in their lives based on their new understanding.

Dream Groups

In recent years, there has also emerged within the popular culture a movement of groups that meet for the purpose of sharing and interpreting dreams (Hillman, 1990). Many groups base their proceedings on the works of Montague Ullman or Jeremy Taylor. Ullman's approach (1987) emphasizes safety and discovery in group dream work. The dreamer must feel safe enough with the group to disclose very intimate material. To engender this sense of safety, it is understood that the dreamer has complete control of the dream work process at every stage. Discovery is facilitated by the group's involvement in adopting the dream as their own. Ullman's group method involves four stages: (a) the dreamer offers a dream and the group ask questions to gain a clear impression of the dream, (b) group members project their own material onto the dream and offer their own associations to particular images, (c) the dreamer is then invited to respond to the group's input, and (d) homework is assigned.

Similarly, Jeremy Taylor (1992, 1998) emphasized that anonymity must be maintained whenever the dreams are discussed outside the group. Furthermore, Taylor suggested that all dreams speak a universal language, the individual dreamer alone has definitive say of the meaning of his or her dream, dreams have more than one meaning, all dreams break new ground, and that group members should always use the phrase, "If it were my dream . . ." when referring to another person's dream.

Donald Wolk (1996) outlined an integrative technique using Ullman's method as a warm-up to using psychodrama. The warm-up facilitates the identification of issues and spontaneous discovery of ways to perceive and work on these issues. During the psychodrama, the dreamer takes on the role of protagonist and reenacts the dream. Although the dreamer has the role of protagonist and primary guide, the director helps in the choice of dream characters and objects from among group members. The director also provides direction during the enactment, empathy for the protagonist, and occasional reflections of feeling. Through psychodramatic reenactment, the dreamer becomes more emotionally and cognitively aware of how underlying motivations affect day-to-day functioning and interpersonal relations.

Another option for group dream work is an adaptation of Hill's cognitive-experiential model (Wonnell, 2004). The three-stage structure is maintained, but group members offer input in all the stages, using the Ullman phrase "If it were my dream," to remind all participants of the dreamer's ultimate control over his or her own dream. The Hill model has some features of the Ullman and Taylor methods, but the more detailed framework, particularly in the exploration stage, provides more direction, which may be beneficial for newly formed groups or new members of established groups.

Summary

In sum, dream theories have been proposed for virtually every theoretical perspective and for individual as well as group therapy. The plethora of theories suggests that there is not one "right" way to work with dreams. Clearly, though, theoreticians and therapists have recognized the value in working with dreams as a therapeutic endeavor.

THE OCCURRENCE OF DREAM WORK IN ONGOING THERAPY

Although many models have been proposed for working with dreams, a crucial question is how much dream work is practiced in ongoing therapy. Survey results indicate that almost all therapists pay at least some attention to dreams in therapy (Crook & Hill, 2003; Fox, 2002; Keller et al., 1995; Schredl, Bohusch, Kahl, Mader, & Somesan, 2000), although it appears that dreams are rarely a major focus. In one survey (Crook & Hill, 2003), therapists reported that only about 15 percent of clients had brought dreams into therapy in the past year, and they spent only about 5 percent of the time in therapy working with dreams.

Both client and therapist variables appear to influence whether dreams are discussed in therapy. Therapists reported they were most likely to focus on dreams when clients presented troubling or recurrent dreams or nightmares, were psychologically minded, were interested in learning about their dreams, had post-traumatic stress syndrome, or were seeking growth; those therapists who valued dreams and who had training in dream work were most likely to do dream work in sessions (Crook & Hill, 2003). Relatedly, clients who reported that they had discussed dreams in therapy had higher dream recall, more positive attitudes toward dreams, and more encouragement from therapists to talk about their dream than clients who did not discuss dreams in therapy (Crook-Lyon & Hill, 2004). Clients who did not bring dreams into sessions indicated that they needed to focus on other more pressing issues than dreams or it had never occurred to them to bring dreams into therapy (Crook-Lyon & Hill, 2004).

In terms of how they actually work with dreams, therapists reported that they most often listened to dreams, explored connections between dream images and waking life, asked for description of images, and collaborated with clients to construct interpretations of dreams (Crook & Hill, 2003). Similarly, clients who brought dreams into sessions indicated that therapists mostly helped them interpret their dreams, relate their dreams to waking life, and associate to dream images (Crook-Lyon & Hill, 2004). Furthermore, there is some preliminary evidence suggesting that it is valuable for therapists to explicitly encourage clients to bring dreams into therapy (Crook-Lyon & Hill, 2004; Halliday, 1992).

Hence, it appears that the average therapist pays some attention to dreams but perhaps does not use them to the fullest depth possible. As anecdotal evidence for this, in a workshop that Clara E. Hill recently did with practicing therapists, all mentioned that they let clients talk about their dreams briefly in therapy but felt uncomfortable knowing how to work with dreams and so did not do much with them. Interestingly, they felt they had to know the "right" way to work with dreams or else felt that they could not approach them. The data presented in this section suggests that therapists might want to mention to clients during early sessions that they enjoy working with dreams and find them beneficial to the therapy process. Then they could allow clients to explore the images and try to gain some meaning about their dreams, working with them in whatever theoretical manner seems to fit best for them. For further ideas about how therapists can incorporate dream work into ongoing therapy, see Cogar (2004).

DOES DREAM WORK HELP? OUTCOMES OF DREAM WORK

The outcomes of dream work in therapy have been examined in case studies as well as in large-sample studies. Case studies provide some preliminary, anecdotal, and often very detailed information about the outcomes of dream work, but of course we have more confidence in the findings from the large-sample studies.

Case Study Research

Case studies have provided evidence of the clinical utility of dreams since the era of Freud. Although they typically include no experimental controls and are thus subject to therapist bias, the sheer number of published case examples attests to therapists' reliance on dream work as an effective therapeutic tool.

Although dream work has been reported as an effective technique across theoretical approaches and treatment modes, it is not surprising that a large percentage of case studies are of individual psychodynamic therapy. In one such study (Merrill & Cary, 1975), two clinical vignettes illustrated the efficacy of dream work in brief analytic therapy with college students. The authors argued that dreams are an effective tool for closing the psychological distance between client and therapist. In another study (Levay & Weissburg, 1979), the authors used four cases to show that integrating dream work into sex therapy can result in briefer, more successful treatment than therapy without dream work. Other psychodynamically oriented case studies have pointed to the use of dream work for childhood trauma (Dowling, 1982); couples' relational and sexual issues (De Domenico, 2002; Nicolo, Norsa, & Carratelli, 2003; Sander, 2004; Scharff & Scharff, 2004); depression (Solis, 1987); dissociation/sleeping during sessions (Geffner, 2004); masochism as a manifestation of excessive relationship (Olivetti, 2005); conflict and defensiveness in an obsessional child (Karush, 1998); family issues (Cirincione, Hart, & Karle, 1980; Buchholz, 1990; Bynum, 1980, 1993); readiness for termination (Grenell, 2002); severe trauma (Stubley, 2003); sex differentiation (Sirois, 2005); and therapist and client illness and death (Calogeras & Alston, 2000; Edwards, 2004). In addition, several case studies (Gabel, 1993; Glucksman, 1988; Merrill & Cary, 1975) have found increases in insight following dream work in psychodynamic therapy.

Case studies have also indicated that psychodynamic dream work can be a multiculturally effective technique. Eisold (2005) focused on the lifelong resilience and adaptability of a young African American woman in psychoanalytic psychotherapy. The client quickly learned to associate to dreams and use them therapeutically. The therapist ascribed this facility with dream work to the client's high intelligence and talent for metaphor combined with an intense desire to be rid of her depression, self-doubt, nightmares, and various somatic symptoms. Another case study (Levounis, 2003) examined the effects of sexual orientation of client and therapist on the course of therapy, particularly the erotic components of the client's transference as manifested in the client's dreams. Another therapist provided several clinical vignettes as evidence of the successful use of dream interpretation with homeless clients (Merlino, 2002). The author argued that with the brief time usually available for working with homeless clients, dreams provide an avenue for quickly getting to the heart of clients' most pressing issues.

Case examples have also provided evidence that group therapy is a fitting treatment mode for dream work. Arons (1978) showed that first-reported dreams in group therapy reflect the client's basic conflict as well as group tensions around issues of trust, support, advice-giving, universality, sexual attraction, rivalry, anger, and transference. Friedman (2000) described an interpersonal approach to group dream work, arguing that the group served as a container to help the dreamers bear the difficult emotions in the dream and to continue exploring them. Reciprocally, the group's response to the dream telling may cause the dreamer to take a particular role in the group or it may influence the individual's dream content. Similarly, Stone and Karterud (2006) presented examples of group dream work from a self-psychology perspective, suggesting that the therapist should focus the group on increasing its capacity for awareness and reflection of emerging abilities as they appear in the dream.

In a case study of the Hill cognitive-experiential dream model, Heaton, Hill, Petersen, Rochlen, and Zack (1998) traced the changes in therapy based on dream work with recurrent and nonrecurrent dreams of a dissociative client. They concluded that working with recurrent dreams helped the client become aware of problematic themes in her waking life and helped her make changes.

A cognitive approach to working with dreams was the subject of a recent case study (Willner, 2004), in which a learning-disabled client with two recurrent posttraumatic nightmares and fearful ruminations during waking hours was taught to conceptualize his dreams and stories and to "rewrite" new, happier endings. Willner suggested that the positive outcome was due to therapist intervention on the second nightmare soon after successfully intervening on the first. In addition, the relationships with therapist and support staff were trusting and supportive, the elements of the newly created endings were true and acceptable, and the "facts" of the new story were easy to assimilate. In another case study of a multimodal behavioral approach (Tanner, 2004), a 23-year-old woman's nightmares were decreased through a combination of relaxation procedures, a mnemonic to increase lucid dreaming, and dream rehearsal upon waking from a nightmare.

In another case (Knudson, 2006), the client's phenomenological understanding of her dream was ignored by her therapist. This case highlighted the dangers of strict adherence to interpreting dreams metaphorically and ignoring the dreamer's experience of the dream. The severely anorectic client had presented the dream to her therapist, who quickly interpreted the dream as a representation of the client's unstable condition and need for hospitalization. The client angrily terminated but was determined to improve without therapy, using her own experience of her dream as an indication that she was capable of getting better.

Finally, Eudell-Simmons and Hilsenroth (2005) reviewed evidence from a number of case studies that dreams themselves change as a function of successful psychotherapy (Caroppo, Dimaggio, Popolo, Salvatore, & Ruggeri, 1997; Cartwright & Wood, 1993; Dimaggio, Popolo, Serio, & Ruggeri, 1997; Glucksman, 1988; Heaton, Hill, Hess, Hoffmann, & Leotta, 1998; Melstrom & Cartwright, 1983; Warner, 1983). For example, in a series of dreams of one client in therapy, Caroppo and colleagues (1997) showed that the last eighteen dreams worked on in therapy reflected more adaptive and integrated methods of dealing with problems and conflicts than did the client's first eighteen dreams. Dimaggio and colleagues (1997) found the pleasant emotions in dreams increased as the client improved. Dreams have also been seen as a signal of a resolution of the client's previously intractable, extremely angry paternal transference (Eyre, 1988). Finally, dreams have been used to assess change over the course of treatment and consolidation of therapy experiences (Carlson, 1986; Glucksman, 1988; Lopez, 1987; Schwartz, 1970; Woltmann, 1968).

Large-Sample Studies of Individual Dream Work

Reviewers of the empirical literature on dream work (Eudell-Simmons & Hilsenroth, 2005; Hill, 1996; Hill & Goates, 2004; Pesant & Zadra, 2004) have suggested several major outcomes of dream work. The first major outcome is the perceived quality of dream sessions. There is convincing and consistent evidence (see review by Hill & Goates, 2004) that clients have rated the quality of sessions using the Hill model of dream work significantly higher than did clients who were in regular therapy. It appears, then, that clients felt better about the quality of the sessions when they focused on dreams than when they focused on other topics. We speculate this is because the gentle structure of the Hill model allows clients to come to some new understandings and then bridge these understandings to action. They bring in a dream that they really want to understand (which provides a clear marker that they are ready to work on this issue) and leave sessions feeling they have accomplished something tangible in terms of understanding their dreams and having an idea of what to do about it.

A second outcome, which is consistent with client goals of gaining understanding of their dreams, is insight gains. Insight gains from dream work have been measured in multiple ways, including open-ended questions, standard measures of insight and understanding, and ratings of insight reflected in the before- and after-session interpretations clients give of their dreams. From the studies using these various approaches to investigating the Hill model comes convincing evidence (see review in Hill & Goates, 2004) that clients gained insight into their dreams. Interestingly, Hill and colleagues (2006) showed that clients started at moderate levels of insight into their dreams and gained insight progressively as a result of both the exploration and insight stages. Hence, rather than clients having no insight about their dreams initially and getting "the" interpretation of their dream during the session, it appears they started with a fairly good understanding of their dreams and gained even more during sessions although they rarely achieved complete insight after a single session.

More recently, Hill and colleagues have assessed the quality of action ideas related to the dream discussed in dream sessions using the Hill model. Based on ratings made by trained judges (similar to those used for insight) (again see review in Hill & Goates, 2004), clients' ideas about what they could do behaviorally in their waking life that related to the dreams discussed in sessions became more clear, articulated, and doable after dream sessions. Hill and colleagues (2006) showed that at the start of the session, clients' action ideas were relatively low in clarity or workability, and their action ideas improved to a moderate level by the end of the action stage. Hence, even before sessions, clients often have some idea of what they should do based on the dream but gained in their conceptualization of what to do during the dream sessions. It makes sense that action ideas would lag behind insight, because theoretically insight is needed before the dreamer can decide what to do differently in life; if there is no understanding of what the dream means, the dreamer cannot very well decide to take action (Hill, 1996, 2004).

In a recent study, Hill and colleagues (2006) also assessed changes in the individualized target problem reflected in the dream. Assessing the target problem in dreams is challenging because clients often do not know what the dream is about before the session. So clients are asked after sessions to describe the target problem reflected in the dream and then rate their functioning on the target problem both for the current time and also retrospectively for how they experienced it before the session. Obviously, such ratings are confounded with client perceptions of the quality of the session, but they still provide some estimate of whether clients feel like they improve on the problem reflected in the dream, which of course is a key concern for dream work (and psychotherapy). Results showed that clients reported increases in functioning after a single dream session, suggesting that clients felt that working with their dreams directly helped them resolve problems in waking life. Similarly, two studies found evidence for changes in the impact of specific events (divorce in Falk & Hill, 1995; loss in Hill et al., 2000).

There is some, albeit less, evidence for changes on more standard outcomes of psychotherapy. Evidence has been found for decreases in general symptoms (Diemer, Lobell, Vivino, & Hill, 1996; Hill et al., 2000; Wonnell & Hill, 2005), decreases in depression (Falk & Hill, 1995), and increases in existential well-being when the focus of the dream work was on spiritual insight (Davis & Hill, 2005). Mixed results have been found for interpersonal functioning (Diemer et al., 1996; Hill et al., 2000). With couples dream work, Kolchakian and Hill (2002) found increases in other dyadic perspective taking but no changes in dyadic adjustment, primary communications, and self-dyadic perspective. No changes were found in anxiety or self-esteem for group dream work (Falk & Hill, 1995). One could argue that systematic changes in symptoms and interpersonal functioning would not necessarily be expected given that dreams might reflect problems in other areas. Based on this argument, we suggest assessing outcomes in areas more likely to be related to dream work, such as those reported earlier in this section (insight, action ideas, change in individualized target problems, and changes in dreams).

Research on Dream Groups

Only two studies have examined the effects of group dream work. Shuttleworth-Jordan, Saayman, & Faber (1988) compared their four-step method of group dream work with Ullman's group dream interpretation method. They found that therapist and clients in the four-step method were highly involved and did not experience overwhelming tension or loss of control, whereas the therapist and the clients in the Ullman method group were frustrated by the projection step of the technique. Falk and Hill (1995) investigated the effects of group dream work with separated and recently divorced women and found that after eight sessions, those in dream interpretation groups were higher in self-esteem and insight than those in the wait-list group.

Summary of Outcomes

Based on empirical evidence, dream work appears to have very positive outcomes. From case studies, we have evidence that individuals make a variety of changes as a result of working on their dreams. In addition, the volume and breadth of scope of case examples of dream work provides further support for its clinical efficacy and continued use. From large-sample studies of individual therapy, we have consistent evidence of an impact on session quality, insight, action ideas, target problems reflected in the dreams, and dream content, with somewhat less consistent evidence about effects on symptoms and interpersonal functioning. We must caution, however, that most of the large-sample studies have been done with the Hill model; we know very little about the efficacy of other dream models. Finally, given that only two large-sample studies have been conducted on dream groups, it is difficult to make major claims about its efficacy.

BUT IS IT FOR EVERYONE? PREDICTORS OF WHO PROFITS FROM DREAM WORK

In three large-sample studies involving a range of attitudes toward dreams (Hill et al., 2001; Hill et al., in press; Zack & Hill, 1998), researchers found evidence that clients with positive attitudes toward dreams had positive outcomes. Taken together with the finding that the people who volunteer for dreams sessions have more positive attitudes toward dreams than those who do not volunteer (Hill, Diemer, & Heaton, 1997), it appears that valuing dreams is an important precondition for dream work. This finding is reminiscent of the work on the importance of client expectations in psychotherapy (Arnkoff, Glass, & Shapiro, 2002). In addition, Hill and colleagues (2006) found that the clients who profited most from dream sessions had poor initial functioning on the problem reflected in the dream, salient dreams, high levels of self-efficacy for working on dreams, low initial insight into the dream, and poor initial action ideas related to the dream. These studies, then, suggest the importance not only of positive attitude toward dreams but of clients having salient, puzzling dreams that they do not understand, having dreams that reflect a specific underlying waking life problem, and feeling confident of their ability to do the tasks involved in dream work.

Less consistent findings have been reported for the valence of dreams. Zack and Hill (1998) found the best session outcomes for clients whose dreams were moderately unpleasant or extremely pleasant and the worst outcomes for clients whose dreams were moderately pleasant or extremely unpleasant. Hill and colleagues (2001) found that session outcomes were best for clients with pleasant dreams. Hill and colleagues (2003) found no relationship between dream valence and session outcome. A recent study (Hill, Spangler, Sim, & Baumann, 2007) suggests that perhaps the reason for the mixed findings with the previous studies was that they rated the dream valence on a simple unipolar dimension of unpleasant to pleasant. Recently, Hill and colleagues categorized interpersonal dreams into four categories: positive, negative, agency, and nightmares; however, many dreams either had no interpersonal content or had multiple interpersonal themes. These results suggested that dreams are often complicated and rarely fall onto a simple unpleasant-pleasant dimension. Their results also suggested that the process (client involvement, therapist competence) and outcome (insight gains, action gains, session evaluation, and change in target problems) of sessions was better for clients who presented positive interpersonal, interpersonal agency, and noninterpersonal dreams than for clients who presented negative dreams and interpersonal nightmares.

Other client characteristics (for example, gender, race/ethnicity, psychological mindedness) have minimal association with the outcome of dream sessions (Hill & Goates, 2004). Similarly, other dream-related characteristics (for example, recency, vividness, arousal, distortion) had minimal impact on the outcome of dream sessions (Hill & Goates, 2004).

In concert then with the findings presented in the section on dream work in naturally occurring therapy, these results suggest that it is best to do dream work with clients who have positive attitudes toward dreams, self-efficacy for working with their dreams, salient dreams that are puzzling, dreams that reflect underlying concerns, low insight and action ideas related to the dreams, who are willing to discuss dreams in therapy, and who are confident about their ability to do the tasks of dream work. A time that might be particularly appropriate to discuss dreams in psychotherapy is when the client has had a recent trauma or is undergoing a major transition (divorce, loss). Again, however, we caution that most of these studies have been done on the Hill model, and we do not yet know whether findings will generalize to other dream models.

HOW DREAMS HELP: THE PROCESS OF DREAM WORK

A number of studies aimed at understanding the effective components of the process of dream work using the Hill model have now been conducted. Thus, for example, four studies (Diemer et al., 1996; Hill et al., 2006; Wonnell & Hill, 2000; 2005) found evidence that client involvement is related to the outcome of individual dream work, although one study (Falk & Hill, 1995) did not find that client involvement was related to outcome of group dream work. In addition, one study (Hill et al., 2006) found evidence that therapist adherence to the model and competence using the model was related to session outcome. Furthermore, two studies (Heaton et al., 1998; Hill et al., 2003) found that volunteer clients gained more from working with a therapist than they did from using the same approach in a self-help format, although it is interesting that a small subgroup of clients in the latter study preferred working by themselves. Liking the therapist and the therapist's input were also mentioned in three qualitative studies (Hill et al., 1997, 2000, 2003) as helpful components of the process. It appears, then, that both client and therapist involvement in the process are key ingredients related to outcome.

Other information was gleaned from the three qualitative studies mentioned in the previous paragraph: clients mentioned that insight and interpretations, links to waking life, and catharsis were helpful components of the process of working with dreams. Interestingly, few clients mentioned hindering aspects and when they did there was no consistency to the things they did not like, suggesting that variables unique to the particular session, client, or therapist rather than the model itself might have been problematic.

Several studies did experimental manipulations of components of the Hill model, such that some components were delivered or not and then the effects on outcome were tested. Experimental manipulations are important because they provide greater confidence in the causal nature of these components than is possible with the naturalistic investigations described above. In a study involving description only, association only, or description and association in the exploration stage, Hill, Nakayama, and Wonnell (1998) found slightly more benefit in terms of outcome for the association-only condition, but in general found that both description and association were helpful. In tests of components of the insight stage, no differences were found in outcomes for waking life versus parts-of-self interpretations (Hill et al., 2001), and no differences were found in nonspiritual outcomes for waking life versus spiritual interpretations, although spiritual interpretations led to more spiritual insight (Davis & Hill, 2005). Hill and colleagues (2003) found mixed outcomes for the provision of therapist empathy and input (interpretations in the insight stage and action ideas in the action stage) versus empathy only (following the client's lead), although the nondirective condition led to better action ideas. Hill and colleagues (in preparation) found no differences between a low input and a high input condition for clients of East Asian descent, although clients who were more anxiously attached and lower on Asian values had better outcomes in the low input condition, whereas clients who were less anxiously attached and higher on Asian values had better outcomes in the high input condition. In terms of the action stage, Wonnell and Hill (2000) found that clients who went through all three stages (exploration, insight, action) had better action ideas and rated sessions higher on problem solving than did clients who only got the exploration and insight stages.

Additional process components were suggested in a series of three case studies examining how insight develops in dream sessions (Hill et al., 2007; Knox, Hill, Hess, & Crook-Lyon, in preparation). The two clients who acquired insight were consistently motivated and involved in the sessions, nonresistant, trusting of others, and affectively present in the sessions but not overwhelmed by affect. In addition, their therapists were able to skillfully use probes for insight and manage their countertransference reactions toward the clients. In contrast, the client who did not gain insight was resistant, untrusting, and emotionally overwhelmed in the session, and her therapist was not skillful in conducting the session and was not able to manage her negative countertransference.

In sum, it appears that therapist and client involvement and motivation are key components of dream work. Furthermore, it seems that it is helpful for clients to gain insight, make links to waking life, and cathart. All components of the Hill model (exploration, insight, and action) appear to be helpful, although therapists need to be responsive to the particular client. Finally, it appears crucial that the client not be overwhelmed by affect in the session and be open to and trusting of the therapist, and that the therapist be able to use probes for insight and monitor countertransference. Once again, these findings need to be replicated to determine whether they will generalize to other dream models than just the Hill model.

OTHER EXCITING AREAS RELATED TO DREAMS AND PSYCHOTHERAPY

There are a number of other ways that dreams can be used in psychotherapy. We focus here on just a few of these applications.

Therapist Use of Dream Content to Understand Clients

In their review of the literature, Eudell-Simmons and Hilsenroth (2005) suggested that therapists use dream content to better understand their clients. They argued that dreams provide information similar to other forms of assessment data but have an advantage because clients often are not as threatened by exploring dreams as they are by other assessment methods. Also, clients are often genuinely more invested in their dreams than in other assessment methods and hence are more willing to engage in dream work. Given that much work has been done comparing dream content for different diagnostic groups (see reviews in Hill, 1996; Van de Castle, 1994), therapists can thus determine whether clients have dreams that are similar to those of clients with depression, hysteria, schizophrenia, chronic brain syndrome, or sex offenders. We would caution, however, against too much reliance on such data, because these data are based on between group comparisons (for example, a comparison of dreams of clients with and without depression) and thus may not be applicable to individuals within groups.

With regard to particular content, research has shown that interpersonal themes are prevalent in dreams. Calvin Hall and Robert Van de Castle (1966) reported that people typically dream about their views of other people and their feelings about them. In addition, three studies (Popp, Luborsky, & Crits-Christoph, 1998; Popp et al., 1998; Stein, Eudell, DeFife,

& Hilsenroth, 2003) using the Core Conflictual Relationship Theme method (CCRT; Luborsky & Crits-Christoph, 1990; 1998) found that dreams were filled with interpersonal content. For example, in studies by Popp and colleagues (1998) and Stein and colleagues (2003), the most typical response of others in dream narratives was to reject and oppose the dreamer, whereas the most typical responses of self were to feel anxious/ashamed and helpless. These results suggest that most interpersonal content of most dreams is negative. Furthermore, results from Popp and colleagues (1998) showed similarities between the central interpersonal patterns in dreams and those in waking life. As mentioned earlier, Hill and colleagues (2006) found four interpersonal types of dreams (positive, negative, agency, and nightmares).

Dreams can also be used to assess the process and outcome of therapy. Some psychodynamic case studies have shown that the first dream presented in analysis is reflective of crucial themes (Bradlow & Bender, 1997). Gillman (1993) presented three types of undisguised transference dreams: a response to a break in the analytic barrier, a defense against an emerging transference neurosis, and reflection of a specific character defense. Sirois (1994) suggested that dreams may signal sensitive moments in therapy and may occur when the therapist's interventions are perceived as traumatic. In addition, Oremland (1973) indicated that clients often dream about termination in successful analyses.

Culture, Dreams, and Psychotherapy

Dream Work with Men

Differences between the dream experiences of men and women have been well documented. Men have lower dream recall than women (Cowen & Levin, 1995; Schredl, 2000), and researchers have found content differences in the dreams of men and women (Van de Castle, 1994; Schredl & Piel, 2005). Men's dreams contain more aggression, anxiety, achievement, and work-related themes than do the dreams of women. Less documented are the processes and outcomes of dream work with men.

Aaron Rochlen (2004) suggested an approach to dream work based on the Hill cognitive-experiential model that integrates gender-specific strategies based on the literature. These strategies include overcoming men's resistance by explaining why each of the stages of dream work are necessary, encouraging men to move beyond concrete thinking when working with dreams, modeling interpretations for men who are emotionally constricted, and recognizing if the client is too focused on the action stage. When the model was tested (Rochlen & Hill, 2005) among men with different levels of gender-role conflict, results showed that men who reported higher gender-role conflict discussed related conflict themes during dream sessions. Themes in sessions included conflicts between work and family, restrictive emotionality, and preoccupation with achievement and competition. Men with both high and low gender-role conflict rated the dream sessions as equally helpful, indicating that once men agree to dream work they will find it helpful regardless of their level of gender role conflict.

Dream Work with East Asian Clients

In a study of dream work with clients and therapists of East Asian descent, Hill and colleagues (in preparation) found no support for the premise often promoted in the literature that Asian clients would benefit more from a directive than nondirective approach (which they labeled as high versus low input only). In fact, there were no overall outcome differences between one condition in which therapists provided only low input (probes and reflections) versus another condition in which therapists provided high input (probes and reflections + interpretations and suggestions for action). They did find, however, that clients who were more anxiously attached and lower on Asian values had better outcomes in the low input condition, whereas clients who were less anxiously attached and higher on Asian values did better in the high input condition. These findings suggest that some East Asians might do better with a more directive approach, whereas others might do better with a more nondirective approach.

Spirituality and Dream Work

Although dreams have long been regarded as reflections of spirituality (Jung, 1964; Van de Castle, 1994), little is known about the relationship between spiritually centered dream work and therapeutic outcome. Hence, Davis and Hill (2005) examined how spiritually centered dream work relates to session evaluation and gains in spiritual insight for clients who are spiritually oriented. Clients whose therapists provided spiritual interpretations in the insight stage gained more spiritual insight and had greater increases in existential well-being than did clients whose therapists offered waking life interpretations of their dreams. The authors concluded that the findings highlight the value of addressing spiritual and existential concerns with spiritually oriented clients.

Client Dreams about Therapists

From a clinical perspective, it can also be very useful to examine clients' dreams about their therapists. When clients dream about their therapists and disclose such dreams in session, therapists are presented with a wealth of material about the client and the therapeutic relationship, usually assumed to relate to the transference. One study (Harris, 1962) found that dreams about the therapist occurred in about 10 percent of all client dreams. These dreams were associated with particularly turbulent transferences, with therapists appearing as real objects the client could make demands upon. The authors suggested that early dreams about therapists indicate a strong desire to fuse with the mother as a defense against castration anxiety. Similarly, Rosenbaum (1965) found that 10 percent of reported dreams were about the therapist. Analyses indicated that frequency of the dreams was not related to outcome, stage of analysis, intensity of the transference or countertransference, eroticism of the transference, or the therapist's strong conscious feelings of toward the client. The author concluded the dreams serve as a signal to go deeper in examining the inner lives of both client and therapist. In another study, Rohde, Geller, and Farber (1992) found themes of separation-rejection, seduction-antagonism, protectiveness-responsiveness, and praise in dreams about the therapist.

Therapist Dreams about Clients

Less attention has been given to the phenomenon of therapists' dreams about clients, despite the fact that the first such dream was recorded and interpreted by Freud himself (1900/1953). Dreams about clients have been the topic of occasional case studies and anecdotal accountings, but little empirical research has been conducted. What is known points to the therapeutic utility of understanding these dreams and how therapists work with them: A survey (Lester, Jodoin, & Robertson, 1989) of psychoanalysts and analysts-in-training indicated that dreams about clients tend to occur at difficult points in analysis and that less experienced therapists and trainees do not dream about clients any more frequently than do experienced therapists. The researchers also found six distinct relational themes for these dreams: sexual/erotic, intrusive, competitive, overwhelming affect, identification or closeness with the client, and sadistic control over the client.

In addition, three qualitative studies examined dreams about clients from a psychoanalytic or Jungian perspective. One study (Karcher, 1999) of the supervisory uses of trainees' dreams about clients in addressing countertransference showed that most of the dreams revealed trainee countertransference and that trainees perceived some benefit from addressing these dreams with their supervisors. Degani (2001) showed that therapist dreams about clients occurred during challenging periods during therapy; that they involved difficult clients; that they functioned as a mode to fulfill wishes, work through relationship problems, and purge unpleasant emotions; and that insight from dream interpretation could elicit therapeutic breakthrough. Kron and Avny (2003) examined Jungian and relational perspectives of therapists' counter-transference dreams and found interpersonal themes similar to themes identified in previous studies.

In a study currently underway, Patricia Spangler is qualitatively investigating the dreams of experienced therapists. Preliminary results indicate several common themes: emotional closeness with the client, concerns about clinical judgment, managing multiple roles, and boundary issues. Participants reported that they used a variety of methods to work with the dreams: early morning contemplation, journaling, drawing, sand art, and talking with someone about the dream.

Training Therapists to Do Dream Work

Montague Ullman (1994) reviewed existing methods for teaching the clinical use of dreams and then outlined an experiential approach, which he suggested provides the necessary structure for learning to make connections between dream images and waking life experiences. The experiential dream group approach stresses the importance of the dialogue that must occur between dreamer and therapist. Although no formal therapeutic techniques are used, the art of listening to and questioning the dreamer are emphasized, because these are the keys to eliciting relevant client information. The safety factor and the discovery factor are used to meet the basic needs of the dreamer. Unfortunately, Ullman's training method has not been tested.

Crook and Hill (2003) found that amount of training in dream work varied according to therapist orientation. Cognitive therapists, for example, reported a low amount of training in dream work compared with psychodynamic or eclectic therapists (Crook, 2004a). As an outgrowth of these findings, Rachel Crook (2004b) described a method for training therapists to use the Hill cognitive-experiential dream model. Training involves having therapists read about the model, participate in discussions of the model, and then practice the model in group and dyadic settings. A recent empirical study found support for changes in self-efficacy as a result of both didactic training and supervisory feedback (Crook-Lyon, Hill, Wimmer, Hess, & Goates-Jones, in preparation).

FUTURE DIRECTIONS

Given the potential effectiveness of dream work, we hope that more therapists will begin to work with dreams in therapy. Ideally, therapists would be trained by experts to work with specific models that have received empirical support. But alternatively, therapists can learn methods for working with dreams from reading texts and practicing on their own.

Clearly, more research is needed on different dream models to determine the effectiveness of these models. Furthermore, work is needed to determine the effective components of the different models. More work is also needed on the best methods for including dream work in therapy and for training therapists.

We conclude by saying that there is strong evidence that working with dreams therapeutically is useful. If we can use dreams to increase self-understanding, and if we can make changes in problems that are troubling us after working with dreams, these are compelling reasons for paying attention to dreams.

NOTES

1. We use the term "dream work" throughout rather than the more commonly used term "dream interpretation," because the latter term implies that therapists actively "interpret" the client's dream, whereas "dream work" just implies that dreams are the focus of attention.

2. In this chapter, we use the term "client" to refer to any person seeking help from a therapist about their dreams. We prefer the term "client" rather than "patient," because the latter has more of a medical connotation.

REFERENCES

Adler, A. (1936). On the interpretation of dreams. *International Journal of Individual Psychology, 2,* 3–16.

Adler, A. (1938). *Social interest: Challenge to mankind.* London: Faber & Faber.

Adler, A. (1958). *What life should mean to you.* New York: Capricorn.

Arnkoff, D. B., Glass, C. R., & Shapiro, S. J. (2002). Expectations and preferences. In J. C. Norcross (Ed.), *Psychotherapy relationships that work: Therapist contributions and responsiveness to patients* (pp. 37–70). New York: Oxford University Press.

Arons, B. S. (1978). First reported dreams in psychoanalytic group psychotherapy. *American Journal of Psychotherapy, 32,* 544–551.

Beck, A. T. (1971). Cognitive patterns in dreams and daydreams. In J. H. Masserman (Ed.), *Dream dynamics: Science and psychoanalysis* (Vol. 19, pp. 2–7). New York: Grune & Stratton.

Beebe, J. (1993). A Jungian approach to working with dreams. In G. Delaney (Ed.), *New directions in dream interpretation* (pp. 77–102). Albany, NY: SUNY Press.

Bird, B. E. I. (2005). Understanding dreams and dreamers: An Adlerian perspective. *Journal of Individual Psychology, 61,* 200–216.

Bonime, W. (1987). Collaborative dream interpretation. In M. L. Glucksman & S. L. Warner (Ed.), *Dreams in a new perspective: The royal road revisited* (pp. 79–96). New York: Human Sciences Press.

Bosnak, R. (1988). *A little course in dreams: A basic handbook of Jungian dreamwork.* Boston, MA: Shambhala.

Boss, M. (1958). *The analysis of dreams.* New York: Philosophical Library.

Boss, M. (1963). *Psychoanalysis and daseinanalysis.* New York: Basic Books.

Bradlow, P. A., & Bender, E. P. (1997). First dreams in psychoanalysis: A case study. *Journal of Clinical Psychoanalysis, 6,* 107–122.

Buchholz, M. B. (1990). Using dreams in family therapy. *Journal of Family Therapy, 12,* 387–396.

Bynum, E. B. (1980). The use of dreams in family therapy. *Psychotherapy: Theory, Research & Practice, 17,* 227–231.

Bynum, E. B. (1993). *Families and the interpretation of dreams: Awakening the intimate web.* New York, NY: Harrington Park Press/Haworth Press.

Calogeras, R. C., & Alston, T. M. (2000). The dreams of a cancer patient: A "royal road" to understanding the somatic illness. *Psychoanalytic Review, 87,* 911–937.

Carlson, R. (1986). After analysis: A study of transference dreams following treatment. *Journal of Consulting and Clinical Psychology, 54,* 246–252.

Caroppo, E., Dimaggio, G. G., Popolo, R., Salvatore, G., & Ruggeri, G. (1997). Recurrent oneiric themes: A clinical research on dream evaluation during psychotherapy. *New Trends in Experimental & Clinical Psychiatry, 8,* 275–278.

Cartwright, R. D., & Wood, E. (1993). The contribution of dream masochism to the sex ration difference in major depression. *Psychiatry Research, 46,* 165–173.

Cirincione, D., Hart, J., & Karle, W. (1980). The functional approach to using dreams in marital and family therapy. *Journal of Marital & Family Therapy, 6,* 147–151.

Cogar, M. C. (2004). Working with dreams in ongoing psychotherapy. In C. E. Hill (Ed.), *Dream work in therapy: Facilitating exploration, insight, and action.* Washington, DC: American Psychological Association.

Cowen, D., & Levin, R. (1995). The use of the Hartmann Boundary Questionnaire with an adolescent population. *Dreaming, 5,* 105–114.

Craig, E., & Walsh, S. J. (1993). The clinical use of dreams. In G. Delaney (Ed.), *New directions in dream interpretation* (pp. 103–154). Albany, NY: SUNY Press.

Crook, R. E. (2004a). A comparison of cognitive, psychodynamic, and eclectic therapists' attitudes and practices in working with dreams in psychotherapy. In R. I. Rosner, W. J. Lyddon, & A. Freeman (Eds.), *Cognitive therapy and dreams* (pp. 33–55). New York: Springer.

Crook, R. E. (2004b). Training therapists to work with dreams in therapy. In C. E. Hill (Ed.), *Dream work in therapy: Facilitating exploration, insight, and action.* Washington, DC: American Psychological Association.

Crook, R. E., & Hill, C. E. (2003). Working with dreams in psychotherapy: The therapists' perspective. *Dreaming, 13,* 83–93.

Crook-Lyon, R. E., & Hill, C. E. (2004). Client reactions to working with dreams in psychotherapy. *Dreaming, 14,* 207–219.

Crook-Lyon, R. E., Hill, C. E., Wimmer, C. L., Hess, S. A., & Goates-Jones, M. K. (in preparation). Training and feedback for dream work: An empirical investigation

Davis, T. L., & Hill, C. E. (2005). Including spirituality in the Hill model of dream interpretation. *Journal of Counseling and Development, 83,* 492–503.

De Domenico, G. S. (2002). Weaving together dream, image and relationship: Moving from anger, to fear, to love. *International Journal of Play Therapy, 11,* 1–18.

Degani, H. (2001). Therapists' dreams about patients and supervisors. *Dissertation Abstracts International, 62*(3-B), 1570.

Delaney, G. (1991). *Breakthrough dreaming.* New York: Bantam Books.

Delaney, G. (1993). The dream interview. In G. Delaney (Ed.), *New directions in dream interpretation* (pp. 195–240). Albany, NY: SUNY Press.

Diemer, R., Lobell, L., Vivino, B., & Hill, C. E. (1996). A comparison of dream interpretation, event interpretation, and unstructured sessions in brief psychotherapy. *Journal of Counseling Psychology, 43,* 99–112.

Dimaggio, G. G., Popolo, R., Serio, A. V., & Ruggeri, G. (1997). Dream emotional experience changes and psychotherapeutic process: An experimental contribution. *New Trends in Experimental & Clinical Psychiatry, 8,* 271–273.

Dowling, S. (1982). Dreams and dreaming in relation to trauma in childhood. *International Journal of Psycho-Analysis, 63,* 157–166.

Edwards, N. (2004). The ailing analyst and the dying patient. *Psychoanalytic Dialogues, 14,* 313–335.

Eisold, B. K. (2005). Notes on life-long resilience: Perceptual and personality factors implicit in a particular adaptive style. *Psychoanalytic Psychology, 22,* 411–425.

Eudell-Simmons, E. M., & Hilsenroth, M. J. (2005). A review of empirical research supporting four conceptual uses of dreams in psychotherapy. *Clinical Psychology and Psychotherapy, 12,* 255–269.

Eyre, D. (1988). The use of the analyst as a dream symbol. *British Journal of Psychotherapy, 5,* 5–18.

Falk, D. R., & Hill, C. E. (1995). The process and outcome of dream interpretation groups for divorcing women. *Dreaming, 5,* 29–42.

Faraday, A. (1972). *Dream power.* New York: Coward, McCann & Geoghegan.

Faraday, A. (1974). *The dream game.* New York: Harper & Row.

Fosshage, J. L. (1983). The psychoanalytic function of dreams: A revised psychoanalytic perspective. *Psychoanalysis and Contemporary Thought, 6,* 641–669.

Fosshage, J. L. (1987). New vistas in dream interpretation. In M. L. Glucksman & S. L. Warner (Eds.), *Dreams in a new perspective: The royal road revisited* (pp. 23–44). New York: Human Sciences Press.

Fox, S. A. (2002). A survey of mental health clinicians' use of dream interpretation in psychotherapy. *Dissertation Abstracts International: Section B. The Sciences & Engineering, 62*(7-B), 3376.

Freeman, A., & White, B. (2004). Dreams and the dream image: Using dreams in cognitive therapy. In R. I. Rosner, W. J. Lyddon, & A. Freeman (Eds.), *Cognitive therapy and dreams* (pp. 69–87). New York: Springer Publishing Company.

Friedman, R. (2000). The interpersonal containment of dreams in group psychotherapy: A contribution to the work with dreams in a group. *Group Analysis, 33,* 221–233.

Freud, S. (1953). *The interpretation of dreams* (J. Strachey, Trans.). London: Hogarth Press. (Original work published 1900)

Gabel, S. (1993). The phenomenology of the self and its subjects in waking and dreaming: Implications for a model of dreaming. *Journal of the American Academy of Psychoanalysis, 21,* 339–362.

Garma, A. (1987). Freudian approach. In J. L. Fosshage & C. A. Loew (Eds.), *Dream interpretation: A comparative study* (pp. 16–51). New York: PMA.

Geffner, A. H. (2004). "To sleep, perchance to dream" . . . on the couch: The interpersonal nature of dreams and other dissociative processes: A case illustration. *Psychoanalytic Dialogues, 14,* 139–162.

Gendlin, E. (1986). *Let your body interpret your dream.* Wilmette, IL: Chiron.

Gillman, R. D. (1993). Dreams in which the analyst appears as himself. In J. Natterson (Ed.), *The dream in clinical practice* (pp. 29–44). Northvale, NJ: Jason Aronson, Inc.

Glucksman, M. L. (1988). The use of successive dreams to facilitate and document change during treatment. *Journal of the American Academy of Psychoanalysis, 16,* 47–69.

Glucksman, M. L., & Warner, S. L. (Eds.). (1987). *Dreams in a new perspective: The royal road revisited.* New York: Human Sciences Press.

Grenell, G. (2002). The termination phase of psychoanalysis as seen through the lens of the dream. *Journal of the American Psychoanalytic Association, 50,* 779–805.

Hall, C., & Van de Castle, R. (1966). *The content analysis of dreams.* New York: Appleton-Century-Crofts.

Halliday, G. (1992). Effect of encouragement on dream recall. *Dreaming, 2,* 39–44.

Harris, I. (1962). Dreams about the analyst. *International Journal of Psycho-Analysis, 43,* 151–158.

Heaton, K. J., Hill, C. E., Hess, S., Hoffman, M. A., & Leotta, C. (1998). Assimilation in therapy involving interpretation of recurrent and nonrecurrent dreams. *Psychotherapy, 35,* 147–162.

Heaton, K. J., Hill, C. E., Petersen, D., Rochlen, A. B., & Zack, J. (1998). A comparison of therapist-facilitated and self-guided dream interpretation sessions. *Journal of Counseling Psychology, 45,* 115–121.

Hill, C. E. (1996). *Working with dreams in psychotherapy.* New York: Guilford Press.

Hill, C. E. (Ed.) (2004). *Dream work in therapy: Facilitating exploration, insight, and action.* Washington, DC: American Psychological Association.

Hill, C. E., Crook-Lyon, R. E., Hess, S., Goates, M. K., Roffman, M., Stahl, J., et al. (in press). Prediction of process and outcome in the Hill dream model: Contributions of client dream-related characteristics and the process of the three stages. *Dreaming, 16, 159–185.*

Hill, C. E., Diemer, R., & Heaton, K. J. (1997). Dream interpretation sessions: Who volunteers, who benefits, and what volunteer clients view as most and least helpful. *Journal of Counseling Psychology, 44,* 53–62.

Hill, C. E., & Goates, M. K. (2004). Research on the Hill cognitive-experiential dream model. In C. E. Hill (Ed.), *Dream work in therapy: Facilitating exploration, insight, and action* (pp. 245–288). Washington, DC: American Psychological Association.

Hill, C. E., Kelley, F. A., Davis, T. L., Crook, R. E., Maldonado, L. E., Turkson, M. A., et al. (2001). Predictors of outcome of dream interpretation sessions: Volunteer client characteristics, dream characteristics, and type of interpretation. *Dreaming, 11,* 53–72.

Hill, C. E., Knox, S., Hess, S., Crook-Lyon, R., Goates-Jones, M., & Sim, W. (2007). The attainment of insight in the Hill dream model: A single case study. In L. Castonguay & C. E. Hill (Eds.), *Insight in psychotherapy.* Washington, DC: American Psychological Association.

Hill, C. E., Nakayama, E., & Wonnell, T. (1998). A comparison of description, association, and combined description/association in exploring dream images. *Dreaming, 8,* 1–13.

Hill, C. E., Rochlen, A. B., Zack, J. S., McCready, T., & Dematatis, A. (2003). Working with dreams using the Hill Cognitive-Experiential Model: A comparison of computer-assisted, therapist empathy, and therapist empathy + input conditions. *Journal of Counseling Psychology, 50,* 211–220.

Hill, C. E., Spangler, P., Sim, W., & Baumann, E. (in preparation). The interpersonal content of dreams: Relation to pre-session client variables, process, and outcome of sessions using the Hill dream model.

Hill, C. E., Tien, H. S., Sheu, H, Sim, W., Ma, Y., Choi, K., et al. (in preparation). Predictors of outcome of dream work with clients and therapists of East Asian descent: Dream factors, anxious attachment, and Asian values.

Hill, C. E., Zack, J., Wonnell, T., Hoffman, M. A., Rochlen, A., Goldberg, J., et al. (2000). Structured brief therapy with a focus on dreams or loss for clients with troubling dreams and recent losses. *Journal of Counseling Psychology, 47,* 90–101.

Hillman, D. J. (1990). The emergence of grassroots dreamwork movement. In S. Krippner (Ed.), *Dream time and dreamwork: Decoding the language of the night* (pp. 13–20). Los Angeles, CA: Jeremy P. Tarcher, Inc.

Johnson, R. (1986). *Inner work.* San Francisco: Harper & Row.

Jung, C. G. (Ed.). (1964). *Man and his symbols.* New York: Dell.

Jung, C. G. (1974). *Dreams* (R. F. C. Hull, Trans.). Princeton, NJ: Princeton University Press.

Karcher, J. E. (1999). Countertransference dreams in supervision. *Dissertation Abstracts International, 59*(9-B), 5090.

Karush, R. J. (1998). The use of dream analysis in the treatment of a nine-year-old obsessional boy. *Psychoanalytic Study of the Child, 53,* 199–211.

Keller, J. W., Brown, G., Maier, K., Steinfurth, K., Hall, S., & Piotrowski, C. (1995). Use of dreams in therapy: A survey of clinicians in private practice. *Psychological Reports, 76,* 1288–1290.

Knox, S., Hill, C. E., Hess, S., & Crook-Lyon, R. (in preparation). The attainment of insight in the Hill dream model: Replication and extension.

Kolchakian, M. R., & Hill, C. E. (2002). Working with unmarried couples with dreams. *Dreaming, 12,* 1–16.

Knudson, R. M. (2006). Anorexia dreaming: A case study. *Dreaming, 16,* 43–52.

Krakow, B. (2004). Imagery rehearsal therapy for chronic posttraumatic nightmares: A mind's eye view. In R. I. Rosner, W. J. Lyddon, & A. Freeman (Eds.), *Cognitive therapy and dreams* (pp. 89–109). New York: Springer Publishing Company.

Kron, T., & Avny, N. (2003). Psychotherapists' dreams about their patients. *Journal of Analytical Psychology, 48,* 317–339.

Lester, E. P., Jodoin, R. M., & Robertson, B. M. (1989). Countertransference dreams reconsidered: A survey. *International Review of Psycho-Analysis, 16,* 305–314.

Levay, A. N., & Weissburg, J. (1979). The role of dreams in sex therapy. *Journal of Sex & Marital Therapy, 5,* 334–339.

Levounis, P. (2003). Gay patient-gay therapist: A case report of Stephen. In J. Drescher, A. D'Ercole, & E. Schoenberg, (Eds.), *Psychotherapy with gay men and lesbians:*

Contemporary dynamic approaches (pp. 15–27) Binghamton, NY: The Harrington Park Press/The Haworth Press, Inc.

Lippman, P. (2000). *Nocturnes: On listening to dreams.* Hillsdale, NJ: The Analytic Press.

Lombardi, D. N., & Elcock, L. E. (1997). Freud versus Adler on dreams. *American Psychologist, 52,* 572–573.

Lopez, R. E. (1987). Transitional dreams: A Kleinian approach. *Journal of the Melanie Klein Society, 5,* 72–85.

Luborsky, L., & Crits-Christoph, P. (1990). *Understanding transference: The CCRT method.* New York: Basic Books.

Luborsky, L., & Crits-Christoph, P. (1998). *Understanding transference: The CCRT method* (2nd ed.). Washington, DC: American Psychological Association.

Mahrer, A. R. (1990). *Dream work in psychotherapy and self-change.* New York: Norton.

Melstrom, M. A., & Cartwright, R. D. (1983). Effects of successful vs. unsuccessful psychotherapy outcome on some dream dimensions. *Psychiatry, 46,* 51–65.

Merlino, J. P. (2002). The royal road from homelessness—the clinical use of dreams. *Journal of the American Academy of Psychoanalysis, 30,* 583–594.

Merrill, S., & Cary, G. L. (1975). Dream analysis in brief psychotherapy. *American Journal of Psychotherapy, 29,* 185–193.

Natterson, J. M. (1980). The dream in group psychotherapy. In J. M. Natterson (Ed.), *The dream in clinical practice* (pp. 434–443). New York: Jason Aronson.

Natterson, J. M. (1993). Dreams: The gateway to consciousness. In G. Delaney (Ed.), *New directions in dream interpretation* (pp. 41–76). Albany, NY: SUNY Press.

Nicolo, A. M., Norsa, D., & Carratelli, T. (2003). Playing with dreams: The introduction of a third party into the transference dynamic of the couple. *Journal of Applied Psychoanalytic Studies, 5,* 283–296.

Olivetti, K. W. (2005). Gorging at Friendly's: A masochist's dream. *Issues in Psychoanalytic Psychology, 27,* 1–16.

Oremland, J. D. (1973). A specific dream during the termination phase of successful psychoanalyses. *Journal of the American Psychoanalytic Association, 21,* 285–302.

Perls, F. (1969). *Gestalt therapy verbatim.* New York: Bantam.

Pesant, N., & Zadra, A. (2004). Working with dreams in therapy: What do we know and what should we do? *Clinical Psychology Review, 24,* 489–512.

Polster, E., & Polster, M. (1973). *Gestalt therapy integrated.* New York: Random House.

Popp, C., Diguer, L., Luborsky, L., Faude, J., Johnson, S., Morris, M., et al. (1998). Study 2: The parallel of the CCRT from waking narratives with the CCRT from dreams: A further validation. In L. Luborsky & P. Crits-Christoph (Eds.) *Understanding transference: The core conflictual relationship theme method* (2nd ed., pp. 187–196). Washington, DC: American Psychological Association.

Popp, C., Luborsky, L., & Crits-Christoph, P. (1998). Study 1: The parallel of the CCRT from waking narratives with the CCRT from dreams. In L. Luborsky & P. Crits-Christoph, (Eds.) *Understanding transference: The core conflictual relationship theme method* (2nd ed., pp. 176–187). Washington, DC: American Psychological Association.

Rochlen, A. B. (2004). Using dreams to work with male clients. In C. E. Hill (Ed.), *Dream work in therapy: Facilitating exploration, insight, and action* (pp. 187–201). Washington DC: American Psychological Association.

Rochlen, A. B., & Hill, C. E. (2005). Gender role conflict and the process and outcome of dream work with men. *Dreaming, 15,* 227–239.

Rohde, A. B., Geller, J. D., & Farber, B. A. (1992). Dreams about the therapist: Mood, interactions, and themes. *Psychotherapy: Theory, Research, Practice, Training, 29,* 536–544.

Rosenbaum, M. (1965). Dreams in which the analyst appears undisguised—a clinical and statistical study. *International Journal of Psycho-Analysis, 46,* 429–437.

Sander, F. M. (2004). Psychoanalytic couple therapy: Classical style. *Psychoanalytic Inquiry, 24*(3), 373–386.

Scharff, D. E., & Scharff, J. S. (2004). Using dreams in treating couples' sexual issues. *Psychoanalytic Inquiry, 24,* 468–482.

Schredl, M. (2000). Gender differences in dream recall. *Journal of Mental Imagery, 24,* 169–176.

Schredl, M., Bohusch, C., Kahl, J., Mader, A., & Somesan, A. (2000). The use of dreams in psychotherapy: A survey of psychotherapists in private practice. *Journal of Psychotherapy Practice & Research, 9,* 81–87.

Schredl, M., & Piel, E. (2005). Gender differences in dreaming: Are they stable over time? *Personality & Individual Differences, 39,* 309–316.

Schwartz, E. (1970). A dream which restructured an important memory. *Psychoanalytic Review, 57,* 259–262.

Schwartz, W. (1990). A psychoanalytic approach to dreamwork. In S. Krippner (Ed.), *Dreamtime and dreamwork: Decoding the language of the night* (pp. 49–58). Los Angeles: Tarcher.

Shuttleworth-Jordan, A. B., Saayman, G. S., & Faber, P. A. (1988). A systemized method for dream analysis in a group setting. *International Journal of Group Psychotherapy, 38,* 473–489.

Sirois, F. (1994). Dreaming about the session. *Psychoanalytic Quarterly, 63,* 332–345.

Sirois, F. (2005). The fantasy of choosing one's sex. *Journal of Canadian Psychoanalysis, 13,* 94–112.

Solis, J. (1987). Dreams and depression: The case of a 65-year-old man. *Clinical Gerontologist, 6,* 54–56.

Stein, M., Eudell, E., DeFife, J., & Hilsenroth, M. (2003, November). Examining the reliability of CCRT ratings of dream narratives following 9/11/01. Poster presented at North American Society for Psychotherapy Research, Newport, RI.

Stone, W. N., & Karterud, S. (2006). Dreams as portraits of self and group interaction. *International Journal of Group Psychotherapy, 56,* 47–61.

Stubley, J. (2003). Bearing the unbearable: Melancholia following severe trauma. *Psychoanalytic Psychotherapy, 17,* 219–240.

Tanner, B. (2004). Multimodal behavioral treatment of nonrepetitive, treatment-resistant nightmares: A case report. *Perceptual and Motor Skills, 99,* 1139–1146.

Taylor, J. (1992). *Where people fly and water runs uphill: Using dreams to tap the wisdom of the unconscious.* New York: Warner.

Taylor, J. (1998). *The living labyrinth: Exploring universal themes in myths, dreams, and the symbolism of waking life.* Mahwah, NJ: Paulist Press.

Ullman, M. (1987). The experiential dream group. In B. B. Wolman (Ed.), *Handbook of dreams* (pp. 407–423). New York: Van Nostrand.

Ullman, M. (1994). The experiential dream group: Its applications in the training of therapists. *Dreaming, 4,* 223–229.

Van de Castle, R. L. (1994). *Our dreaming mind.* New York: Ballantine Books.

Warner, S. L. (1983). Can psychoanalytic treatment change dreams? *Journal of the American Academy of Psychoanalysis, 11,* 299–316.

Warner, S. L. (1987). Can psychoanalytic treatment change dreams? *Journal of the American Academy of Psychoanalysis, 11,* 299–316.

Weiss, L. (1986). *Dream analysis in psychotherapy.* New York: Pergamon.

Weiss, L. (1999). *Practical dreaming: Awakening the power of dreams in your life.* Oakland, CA: New Harbinger Press.

Willner, P. (2004). Brief cognitive therapy of nightmares and posttraumatic ruminations in a man with a learning disability. *British Journal of Clinical Psychology, 43,* 459–464.

Wolk, Donald J. (1996). The psychodramatic reenactment of a dream. *Journal of Group Psychotherapy, Psychodrama & Sociometry, 49,* 3–9.

Woltmann, A. G. (1968). Resistance and dreams. *Psychoanalytic Review, 55,* 115–120.

Wonnell, T. L. (2004). Working with dreams in groups. In C. E. Hill (Ed.), *Dream work in therapy: Facilitating exploration, insight, and action* (pp. 14–168). Washington, DC: American Psychological Association.

Wonnell, T. L., & Hill, C. E. (2000). The effects of including the action stage in dream interpretation. *Journal of Counseling Psychology, 47,* 372–379.

Wonnell, T. L., & Hill, C. E. (2005). Predictors of intention to act and implementation of action in dream sessions: Therapist skills, level of difficulty of action plan, and client involvement. *Dreaming, 15,* 129–141.

Zack, J., & Hill, C. E. (1998). Predicting dream interpretation outcome by attitudes, stress, and emotion. *Dreaming, 8,* 169–185.

Seven

Nightmares and Suicidality

Mehmet Yücel Agargün

[Abraham said,] "Grant me a son, Lord, and let him be a righteous man." We [Allah] gave him news of a gentle son. And when he reached the age when he could work with him his father said to him: "My son, I dreamt that I was sacrificing you. Tell me what you think." He replied: "Father, do as you are bidden. Allah willing, you shall find me faithful." And when they had both surrendered themselves to Allah's will, and Abraham had laid down his son prostrate upon his face, We called out to him, saying: "Abraham, you have fulfilled your vision." Thus did We reward the righteous. That was indeed a bitter test.

The Holy Koran 37; 100–106

Everyone knows what a nightmare is. But it is difficult to explain what the exact functions of a nightmare are. If a dream, basically, is the recall of mental activity that has occurred during sleep, what kind of mental activity is recalled just after a nightmare: an emotion, a threatening action, a mental imagery, or all of them?

WHAT IS A NIGHTMARE?

"A nightmare is a long, frightening dream that awakens the sleeper," "nightmares are vivid and terrifying nocturnal episodes," "after nightmares, typically, the dreamer wakes from sleep," or "returning to sleep is a bit difficult depending on high anxiety level of dream narrative." All explanations describe correctly what a nightmare is, but none of them is satisfactory, because a nightmare is considered an event; an ordinary dream in response to traumatic events, an anxiety symptom, or a sleep disorder.

NIGHTMARE AS A SLEEP DISORDER

Primary sleep disorders are divided into two subcategories. Dyssomnias are disorders relating to the amount, quality, and timing of sleep. Parasomnias relate to abnormal behavior or physiological events that occur during the process of sleep or sleep-wake transitions. From a diagnostic point of view, nightmares are the most prevalent and commonly appreciated form of dream disturbance.

The widely accepted definition of a nightmare is a long, frightening dream that awakens the sleeper (Hartmann, 1984; Levin & Fireman, 2002). This definition is also used in standard diagnostic texts such as the *Diagnostic and Statistical Manual for Mental Disorders* (DSM-IV-TR; American Psychiatric Association, 2000), the *International Classification of Diseases* (ICD-10; World Health Organization, 1993), and the *International Classification of Sleep Disorders* (ICSD-R; American Academy of Sleep Medicine, 2005).

DSM-IV-TR DIAGNOSTIC CRITERIA FOR 307.47 NIGHTMARE DISORDER

A. Repeated awakenings from the major sleep period or naps with detailed recall of extended and extremely frightening dreams, usually involving threats to survival, security, or self-esteem. The awakenings generally occur during the second half of the sleep period.

B. On awakening from the frightening dreams, the person rapidly becomes oriented and alert (in contrast to the confusion and disorientation seen in sleep terror disorder and some forms of epilepsy).

C. The dream experience, or the sleep disturbance resulting from the awakening, causes clinically significant distress or impairment in social, occupational, or other important areas of functioning.

D. The nightmares do not occur exclusively during the course of another mental disorder (for example, posttraumatic stress disorder) and are not due to the direct physiological effects of a substance (e.g., a drug of abuse, a medication) or a general medical condition.

ICD-10 DIAGNOSTIC CRITERIA FOR 307.47 NIGHTMARES

The following clinical features are essential for a definite diagnosis:

A. Awakening from nocturnal sleep or naps with detailed and vivid recall of intensely frightening dreams, usually involving threats to survival, security, or self-esteem; the awakening may occur at any time during the sleep period, but typically during the second half;

B. Upon awakening from the frightening dreams, the individual rapidly becomes oriented and alert;

C. The dream experience itself, and the resulting disturbance of sleep, cause marked distress to the individual.

ICSD-R DIAGNOSTIC CRITERIA FOR 307.47 NIGHTMARES

A. The patient has at least one episode of sudden awakening from sleep with intense fear, anxiety, and feeling of impeding harm.

B. The patient has immediate recall of frightening dream context.

C. Full alertness occurs immediately upon awakening, with little confusion or disorientation.

D. Associated features include at least one of the following:

1. Return to sleep after episode is delayed and not rapid

2. The episode occurs during the latter half of an habitual sleep period

NIGHTMARE AS A SYMPTOM FOR ANXIETY

Is a nightmare an equivalent of anxiety? Most people experience a certain amount of anxiety and fear in their lifetimes; it is a normal part of living. For millions of people, however, anxieties and fear are persistent and over-whelming and can interfere with daily life.

If anxiety becomes pronounced, it can express itself in various ways. For example, a person who has anxiety may have the following symptoms: has trouble falling asleep; dwells on a particular situation and finds it difficult to think of something else; feels tense, restless, jittery, dizzy, and sweaty; has trouble concentrating; overeats or loses appetite; is overly vigilant and startles easily; has a feeling of impending disaster, as if something bad is going to happen.

Dreams may cause anxiety in healthy people. Recall of extended and extremely frightening dreams, usually involving threats to survival, security, or self-esteem, results in marked distress and anxiety in even healthy individuals. After a night of serious nightmaress, one may feel fear, as well as heart palpitations, trembling, dry mouth, dizziness, and nausea. The following night, the dreamer may fail to go to sleep and maintain sleep efficiently.

Nightmares may be considered a variant of trait anxiety in the sufferers. Nightmares seem to be an almost trait-like variable with correlations to trait but not state anxiety. Individuals with frequent nightmares who also report high levels of global nightmare distress may demonstrate particularly active hypervigilant perceptual threat schemas, much in the way chronic posttraumatic stress disorder (PTSD) victims do, but without an as yet identifiable discrete trigger event (McNally, 1998; Zoellner, Foa, Brigidi, & Przeeworski, 2000).

WHEN IS A DREAM A NIGHTMARE?

Should all kinds of disturbing or frightening dreams be called nightmares? All dreams that are bad are not nightmares. We dream a lot of negative narrative dreams in everyday life, but some of them are real nightmares. The presence of two parameters, intense anxiety or fear and awakening with full alertness, are important to consider a dream as a nightmare (Nielsen & Zadra, 2005). If awakening does not follow a bad dream, some researchers prefer to call it just that, a "bad dream" (Halliday, 1987). On the other hand, some researchers prefer to define a nightmare as any dream accompanied by an unpleasant emotion (Belicki, 1992a), most frequently fear, but also extreme anger or sadness (Zadra & Donderi, 1993). In summary, *nightmares* are very disturbing dreams that awaken the sleeper; *bad dreams* are very disturbing dreams that do not awaken the sleeper, although negative emotions may exist both in bad dreams and nightmares.

NIGHTMARES DIFFERS FROM OTHER PARASOMNIAS

Primary sleep disorders can be divided into two subcategories. Dyssomnias are disorders relating to the amount, quality, and timing of sleep. Parasomnias relate to abnormal behavior or physiological events that occur during the process of sleep or sleep-wake transitions.

Parasomnias are unpleasant or undesirable behavioral or experiential phenomena that occur predominately or exclusively during the sleep period. They may be categorized conveniently as primary (disorders of the sleep states, per se) and secondary (disorders of other organ systems that manifest themselves during sleep). The primary sleep parasomnias can be classified according to the sleep state of origin: rapid eye movement (REM) sleep, non-REM (NREM) sleep, or miscellaneous (that is, those not respecting sleep state) (Mahowald & Schenck, 2005a).

Nightmares are considered traditionally as REM sleep-parasomnias, although they can also occur during NREM sleep. They are long frightening dreams involving threats to survival or security, from which the sleeper awakens. Apparently, nightmares relate to sleep-related violence as well. Nightmares should be differentiated from sleep terrors, narcolepsy, sleep panic attacks, REM Behavior Disorder (RBD), sleep-related dissociative episodes, and other awakenings relating violence during sleep. Nightmares typically occur later in the night during REM sleep and produce vivid dream imagery, complete awakenings, autonomic arousal, and detailed recall of the event.

Sleep terrors are the most dramatic disorder of arousal. They frequently are initiated by a loud, blood-curdling scream associated with extreme panic, followed by prominent motor activity such as hitting the wall, running around or out of the bedroom, or even out of the house, and result in bodily injury or property damage. A universal feature is inconsolability. Although victims seem to be awake, they usually misperceive the environment, and attempts at consolation are fruitless and may serve only to prolong or even intensify the confusional state. Some degree of perception may be evident, for example, running for and opening a door or window. Complete amnesia for the activity is typical but may be incomplete (Mahowald & Schenck, 2005b).

Sleepwalking is a disorder of arousal in which the subject arises from deep sleep displaying short and simple behavior or longer complex behavior, including leaving the bed and walking, with memory impairment of the event (American Academy of Sleep Medicine, 2005). Sleepwalking episodes usually occur abruptly during the first two or three hours of sleep, with patients showing a blank facial expression with a low level of awareness and reactivity. Eyes are often held open, and patients may appear awake during sleepwalking, but motor behavior is usually clumsy and purposeless, with slowing in speech and mentation and poor response to stimulation, and, noteworthy, without screaming, tremors, or autonomic signs such as sweating (Plazzi, Vetrugno, Provini, & Montagna, 2005).

RBD most commonly affects middle-aged men. Patients with this disorder often present with a history of sleep-associated injuries to themselves or a sleeping partner. RBD is characterized by vivid, action-filled, violent dreams that the dreamer acts out, sometimes resulting in injury to the dreamer or the sleeping partner (Schenck & Mahowald, 1996).

Complex, potentially injurious behavior, occasionally confined to the sleep period, may be the manifestation of a psychogenic dissociative state. A history of childhood physical or sexual abuse almost always is positive (Agargün et al., 2001; Agargün et al., 2002a). Nocturnal dissociative episodes usually involve elaborate behaviors that appear to represent attempted reenactments of previous abuse situations (for example, being choked or punched by a sibling, being beaten or sexually abused by a parent). What is perceived to be dream enactment is actually a dissociated wakeful memory of past abuse. Sexualized behavior (pelvic thrusting, rocking) is not uncommon and is often paired with defensive behavior (trying to push or ward someone off, with congruent verbalization, such as "Don't do that, you're hurting me, get away") (Schenck, Milner, Hurwitz, Bundlie, & Mahowald, 1989).

Nocturnal panic attack refers to waking from sleep in a state of panic. Sleep panic attacks may affect clinical variables and modify the severity of illness in patients with panic disorder (Agargün & Kara, 1998). During a panic attack, an abrupt and discrete period of intense fear or discomfort is accompanied by cognitive and physical symptoms of arousal including tachycardia, sweating, shortness of breath, chest pressure, choking sensations, dizziness or lightheadedness, depersonalization or derealization, stomach discomfort, and fears of dying or going crazy. Nocturnal panic does not refer to waking from sleep and panicking after a lapse of waking time, or nighttime arousals induced by nightmares. Instead, nocturnal panic is an abrupt waking from sleep in a state of panic without an obvious trigger (Craske & Tsao, 2005).

ASSESSMENT OF NIGHTMARES

Nightmares can be assessed and diagnosed on the basis of the patient's history. It is not necessary to assess the subject who is suspected to have nightmare disorder polysomnographically in order to confirm the diagnosis. Neither ICSD nor DSM-IV-TR requires a sleep laboratory assessment to diagnose a nightmare disorder. A diagnosis of nightmare disorder involves merely clinical criteria.

Polysomnographic recording in the sleep laboratory relating nightmares is problematic. First of all, the artificial setting of the sleep laboratory may influence the contents of dreams. Thus, nightmares tend to occur less often in this setting (Fisher, Byrne, Edwards, & Kahn, 1970). The best way(s) to adequately measure nightmares with polysomnographic recordings could be to conduct polysomnography for a longer period so participants can adjust to the artificial setting and/or to conduct polysomnographic recordings with an ambulant method in the home environment (Spoormaker, Schredl, & van den Bout, 2006).

The characteristics associated with nightmares can be delimited via standardized assessment methods. Retrospective questionnaires and prospective logs are the most common instruments for assessing various nightmares, although they have limitations. Among the instruments that focus on the negative impact of stressful dreams, the following stand out: the *Nightmare Distress Questionnaire* (NDQ; Belicki, 1992b), which analyzes emotional disturbance associated with these types of dreams; and *Nightmare Effects Survey*

(NES; Krakow et al., 2000b), which examines the areas of daily life that are affected by nightmares. A recent study (Martinez, Miro, & Arriaza, 2005) showed that the NDQ and NES are reliable and valid measures that successfully examine the repercussions of nightmares.

The Van Dream Anxiety Scale (VDAS) was developed by Agargün et al. in 1999 to measure anxiety levels resulting from nightmares (Agargün et al., 1999). It establishes a reliable and valid measure of dream anxiety. It is a scale that is easy for subjects to use and for clinicians and researchers to provide a longitudinal assessment of dream anxiety and treatment response in subjects with nightmares, as well as to provide an examination of dream anxiety relevant to adult psychopathology. The questions in the scale were internally consistent. The scale had a good level of internal consistency (Cronbach's α = 0.87). Global scores and individual responses were stable across time. The VDAS consists of seventeen self-rated questions. Four questions (questions 7–10) are used for clinical information only and are not tabulated in the scoring VDAS. These questions are concerned with bedtime, getting up time, sleep latency, and sleep duration, respectively. Twelve questions are concerned with nightmare frequency (q.1), difficulty in falling asleep after a nightmare (q.2), fear of sleeping because of anticipated nightmare (q.3), trouble sleeping (q.4), dream recall frequency (q.6), daytime sleepiness (q.11), daytime anxiety (q.12), occupational distress (q.13), familial distress (q.14), social distress (q.15), psychological problems (q.16), and memory/concentration problems (q.17). The items are weighted equally on a 0–4 scale (never, 0; rarely, 1; sometimes, 2; usually, 3; and often, 4). Question 5 is related to autonomic hyperactivity, such as palpitation, breathing difficulty, dizziness, dry mouth, and sore throat. The scores for the thirteen questions are summed to yield a global VDAS score, which ranges from 0 to 52.

PREVALENCE OF NIGHTMARES AND NIGHTMARE DISORDER

Nightmares often begin between three and six years of age, with 50 percent of cases starting before age ten, and two-thirds before age twenty. A major stressful life event precedes onset in 60 percent of cases. Children usually outgrow nightmares, but in adults, they tend to be chronic. In addition, they are more common in females than in males (American Psychiatric Association, 1994).

In the general population, lifetime prevalence for a nightmare experience is unknown. However, it has been suggested that prevalence rate may well approach 100 percent. If we consider nightmare to be a highly disturbing theme in a terrifying dream, lifetime prevalence is 92 percent among women and 85 percent among men (Nielsen & Zadra, 2005). Vgontzas and Kales

(1999) reached the conclusion that nightmares are a current problem for approximately 5 percent of the general population, and a past problem for another 5 percent. About 4 percent of general practice patients spontaneously report a problem with nightmares to their physician (Bixler, Kales, & Soldatos, 1979).

Age is known to be a mediating factor: children, young adults, and groups of adults and older adults have nightmares "at least sometimes," with a prevalence of 30 to 90 percent, 40 to 60 percent, and 60 to 68 percent, respectively (Partinen, 1994). Nightmares are especially frequent at the ages of three to six. Numbers vary, but 20 to 50 percent of children in this age group are reported to have frequent nightmares. At least one-fifth of children five to twelve years old are reported to have a minimum of one nightmare in any six-month period (Simonds & Parraga, 1982). Approximately, 60 to 80 percent of adults report having had nightmares in childhood (Hartman, 1982, 1992). Nielsen et al. (2000) found a large gender difference in the recall ("sometimes" or "often") of bad dreams at age thirteen (boys: 25 percent versus girls: 40 percent) and age sixteen (20 percent versus 40 percent). In the DSM-IV, females report having nightmares more often than do men at a ratio of approximately 2–4 : 1 (American Psychiatric Association, 1994). Agargün et al. (2003b) found a gender difference in their study: girls had a higher prevalence of nightmare disorder than boys among college students.

Recently, we interviewed 971 preadolescent school-aged children and their parents in order to survey the prevalence of parasomnias in a preadolescent school-aged population of children aged seven to eleven years (Agargün et al., 2004). We found a 1 percent prevalence of nightmare disorder according to DSM-IV criteria in their sample. This was unexpectedly low compared to data from the literature. In a clinical context, where nightmare disorder problems were defined as lasting for more than three months, Salzarulo and Chevalier (1983) found a prevalence of 41 percent for children aged six to ten years and 22 percent for children aged eleven years. They also indicated that 20 to 30 percent of 5- to 12-year-old children had at least one nightmare in any six-month period. However, in that study, they used a diagnosis of nightmare disorder rather than nightmare and considered only cases of nightmare disorder. Another issue is that the response categories (for example,, once a week, frequently/always) differ from those of the other studies. This may affect the prevalence rates considerably. In addition, the low prevalence rate of nightmare disorder might be partly related to the underestimation of parent questionnaires (Richman, 1987). Agargün and colleagues (2003a) found 7.5 percent prevalence of "often" and a 58.2 percent prevalence of "sometimes" for nightmares among college students.

A community-based study of 6,103 older subjects (Asplund, 2003) showed frequent nightmares were reported by 9.0 percent of the men and 11.9 percent of the women. Among men, frequent nightmares were reported 4.1 (2.1–7.9) times more often by those who experienced such pain very seldom or never, and this figure among women was 5.0 (2.0–8.5) times. Nightmares were reportedly common among those who experienced pain—both men and women.

GENETIC OF NIGHTMARES

Many parasomnias are known to run in families, and genetic effects have long been suggested to be involved in their occurrence. Nightmares are a common and persistent trait, affected substantially by genetic factors. The estimated proportion of genetic effects in childhood was 44 percent of the phenotypic variance in males and 45 percent in females.. As adults, the values were 36 percent in males and 38 percent in females. Nightmares are quite a stable trait from childhood to middle age (Hublin, Kaprio, Partinen, & Koskenvuo, 1999). However, recent data indicated dissimilarity in the genetic background of nightmares and the other parasomnias studied here, and this may be a reflection of the different pathophysiological background (nightmares are considered to be a REM sleep-related parasomnia, the others are not) (Hublin, Kaprio, Partinen, & Koskenvuo, 2001).

NIGHTMARES AND PSYCHOPATHOLOGY

Nightmares may be associated with psychopathology, in particular, in young adults and adults. Nightmares are common among patients with psychiatric disorders (the higher the frequency of nightmares, the higher the likelihood of a comorbid psychiatric disorder) (Hublin et al., 1999). They are also related to the general level of mental complaints or general psychopathology. Recently, completing the Minnesota Multiphasic Personality Inventory (MMPI) and the Eysenck Personality Questionnaire (EPQ), nightmare subjects were scored significantly higher on the EPQ Neuroticism scale and on eight MMPI clinical scales than did the control group. This may be interpreted as a reflection of global maladjustment rather than of specific psychotic symptomatology (Berquier & Ashton, 1992). Contextualized images (central dream images providing a picture context for the dominant emotion) in nightmares have also been associated with elevated subscales on the Symptom Check List-90 (SCL-90) in community samples, suggesting a relation to psychopathology, while contextualized images in ordinary dreams are not associated with psychopathology (Levin & Basile, 2003).

Recently, Schredl (2003) showed that the association between neuroticism and nightmares is mediated by state anxiety. He suggested that persons who score high on neuroticism experience more stress and, therefore, more nightmares, although the nature of this process remains unclear and needs more theoretical and empirical attention. On the other hand, persons who score high on neuroticism are more likely to remember and report their nightmares with retrospective measurements (Wood & Bootzin, 1990).

There are several reports that suggest a relationship between nightmares and anxiety, (Spoormaker et al., 2006). Using daily dream logs, Wood and Bootzin (1990) monitored nightmare frequency in 220 undergraduates; 47 percent of students reported at least one nightmare during the study period. Nightmare frequency and anxiety were found to be uncorrelated. These findings suggest that nightmares are more prevalent than has been reported and their frequency unrelated to self-reported anxiety.

Recurrent nightmares are characterized by a high comorbidity of mood and anxiety disorder. In major depressive disorder, nightmares often occur during the illness and dramatically decrease in the treatment period. Nightmares were also found to be associated with personality disorders (Hartmann, Russ, Oldfield, Sivan, & Cooper, 1987), schizotipy (Levin, 1998), alexithymia (Nielsen et al., 1997), and drug and alcohol dependence (Hershon, 1977).

Recurrent frightening anxiety dreams also occur in most PTSD patients. The relationship between recurrent nightmares and PTSD is also causal. Disturbed dreaming may, in fact, be the hallmark of delayed PTSD; the content of disturbing dreams (for example, reliving combat), as well as associated sleep disruptions (nocturnal awakenings, fear of sleep), may reinforce the illness (Nielsen & Zadra, 2005). The association of dream disturbances with flashbacks related to the trauma and the fact that Vietnam veterans with disturbed dreaming suffered from a more severe form of PTSD are congruent with the suggestion that disturbed dreaming may be at the core of the PTSD (Kaminer & Lavie, 1991). PTSD consists of three clusters: (a) intrusion: re-experiencing the traumatic event in nightmares or flashbacks; (b) avoidance of stimuli that could be reminders of the traumatic event; and (c) hyperarousal (for example,, insomnia, increased tension during the day) (American Psychiatric Association, 2000). Posttraumatic nightmares are part of the re-experiencing cluster and are one of the major complaints of persons who have PTSD (Ross, Ball, Sullivan, & Caroff, 1989). A prevalence for nightmares is 40 to 56 percent among PTSD patients (Kilpatrick, Resnick, & Freedy, 1998; Schreuder, Kleijn, & Rooijmans, 2000). Recurrent traumatic dreams also occur in acute stress disorder patients. Thus, it may be suggested that nightmares seem to be an effective copy mechanism in trauma victims (Agargün et al., 2003a).

DRUGS AND NIGHTMARES

Pharmacological agents affecting the neurotransmitters norepinephrine, serotonin, and dopamine are clearly associated with patient reports of nightmares. Agents affecting immunological response to infectious disease are likely to induce nightmares in some patients. A possible association exists between reports of nightmares and agents affecting the neurotransmitters acetylcholine, gamma-aminobutyric acid (GABA) and histamine, as well as for some anesthetics, antipsychotics, and antiepileptic agents (Pagel & Helfter, 2003). Drugs that affect the dopaminergic and cholinergic systems are also known to increase the vividness and frightening quality of dreams (Wichlinski, 2000).

NIGHTMARES AND PSYCHOLOGICAL TRAUMA

There is a relationship between nightmares and psychological trauma, in particular childhood traumatic events. In a recent study, two important results were useful in understanding the relationship between nightmares and childhood events. First, we found that the rate of childhood traumatic experiences (in general) and the rate of physical abuse (in particular) were higher in the "often" nightmare sufferers than in the "sometimes" nightmare sufferers and in those without nightmares. Second, we demonstrated that subjects who had experienced physical abuse and sexual abuse had higher VDAS global and item scores. In general, subjects with childhood traumatic experiences had higher VDAS scores than the others. These results indicate a strong association between nightmares and childhood traumatic experiences. The association between traumatic dreams and traumatic events is well described, and there is also a paradigm for nightmares (Hartmann, 1999). Traumatic nightmares may arise out of varying stages of sleep and are not confined to REM sleep alone. Sleep disturbances and disturbed dreaming are among the hallmarks of the long-term effects of traumatic events (Kaminer & Lavie, 1991; van der Kolk, Blitz, Burr, Sherry, & Hartmann, 1984). In that study, we showed that subjects with reported childhood histories of trauma were not different from other subjects for dream recall frequency, but they did have a higher nightmare frequency. This finding confirms a suggestion that dream recall decreased in subjects with trauma. A successful adjustment to traumatic life events includes a protective dampening of the recall of all dreams in comparison to control subjects even many years later. A decrease in dream recall that minimizes the probability of anxiety dreams and nightmares appears to be an effective coping mechanism in trauma victims (Kaminer & Lavie, 1991).

NIGHTMARES, DISSOCIATIVE EXPERIENCES, AND DISSOCIATIVE DISORDERS

Dissociation is a fundamental pathogenetic mechanism of many psychiatric disorders, such as dissociative disorders, somatoform disorders and, more recently, acute stress disorder and PTSD. A strong relationship was found between childhood traumatic events and the development of dissociative symptomatology (Putnam, 1985; van der Kolk, Herron, & Hostetler, 1994). During the developmental course, children and young adolescents are particularly prone to dissociative experiences and use dissociation as a defense mechanism (Butler, Duran, Jasiukaitis, Koopman, & Spiegel, 1996). The dissociative experiences scale (DES) was developed by Bernstein and Putnam (1986) to assess a variety of dissociative experiences, many of which are normal experiences. The DES is a 28-item self-report instrument that can be completed in ten minutes and scored in less than five minutes. It is easy to understand, and the questions are framed in a normative way that does not stigmatize the respondent for positive responses. The respondent then slashes the line, which is anchored at 0 percent on the left and 100 percent on the right to show how often he or she has this experience. The overall DES score is obtained by adding up the twenty-eight item scores and dividing by twenty-eight; this yields an overall score ranging from 0 to 100.

A recent study (Agargün et al., 2003a) showed that the subjects with a history of physical abuse and with a history of sexual abuse had higher DES score than the others. The subjects who experienced at least one childhood traumatic event also had a higher mean DES score than those who had not. The relationship between traumatic events in childhood and high DES scores is well known. DES scores are highly correlated with reported childhood histories of trauma (Chu & Dill, 1990). In a recent study by Agargün et al. (2003a), the subjects with nightmares had significantly higher scores on the DES than those without nightmares. DES scores negatively correlated with duration of nightmares in subjects with childhood traumatic experiences. These findings suggest that the subjects with reported childhood histories of trauma have failed to psychologically integrate their traumatic experiences and use dissociation as a way of dealing with strong affects. It may be suggested that dreams, particularly those that focus on an emotionally disturbing event, are necessary to emotional adaptation in childhood traumatic events, and nightmares have an adaptive function in this process.

Nightmare disorder is common among patients with dissociative disorders. In a recent study (Agargün et al., 2003b), thirty patients with dissociative disorders (five male and twenty-five female) were recruited over twelve months. The subjects were diagnosed according to the *Diagnostic and Statistical Manual of Mental Disorders* (4th edition) criteria for nightmare disorder. The Dissociative Experiences scale, Beck Depression Inventory, and a semistructured interview schedule for childhood traumatic events were administered to the subjects. A 57 percent prevalence of nightmare disorder was found among patients with dissociative disorders. Among patients with dissociative disorders, those with nightmare disorder had a higher rate of self-mutilative behavior, a history of suicide attempt in the last year, and comorbidity with borderline personality disorder than those without nightmare disorder. It may be reasonable to attribute a role to nightmares as an adaptive coping strategy in dissociative disorders. The dreams reduce the intensity of the emotional distress by juxtaposing the current trauma with various other events in the person's life, making connections to other similar or not so similar events. When trauma is dreamt about, it is no longer uniquely distressing; it gradually becomes part of a fabric or network. Thus, dreaming has an adaptive function and nightmares are common following a trauma (Hartmann, 1999). Nightmares or dreams of dissociative disorders patients can be used to facilitate the therapy of these disorders.

DREAMS, MOOD, AND DEPRESSION

Among the proposed psychological functions of dreaming, perhaps the one with the most research support is mood regulation. Mood regulatory function of dreaming is a hypothesis that states that the effect of the slow wave sleep to REM sleep sequence is to downregulate affect carried over from previous waking (Cartwright, Agargün, Kirkby, & Friedman, 2006). This is accomplished by "contextualizing" the central affect in a metaphoric image and relating it to a network of previously stored images (Hartmann, 2002). Dreams are an intervening variable between waking emotional concerns and postsleep mood. As such, they may become dysfunctional because of an overload of disturbed affect or a failure to accomplish the linkage to past memories, which is essential to the reduction of disturbed mood (Cartwright, 2005). Dream content is related to the ongoing emotional concerns of the dreamer and contributes to the down-regulation of disturbed mood, when affect is within a defined range (Cartwright et al., 2006). On the other hand, dream characteristics appear to respond adaptively during life changes, but this is delayed when subjects are depressed (Cartwright, Lloyd, Knight, & Trenholme, 1984). Those who are severely depressed are reported to have poorer dream recall and blunted dream affect (Armitage, Rochler, Fitch, Trivedi, & Rush, 1995). In contrast, those who have less severe depression, particularly females, report higher rates of unpleasant dreams than other psychiatric patients or normal subjects (Cartwright, 1992).

Recently, Cartwright, Young, Mercer, and Bears (1998) found that subjects reporting more negative dreams at the beginning of the night and fewer at the night's end were more likely to be in remission one year later than were those with few negative dreams at the beginning and more at the end of the night. Hence, it is favorable to suggest that early negative dreams reflect a within-sleep mood-regulation process taking place, while those that occur later may indicate a failure in the completion of this process. Agargün and Cartwright (2003) found that when end-of-night dream narratives were more negative in affect type but low in narrative quality, the affect appeared to be less integrated with older affective memory material close to the morning awaking, indicating a failure to regulate negative mood. It might be that this pattern of affect processing is pathogenic. Thus, Agargün and Cartwright also noted that early negative dreams reflect a within-sleep mood-regulation process taking place while those that occur later may indicate a failure in the completion of this process.

NIGHTMARES, MOOD, AND DEPRESSION

In addition to the relationship between dreams and mood and depression, recent research indicates that nightmares are also associated with mood changes and depression. Recently, Agargün, Kara, and Inci (2003) reported three cases who had nightmare-induced manic episodes and suggested mood-regulatory function of dreaming. A dysregulation in neural circuits and monoaminergic systems in brain may precede mood shift during REM sleep dreaming and result in manic episode. Previously, Beauchemin and Hays (1995) demonstrated that dream content is related to prevailing mood state and that certain types of dream precede upward mood changes in bipolar disorder (manic depression). In another study (1996), these two authors found that: (1) REM latency tends to increase as the mood improves in patients with bipolar disorder but is stable (and even decreases with mood improvements) in patients who are unipolar depressive; (2) dream content continues to systematically relate to prevailing mood state, but the patterns seen are different in patients with unipolar and bipolar disorders; and (3) dreams of death are frequent in patients with bipolar disorder and mark the transition of a mood shift upward.

With regard to depression, nightmares are significantly more frequent in depressed patients, in particular with melancholic features such as terminal insomnia, pervasive anhedonia, unreactive mood, and appetite loss (Besir-oglu, Agargün, & Inci, 2005). All these symptoms were reported to be related to short REM latency and increased REM density in depressed patients (Giles, Rush, & Roffwarg, 1986). As an essential feature of melancholia, negative affective state in the morning might be related to the intervening dream content and affect. Recently, our group (Besiroglu et al., 2005) hypothesized terminal insomnia occurs adaptively in depressed patients with melancholic features to have a therapeutic effect on mood regulation and improve negative dream affect and content. The results of the study suggest an adaptive function for spontaneous early morning awakening may shield mood from the effects of negative dream affect. On the other hand, this reflects a within-sleep, mood-regulation process taking place. Nightmares might reflect a negative dream affect, and terminal insomnia might play a role in preventing depressed morning mood, although a failure in the completion of this process takes place during a depressive episode, in particular with melancholic features.

On the other hand, the masochistic dreams in melancholic depressed individuals may be regarded as a manifestation of the individual's negative bias in interpreting this experience and in his or her expectations (Beck, 1967). It may be suggested that masochism in frightening dreams such as nightmares is associated with a deeper level of self-criticism and self-blaming in melancholic depressed individuals. Feeling worse in the morning than later in the day may be related to the intervening dream content and affect. Thus, REM sleep deprivation that occurs closer to morning may have a therapeutic effect on mood regulation and diminish negative dream affect and content in depressed subjects with melancholic features or diurnal mood symptoms.

VIOLENT BEHAVIORS DURING SLEEP

Violent behavior during sleep (VBS) include a broad range of behaviors: benign dream enactment (kicking, jumping out of bed, and running), self-mutilation, sexual assault, attempted murder, murder, and suicide. The VBS can be directed to other subjects, to objects, or to self (Ohayon, 2000). In 1989, Schenck et al. published a clinical and polysomnographic study on one hundred consecutive adult patients complaining of sleep-related injury. They identified several disorders as being responsible for causing nocturnal violence: sleepwalking, sleep terrors, REM sleep behavior disorder, nocturnal psychogenic dissociative disorders, nocturnal seizures, obstructive sleep apnea, and periodic limb movement disorder. More recently, Ohayon, Malijai, and Priets (1997) reported that VBS during sleep affected 2 percent of the population. They identified a number of sleep factors, mental disorders, and other general health factors that characterize those experiencing episodes of VBS. Night terrors, daytime sleepiness, sleep talking, bruxism, and hypnic jerks were more frequent in subjects with violent or harmful behavior during sleep than the nonviolent subjects, as were hypnagogic hallucinations and the incidence of smoking, caffeine, and bedtime alcohol intake. Many neurologic and psychogenic causes of sleep-related violence were described in the literature (Pareja, Schenck, & Mahowald, 2000). Recently, Agargün et al. (2002b) reported a series of sleep-related violent subjects. They identified nightmares were among the causes of VBS. They reported patients with nightmares who had also nocturnal dissociative disorder or RBD.

SLEEP DISTURBANCES AND SUICIDALITY

There has been an increasing interest in the relationship between sleep and suicidality in depression over the past fifteen years. Sleep disturbances have prognostic significance in predicting suicide among patients with mood disorders.

Among sleep disturbance, both insomnia and hypersomnia are associated with suicidal behavior in patients with major depression (Agargün, Kara, & Solmaz, 1997a; Fawcett et al., 1990). In another clinical study, Agargün, Kara, and Solmaz (1997b), evaluated forty-one patients with major depression by using the Pittsburgh Sleep Quality Index (PSQI) (Buysse, Reynolds, Monk, & Kupfer, 1989) and the Schedule for Affective Disorders and Schizophrenia (SADS) (Endicott & Spitzer, 1978) suicide subscale. They found that suicidal depressive patients had significantly higher scores of subjective sleep quality, sleep latency, sleep duration, habitual sleep efficiency, and PSQI global scores than nonsuicidal patients. They also found significant correlations between the SADS suicide subscale scores and most measures of the PSQI.

In an electroencephalographic (EEG) sleep study, Sabo, Reynolds, Kupfer, and Berman (1991) compared major depressives with and without a history of suicidal behavior and found suicide attempters had longer sleep latency, lower sleep efficiency, and fewer late-night delta wave counts than normal controls. Nonattempters, compared with attempters, had less REM time and activity in the second REM period, but more delta wave counts in the fourth non-REM period in the same study.

With regard to sleep-disordered breathing, only one study has investigated the relationship between sleep-disordered breathing, suicidal ideation, and depressive symptoms. Krakow et al. (2000a) examined subjective sleep disturbances in female sexual assault survivors with PTSD. The results of the study indicated that women who experienced a potential sleep breathing disorder also suffered significantly greater levels of depression and suicidality. The authors suggested that physiological sleep fragmentation might contribute to "emotional exhaustion" in terms of occurrence of suicidal behavior.

Apart from depression, among panic disorder patients, the presence of nocturnal panic attacks may modify the severity of illness in patients with panic disorder. In a recent study, Agargün and Kara (1998) examined the association between recurrent sleep panic and suicidal behavior in panic disorder. They found that patients with recurrent sleep panic had a higher percentage of insomnia and comorbid major depression than the other patients. A multivariate analysis demonstrated an association between recurrent sleep panic and suicidal tendencies in patients with panic disorder.

PARASOMNIAS AND SUICIDAL BEHAVIOR

RBD is a parasomnia, which is another dreaming disorder involving disruptive and violent behaviors during REM sleep. Yeh and Schenck (2004) recently reported a 35-year-old woman with childhood-onset parasomnia, marked by arm waving with talking and shouting, who developed marital discord solely because her parasomnia disrupted her husband's sleep. This was the first report of a suicide attempt directly related to RBD. In this case, marital discord emerged (apparently exclusively) because of the RBD behaviors, resulting in secondary depression and an eventual suicide attempt.

DREAMS, NIGHTMARES, AND SUICIDAL BEHAVIOR

With regard to relationship between nightmares and suicide, there are two recent clinical studies. Agargün et al. (1998) examined the association between repetitive and frightening dreams and suicidal tendency in patients with major depression by using the SADS suicide subscale. The patients with frequent nightmares, particularly women, had higher mean suicide subscale scores and were more likely to be classified as more suicidal than the others. A prospective follow-up study in a sample drawn from the general population (Tanskanen et al., 2001) also reported that the frequency of nightmares is directly related to the risk of suicide. A more recent study (Agargün & Cartwright, 2003) hypothesized that dream variables such as the nature and sequence of the affect reported from dreams collected during REM interruptions and REM sleep abnormalities are related to suicidal tendencies in depressed individuals. Agargün and Cartwright also hypothesized those with a higher proportion of negative dreams in the second half of the night and whose REM latency was abnormally reduced would be more likely to score higher on suicidality. They found a significant negative correlation between suicidality scores and REM latency and a positive correlation between suicidality and REM percent. Suicidal subjects had a significantly shorter mean REM latency and a higher mean REM percentage than the nonsuicidal subjects. The six subjects with a negative dream-like quality (DLQ) difference also scored as suicidal. A reduction in DLQ of the REM content reports between the first and second halves of the night was found to be associated with suicidal tendency.

Is this link largely explained by depressive symptoms or how are specific symptoms of sleep disturbance related to suicidal symptoms when controlling for depression? Recently, Bernert and colleagues (2005) directly addressed this real question regarding research indicating that sleep disturbances may be specifically linked to suicidal behaviors.

They found insomnia and nightmare symptoms were associated with both depressive symptoms and suicidality before controlling for depressive symptoms. After controlling for depressive symptoms, only nightmares demonstrated an association with suicidal ideation. Another new finding was that nightmares were particularly associated with suicidality among women compared to men. Before controlling for gender, a nonsignificant trend emerged between nightmare symptoms and suicidality, and this relationship remained after controlling for depression. After controlling for gender, the link between nightmare symptoms and suicidal ideation was statistically significant. This finding indicates that the association between nightmares and suicidality, while controlling for depression, was somewhat stronger among women versus among men.

On the other hand, as stated above, nightmares are common among patients with dissociative disorders. A clinical study (Agargün et al., 2003b) showed, among patients with dissociative disorders, those with nightmare disorder had a higher rate of history of suicide attempt in the past year than those without nightmares. This finding suggests a relationship between nightmares and suicidal behavior apart from depression.

CONCLUSIONS

There is a considerable association between nightmares and suicidal behavior. This association is bilateral. On one side, nightmares or nightmare disorder represent examples of violent behavior during sleep. On the other side, nightmares are correlated with suicidal tendency both in clinical and in nonclinical populations. Moreover, nightmares are the most useful dreams. Hence, nightmares should be considered in therapy of various specific conditions including dissociation, acute stress reactions, PTSD, divorce, grief, depression, and suicide.

Although the direction of causality between sleep disturbances and suicidal behavior has been somewhat well documented, the causality between dreaming and suicidal behavior in depression is controversial. Serotonin (5-HT) may play a key role in this association because it plays an important role in sleep regulation. Abnormalities in 5-HT neurotransmission or serotonergic dysregulation may play key roles in underlying mechanisms of the association with suicidal tendency and sleep disturbances in depressed patients. It was speculated that low serotonergic turnover may be more closely related to difficulties inhibiting aggressive or destructive behavior, that is, aggression dyscontrol rather than general impulsiveness and that aggression dyscontrol might be the intervening factor relating serotonin to suicide (Asberg, 1997). In addition to its role in suicide, 5-HT seems to be involved in regulating the sleep-wake cycle. 5-HT is thought to facilitate the onset of slow-wave sleep (Singareddy & Balon, 2001). Although the serotonergic mechanisms may somewhat explain the direction of causality between dreaming and suicidal behavior in depression, this association may equally be related to mood-regulatory and adaptive function of dreaming and cognitive-affective processing (Agargün et al., 1998).

Nightmares reflect a negative dream affect. Terminal insomnia may play a role in preventing depressed morning mood. Feeling worse in the morning than later in the day seems to be related to negative dream content and affect. Terminal insomnia reflects REM sleep deprivation closer to morning and diminishes negative dream affect and content in depressed subjects with diurnal mood symptoms (Agargün & Besiroglu, 2005). An investigation of relationship of suicidal behavior with terminal insomnia or nightmares in melancholic depression will be helpful in understanding the sleep-suicide association. On the other hand, it seems to be necessary to evaluate chronobiological correlates of suicidality. Suicidal acts at night are more severe than daytime acts. Thus, eveningness-morningness preference may be important for deducing suicide risk in normal and clinical populations in terms of dreaming and nightmares.

REFERENCES

Agargün, M. Y., & Besiroglu, L. (2005). Sleep and suicidality: Do sleep disturbances predict suicide risk? *Sleep, 28,* 1039–1040.

Agargün, M. Y., & Cartwright, R. (2003). REM sleep, dream variables and suicidality in depressed patients. *Psychiatry Research, 15,* 33–39.

Agargün, M. Y., Cilli, A. S., Kara, H., Tarhan, N., Kincir, F., & Oz, H. (1998). Repetitive and frightening dreams and suicidal behavior in patients with major depression. *Comprehensive Psychiatry, 39,* 198–202.

Agargün, M. Y., Cilli, A. S., Sener, S., Bilici, M., Ozer O. A., Selvi, Y., et al. (2004). The prevalence of parasomnias in preadolescent school-aged children: A Turkish sample. *Sleep, 27,* 701–705.

Agargün, M. Y., & Kara, H. (1998). Recurrent sleep panic, insomnia, and suicidal behavior in patients with panic disorder. *Comprehensive Psychiatry, 39,* 149–151.

Agargün, M. Y., Kara, H., Bilici, M., Cilli, A. S., Telci, M., Semiz, U. B., et al. (1999). The Van Dream Anxiety Scale: A subjective measure of dream anxiety in nightmare sufferers. *Sleep and Hypnosis, 4,* 204–211.

Agargün, M. Y., Kara, H., & Inci, R. (2003). Nightmares associated with the onset of mania: Three case reports. *Sleep and Hypnosis, 5,* 192–196.

Agargün, M. Y., Kara, H., Ozer, O. A., Selvi, Y., Kiran, U., & Kiran, S. (2002a). Sleep-related violence, dissociative experiences, and childhood traumatic events. *Sleep and Hypnosis, 4,* 52–57.

Agargün, M. Y., Kara, H., Ozer, O. A., Selvi, Y., Kiran, U., & Kiran, S. (2003a). Nightmares and dissociative experiences: The key role of childhood traumatic events. *Psychiatry and Clinical Neurosciences, 57,* 139–145.

Agargün, M. Y., Kara, H., Ozer, O. A., Selvi, Y., Kiran, U., & Ozer, B. (2003b). Clinical importance of nightmare disorder in patients with dissociative disorders. *Psychiatry and Clinical Neurosciences, 57,* 575–579.

Agargün, M. Y., Kara, H., Ozer, O. A., Semiz, U., Selvi, Y., Kiran, U., et al. (2001). Characteristics of patients with nocturnal dissociative disorders. *Sleep and Hypnosis, 3,* 131–134.

Agargün, M. Y., Kara, H., & Solmaz, M. (1997a). Sleep disturbances and suicidal behavior in patients with major depression. *Journal of Clinical Psychiatry, 58,* 249–251.

Agargün, M. Y., Kara, H., & Solmaz, M. (1997b). Subjective sleep quality and suicidality in patients with major depression. *Journal of Psychiatric Research, 31,* 377–381.

Agargün, M. Y., Sekeroglu, R., Kara, H., Ozer, O. A., Tombul, T., Kiran, U., et al. (2002b). Sleep-related violence and low serum cholesterol: A preliminary study. *Psychiatry and Clinical Neurosciences, 56,* 195–198.

American Academy of Sleep Medicine. (2005). *International classification of sleep disorders. Diagnostic and coding manual* (2nd ed.). Westchester, IL: American Academy of Sleep Medicine.

American Psychiatric Association. (1994). *Diagnostic and statistical manual of mental disorders* (4th ed.). Washington, DC: American Psychiatric Press.

American Psychiatric Association (2000). *Diagnostic and statistical manual of mental disorders* (4th ed.) Washington, DC: American Psychiatric Press.

Armitage, R., Rochler, A., Fitch, T., Trivedi, M., & Rush, J. (1995). Dream recall and major depression: A preliminary report. *Dreaming, 5,* 189–198.

Asberg, M. (1997). Neurotransmitters and suicidal behavior. The evidence from cerebrospinal fluid studies. *Annual New York Academy of Sciences, 836,* 158–181.

Asplund, R. (2003). Nightmares in relation to health, sleep and somatic symptoms in the elderly. *Sleep and Hypnosis, 5,* 175–181.

Beauchemin, K. M., & Hays, P. (1995). Prevailing mood, mood changes and dreams in bipolar disorder. *Journal of Affective Disorders, 9,* 41–49.

Beauchemin, K. M., & Hays, P. (1996). Dreaming away depression: The role of REM sleep and dreaming in affective disorders. *Journal of Affective Disorders, 25,* 125–133.

Beck, A. T. (1967). *Depression.* New York: Harper & Row.

Belicki, K. (1992a). The relationship of nightmare frequency to nightmare suffering with implications for treatment and research. *Dreaming, 2,* 143–148.

Belicki, K. (1992b). Nightmare frequency versus nightmare distress: Relations to psycho-pathology and cognitive style. *Journal of Abnormal Psychology, 101,* 592–597.

Bernert, R. A., Joiner, T. E. Jr., Cukrowicz, K. C., Schmidt, N. B., & Krakow, B. (2005). Suicidality and sleep disturbances. *Sleep, 28,* 1135–1141.

Bernstein, E. M., & Putnam, F. W. (1986). Development, reliability, and validity, of a dissociation scale. *Journal of Nervous and Mental Disorders, 174,* 727–735.

Berquier, A., & Ashton, R. (1992). Characteristics of the frequent nightmare sufferer. *Journal of Abnormal Psychology, 101,* 246–250.

Besiroglu, L., Agargün, M. Y., & Inci, R. (2005). Nightmares and terminal insomnia in depressed patients with and without melancholic features. *Psychiatry Research, 28,* 285–287.

Bixler, E. O., Kales, A., & Soldatos, C. R. (1979). Sleep disorders encountered in medical practice. *Behavioral Medicine, 6,* 1–6.

Butler, L. D., Duran, R. E. F., Jasiukaitis, P., Koopman, C., & Spiegel, D. (1996). Hyp-notizability and traumatic experience: A diathesis-stress model of dissociative symp-tomatology. *American Journal of Psychiatry, 153,* 42–63.

Buysse, D., Reynolds, C. F., Monk, T. H., & Kupfer, D. J. (1989). The Pittsburgh Sleep Quality Index: A new instrument for psychiatric practice and research. *Psychiatry Research, 28,* 193–213.

Cartwright, R. (1992). Masochism in dreaming and its relation to depression. *Dreaming, 3,* 79–84.

Cartwright, R. (2005). Dreaming as a mood regulation system. In M. Kryger, T. Roth, & W. C. Dement (Eds.), *Principles and practice of sleep medicine* (4th ed., pp. 565–572). Philadelphia, PA: W. B. Saunders Company.

Cartwright, R., Agargün, M. Y., Kirkby, J., & Friedman J. K. (2006). Relation of dreams to waking concerns. *Psychiatry Research, 30,* 261–270.

Cartwright, R., Lloyd, S., Knight, S., & Trenholme, I. (1984). Broken dreams: A study of the effects of divorce and depression on dream content. *Psychiatry, 47,* 251–259.

Cartwright, R., Young M. A., Mercer, P., & Bears E. (1998). Role of REM sleep and dream variables in the prediction of remission from depression. *Psychiatry Research, 80,* 249–255.

Chu, J. A., & Dill, D. L. (1990). Dissociative symptoms in relation to childhood physical and sexual abuse. *American Journal of Psychiatry, 147,* 887–892.

Craske, M. G., & Tsao, J. C. (2005). Assessment and treatment of nocturnal panic attacks. *Sleep Medicine, 9,* 173–184.

Endicott, J., & Spitzer, R. L. (1978). A diagnostic interview: The Schedule for Affective Disorders and Schizophrenia. *Archives of General Psychiatry, 35,* 837–844.

Fawcett, J., Scheftner, W. A., Fogg, L., Clark, D. C., Young, M. A., Hedeker, D., et al. (1990). Time-related predictors of suicide in major affective disorder. *American Journal of Psychiatry, 147,* 1189–1194.

Fisher, C. J., Byrne, J., Edwards, A., & Kahn, E. (1970). A psychophysiological study of nightmares, *Journal of American Psychoanalytic Association, 18,* 747–782.

Giles, D., Rush, A. J., & Roffwarg, H. P. (1986). Sleep parameters in bipolar I, bipolar II, and unipolar depressions, *Biological Psychiatry, 2,* 1340–1343.

Halliday, G. (1987). Direct psychological therapies for nightmares: A review. *Clinical Psychological Review, 7,* 501–552.

Hartmann, E. (1982). From the biology of dreaming to the biology of the mind. *Psychoanalytic Study of the Child, 37,* 303–335.

Hartmann, E. (1984). *The nightmare: The psychology and biology of terrifying dreams.* New York: Basic Books.

Hartmann, E. (1992). Nightmares and boundaries of the mind. In M. R. Lansky (Ed.), *Essential papers on dreams* (pp. 376–400). New York: University Press.

Hartmann, E. (1999). The nightmare is the most useful dream. *Sleep and Hypnosis, 1,* 199–203.

Hartmann, E. (2002). Dreaming. In T. Lee-Chiong, M. Sateia, & M. Carskadon (Eds.), *Sleep medicine* (pp. 93–98). Philadelphia, PA: Hanley and Belfus, Inc.

Hartmann, E., Russ, D., Oldfield, M., Sivan, I., & Cooper, S. (1987). Who has nightmares? The personality of the lifelong nightmare sufferer. *Archives of General Psychiatry, 44,* 49–56.

Hershon, H. I. (1977). Alcohol withdrawal symptoms and drinking behavior. *Journal of Studies of Alcohol, 38,* 953–971.

Hublin, C., Kaprio, J., Partinen, M., & Koskenvuo, M. (1999). Nightmares: Familial aggregation and association with psychiatric disorders in a nationwide twin cohort. *American Journal of Medical Genetic, 20,* 329–336.

Hublin, C., Kaprio, J., Partinen, M., & Koskenvuo, M. (2001). Parasomnias: Co-occurrence and genetics. *Psychiatric Genetics, 11,* 65–70.

Kaminer, H., & Lavie, P. (1991). Sleep and dreaming in Holocaust survivors. *Journal of Nervous and Mental Disorders, 179,* 664–669.

Kilpatrick, D. G., Resnick, H. S., & Freedy, J. R. (1998). Posttraumatic stress disorder field trial: Evaluation of the PTSD construct-criteria A through E. In T. A. Widiger, A. J. Frances, & H. A. Pincus (Eds.), *DSM-IV sourcebook* (pp. 803–846). Washington, DC: American Psychiatric Press.

Krakow, B., Artar, A., Warner, T. D., Melendrez, D., Johnston, L., Hollifield, M., et al. (2000a). Sleep disorder, depression, and suicidality in female sexual assault survivors. *Crisis, 21,* 163–170.

Krakow, B., Hollifield, M., Schrader, R., Koss, M., Tandberg, D., Lauriello, J., et al. (2000b). A controlled study of imagery rehearsal for chronic nightmares in sexual assault survivors with PTSD: A preliminary report. *Journal of Trauma and Stress, 13,* 589–609.

Levin, R. (1998). Nightmares and schizotpy. *Psychiatry, 61,* 206–216.

Levin, R., & Basile, R. (2003). Psychopathological correlates of contextualized images in dreams. *Perceptual and Motor Skills, 96,* 224–226.

Levin, R., & Fireman, G. (2002). Nightmare prevalence, nightmare distress and self-reported psychological disturbance. *Sleep, 25,* 205–212.

Mahowald, M. W., & Schenck, C. H. (2005a). Non-rapid eye movement sleep parasomnias. *Neurology Clinics, 23,* 1107–1126.

Mahowald, M. W., & Schenck, C. H. (2005b). Rapid eye movement sleep parasomnias. *Neurology Clinics, 23,* 1077–1106.

Martinez, M. P., Miro, E., & Arriaza, R. (2005). Evaluation of the distress and effects caused by nightmares: A study of the psychometric properties of the Nightmare Distress Questionnaire and the Nightmare Effects Survey. *Sleep and Hypnosis, 7,* pp. 29–41.

McNally, R. (1998). Experimental approaches to cognitive abnormality in posttraumatic stress disorder. *Clinical Psychology Review, 18,* 971–982.

Nielsen, T. A., LaBerge, L., Paquet, J., Tremblay, R. E., Vitaro, F., & Montplaisir, J. (2000). Development of disturbing dreams during adolescence and their relationship to anxiety symptoms. *Sleep, 23,* 727–736.

Nielsen, T. A., Oulelet, L., Warnes, H., Cartier, A., Malo, J. L., & Montplaisir, J. (1997). Alexithymia and impoverished dream recall in asthmatic patients: Evidence from self-report measures. *Journal of Psychosomatic Research, 42,* 53–59.

Nielsen, T. A., & Zadra, A. (2005). Dreaming disorders. In M. H. Kryger, T. Roth, & W. C. Dement (Eds.), *Principles and practice of sleep medicine* (4th ed., pp. 926–935). Philadelphia: W. B. Saunders Company.

Ohayon, M. M. (2000). Violence and sleep. *Sleep and Hypnosis, 2,* 1–7.

Ohayon, M. M., Malijai, C., & Priets, R. G. (1997). Violent behavior during sleep. *Journal of Clinical Psychiatry, 58,* 369–376.

Pagel, J. F., & Helfter, P. (2003) Drug-induced nightmares: An etiology based review. *Human Psychopharmacology, 18,* 59–67.

Pareja, J. A., Schenck, C. H., & Mahowald, M. W. (2000). Current perspectives on sleep-related injury, its updated differential diagnosis and its treatment. *Sleep and Hypnosis, 2,* 8–21.

Partinen, M. (1994). Epidemiology of sleep disorders. In M. H. Kryger, T. Roth, & W. C. Dement (Eds.), *Principles and practice of sleep medicine* (2nd ed., pp. 437–452). Philadelphia: W. B. Saunders Company.

Plazzi, G., Vetrugno, R., Provini, F., & Montagna, P. (2005). Sleepwalking and other ambulatory behaviours during sleep. *Neurological Sciences, 26,* 193–198.

Putnam, P. W. (1985). Dissociation as a response to extreme trauma. In R. P. Kluft (Ed.), *Childhood antecedents of multiple personality disorder* (pp. 65–97). Washington, DC: American Psychiatric Press.

Richman, N. (1987). Surveys of sleep disorders in children in a general population. In C. Guilleminault (Ed.), *Sleep and its disorders in children* (pp. 115–127). New York: Raven Press.

Ross, J. W., Ball, W. A., Sullivan, K. A., & Caroff, S. N. (1989). Sleep disturbance as the hallmark of posttraumatic stress disorder. *American Journal of Psychiatry, 146,* 697–707.

Sabo, E., Reynolds, C. F., Kupfer, D. J., & Berman, S. R. (1991). Sleep, depression, and suicide. *Psychiatry Research, 36,* 265–277.

Salzarulo, P., & Chevalier, A. (1983). Sleep problems in children and their relationship with early distrurbances of the waking-sleeping rhythms. *Sleep, 6,* 47–51.

Schenck, C. H., & Mahowald, M. W. (1996). REM sleep parasomnias. *Neurology Clinics, 14,* 697–720.

Schenck, C. H., Milner, D. M., Hurwitz, T. D., Bundlie, S. R., & Mahowald, M. W. (1989). Dissociative disorders presenting as somnambulism: Polysomnographic, video and clinical documentation (8 cases). *Dissociation, 2,* 194–204.

Schredl, M. (2003). Effects of state and trait factors on nightmare frequency. *European Archives of Psychiatry and Clinical Neurosciences, 253,* 241–247.

Schreuder, J. N., Kleijn, W. C., & Rooijmans, H. G. M. (2000). Nocturnal re-experiencing more than forty years after war trauma. *Journal Traumatic Stress, 13,* 453–463.

Simonds, J. F., & Parraga, H. (1982). Prevalence of sleep disorders and sleep behaviors in children and adolescents. *Journal of American Academy of Child and Adolescent Psychiatry, 21,* 383–388.

Singareddy, R. K., & Balon, R. (2001). Sleep and suicide in psychiatric patients. *Annals of Clinical Psychiatry, 13,* 93–101.

Spoormaker, V. I., Schredl, M., & van den Bout, V. (2006). Nightmares: From anxiety symptom to sleep disorder. *Sleep Medicine Reviews, 10,* 19–31.

Tanskanen, A., Tuomilehto, J., Viinamaki, H., Vartiainen, E., Lehtonen, J., & Puska, P. (2001). Nightmares as predictors of suicide. *Sleep, 24,* 844–847.

van der Kolk, B., Blitz, R., Burr, W., Sherry, S., & Hartmann, E. (1984). Nightmares and trauma: A comparison of nightmares after combat with lifelong nightmares in veterans. *American Journal of Psychiatry, 141,* 187–190.

van der Kolk, B. A., Herron, N., & Hostetler, A. (1994). The history of trauma in psychiatry. *Psychiatry Clinics of North America, 17,* 588–600.

Vgontzas, A. N., & Kales, A. (1999). Sleep and its disorders. *Annual Review of Medicine, 50,* 387–400.

Wichlinski, L. J. (2000). The pharmacology of threatening dreams. *Behavioural and Brain Sciences, 23,* 1016–1017.

Wood, J. M., & Bootzin, R. R. (1990). The prevalence of nightmares and their independence from anxiety. *Journal of Abnormal Psychology, 99,* 64–68.

World Health Organization. (1993). *The 10th revision of the International Classification of Diseases. Chapter V (F): Mental and behavioral disorders.* Huber: Göttingen.

Yeh, S. B., & Schenck, C. H. (2004). A case of marital discord and secondary depression with attempted suicide resulting from REM sleep behavior disorder in a 35-year-old woman. *Sleep Medicine, 5,* 151–154.

Zadra, A., & Donderi, D. C. (1993). Variety and intensity of emotions in bad dreams and nightmares. *Canadian Psychology, 34,* 294.

Zoellner, L., Foa, E., Brigidi, B., & Przeeworski, A. (2000). Are trauma victims susceptible to "false memories"? *Journal of Abnormal Psychology, 109,* 517–524.

Eight

Trauma and Dreaming: Trauma Impact on Dream Recall, Content and Patterns, and the Mental Health Function of Dreams

Raija-Leena Punamäki

INTRODUCTION

Two accounts from our field work among war-traumatized families in the Middle East evoked my interest in dreaming. Palestinian school children had been demonstrating against Israeli military occupation in the West Bank town of Hebron. One child was shot dead and two were wounded. As usual, children gathered in their schoolyard, showing victory signs and singing about national commitment and invincibility. The school headmaster sadly said: "If you really want to understand what violence and death do to these children, you should come back here in the night and hear how they scream in their sleep." An Israeli friend who spent her childhood and youth in Kibbutz where a majority of members were Holocaust survivors, recalled: "I remember the strange feeling when you, as an adolescent, were returning late home, and in every house you could hear people screaming in their sleep." Whenever, we, the postwar generation in Europe remember our childhood, one or two recall: "I still feel in my skin the terrible roaring and shouting of our father in his sleep, or can see the mother preparing the countless cups of warm milk for her sleepless spouse." Nighttime seems to create a momentum for the traumas to return and exercise their impact on human life. This chapter seeks answers to questions about how traumatic experiences, such as war and military violence, impact dreaming and whether dreams have mental health and developmental function. The analysis focuses on dream recall and content, structure, and patterns of dreaming among trauma victims.

The basic assumption of life is that human beings are rational creatures aiming at meaningfulness, integration, and happiness. Our innocent belief, whether based on science or divine order, is that humans are psychological and biologically "well-built," and mental and physiological processes ultimately serve survival, blossoming, and progress. Because we spend about one-third of our lives in sleep, it is necessary to understand whether and how dreaming quality contributes to our well-being and balance. Even more, it is important to know whether certain dream characteristics can protect trauma victims from psychological distress in life-endangering conditions.

WHY IS DREAMING IMPORTANT IN TRAUMATIC CONDITIONS?

Traumatic events are exceptionally threatening and catastrophic, and they involve a deep sense of helplessness, fear of death, and distress (American Psychiatric Association, 1994). Epidemiological studies in peaceful societies reveal multiple trauma exposures, typical being traffic and fire accidents, natural disasters, and military and civilian violence among men, and sexual and domestic violence among women (Breslau, 1998; Stein, Walker, Haze, & Forde, 1997). In unstable societies, military violence, combat experiences, human rights abuses, and witnessing or participation in killing, injury, and destruction are common sources of trauma. Both the human-made and natural disasters thoroughly impact the victims' lives.

Trauma survivors often say that "nothing was the same after that event," indicating that trauma has a comprehensive impact on their lives and overloads their normal capacity to process the painful and shattering experience. To get an idea about the exhaustiveness of trauma impact, Table 8.1 summarizes trauma-related changes in victims' cognitive, emotional, neurophysiological, and social spheres of life. Common characteristics are narrowing, fragmenting, and lack of synchrony in trauma victims' thinking, remembering, and feeling. Traumatic experiences are difficult to share and may lead to social isolation and family problems. The comprehensive and multilevel changes tell about difficulties that trauma victims face in attempting to integrate the painful and often shameful experience as part of their own life history and identity. Traumatic memories do not easily fit with experiences of normal life, and two seemingly contradictory phenomena follow. On the one hand, the unfit visual images of trauma continue to bombard the mind in the form of intrusive images, nightmares, and flashbacks. On the other hand, trauma victims tend to block out the memories, numb the related feelings and delay realization and awareness of the trauma (Brewin & Holmes, 2003; Horowitz, 1997).

Dreams are hallucinatory, complex, and temporally progressing multimodal sequences of experiences during sleep. Although they are internally

TABLE 8.1

Impact of Traumatic Experiences on Cognitive, Emotional, Psychophysiological, and Social Domains of Functioning

Levels of functioning	Trauma-related changes
Cognitive processes	
Attention	• Vigilance for threat and danger • Automatic activation of fear responses • Generalization of negative feelings into neutral cues
Memory	• Realistic and long-lasting recollections of the trauma scene • Vivid and intensive memories do not fade out • Experience as if the trauma is happening here and now • Sensory (smell, sound) and kinaesthetic (body) memories • Incoherent, inaccurate, oddly detailed reminiscences • Lack of narrative quality and verbal access to memories • Difficult to share with others
Thinking, attribution, & problem solving	• Expecting people to be unpredictable, bad, and dangerous • Perceiving environment as globally unsafe • Confused causal explanations for the event • Narrowing range of coping alternatives • Diminishing flexibility in thinking • Concentration problems
Emotional processing	
Emotion experience	• Lack of synchrony between appraisals, feeling states, and behavioral and physiological dimensions of emotion • Domination of behavioral urge to act at the expense of more reflecting emotions • Difficulty to name one's own mental and bodily feeling states
Emotion recognition & discrimination Emotion expression	• Emotion recognition biased towards fear and anger • Diminished discrimination of own and other's feeling states • Numbing versus overwhelming feelings • Negative valence • Narrowed repertoire: fear and anger dominate
Neurophysiological	
Brain functioning	• Reduced hippocampal volume • Hyperactivity of amygdala and hypoactivity of frontal areas
Neurohormonal modulation	• HPA-axis alterations: no attenuation during the day • Elevated heart beat and difficulties in soothening arousal • Acoustic startle responses
Social relations	
Family communication	• Silence: family members protect each other from painful awareness of trauma • Role reversals: children take adult responsibilities before ample maturation • Guilt: parents feel unable to protect their offspring from dangers
Human relations	• Horrific memories interfere with intimate relations • Difficulty sharing experiences • Feeling that nobody understands the traumatic experience • Social isolation

generated by the brain, they involve subjective experiences of sensations, perceptions, thoughts, emotions, and social encounters (Hartmann, 1996; Kahn, Pace-Schott, & Hobson, 2002; Revonsuo, 2000). The question concerning trauma survivors is whether processing traumatic memories in the altered conscious state of dreaming matters and, if so, how. Two opposing alternatives emerge. The dreaming is simply a reflection and continuation of waking everyday life and, therefore, the fragmented, desynchronized, and frightening trauma scenes are repeated without solution. Or, the altered nighttime state of consciousness allows the dreamer to process the painful, helpless, and shameful events emotionally, frame the overwhelming emotions and arousals cognitively, and seek a wider range of associations in order to integrate the alien horrifying experience as a part of earlier memories. In other words, the function of dreaming is a crucial question in dream research.

Posttraumatic stress disorder (PTSD) can result from failed and biased attempts to process the traumatic experience. The PTSD depicts the bewildered and conflicting states of mind that, on the one hand, involve re-experiencing the trauma in nightmares, intrusive feelings, involuntary and intensively vivid memories and flashbacks, unbidden thoughts, and repetitive behavioral impulses, and on the other hand, avoiding the trauma-related reminders, numbing feelings, blunting sensations, and denying memories. In addition, PTSD depicts trauma victims' constant vigilance for dangers and hyperarousal, which results in memory and concentration problems, oversensitivity to trauma-related cues, and startle responses (American Psychiatric Association, 1994; Horowitz, 1997). The original concept of PTSD by Horowitz (1979) understood trauma responses as the "wise psyche" struggling for balance: the intensive repetitive and intrusive trauma memories functioning as a kind of in vivo stress inoculation, and avoidance, in turn, providing the overwhelmed mind a lacuna of temporary relief and numbing. The mental processing would oscillate between intrusion and avoidance until the experiences of pain, helplessness, and shame are neutralized and no provocative and shattering memories are left to bombard the mind. Understanding trauma responses as an oscillating process aiming at balance and healing has not gained empirical support, whereas PTSD as a diagnostic psychopathology enjoys empirical and theoretical consensus (American Psychiatric Association, 1994; Yehuda, 1995).

Sleeping and dreaming seem to be especially vulnerable in trauma. Augmenting evidence shows that traumatic experiences increase distressing dreams, nightmares, and sleep disturbances among adults (for example, Koren, Arnon, Lavie, & Klein, 2002; Wilmer, 1996) and children (Nader, 1996; Qouta, Punamäki, & El-Sarraj, 2003). However, the role of dreaming in trauma is still largely undecided. The crucial question is whether alterations in sleeping and dreaming indicate emotional-cognitive processes of attempted mastery or simply equate with or predict psychopathology. We should know more about how and why dreaming changes as a consequence of trauma. Understanding how traumatic events impact dream recall, dream content, and structure, as well as sleeping architecture serve both theoretical and clinical work. The associations between trauma and dreaming evoke intriguing questions about the ways through which psychological experience interacts with biological processes such as sleeping. Clinicians need to know whether dreams are relevant for mental health and what kind of dreams can enhance psychological healing among trauma victims.

HOW DOES TRAUMA IMPACT DREAM RECALL?

People greatly differ in how frequently they remember their dreams and how salient, vivid, emotional, intensive, and complete their dream recalls are. Reasons for these differences are not, however, well understood or agreed upon (for review, see Schredl & Hoffman, 2003). The question about remembering or forgetting dreams is vital among trauma survivors, because the access to nocturnal life of dreams may either poison (Lavie & Kaminer, 1991) or protect their sleep (Freud, 1900/1953).

Research is still discrepant about the impact of traumatic experiences on dream recall, showing both decrease and increase. Trauma-related decrease in remembering dreams has been found among adult combat soldiers and Holocaust survivors and children living in conditions of war and military violence. An early study found only 50 percent dream recall of awakenings from REM sleep among Vietnam combat veterans (Kramer, Schoen, & Kinney, 1984), while normative REM sleep dream recall amounts between 85 to 90 percent (Foulkes, 1985; Nielsen, 2000). Also, in a sleep laboratory setting, Holocaust survivors had a significantly lower recall of dreams than their age-matched controls or were unaware of having dreamt at all (Kaminer & Lavie, 1991). Similarly, early research using dream diary methods confirmed decreased dream recall among Middle Eastern children exposed to military violence (Nashef, 1992; Rofe & Lewin, 1982). Children who lived in life-endangering environments showed an especially low level of remembering horrific, aggressive, and unpleasant dreams.

On the contrary, more recent research maintains that traumatic and stressful experiences increase dream recall, which has been substantiated among Vietnam veterans (Mellman, Kumar, Kulick-Bell, Kumar, & Nolan, 1995a; Ross et al., 1994a) and stressed women (Cartwright, 1983) and students (Duke & Davidson, 2002). Increased dream recall was also found among Middle Eastern children living in acutely dangerous and life-threatening conditions. Children exposed to multiple and severe traumas of losing family members and witnessing shooting, killing, and destruction more frequently remembered and reported their dreams than did less exposed children in Palestine (Punamäki, 1997) and Kurdistan (Punamäki, Ali, Ismahil, & Nuutinen, 2005). The recalled dreams were also longer among traumatized than non-traumatized children (Valli et al., 2005; Valli, Revonsuo, Pälkäs, & Punamäki, 2006). Similarly, Cartwright (1984) found that exposure to stress increased the length of women's dream reports.

WHY TRAUMA SURVIVORS REMEMBER OR FORGET THEIR DREAMS

To understand the role of dream recall among children exposed to trauma, it is wise to consider the general determinants and function of dream recall. Psychodynamic, cognitive, and neurological models are all informative in explaining both good remembering of nocturnal dreams and loss of dream recall. However, empirical testing is scarce concerning the reasons for the variation in dream recall among trauma survivors.

Psychodynamic dream researchers would explain the decrease of dream recall by repression model by Freud (1900/1953; 1920/1955) and the increase by compensation model by Jung (1974). The failure to recall dreams is associated with a human tendency to repress dream contents because they are shameful, provocative, and undesired. There is some evidence that stressful and threatening laboratory manipulations of an aggressive and sexual nature lead to a low dream recall, because this kind of dream material is typically repressed (Cartwight, Bernick, Borowitz, & Kling, 1969). Repression or suppression models are lacking empirical support generally (Domhoff, 2004) but are still used to explain lack of recalled dreams among trauma victims. They are good candidates for suppressing the memory of the dreams because of their painful, frightening, and often shameful contents.

There is evidence that children living in a violent and life-endangering environment frequently show repressive personality traits, characterized by a tendency to avoid perceiving, seeing, or thinking about the stress and danger, and that the repressive style is correlated with infrequent dream recall (Rofe & Lewin, 1982). Similarly, Terr (1981) observed that some children coped with the extreme trauma of kidnapping by repressing their memories and forgetting the experience. Traumatized children tended to develop generalized repressive personality style, which, in turn, was associated with low dream recall. Lavie and Kaminer (1991) evidenced that among Holocaust survivors, low dream recall was associated with repressive personality style and high recall with sensitizing personality. The repression model of low dream recall among trauma survivors is based on the continuity hypothesis of dreams, which argues that dreaming reflects waking experiences, personality, behavior, and cognitive-emotional processes (Domhoff, 1996, 2001; Schredl & Hofmann, 2003). The repressive personality and coping styles are visible both during the day when survivors attempt to distance themselves from their threatening and dangerous events and numb the related emotions, and in the night, when there is no dream recall.

Elevated dream recall among traumatized people can be interpreted as an urge or pressure to dream. Abundant and bothering trauma memories lead to more intensive, emotionally loaded, and vivid dreams, which are easier to remember (Cohen, 1974). Compensatory dynamics suggest that dreaming, as a cathartic state, permits painful and traumatic memories to be experienced and solved in "a safe place" and provides wider and more complex associations between thoughts and emotions than is possible during the waking life (Hartmann, 1996). The intensity of this connecting is guided by the dominant concerns of the dreamer. Accordingly, the elevation of dream work, as reflected in an increased dream recall, should occur after traumatic events when people have abundantly emotionally salient material to be processed, that is, connected with the previous memory stores.

As a support for compensatory hypothesis, research among Palestinian children in conditions of military violence and acute life threat showed that the more they used suppressive, avoidant, and denying coping modes (in the day), the more frequently they recalled their dreams (Punamäki, 1998a). One may suggest that children need twenty-four hours to work through, process, and integrate their extremely painful and frightening experiences. Suppressive and avoidant coping strategies may have served their survival and helped them to endure daytime dangers and threats. Feelings of fear, anger, and pain that children could not afford to show during the day were, however, possible to be ventilated in memorable dreams that emerged at night.

It might be fruitful to consider dream recall as a part of comprehensive emotional-cognitive regulation process among traumatized people. To survive mentally and gain a psychic balance, trauma victims must go through phases of intensified working through and repression of painful experiences, and dreaming can provide a safe heaven and perfect timing for both (Hartmann, 1991). Koulack and Goodenough (1976) suggest that there may not be a linear association between repression tendencies and dream recall, but the association depends on the emotional intensity of dream content. They hypothesize that highly affective dreams are more subject to repression, and neutral dreams are subject to interference, while moderately affective dreams are remembered, because they are salient enough, but not too threatening to be repressed.

Rather than focusing on the cathartic nature of dream content, *cognitive models* of dream recall focus on the encoding, interpretation, and retrieval processes as explanations for why dreams are remembered and forgotten. The same rules are valid in dream recall as waking time remembering. The saliency model of dream recall, for instance, states that peculiar, unusual, vivid, emotionally meaningful, and visually provocative pictures can be easily remembered (Cohen, 1974). Dreaming about a shattering and emotionally loaded traumatic experience would thus predict a high recall. On the other hand, because of intensive affect arousal and dissociation, memories of traumatic events are typically inaccurate, fragmented, and detail-focused and lack comprehensive narratives (van der Kolk & Fisler, 1995). These dream characteristics would in turn predict a low recall. Recall depends also on dreamers' cognitive style and habitual ways of processing experiences. A high level of dream recall was found to correlate with creativity (Wesley, Clark & Monroe, 1978), divergent thinking (Austin, 1971), nonverbal mode of representations, and holistic perception (Galin, 1974).

Classic cognitive memory models can help us further understand recall in conscious and unconscious states. According to the interactive memory model (Tulving, 1983), the level of remembering depends on the nature of the information and how it is encoded and maintained in memory, in addition to the circumstances that surround its retrieval. The theory of state dependent memory predicts that what has been learned in a certain state of mind or brain functioning is best remembered in a similar state (Bartlett & Santrock, 1979; Eich, 1995). Applied to the dream research, a match between the dream content and the external reality in which the dreamer is waking up would predict higher dream recall than a mismatch. Discrepancies between a dreamer's feeling and his/her waking-up mood, and between dream content and waking-up circumstances, would predict a decreased dream recall. This kind of "mood congruency" dynamics between dream emotions and morning mood was substantiated among Palestinian children in conditions of war and military violence. Dream recall was high among children whose dream atmosphere and feelings and morning mood were sad and among those whose dreams incorporated fear and terror and whose morning mood was worrying (Punamäki, 1999). Findings that decreased dream recall occurs among trauma victims whose current environment is safe and lacks traumatic reminders provide implicit evidence for the theory of state dependent memory. The dream contents of Holocaust survivors (Lavie & Kaminer, 1991) and war veterans (Ross, Ball, Sullivan, & Caroff, 1989) often were past-oriented and replicated the trauma scene, and thus were outside the realm of their current waking experience. On the contrary, frequent recalling of dreams was common among children who continued to live in life-endangering conditions that corresponded to their dream contents (Punamäki, 1997; Punamäki et al., 2005).

Other researchers remind us that dream recall depends also on interpretation and organization of dream material during sleep (Cipolli, Bolzani, Cornoldi, De Beni, & Fagioli, 1993; Cipolli & Poli, 1992). If existing memory schemes are not adequate for interpreting the burst of traumatic and intrusive contents of dream impulses, the sleep-time interpretation process is disturbed, and no coherent dream is available to be recalled on awaking. Research showed that Vietnam combat veterans with PTSD had greater difficulty retrieving specific memories in response to neutral cues than did controls. Their over-general memory refers to a diminished cognitive capacity arising from intrusive preoccupation with trauma-related memories (Zeitlin & McNally, 1991). Trauma victims may face special difficulties in organizing their memory in a narrative form and, therefore, they show diminished recall and fail to produce narratives of their dreams.

Recalling versus forgetting dreams among trauma victims should be examined as a process over time and at different stages of recovery. At the early stage of recovery, the survivor attempts to integrate the memories of traumatic scenes with earlier memories. In this integration process, dreams apparently gain more and more narrative form, which enhances remembering and increases dream recall (Cicogna, Cavallero, & Bosinelli, 1986; Cohen, 1974). In the later stage of successful recovery, the survivor gradually manages to extinguish or suppress reactivation of traumatic scenes, and there is less "emotional surge" left to be remembered and recalled (Kramer, 1991a). Accordingly, one may hypothesize a low dream recall during both the early and late stages of recovery from trauma, while a high dream recall occurs in the middle. The underlining mechanisms explaining the dream recall differ, however, in the early and late stages of recovery: a lack of narrative dream structure being salient at the beginning and diminished emotional impact at the end.

The dynamics of dream recall among trauma survivors depict the core contradiction and conflict in their lives. Traumatic events bring about a surplus of emotionally loaded and meaningful material to be processed during the night, demanding activation of dream production systems and resulting in increased dreaming and dream recall (Revonsuo, 2000). However, the painful and provocative content of dream material concurrently leads to avoidance, inhibition, repression, and suppression of these visual images, resulting in low dream recall.

HOW TRAUMA IMPACTS DREAM CONTENT AND STRUCTURE

Researchers agree that traumatic and stressful experiences are incorporated in dreams, although the mechanism through which the transition occurs is inconclusive (Barrett, 1996; Newell & Cartwright, 2000; Siegel,

1996; Strauch & Meier, 1996). Empirical analyses of contents and themes of trauma survivors' dreams are still rare, and a majority of the studies focus on self-reports of the occurrence of nightmares and posttraumatic anxiety dreams. Content analyses of trauma victims' dreams have revealed three phenomena: (1) generally negative tone and anxious, hostile, and persecuting themes, (2) lack of dreamlike characteristics of bizarreness, condensation, and shifts of place and time, and (3) domination of past traumatic scenes and repetition of horrific contents without progress and resolving.

Trauma victims tend to have negative and frightening dreams years after the trauma. Holocaust survivors reported more anxiety and persecution dreams than did controls, and their dreams frequently incorporated danger to the dreamer and direct scenes from concentration camp experiences (Lavie & Kaminer, 1991). Research showed that about one-quarter of dreams of Dutch war victims (World War II) incorporated vivid war-related anxiety, life dangers, and personal trauma (Schreuder, Kleijn, & Rooijmans, 2000). Themes of anxiety, persecution, and being haunted and suffocated are also common in dreams of victims of rape and sexual abuse (Krakow et al., 2001).

Similarly, children exposed to war-related traumatic events report dreams involving feelings of anxiety and hostility (Bilu, 1989; Levine, 1991; Masalha, 2003; Nader, 1996; Nashef, 1992). The dreams of Palestinian children living in conditions of military violence and life threat incorporated more frequently themes of anxiety, persecution, aggression, and hostility, as well as attacks and malevolence in human relationships, compared to children in peaceful areas (Punamäki, 1998b). Kurdish children who were exposed to multiple and severe traumatic events, such as a family member killed and wounded, destruction of home, and separations in family, reported dreams incorporating high levels of hostile, frightening, and horrifying themes. Typical dream contents and scenes incorporated children's own death, falling in graves and holes, and being persecuted by humans, animals, and fantasy figures (Punamäki et al., 2005).

Research by Hartmann (2001) on contextualizing images in adult trauma victims' dreams showed that their aggressive, frightening, and horrifying experiences are not directly portrayed in dreams, but emerge through associations, symbols, and metaphors. Common metaphors among combat soldiers and rape victims were, for instance, tidal waves, escaping fire, drowning, and being captured. Hartmann's research team found that the emotional intensity of dream imagery increased after the September 11th terrorist attack among American dreamers. Noteworthy enough, the post-terrorist attack dreams neither incorporated increased levels of direct negative emotions of fear and terror, nor manifested themes of attacks and images of buildings and airplanes (Hartmann & Basile, 2003).

Research in war conditions confirms that the dreams of both adults and children incorporate themes of one's own and comrade's death, being wounded, and witnessing killing and destruction. A striking characteristic of these dreams is the lack of dreamlike qualities, such as bizarreness, shifts of scenes and characteristics, and metaphoric, symbolic, and fantastic themes. On the contrary, dreams of traumatized war veterans often precisely mirrored the original traumatic scene. For instance, repetitive anxiety dreams of Vietnam veterans were exact replicas of actual combat events represented in a very vivid, realistic, and paralyzing form (Ross, Ball, Sullivan, & Cardoff, 1990; van der Kolk, Blitz, Burr, Sherry, & Hartmann, 1984). Others have confirmed that veterans' dreams contain excessively realistic military references (Esposito, Benitez, Barza, & Mellman, 1999; Neylan et al., 1998), and the same phenomenon was also found among civilian war victims (Scheuder et al., 2000). War veterans and civilian victims' dreams are portrayed as a kind of news report, consisting of emotionless, factual, "businesslike," and mundane reporting. The findings contradict Hartmann (2001), who found that trauma, although not being completely camouflaged or disguised, often received a metaphoric, symbolic, and veiled form in victims' dreams. A probable explanation for the discrepancy may be the fact that Hartmann's (2001) sample included therapy participants whose dreams apparently showed already characteristics of successful recovery from trauma.

The dreams of children living in acutely life-endangering conditions of military violence typically incorporated realistic scenes of confrontations with enemy soldiers, hiding and fleeing because of shooting, destruction of property, and various scenes of persecution. Palestinian and Kurdish children exposed to multiple and severe traumas such as losing family members, being wounded, and witnessing killing and destruction reported less bizarre, symbolic, and narrative dreams than did less-exposed children. The dreams of trauma-exposed children were mundane replications of their experiences of violence, losses, and dangers, and nightmarish fears frequently interrupted their sleeping (Punamäki, 1998b; Punamäki et al., 2005). Table 8.2 provides examples of Palestinian children's dreams. The examples illustrate how severe trauma can strip children's dreams of dreamlike, symbolic, and fantasy characteristics and replace them with mundane, factual, and emotionless scenes of violence.

The lack of dreamlike quality among children in immediate trauma accords with studies by Terr (1981, 1990), who observed children's dreams to proceed in four stages after a severe life-endangering experience of kidnapping. Immediately after trauma, children showed contentless night terrors, then their dreams frequently repeated the original traumatic scene in an

TABLE 8.2

Examples of How Palestinian Children's Dream Content and Structure Differ among Those Exposed to (a) Less Severe and (b) Severe Trauma of War and Military Violence

(a) Less severe trauma	(b) Severe trauma	Dream content and structure
I was walking in a very dark forest alone. I was afraid and tears were on my face. Suddenly, two big, black panthers came toward me and stopped. Their eyes were very sad as if they were asking me something.	I dreamed that I went to school and the bell rang. Suddenly I saw myself walking on the playground and heard shooting of the bullets. I try to run away but my legs were fixed as if from fear. At this moment I saw a bird that was wounded and was in great pain. I got hold of him in my two hands and tried to treat him, so I went slowly full of terror and fear to the water tap which was near the toilet. But I found the soldiers sitting there. I was terrified and fell unconscious. So I woke up frightened.	*Neutral and consoling dream content* *vs.* *Anxiety, persecution and horror dream*
I dreamed last night that I and my mother and my brothers and sisters and my grandmother went to the sea. We were playing and running and swimming. I dreamed that I took a fish to our house and brought it up until it became so big it didn't fit in the box any more. Then one day I came back from school to find that my mum had taken it out of the box and eaten it, thinking it was the kind of fish you eat. I woke up laughing a lot, and everyone asked me why I was laughing, but I couldn't tell them.	I dreamed that I was going to school and the streets were full of people. I saw some occupation soldiers, running among the people. I got scared I run away I fell in a deep hole, nobody saw me, I started to cry. Save me I shouted, nobody heard me, I woke up.	

(continued)

TABLE 8.2 (continued)

(a) Less severe trauma	(b) Severe trauma	Dream content and structure
I dreamed that I went to school and found the occupation soldiers in front of me. I went back home and found them in front of me. I returned to the school through alleys and entered the classroom and started to study. The teacher came, but he was not our teacher. He was a soldier. He started to write on the blackboard and the chalk fell on the floor. When he bent over to pick it up, his mask fell off. We realized that he was a soldier. Everyone was scared and ran away. The soldier caught us and beat us up. We ran to every direction, shouting, confused.	I was dreaming that a dog was running after me and I try to run faster and dog bite my arm. I dreamed at night that I fell down into a hole. I dreamed fearful dreams, as if they were nightmares. I was in darkness and forest but I don't remember the people and the things that happened there. I dreamed that snakes were outside our house.	*Complete narrative as the dream story* *vs.* *Fragmented, intrusive and contentless dream*
Last night I dreamed that I stepped out of the house to find out that it was raining outside. In the middle of the street I found a big stone, and next to it was an egg. I put the egg in our neighbor's shack. Soon it became very big and a small child came out of it. The child was laughing, but I didn't know him. I woke up thinking this was a strange dream.	I dreamed that the forest was full of giant animals like dinosaurs, dragons, lions, and tigers. I was horrified. The lion tried to eat me. I was running away but the animals blocked my way from every side. I woke up without finishing the dream, and I slept again until the morning.	*Dream involving plot and story* *vs.* *Nightmare is waking up the dreamer*

(continued)

223

TABLE 8.2 (*continued*)

(a) Less severe trauma	(b) Severe trauma	Dream content and structure
Last night I dreamed that I was travelling to France. I was crying a lot because I was going to travel. When I got to the airport, the plane was stuck and couldn't move. I was very happy and I came back to my family. My mother was in the house and she laughed at me as if she had known that I wasn't travelling. I dreamed also another dream that was scary. The monster was chasing me and he wanted to eat me. I saw him and he was really ugly. I woke up suddenly and cried. I dreamed that I was drowned in the sea and couldn't get out into the surface. The waves were high.... A big fish came near to me, I was afraid of it, but it took me on its back and carried me to the shore. I was very happy, and because of my happiness I woke up and was not worried.	I dreamed that I was carrying my brother in my hand. He fell and blood came down from him. My mother hit me and my father scolded me, and my mother said that this is the first and the last time. If you let your brother fall, I will beat you up. And she told to me: Take care of your brother. I dreamed that the occupation soldiers followed me and I was running away from them and they were running after me until they caught me. They beat me very much. My blood came down from my head and they broke my arm. The people took me to Sefad-hospital. When I become better, my friends came to visit me and told me, thanks to God that you are safe. That moment I woke up and drank water.	*Multiple emotions, both negative and positive feelings* *vs.* *Lack of emotions and alienated feelings*

(continued)

TABLE 8.2 (continued)

(a) Less severe trauma	(b) Severe trauma	Dream content and structure
I dreamed last night that my uncle S. was distributing mangos near the market . . . there was a man near him digging the earth, and there was a big sack full of mangos. He was putting five mangos in every hole. Suddenly light came from the opening of the holes, and they started to dig and a well came. I looked around me and saw that the whole world was green, full of trees. I found that the trees were burning with fire. I went to look for water and found that the well was empty. Instead of water the occupation soldiers were coming out of it. So I and my friend E. and my cousin M. and our relative H. and daughter of my uncle H. were running and running very quickly and all the people were running and running. The soldiers came and followed us and told us to stop, and the soldiers gathered around us. When I saw it I started to read verses from the Koran. When I read them, the soldiers left us and didn't do us anything. . . . After that I looked around me and saw that the fire went out and after that I waked from my dream and I was terrified.	I dreamed that we were having curfew. I went out to visit my sister in the camp. A soldier followed me, I was afraid and I ran away from him. I took a taxi, and when I entered the seat I saw the soldier was sitting in the taxi. So I ran away from the taxi and from him. But he held me and took my sister away from me. I cried and asked him to let us go.

I dreamed that I went to the beach with my father and my brothers. My mother was with us, and we had food. There was a ship which took me far away and I was about to drown but my father hurried to the place and saved me.

I dreamed last night that I went to the sea. I got a big fish, I took it to my home and cleaned it and ate it. After that I drank tea and went to sleep.

I dreamed that my father bought me a bike, I got on it and drove until I reached the school. While I was driving, I fell down from the bike, a man had seen me and told me, if you don't know how to drive a bike don't drive. I woke up from my sleep. | *Symbolic and metaphoric content and bizarre events*

vs.

Realistic and profane content and dream characters |

225

exact replication, followed by modified repetitions of the traumatic scene, and finally dreams involved symbolic narratives incorporating feelings of horror and fear in more disguised forms. We may regard camouflaging and symbolizing of traumatic material in dreams as a sign of recovery, achieved either by therapy or natural healing of dream work.

Frightening, repetitive, replicating, and recurrent dreams are sometimes considered to be synonyms of traumatic dream pattern. It involves a restatement of the vital conflict of one's life or repetition of painful and frightening trauma scenes within a narrow range and without the progression observed in the normal dream pattern (Brown & Donderi, 1986; Domhoff, 1993; Kramer, 1993). Research has evidenced the occurrence of the recurrent dream contents among war veterans (Kramer et al., 1987: Mellman et al., 1995a; Mellman, Kulick-Bell, Aslock, & Nolan, 1995b; Mellman, 1997) and other trauma victims (Breslau et al., 2004; Herman, 1992; Terr, 1990). Generally, there is little variation in people's dreaming, and similar themes are repeated both across cultures, historical times, and the lifespan of an individual (Domhoff, 1999). However, the occurrence of trauma-related repetitive dream is a more complex phenomenon. Both Freudian dream researchers (Adam-Silvan & Silvan, 1990) and contemporary cognitive trauma researchers (Brewin & Holmes, 2003) emphasize the repetition principle: the unfit, provocative, overwhelming, and traumatic experience must be encountered, remembered, and processed, as long as it is not neutralized. Only when the experience is neutralized and integrated will it cease burdening psychic energy.

Again, research is lacking about the concrete night-by-night documentation of repeated dreams among trauma victims. Our research confirmed that Palestinian and Kurdish children exposed to severe war trauma often reported nightmares that frequently interrupted the dream narratives (Punamäki, 1998a; Punamäki et al., 2005). The repetitive themes were, for instance, interaction with the deceased parent, shouting for help and realizing that no voice was coming out, and trying to flee the enemy but realizing that their feet were paralyzed or glued to the ground. Table 8.3 shows examples of repetitive dream themes across seven nights of a Kurdish girl who lost her family in military atrocities.

MECHANISMS OF INCORPORATING TRAUMA INTO DREAMS

The process of fusion of experiences into dream content is not well understood, and knowledge about the integration of traumatic events into dreams is particularly scarce. Researchers are fairly unanimous about three interdependent dream phenomena that may contribute to understanding

TABLE 8.3
Examples of Repetitious Themes in the Dreams of a 10-Year-Old Kurdish Girl Who Has Lost Her Family in War

Dream during 7 nights	Repetitive themes
1st Night: I dreamed that Mrs. Simeh [the school director, name changed] came and we went to visit my brother. Then she said to me: "We go to picnic," but then Mrs. Suzi [a caretaker in the orphanage, name changed] became angry and told us "I don't come with you." I told Mrs. Suzi "Please agree to come with us to the picnic." Then another girl came and said to us: "What happened?" We told her: "There is a problem." She became angry.	• Conflict in human relations • Negative emotions of anger
2nd Night: I dreamed that my sister Sakaria [name changed] was crying. I told her "why are you crying? " She told me "I have heart disease." Then I woke up.	• Illness
3rd Night: I dreamed that my father and my mother came to me and told me: "Change your clothes, we will go away." I cry more and more because they were bad and beat me. Then my brother came and told us "Never mind, change your clothes, if they try do bad things and hit you, I will bring you to my house."	• Conflict in human relations • Negative emotions of aggression and threat • Protective human relation
4th Night: I dreamed that my uncle came and brought me presents. Then a ghost followed me and I ran away. He said this is the end.	• Persecution and haunting by ghost • Fleeing and escaping
5th Night: I dreamed that I went to a room to wash myself. Then suddenly a ghost was present there and he didn't go away. Then I could not wash and had to wear dirty clothes. After that my caretaker came and said "Come here, I'll comb your hair, and make your head, whether it is dirty or not."	• Persecution and haunting by ghost • Protective human relation
6th Night: I dreamed that I was in a place in which nobody was present, and I had lost my mother. Suddenly a scorpion was there, and I became very unhappy because I thought that I will also die.	• Death and loss • Threat and danger • Negative emotion of fear
7th Night: I dreamed that a person was burning by fire. I was afraid. Then a man came to say that he will burn me, too. Then I lost myself.	• Death and loss • Threat and danger

how trauma is incorporated into dreams. First, dreams contain an abundance of emotional material (Domhoff, 2000; Fosse, Stickgold, & Hobson, 2001; Schredl & Doll, 1998), and second, dream content mirrors the dreamer's emotional experience of the stress and trauma rather than the actual event (Delorme, Lortie-Lussier, & De Koninck, 2002; Schredl & Hofmann, 2003; Strauch & Meier, 1996). Third, although less agreed, waking experiences are reflected in dreams, conceptualized as the continuity hypothesis (Domhoff, 1996; Schredl, 2003; Strauch & Meier, 1996).

Hartmann and colleagues (1996; Hartmann, Kunzendorf, & Rosen, 2001a; Hartmann, Zborowski, & Kunzendorf, 2001b; Hartmann, Zborowski, Rosen, & Grace, 2001c) have analyzed the meaning of the content, plot, and narrative of dreams in general and especially after traumatic experiences. They suggest that the current emotional concern of the dreamer guides and determines the images of the dreams, both what he/she dreams about and how he/she dream abouts it. In dreams, the contextualizing image depicts a powerful central theme and provides a visual and narrative presentation for a dominant core emotion of the dreamer (Hartmann et al., 2001a; Hartmann, Rosen, & Grace, 1998). The emotional intensity of the contextualized image in a dream reflects the extent of how active and unresolved versus resolved is the current emotional concern (Hartmann et al., 2001b).

Some evidence is available to indicate that the dreams of traumatized individuals include intensive contextualized images that portray vividly their core emotional concern of safety versus danger, self-respect versus humiliation, and competence versus helplessness. The intense contextualized emotional images can be understood as an urge to work trough the painful and traumatic experiences by framing them in controllable pictorial images and thematic narratives. Hartmann et al. (2001a) illustrated how trauma victims' core emotions of terror, anger, and shame were contextualized into dream images of fire, a gang of monsters, and a tidal wave. Fear can be portrayed in dream images in various threatening elements and symbols, for example, being chased, the presence of a threatening unknown figure, or falling into a deep hole.

A replication of Hartmann's contextualizing emotional image procedure substantiated that children exposed to severe military trauma showed a high intensity of emotional contextualized images in their dreams (Helminen & Punamäki, 2006). The contents of contextualized images correspond with those found earlier among adult trauma victims: being chased, falling, and being paralyzed. Severe and multiple exposures to trauma did not only increase the negative but also the positive valence of emotional contextualizing images in dreams. The intensified imagery of emotionally salient material in dreams may illustrate the reality of children whose days are filled with horrors, destruction, and near escapes from death. Children's minds must work intensively during the night in order to maintain psychological balance and integrate the core emotional concerns of fear, worry, and hope.

The process through which traumatic experiences are incorporated into dream contents may differ from the fusion of more neutral experiences, reflecting the victims' conflicting tendencies either to avoid or be overwhelmed by traumatic memories. Research shows that intensive emotional experiences of the previous day are likely to appear in the dreams during the following night (Piccone, Jacobs, Kramer, & Roth, 1977; Strauch & Meier, 1996). The occurrence of repetitious, narrowly focused, and past-oriented dreams among trauma victims hints that day residues fail to penetrate into their dreams. This was evidenced in a sleep laboratory study by Kramer (1991b). If past trauma continues to be the dominant core emotion, new daily experiences, day residues, are unable to evoke a broad arrow of memories and, therefore, dreams fail to juxtaposition the narrative elements from existing affective memory sources (Breger, Hunter, & Lane, 1971; Kuiken, Rindslisbacher, & Nielsen, 1990–1991). As a consequence, the process of integrating traumatic events with old adaptive and adequate memories fails, and the formation of novel, symbolic, and metaphoric dream narratives is prevented.

Evening mood and emotional expressions form additional mnemonic linkages, which result in dreams being formed by the fusion of a broadened array of memories. Traumatic events have a strong impact on victims' emotional responses, characterized by dominance of negative emotions such as fear and anger and lack of synchrony between feeling states, behavioral urges to act, and physiological arousals (Frijda, 1986; Näätänen, Kanninen, Qouta, & Punamäki, 1996). The conflicting and desynchronized emotional experience may explain the repetitive, fragmented, mundane, and emotionless dreams among trauma victims. Characteristic of trauma-related emotional expression is both lacking and overwhelming feeling states, reflecting concurrent hypo- and hyperemotionality. Trauma victims commonly show narrowed, avoidant, and repressive behavior patterns and minimized emotional expression (Näätänen et al., 1996; Rofe & Lewin, 1982). Repression, in turn, prevents the availability of broad arrows of memories, which is reflected in the occurrence of repetitive and mundane dreams that involve narrow memory patterns. On the other hand, trauma victims tend to pay vigilant attention to possible threatening and trauma-related cues in their daily lives. Their memory functioning is characterized by virtue of hyperaccessibilty and hypervigilance (Litz & Keane, 1989; Wolfe, 1995). In other words, the day residues and not only the past memories of trauma victims can be emotionally overwhelming and intrusive. As a consequence of assimilation of the strong emotions, dream content is characterized by intensive, threatening, and persecuting themes that are, however, monotonous and trauma-oriented.

The burden and overflow of emotion-loaded memories seem to be the core determinant of changes in dream content during adjustment to traumatic stress. Kramer's (1993) ideas about assimilative and accommodative dream functions are informative in understanding these changes. Repetitious trauma-related dreams apparently refer to an intensified dream work or attempts to incorporate overwhelming emotions into a coherent dream narrative. However, they are lacking the accommodating function, that is, transmitting the problem-solving dreams to benefit recovery process. We may hypothesize that in acute trauma, assimilating day residues and current emotional concerns is an intensified process, whereas integration, synchronization, and working through experiences in dreams are less effective. A balance between assimilating and accommodating dream functions can be considered a sign of recovery from trauma. It means that the emotional urge to dream attenuates through gradual integration of the traumatic and provocative experiences into existing memory schemes, and thus it is possible to create symbolic dream narratives that accommodate messages of mastering, consoling, and strengthening.

The question of similar versus different dynamics between waking and sleeping realities is crucial for understanding the dream content among trauma victims. Empirical evidence seems to support the continuation hypothesis of trauma-related dreams mirroring waking experiences. Evidence is scarce about possible discontinuation depicted in compensation hypothesis, suggesting that thoughts, feelings, and behavioral patterns that are neglected in waking life will find their expression within dreams. Research comparing Palestinian children's coping strategies in waking-life traumatic stress and coping themes in their dreams (Punamäki, 1998a) found evidence for compensatory dynamics in general and among severely traumatized persons in particular. Children who responded with passive, withdrawing, and emotion-focused coping modes in daytime dangers showed active, heroic, and problem-focused coping responses in their dreams, and vice versa, children whose daytime coping was active and heroic expressed fear, helplessness, and reliance during the night in their dreams.

DOES TRAUMA IMPACT SLEEP ARCHITECTURE AND DREAM PATTERNS?

Normal adults sleep six to nine hours, and their sleep involves multiple periods across the night. The sleep patterns involve, most notably, alternations of

REM sleep and non-REM or deep sleep on an approximately 90-minute rhythm, an increase in the length of REM periods, and an increase in the density of eye movements within these REM periods throughout the night (Antrobus, 1991; Aserinsky & Kleitman, 1953; Empson, 1993; Nielsen, 2000). Adults spend 20 to 25 percent of their sleep in the REM stages, latency to enter the first REM sleep stage is between seventy and one hundred minutes, and normal sleepers spend less than 5 percent of time awake in the night (Carscadon & Dement, 1989; Nielsen, 2000). The REM and non-REM sleep stages share distinct physiological (electroencephalogram [EEG], electromyographic, and electro-oculographic indicators, body temperature, and brain metabolism), cognitive (sensations, perception, and thought) and emotional (intensity and valence of dream atmosphere and feelings) characteristics and differ in the responsiveness to dream and waking stimuli, body movements, and thresholds for waking up (Hartmann, 1984; Hobson, 1990; Kramer, 1993; Ross et al., 1989).

Exposure to trauma and especially diagnosis of posttraumatic stress disorder (PTSD) seem to associate with changes in the majority of these sleep domains, although findings concerning the nature of these changes are discrepant. Considering dreaming, relations between REM and deep sleep, as well as sleep phases are of great interest. REM latency refers to the time of the onset of the first REM period and REM density to rapid eye movements per REM sleep period (Empson, 1993). The short REM latency and increased REM density are the physiological correlates of pressure to dreaming and may indicate the occurrence of trauma-related anxiety dreams (Pillar, Malhotra, & Lavie, 2000). Findings are contradictory, showing both increase and decrease in REM latency and REM density among trauma victims. Lavie, Hefez, Halperin, and Enoch (1979) found that Israeli war veterans with combat neurosis showed increased REM latency, diminished average REM sleep episode duration, and reduced percentages of REM sleep compared to healthy controls. Holocaust trauma had a similar impact on the sleep patterns of elderly survivors (Kaminer & Lavie, 1991).

Opposite results evidenced shortened REM sleep latency, increased REM density, and sleep containing more and longer REM periods among war veterans (Greenberg, Pearlman, & Gampel, 1972; Ross et al., 1994a). Similarly, stressful life events were shown to be related to shortened REM latency and increased REM density (Cartwright, 1983; Reynolds et al., 1993). Ross et al. (1994a) showed that the veterans with PTSD had a higher percentage of sleep time spent in REM, a longer mean REM period duration, as well as more heightened REM activity than the controls. However, more recent studies deny that PTSD patients show pressure to dream as indicated by decreased REM latency and time spent in REM sleep in comparison to deep sleep (for review, see Pillar et al., 2000; Bader & Schäfer, 2005). Instead, increased REM density among trauma victims with PTSD has been docu- mented in a considerable number of studies. Mellman and his research group (1995a, 1997) found intensified REM density among both PTSD vic- tims of both natural disaster and man-made trauma of war. Mellman (1997) concluded that mean measurement of REM latency may not distinguish PTSD patients from controls, but rather the very high and very low values of REM latency are typical of the PTSD group. The discrepancy illustrates the core phenomenon of PTSD, in which patients experience both height- ened arousal and awareness of trauma and inhibited consciousness of it.

Ross et al. (1994a, 1994b) proposed that PTSD involves fundamental REM sleep disturbance with the specific characteristics of elevated tonic REM sleep measures that include an increase in time spent in REM sleep, REM density, periods of longer duration, and heightened REM sleep phasic event generation, conceptualized as REM dysfunction theory of PTSD. The dysre- gulation of the REM sleep control system results in threatening anxiety dreams and repetitive replicating nightmares and increased body movements in REM sleep among trauma victims with PTSD.

Normally, the rates of body movement are closely associated with the sleep states and are under the control of a unique neural oscillator, whose activity is synchronized with the sleep stage rhythms (Pillar et al., 2000). Yet, increased body movements accompanying the nightmares, and noctur- nal motility associated with increased autonomic activity, are found among trauma victims (Lavie & Hertz, 1979; van der Kolk et al., 1984). These sleep characteristics lead to subjective complaints of severe fatigue and sleepi- ness upon rising in the morning. Lavie and Hertz (1979) propose that this represents a distinct type of sleep disorder, which they called nonrestorative sleep syndrome. It concurs with the suggestion that normally there is a decrease of emotional intensity across the night from evening to morning (Kramer, 1993), but the decline does not happen among trauma victims.

Dreaming is linked to a process of repeated arousals, and people vary in their responsiveness to them. There is evidence that trauma victims with PTSD show a lowered threshold for awaking and increased arousals during the sleep (Breslau et al., 2004; Mellman et al., 1995b). This concurs with trauma victims' subjective complaints about their easily disturbed sleep and the hyperarousal theory of PTSD, suggesting overreactive and biased process- ing of fear (van der Kolk, 1997). Again, opposite evidence shows elevated awaking thresholds among traumatized war veterans (Dagan, Lavie, & Bleich, 1991; Lavie, Katz, Pillar, & Zinger, 1998).

Discrepant results suggest that the relationship between trauma and REM sleep characteristics may vary according to the acuteness of trauma, ways of coping with traumatic memories, and the mental health status of the survivor. Hefez et al. (1987) suggested that decreased dream intensity was a typical long-term alteration in dream sequence resulting from traumatic events. People who were traumatized in the distant past showed nearly complete suppression of dream recall, concomitant with shorter REM time and low REM density. Instead, characteristic to people who were more recently exposed to traumatic experience were intense REM-related nightmares and multiple awakenings from REM sleep.

Insightfully, Pillar et al. (2000) suggested that the discrepancies found in the PTSD-related sleep architecture reveal the very phenomenon of being traumatized. Hyperarousal and a sleep-deepening mechanism may exist simultaneously. Evidence about increased sleep latency and subjective experiences of insomnia and transparent, easily disturbed sleep are true. But once PTSD sufferers fall asleep, their sleep is deeper, as evidenced by higher awakening threshold. PTSD sufferers frequently claim that they feel like they have not slept at all. This is no wonder, if there are such conflicting processes going on in the night. One may speculate that the sleep architecture of PTSD patients shows typical elements of their symptoms: memory intrusions, flashbacks, and pressure to REM sleep, combined with numbing, repressing, and avoidance. Mellman (1999) showed that victims with PTSD showed the lowest and highest levels of latency to REM sleep, so there might be the coexistence of pressure to REM sleep and dreaming, while heightened arousals during the night are inhibiting the onset of REM.

PSYCHOLOGICAL ASPECTS OF SLEEP ARCHITECTURE

The question is open whether there is a psychological correspondence in dream content and structure with the biological sleep architecture. Empirical evidence is scarce and old. The argument that "real, dream-like" dreaming is more characteristic to REM than non-REM sleep periods is substantiated in results showing that dreams become longer and their dreamlike quality (bizarreness, condensation, and shifts in time and space) increases towards the morning (Cartwright, 1983). Furthermore, emotionally loaded dreams occur more frequently at the end of sleep than at the onset (French & Fromm, 1964; Trosman, Rechtschaffen, Offenkrantz, & Wolpert, 1960). Dream contents are suggested to develop across the night. The dreams in the first half of the night tend to be more related to the dreamer's present anxieties and concern, while the following dreams relate to significant emotional experiences in the past. The morning dreams also incorporate more contemplated solutions than early dreams (Cartwright, 1977).

Some evidence is available of traumatic experiences disturbing the progress and development of dreaming across the night. Intensive dreaming is found to occur already at the beginning of the night among traumatized (van der Kolk et al., 1984) and stressed (Cartwright & Lloyd, 1994) people. Cartwright and Lloyd (1994) showed an association between the physiological signs of shortened latency to REM sleep and heightening of the dream-like quality of the dream reports collected from the first REM period compared to dreams collected during the rest of the night.

Kramer (1993) suggests that disturbing themes and tensions often accumulate alternatively with dreams discharging that tension, and subsequently the progressive-sequential dream process leads to a decrease in mood intensity across the night. However, characteristic of the trauma-related disturbed sleep is that the problem or conflict shows no resolution from dream to dream but is repetitively restated (Kramer, 1991b). Cartwright (1986) further evidenced that masochistic and negative themes even increased among divorced and depressed women between the first and last dreams during the night. As compared with the controls, stressed women also woke up frequently from a negative dream at the end of the night.

In the normal population, the recall rate of dreams occurring during REM sleep is higher than the recall from non-REM sleep dreams, and the recalled REM dreams are more vivid, bizarre, and incorporate more dreamlike contents (Porte & Hobson, 1987). However, typical for the trauma-related distorted dream process is that dreaming can also occur in the non-REM sleep (Hartmann, 1984; Kramer et al., 1984). The dream overflow to non-REM sleep may be explained by the "intensity surge" exceeding the integrative capacity of dreaming among trauma victims (Kramer, 1991a). The traumatic affect exceeds especially if the existing memory schemes are not adequate for assimilating within the usual REM time frame (Cartwright, 1983). As a consequence, the intrusive re-experiencing of the traumatic event actually is manifested in both REM and non-REM sleep (Hartmann, 1984).

To understand the realities of trauma victims, it is crucial to bring together knowledge about trauma-related changes in sleep architecture and dream recall, content, and structure. There have been some attempts at explaining the paradoxical findings of physiological sleep characteristics as correlates of trauma victims' struggles of seeking balance, meaningfulness, and safety. The idea that a psychological experience such as trauma can possibly change some aspects of sleeping is intriguing, providing an example of interaction between psychological and biological domains of life.

MENTAL HEALTH FUNCTION OF DREAMING

Different dream theorists present dreaming as a kind of homeostatic process integrating a person's sleeping and waking realities. Psychodynamic theorists understand the dreaming process as consisting of discharging emotional surge and mastering pivotal experiences (Freud, 1920/1953; Jung, 1974). Cognitive theorists admit that one possible function of dreaming involves the imposing of expressive and thematic coherence on mnemonic activation, and physiologists conceptualize dreaming as an expression of biological rhythm and balancing control over brain activation (Hobson, 2003; Hunt, 1989). All theoretical considerations of dream functions are informative for trauma research, because integration, balancing, and mastering of daytime and nighttime realities are vital for the mental health of survivors.

Integration of multiple discrepancies on different domains of life constitutes an essential element in successful recovery from trauma. Table 8.1 describes the comprehensive negative impacts of trauma on cognitive, emotional, psychophysiological, and social domains of life, revealing that fragmentation, disintegration, biases. and asymmetries were their core characteristics. Dreaming functions as a meeting point between conscious and unconscious states of mind, between waking and sleeping, between present and past, between emotional regulation and cognitive framing, and is, therefore, a good candidate for playing an important mental health role after trauma. The idea that dreaming has a mental health function suggests that certain kinds of dream recall, content, structure, and progress across a night would predict good mental health, for example, the absence of PTSD and depression, and the presence of posttraumatic growth and resiliency. One possible route for mental health function of dreaming among trauma victims would be through increased integration between these shattered mental, physiological, and social processes.

If dreaming can provide any healing potential, it must realize integration and synchrony as preconditions for full recovery from trauma. The idea that dreaming provides a state of mind for an intensive working through, rehearsal, and solving of the dreamer's current concerns and problems, including traumatic experience, is present in early dream theories. According to Freud (1900/1953), dreams are generated to protect consciousness and sleep from the disruptive effects of unconscious wishes that are realized in dreaming. The purpose of dreams is to maintain psychic equilibrium, and if dreaming is prevented or dreams lack adequate characteristics, there is an increased risk for emotional disturbances or even psychiatric illness. The perfect realization of the dream work of condensing, distorting, camouflaging, and symbolizing traumatic experiences would predict successful mastery and good mental health. However, the repetitious and mundane dreams replicating the trauma scene and lacking progress across the night provide an example of the failure to translate traumatic and painful events into new symbolized and masked narratives. This failure of dream work explains the impairment of waking-time mental processes and psychological adjustment (Adam-Silvan & Silvan, 1990; Freud, 1920/1955).

The emotional information-processing model by Breger, Hunter, and Lane (1971) suggested that dreaming allows the integration of stressful themes into an organized network of memories, and as a result, the current stress is transformed into familiar terms, which opens up possibilities for adequate and successful coping strategies. The mental health function of dreaming is to integrate affect-related information into existing memory systems that have earlier proved satisfactory in dealing with similar material (Breger, 1967).

Two contemporary dream researchers consider trauma-related dreaming as a kind of prototype of dreaming, reflecting the core attuning function of dreams of facilitating adjustment and survival, balancing shattering experiences, and integrating changing patterns according to outer and inner realities of trauma. Hartmann (1991, 1995, 2001) understands dreams as contextualized images of the dreamers' core emotional concern, and Revonsuo (2000) considers them as an evolutionarily wise process of simulation of threatening and life-endangering experiences in order to accommodate the dream solutions into better coping strategies in waking realities. The prominent dream theorists, Hobson (Hobson & McCarley, 1977; Hobson, 1990, 2003) and Domhoff (1999, 2001) are less convinced that dreaming has any psychological function, not to mention the purpose of maintaining mental health and psychic integrity. Also, others have criticized the assumption of dreams serving problem-solving and healing functions for empirical and theoretical deficits (Blagrove, 1992; Foulkes, 1982, 1985, 1990).

Based on extensive clinical, sleep laboratory, and dream diary analyses, Hartmann (1996, 2001) revealed changes in dreaming after trauma, which he interpreted as indicating attempts for psychological healing. At first, the dreams picture the trauma as it has happened, involving typically the images of extreme fear, helplessness, and terror. Then, gradually, other themes emerge involving a variety of past experiences, although dreams still contain images of the trauma. Finally, dreams increasingly contain other, everyday experiences from the dreamer's life, and both the images and emotional impact of trauma are gradually resolved and neutralized. It is also possible that the dream process fails in psychological healing. PTSD is an illustrative example in which the integrating and neutralizing process is seized up, and the person is afflicted by distressing, threatening, hostile, replicating, and repetitive dreams and posttraumatic nightmares.

One reason for the failure of integrating and neutralizing dream processes lies in the fact that trauma evokes dream images that mismatch with existing memory systems (Hartmann, 1991). The images exceed the existing memory schemes, or these schemes are not adequate for assimilating the images within the usual REM sleep and dreaming (Cartwright, 1983). The repeating dream pattern may signify attempts to solve the problem, but the mind fails to connect trauma-related thoughts, images, memories, wishes, and fears in new ways. As a consequence, disturbed sleep and subjectively bad dreams occur, which in turn predict poor mental health and psychiatric distress.

The integrative process is possible because memory and other cognitive, chemical, and neural associative processing systems in the brain are closely connected during dreaming, while they function more separately during waking consciousness (Hartmann, 1995; 2001). Both older and contemporary neurophysiological studies provide some evidence for a high "associative status of brain" in sleep. An increased hemispheric symmetry has been found during REM sleep compared with wakefulness (Lavie & Tzischinsky, 1985; Morel et al., 1991; Pivik, Bysma, Busby, & Sawyer, 1982). The dreaming state allows a regulatory function, thus the dreamer makes connections between new experiences and old schemas in an auto-associative manner (Hartmann, 1995, 1996). The process of making connections happens in neural networks, where the associations of past and recent memories are triggered by current emotional concerns. Hartmann conceptualizes dreaming as a safe place similar to psychotherapy that makes it possible for dreamers to form new and healing contextualizing images of their dominant emotional concerns and dangerous experiences. Intensive emotional contextualizing in dreams is beneficial because it enables neutralizing of trauma-related overwhelming emotions. Making connections and integrating multiple conflicting experiences may facilitate recovery from trauma and, therefore, trauma-related therapies include training for cognitive framing and emotional regulation of highly shattering and disintegrating experiences (Brewin & Holmes, 2003; Janoff-Bulman, 1989).

The Threat Simulation Theory of dreaming (TST) by Revonsuo (2000) postulates that the function of dreaming is to simulate threatening events in the form of the repeated nocturnal rehearsal, which salient neurocognitive mechanisms make possible. Activation of successful simulation and rehearsal of life-endangering experiences prepares the dreamer to perceive and avoid real threats in walking lives. The evolutionary origin of the nocturnal threat simulation and danger rehearsal refers to the life-endangering living conditions of our ancestors. When dangers such as snakes, strangers, floods, and fires were life-threatening and plentiful, survival was more probable for species whose dream production system was effective enough to select memory traces containing simulated solutions of successful escape or attack. These characteristics of trauma-related dreams are still, to a great extent, present in contemporary people's dreams, including universally negative dream themes, recurrent dream themes, bad dreams, nightmares, and posttraumatic dreams. Facing stress, trauma, and threat should activate the threat simulation mechanism in order to guarantee effective and successful coping and healthy ways of defending one's psychic integrity.

The argument that nightmares and posttraumatic dreams serve some evolutionally beneficial and balancing function has evoked controversies (Malcolm-Smith & Solms, 2004). Repetitious replicating anxiety dreams and nightmares are considered equal to symptoms of PTSD that are understood to lack any psychological healing function. The consensus about distressing dreams is along the line of Freud conceptualizing distressing dreams as failures of dream functioning as the negative, frightening, and shameful emotions break through into consciousness. Revonsuo (2000) suggests, however, that the most salient memory traces for the dream production mechanism are the ones encoding the most threatening events that are most recently encountered, often marking situations critical for physical survival and reproductive success. Consequently, the reason traumatic experiences are incorporated into dreams more effectively than other experiences indicates a mental health function. The bad dreams tend to persist and recur in dreams over and over again until neutralized, which signifies recovery from trauma.

Revonsuo and colleagues provided some empirical evidence about the activation of the threat simulation mechanism, when salient threat and dangers are present, as is the case among children growing up in life-endangering environments of war and military violence (Valli et al., 2005; 2006). The activation was evidenced by more frequent, intensive, and detailed incorporation of life-threatening events into dream narratives among severely traumatized children compared to less traumatized and nontraumatized groups. However, no research is available on whether the high activation of the threat simulation mechanism in trauma victims' dreams can protect their mental health.

It is plausible that dreams serve multiple functions, that is, they have mastering, avoiding, and compensating roles in adaptation to stress and recovery from trauma (Hunt, 1989; Koulack, 1993; Stewart & Koulack, 1993; Wright & Koulack, 1987). Mastery dreams incorporate painful scenes and feelings, and the dream atmosphere presents a continuation of the trauma victim's waking life and emotional concerns. They entail re-experiencing the trauma and associated emotions in "a safe place" of dreaming (Freud, 1900/1953; Hartmann, 1995; Perlis & Nielsen, 1993), or, in physiological terms, in a state of low brain activity and inhibition of external sensory stimuli (Antrobus, 1991; Hobson, 1990). Avoidance dreams, on the contrary, incorporate harmonious, calming, and safe scenes that provide the dreamer with consolation and compensation for traumatic experiences. They involve

coherent thoughts, positive emotions, and successful solutions that are missing from trauma victims' real life, thus alleviating their overwhelming pain
and arousal. The disruption-avoidance-adaptation (DAA) model by Wright
and Koulack (1987) depicts mastery and avoidance of compensatory dream
functions and assumes them to alternate, reflecting the process of adaptation
to the stressful experience. The alternating process of dreaming aimed at
mastery and compensation continues until the traumatic impacts have been
neutralized and the dreamer has successfully adapted to the stress.

The mood regulatory theory of sleep and dreams by Kramer (1991b,
1993) further contributes to our understanding of processing traumatic
experiences in dreams. Kramer suggests that dreaming serves a selective and
affective regulatory function by correcting the level and intensity of the person's mood. Two principal patterns of thematic dream development were
found that result in different morning mood. A progressive-sequential dream
pattern involves a problem statement that is worked on and resolved, which
then results in a positive alteration in the dreamer's emotional state. A
repetitive-traumatic dream pattern, on the contrary, involves a restating of
trauma and conflict in a narrow range without progression and without positive mood change. The problem-solving dream patterns naturally fulfill the
function of maintaining mental health. Traumatic events may thus constitute a risk for mental health through dreams failing to correct the person's
intensive negative mood, which leads to agitated morning mood and disturbed emotions. As shown earlier, the core characteristics of trauma victims' dreams are their narrow and frightening contents, fragmentation, and
physiological indicators of dysfunctional sleep architecture, as well as lack of
sequential progress across the night. Their dreams fail to restore the sleep or
integrate traumatic events into personal memory and identity. As a consequence, dreaming does not result in decreased feeling intensity and increased
sense of rest.

EMPIRICAL EVIDENCE ABOUT DREAMING AND MENTAL HEALTH

There is some consensus that the processing of waking life emotional
concerns in dreams is linked with psychological well-being (Cartwright,
Luten, Young, Mercer, & Bears, 1998; Hartmann, 1996; Koulack, 1993;
Kramer, 1993; Zadra & Donderi, 2000). Empirical evidence is scarce about
what kind of dream content, structure, and patterns would be beneficial for
successful recovery from trauma.

Findings are discrepant about whether incorporating traumatic memories
in dreams is beneficial or malevolent for mental health. On the one hand,
results show that poorly adjusted trauma victims show more dream themes

involving anxiety, hostility, and interpersonal conflicts. Holocaust survivors with severe psychiatric distress dreamt more about their past and traumatic events than the controls and better-adjusted survivors. The orientation to the past interferes with integration of present positive experiences with traumatic long-term memories (Lavie & Kaminer, 1991).

On the contrary, some evidence supports the theoretical idea that emotional working through and incorporating vital conflict and concerns into dreams predict good psychological adaptation. Breger, Hunter, and Lane (1971) showed that successful dreaming in facing a stressful event, such as surgery and childbirth, was characterized by transforming the event into the thoughts and feelings aroused by it and integrating them into an organized network of memories. Cohen and Cox (1975) showed that the more subjects' dreaming revealed "dream working" and incorporation of the stressful events (laboratory-induced horrific and shameful events), the greater was the positive affective change across the night. Cartwright (1984, 1986) showed that the adaptive dream content was characterized by a wide time perspective, incorporation of themes of self-esteem, and control over events and self in significant roles. Furthermore, long dream reports and dreams involving positive motives in the last REM periods were associated with good mental health. Cartwright (1991) was also able to specify which dream characteristics would predict later good psychological adjustment; they incorporated important human relationships and vital stressful events.

Research by Cartwright and her colleagues (Cartwright, Kravitz, Eastman, & Wood, 1991; Cartwright & Lloyd, 1994; Newell & Cartwright, 2000) is promising, because it combines both dream content and physiological changes in sleep architecture in determining beneficial dream patterns. They confirmed in a follow-up study that the physiological and psychological dream changes as a consequence of stress might signify adaptive dream function. Depressed persons with decreased REM latency and more bizarre and dreamlike quality in the first REM period had a higher rate of recovery over a period of one year than did those who showed normal REM latency and mundane dreams. They suggest that the association between more intense and bizarre early dreaming and the subsequent resolution of depression may represent a compensatory dream mechanism. This dream pattern can balance the burdening negative emotions by increasing the dreamer's coping capacity through intensive simulating of solutions that are carried out into waking life stress. The logic concurs with the theory of threat simulating mechanisms by Revonsuo (2000).

Research among Palestinian and Kurdish children in conditions of war and military violence supported the idea of intensified and compensatory dream dynamics protecting mental health. Severe and multiple exposures to trauma were not associated with PTSD, anxiety, or depressive and aggressive symptoms if children's dreams incorporated bizarre, vivid, and symbolic scenes and themes, joyful feelings, and happy endings, and the dreamer was active and the narrative was complete (Punamäki, 1998b). The results also support the hypothesis of intensified dream work serving the mental health function among traumatized children, provided that dreams incorporated positive emotions. The intensive contextualized images of dream emotions, combined with positive emotional valence, could protect children from developing PTSD and aggressive symptoms, even if they were exposed to severe trauma (Helminen & Punamäki, in press). Results are similar to those of Newell and Cartwright (2000), who found intensive contextualized images combined with positive emotions to be beneficial for stressed adults.

Elevated recall of dreams can be considered proof that the dreaming mind is intensively trying to process and work with the traumatic material (Revonsuo, 2000). Generally, bizarre, vivid, frightening, and meaningful dreams are more easily remembered (Schredl, Kleinferchner, & Gell, 1996), and high dream recall can be considered as an indicator of intensive dreaming. Research among adults confirmed that high recall of stress-related dreams is related to good mental health in the long run but not immediately (Brown & Donderi, 1993). Moreover, among Palestinian children living in life-endangering environments, high recall could protect mental health from negative trauma impact (Punamäki, 1997). Exposure to multiple and severe traumatic events, such as witnessing death, wounding, and destruction, was relatively less associated with aggressive and depressive symptoms among Kurdish children who frequent recalled and reported their dreams (Punamäki et al., 2005). The integration process of framing provocative and shattered trauma scenes into more controllable narrative is expected to result in high dream recall, which partly explains the association between high dream recall and good psychological adjustment.

The results from elderly Holocaust survivors showed the opposite dynamics (Lavie & Kaminer, 1991). The well-adjusted Holocaust survivors had considerably lower dream recall, were often unconscious of having dreamt at all, and reported less complex and less vivid dreams compared to survivors with psychological distress. Repression of painful memories and suppression as a psychological defense thus seemed to be effective in the long-run adjustment after a severe life endangering experience.

The occurrence of frequent recurrent dreams provides another example of discrepant understanding of mental health function of dreaming among trauma victims. On the one hand, the re-experiencing of the traumatic event in the form of repetitive, replicating, and emotionally loaded anxiety dreams is a hallmark of PTSD (Ross et al., 1994b; van der Kolk et al., 1984), thus indicating psychopathology and failure of dream process. On the other hand, recurrent and even repetitious dreams are understood to reveal an intensified dream work attempting to integrate overwhelming and frightening experiences as a part of personal history (Hartmann, 1998). That "psychological work" and integration process may result in positive mental health once the conflict is solved and the recurrent dreams have ceased. The timing of recurrent dreams seems to be important in determining whether they can be considered pathological or beneficial in the recovery from traumatic events. Brown and Donderi (1986) showed that recurrent dreams serve a psychological adjustment function in the long run. While recurrent dreams were related to the negative emotional status in the short run, maintained cessation of a previously recurrent dream correlated with psychological well-being. Past recurrent dreamers did not only show a better psychological adjustment than the recurrent dreamers, but they showed a better psychological adjustment than the control group and general population. The finding was replicated in a student sample (Zadra, O'Brien, & Donderi, 1997–1998) and case studies reported by Hartmann (2001).

Mental health function of dreaming must also take into account the association between continuation versus discontinuation between waking and dreaming realities. Blagrove (1992) proposed a categorization of problem-solving dreams in three types according to their affect on the waking life adjustment. Applied to trauma victims, "real problem solving" dreams create new solutions for the painful experience, which facilitates effective coping and successful recovery. "Dreams containing solutions" may be consoling and rewarding in the dream, but they do not have any positive effects on the recovery process. Finally, dreams can simply reflect the changes in waking-time emotional and cognitive processes, which are translated into dreamlike language. Again, timing is important, because recovery from trauma is a process and the mental health function of dreams apparently is different in acute and chronic stages. Stewart and Koulack (1993) suggested, for instance, that avoidant dreams would be beneficial in the acute and mastery dreams in the later recovery from trauma and stress. Exposure to trauma is a dynamic process in which disruptive mastery and pleasant avoidance dreams oscillate until adaption is successful (Stewart & Koulack, 1993). It is also possible, as Blagrove (1992) suggests, that in the acute stage of trauma, the "reflective dreams" appear in the form of repetitious anxiety and persecution themes. As the recovery proceeds, "containing dreams" appear, and finally, "real problem solving dreams" signify successful recovery from trauma.

CONCLUSIONS

Trauma has a comprehensive impact on the victim, evidenced by negative changes in social, cognitive, emotional, and mental health domains of life. It is urgent that we learn about processes that can alleviate the pain experienced by trauma victims and reveal their healing resources. Dreaming, a meeting point between conscious and unconscious states of mind, can be good for mending trauma-shattered experiences. The beneficial role of dreaming in healing trauma is based on its integrating potentials between waking and sleeping realities, present and past experiences, and emotional and cognitive processes. However, we lack consensus about the mental health function of dreaming both in general and among trauma victims. Subsequently, there is a paucity of research showing which kind of dream characteristics may protect trauma victims from suffering from PTSD, depression, and dissociation.

To understand the realities faced by trauma victims, it is crucial to bring together knowledge about trauma-related changes in sleep architecture and dream recall, content, and structure. Some evidence shows that narrative and bizarre dreams incorporating symbolic, metaphoric, and emotionally-loaded material are associated with good mental health and can even protect child development. Tragically, trauma deprives the dreamer of exactly those dream characteristics: the trauma victims' dreams are typically mundane, fragmented, persecuting, and emotionless. In other words, trauma constitutes a trap or vicious circle for victims: the more they need bizarre and narrative dreams for their mental health, the more the very trauma prevents the healing dreams.

REFERENCES

Adam-Silvan, A., & Silvan, M. (1990). "A dream is the fulfilment of a wish": Traumatic dream, repetition compulsion, and pleasure principle. *International Journal of Psycho-Analysis, 71,* 513–522.

American Psychiatric Association. (1994). *Diagnostic and statistical manual of mental disorders* (4th ed.). Washington, DC: American Psychological Association.

Antrobus, J. (1991). Dreaming: Cognitive processes during cortical activation and high afferent thresholds. *Psychological Review, 98,* 96–121.

Aserinsky, E., & Kleitman, N. (1953). Regularly appearing periods of eye motility and concomitant phenomena. *Science, 118,* 273–274.

Austin, M. D. (1971). Dream recall and the bias of intellectual ability. *Nature, 231,* 59.

Bader, K., & Schäfer, V. (2005). Trauma und Schlaf: Ein Uberblick [Trauma and sleep: An overview]. *Verhaltenstherapie, 15,* 244–253.

Barrett, D. (1996). Introduction. In D. Barrett (Ed.), *Trauma and dreams* (Vols. 1–6). Cambridge, MA: Harvard University Press.

Bartlett, J. C., & Santrock, J. W. (1979). Affect-dependent episodic memory in young children. *Child Development, 50,* 513–518.

Bilu, Y. (1989). The other as a nightmare: The Israeli-Arab encounter as reflected in children's dreams in Israel and the West Bank. *Political Psychology, 10,* 365–389.

Blagrove, M. (1992). Dreams as the reflection of our waking concerns and abilities: A critique of the problem-solving paradigm in dream research. *Dreaming, 2,* 205–220.

Breger, L. (1967). Function of dreams. *Journal of Abnormal Psychological Monograph, 72,* 1–28.

Breger, L., Hunter, I., & Lane, R. W. (1971). The effect of stress on dreams. *Psychological Issues, VII,* Monograph 27.

Breslau, N. (1998). Epidemiology of trauma and posttraumatic stress disorder. In R. Yehuda (Ed.), *Psychological trauma: Review of psychiatry* (Vol. 17, pp. 1–29). Washington, DC: American Psychiatric Press, Inc.

Breslau, N., Roth, T., Burduvali, E., Kapke, A., Schultz, L. R., & Roerhrs, T. (2004). Sleep in lifetime posttraumatic stress disorder. A community-based polysomnographic study. *Archives of General Psychiatry, 61,* 508–516.

Brewin, C. R., & Holmes, E. A. (2003). Psychological theories of posttraumatic stress disorder. *Clinical Psychology Review, 23,* 339–376.

Brown, R. J., & Donderi, D. (1986). Dream content and self-reported well-being among recurrent dreamers, past-recurrent dreamers, and nonrecurrent dreamers. *Journal of Personality & Social Psychology, 50,* 612–623.

Cartwright, R. D. (1977). *Night life. Explorations in dreaming.* Englewood Cliffs, NJ: Prentice-Hall, Inc.

Cartwright, R. D. (1983). Rapid eye movement sleep characteristics during and after mood-disturbing events. *Archives of General Psychiatry, 40,* 197–201.

Cartwright, R. D. (1984). Broken dreams: A study of the effects of divorce and depression on dream content. *Psychiatry, 47,* 51–259.

Cartwright, R. D. (1986). Affect and dream work from an information processing point of view. *Journal of Mind & Behavior, 7,* 411–427.

Cartwright, R. D. (1991). Dreams that work: The relations of dream incorporation to adaptation to stressful events. *Dreaming, 1,* 3–9.

Cartwight, R. D., Bernick, N., Borowitz, O., & Kling, A. (1969). Effect of an erotic movie on the sleep and dreams of young men. *Archives of General Psychiatry, 20,* 263–271.

Cartwright, R. D., Kravitz, H. M., Eastman, C. I., & Wood, E. (1991). REM latency and the recovery from depression. *American Journal of Psychiatry, 148,* 1530–1535.

Cartwright, R. D., & Lloyd, S. R. (1994). Early REM sleep: A compensatory change in depression? *Psychiatry Research, 51,* 245–252.

Cartwright, R., Luten, A., Young, M., Mercer, P., & Bears, M. (1998). Role of REM sleep and dream affect in overnight mood regulation: A study of normal volunteers. *Psychiatry Research, 81,* 1–8.

Carscadon, M. A, & Dement, W. C. (1989). *Normal human sleep: An overview.* Philadelphia, PA: Saunders Company.

Cicogna, P., Cavallero, C., & Bosinelli, M. (1986). Differential access to memory traces in the production of mental experience. *International Journal of Psychophysiology, 4,* 209–216.

Cipolli, C., Bolzani, R., Cornoldi, C., De Beni, R., & Fagioli, I. (1993). Bizarreness effect in dream recall. *Sleep, 16,* 163–170.

Cipolli C., & Poli, D. (1992). Story structure in verbal reports of mental sleep experience after awakening in REM sleep. *Sleep, 15,* 133–142.

Cohen, D. (1974). Toward a theory of dream recall. *Psychological Bulletin, 81,* 138–154.

Cohen, D., & Cox, C. (1975). Neuroticism in the sleep laboratory: Implications for representational and adaptive properties of dreaming. *Journal of Abnormal Psychology, 84,* 91–108.

Dagan, Y., Lavie, P., & Bleich, A. (1991). Elevated awakening thresholds in sleep stage 3–4 in war related post-traumatic stress disorder. *Biological Psychiatry, 30,* 618–622.

Delorme, M. A., Lortie-Lussier, M., & De Koninck, J. (2002). Stress and coping in the waking mid-dreaming states during an examination period. *Dreaming, 12,* 171–183.

Domhoff, G. W. (1993). The repetition of dreams and dream elements: A possible clue to a function of dreams. In A. Moffit, M. Kramer, & R. Hoffman (Eds.), *The function of dreaming* (pp. 293–320). Albany: SUNY Press.

Domhoff, G. W. (1996). *Finding meaning in dreams: A quantitative approach.* New York: Plenum Press.

Domhoff, G. W. (1999). Drawing theoretical implications from descriptive empirical findings on dream content. *Dreaming, 9,* 201–210.

Domhoff, G. W. (2000). The repetition function in dreams: Is it a possible clue to a function of dreams. Retrieved November 6, 2006, from http://psych.ucsc.edu/dreams/Articles/domhoff_2000b.html

Domhoff, G. W. (2001). A new neurocognitive theory of dreams. *Dreaming, 11,* 13–33.

Domhoff, G. W. (2004). Why did empirical dream researchers reject Freud? A critique of historical claims by Mark Soms. *Dreaming, 14,* 3–17.

Duke, T., & Davidson, J. (2002). Ordinary and recurrent dream recall of active, past and non-recurrent dreamers during and after academic stress. *Dreaming, 12,* 185–197.

Eich, E. (1989). Theoretical issue in state dependent memory. In H. L. Roediger, III, & F. I. M. Craik (Eds.), *Varieties of memory and consciousness. Essays in honour of Endel Tulving* (pp. 331–354). Hillsdale, NJ: Lawrence Erlbaum Publishers.

Empson, J. (1993). *Sleep and dreaming* (2nd Rev. Ed.). New York: Harvester Wheatsheaf.

Esposito, K., Benitez, A., Barza, L., & Mellman, T. (1999). Evaluation of dream content in combat-related PTSD. *Journal of Traumatic Stress, 6,* 681–687.

Fosse, R., Stickgold, R., & Hobson, J. A. (2001). The mind in REM sleep: Reports of emotional experience. *Sleep, 24,* 947–955.

Foulkes, D. (1982). *Children's dreams: Longitudinal studies.* New York: Wiley and Sons.

Foulkes, D. (1985). *Dreaming: A cognitive-psychological analysis.* Hillsdale, NJ: Lawrence Erlbaum Associates.

Foulkes, D. (1990). Dreaming and consciousness. *European Journal of Cognitive Psychology, 2,* 39–55.

French, T. M. & Fromm, E. (1964). *Dream interpretation: A new approach.* New York: Basic Books.

Freud, S. (1953). The interpretation of dreams. In J. Strachey (Ed. and Trans.), *The standard edition* (Vols. 4 and 5). London: Hogarth Press. (Original work published 1900)

Freud, S. (1955). Beyond the pleasure principle. In J. Strachey (Ed. and Trans.), *The standard edition* (Vol. 18). London: Hogarth Press. (Original work published 1920)

Frijda, N. (1986). *The emotions.* New York: Cambridge University Press.

Galin, D. (1974). Implications for psychiatry of left and right cerebral specialization. *Archives of General Psychiatry, 31,* 572–583.

Greenberg, R., Pearlman, C., & Gampel, D. (1972). War neuroses and the adaptive function of REM sleep. *British Journal of Medical Psychology, 45,* 7–33.

Hartmann, E. (1984). *The nightmare: The psychology and biology of terrifying dreams.* New York: Basic Books.

Hartmann, E. (1991). *Boundaries in the mind: A new psychology of personality.* New York: Basic Books.

Hartmann, E. (1995). Making connections in a safe place: Is dreaming psychotherapy? *Dreaming, 5,* 213–228.

Hartmann, E. (1996). Outline for a theory on the nature and functions of dreaming. *Dreaming, 6,* 147–170.

Hartmann, E. (1998). *Dreams and nightmares: The new theory on the origin and meaning of dreams* (Rev. paperback ed.). New York: Plenum Press.

Hartmann, E. (2001). *Dreams and nightmares. The origin and meaning of dreams* (2nd ed.). Cambridge, Mass: Perseus Publishing.

Hartmann E., & Basile, R. (2003). Dream imagery becomes more intense after 9/11/01. *Dreaming, 13,* 61–66.

Hartmann, E., Kunzendorf, R., Rosen, R., & Grace, N. (2001a). Contextualizing images in dreams and daydreams. *Dreaming, 11,* 97–104.

Hartmann, E., Rosen, R., & Grace, N. (1998). Contextualizing images in dreams: More frequent and more intense after trauma. *Sleep, 21, suppl,* 284.

Hartmann, E., Zborowski, M., & Kunzendorf, R. (2001b). The emotion pictured by a dream: An examination of emotions contextualized in dreams. *Sleep & Hypnosis, 3,* 33–43.

Hartmann, E., Zborowski, M., Rosen, R., & Grace, N. (2001c). Contextualizing images in dreams: More intense after abuse and trauma. *Dreaming, 11,* 115–126.

Hefez, A., Metz, L., & Lavie, P. (1987). Long-term effects of extreme situational stress on sleep and dreaming. *American Journal of Psychiatry, 144,* 344–347.

Helminen, E., & Punamäki, R.-L. (2006). Emotional images in children's dreams: The impact of political violence and mental health function. Manuscript submitted for publication.

Herman, J. L. (1992). *Trauma and recovery.* New York: Basic Books.

Hobson, J. A. (1990). Sleep and dreaming. *Journal of Neuroscience, 10,* 371–382.

Hobson, J. A. (2003). *Dreaming: An introduction to the science of sleep.* Oxford: Oxford University Press.

Hobson, J., & McCarley, R. (1977). The brain as a dream state generator: An activation-synthesis hypothesis of the dream process. *The American Journal of Psychiatry, 134,* 1335–1348.

Horowitz, M. J. (1979). Psychological response to serious life events. In D. M. W. V. Hamilton (Ed.), *Human stress and cognition: An information processing approach* (pp. 235–263). Chichester, United Kingdom: John Wiley & Sons.

Horowitz, M. J. (1997). *Stress response syndromes* (3rd ed.). Northvale, NJ: Jason Aronson.

Hunt, H. T. (1989). *The multiplicity of dreams: A cognitive psychological perspective.* New Haven, CT: Yale University Press.

Janoff-Bulman, R. (1989). Assumptive words and the stress of traumatic events: Application of the schema construct. *Social Cogniton*, 113–136.

Jung, C. (1974). *Dreams*. Princeton, NJ: Princeton University Press.

Kahn, D., Pace-Schott, E. F., & Hobson, J. A. (2002). Emotion and cognition: Feeling and character identification in dreaming. *Consciousness and Cognition, 11*, 34–50.

Kaminer, H., & Lavie, P. (1991). Sleep and dreaming in Holocaust survivors: Dramatic decrease in dream recall in well-adjusted survivors. *Journal of Nervous and Mental Disease, 179*, 664–669.

Koren, D., Arnon, I., Lavie, P. & Klein, E. (2002). Sleep complaints as early predictors of posttraumatic stress disorder: A 1-year prospective study of injured survivors of motor vehicle accidents. *American Journal of Psychiatry, 159*, 855–657.

Koulack, D. (1993). Dreams and adaption to contemporary stress. In A. Moffit, M. Kramer, & R. Hoffman (Eds.), *The function of dreaming* (pp. 321–340). Albany: SUNY Press.

Koulack, D. & Goodenough, D. R. (1976). Dream recall and dream recall failure: An arousal-retrieval model. *Psychological Bulletin, 83*, 975–984.

Krakow, B., German, A., Warner, T. D., Schrader, R., Koss, M., Hollifield, M., et al. (2001). The relationship of sleep quality and posttraumatic stress to potential sleep disorders in sexual assault survivors with nightmares. *Journal of Traumatic Stress, 14*, 647–655.

Kramer, M. (1991a). The nightmare: A failure in dream function. *Dreaming, 1*, 277–285.

Kramer, M. (1991b). Dream translation: A nonassociative method for understanding the dream. *Dreaming, 1*, 147–159.

Kramer, M. (1993). The mood regulatory function of sleep. In A. Moffit, M. Kramer, & R. Hoffman (Eds.), *The function of dreaming* (pp. 139–195). Albany, NY: SUNY Press.

Kramer, M. Schoen, L. S., & Kinney, L. (1984). The dream experience in dream-disturbed Vietnam veterans. In B. A. Van der Kolk, (Ed.), *Post-traumatic stress disorder: Psychological and biological sequelae* (pp. 204–211). Washington, DC: American Psychiatric Press.

Kuiken, D., Rindlisbacher, P., & Nielsen, T. (1990–1991). Feeling expressions and the incorporation of presleep events into dreams. *Imagination, Cognition & Personality, 10*, 157–166.

Lavie, P., Hefez, A., Halperin, G., & Enoch, D. (1979). Long-term effects of traumatic war-related events on sleep. *American Journal of Psychiatry, 136*, 175–178.

Lavie, P., & Hertz, G. (1979). Increased sleep motility and respiration rates in combat neurotic patients. *Biological Psychiatry, 14*, 983–987.

Lavie, P., & Kaminer, H. (1991). Dreams that poison sleep: Dreaming in Holocaust. *Dreaming, 1*, 11–21.

Lavie, P., Katz, N., Pillar, G., & Zinger, Y. (1998). Elevated awaking thresholds in sleep stage 3–4 in war related post-traumatic stress disorder. *Biological Psychiatry, 44*, 1060–1065.

Lavie, P., & Tzischinsky, O. (1985). Cognitive asymmetry and dreaming: Lack of relationship. *American Journal of Psychology, 98*, 53–361.

Levine, J. B. (1991). The role of culture in the representation of conflict in dreams: A comparison of Bedouin, Irish, and Israeli children. *Journal of Cross-Cultural Psychology, 22*, 472–490.

Litz, B. T., & Keane, T. M. (1989). Information processing in anxiety disorder: Application to the understanding of posttraumatic stress disorder. *Clinical Psychology Review*, 9, 243–257.

Malcolm-Smith, S., & Solms, M. (2004). Incidence of threat in dreams: A response to Revonsuo's Threat Simulation Theory. *Dreaming, 14*, 220–229.

Masalha, S. (2003). Children and violent conflict: A look at the inner world of Palestinian children via their dreams. *Palestine-Israel Journal of Politics, Economics & Culture, 10*, 62.

Mellen, R. R., Duffey, T. H., & Craig, S. M. (1993). Manifest content in the dreams of clinical populations. *Journal of Mental Health & Counseling, 15*, 170–183.

Mellman, T. A. (1997). Psychobiology of sleep disturbances in posttraumatic stress disorders. In R. Yehuda & A. C. McFarlane (Eds.), *Psychobiology of posttraumatic stress diorder. Annals of the New York Academy of Science* (Vol. 821; pp. 142–149). New York: The New York Academy of Science.

Mellman, T. A., Kulick-Bell, R. L., Aslock, L. E., & Nolan, B. (1995b). Sleep events among veterans with combat-related posttraumatic stress disorder. *American Journal of Psychiatry, 152*, 110–115.

Mellman, T. A., Kumar, A., Kulick-Bell, R. L., Kumar, M., & Nolan, B. (1995a). Nocturnal/daytime urine noradrenergic measure and sleep in combat-related PTSD. *Biological Psychiatry, 38*, 174–179.

Mellman, T. A., Nolan, B., Hebding, J., Kulick-Bell, R. L., & Dominguez, R. (1997). A polysomnic comparison of veterans with combat-related PTSD, depressed men, and non-ill controls. *Sleep, 20*, 46–51.

Morel, C. R., Hoffmann, R. F., & Moffitt, A. R. (1991). The electrophysiological correlates of dream recall and nonrecall from stage 2 sleep. *Canadian Journal of Psychology, 45*, 140–147.

Näätänen, P., Kanninen, K., Punamäki, R-L, & Qouta, S. (2002). Trauma-related emotional patterns and their association with post-traumatic and somatic symptoms. *Anxiety, Stress, & Coping, 13*, 1–17.

Nader, K. (1996). Children's traumatic dreams. In D. Barrett (Ed.), *Trauma and dreams* (pp. 9–24). Cambridge, MA: Harvard University Press.

Nashef, Y. (1992). *The psychological impact of the Intifada on Palestinian children living in refugee camps in the West Bank, as reflected in their dreams, drawings and behaviour*. Frankfurt am Main: Peter Lang.

Newell, P. T., & Cartwright, R. D. (2000). Affect and cognition in dreams: A critique of the cognitive role in adaptive dream functioning and support for associative models. *Psychiatry, 63*, 34–44.

Neylan, T. C., Marmar, C. R., Melzler, T. J., Weiss, D. S., Zatzick, D. F., Delucchi, K. L., et al. (1998). Sleep disturbances in the Vietnam generation: Findings from a nationally representative sample of male Vietnam veterans. *American Journal of Psychiatry, 155*, 929–933.

Nielsen, T. A. (2000). A review of mentation in REM and NREM sleep: "Convert" REM sleep as a possible reconciliation between two opposing models. *Behavioral and Brain Sciences, 23*, 851–866.

Perlis, M. L., & Nielsen, T. A. (1993). Mood regulation, dreaming and nightmares: Evaluation of desensitization function for REM sleep. *Dreaming, 3*, 243–256.

Piccone, P., Jacobs, G., Kramer, M., & Roth, T. (1977). The relationship between daily activities, emotions and dream content. *Sleep Research, 6,* 133.

Pillar, G., Malhotra, A., & Lavie, P. (2000). Post-traumatic stress disorder and sleep: What a nightmare! *Sleep Medicine Reviews, 4,* 183–200.

Pivik, R. T., Bysma, F., Busby, K., & Sawyer, S. (1982). Interhemispheric EEG changes: Relationship to sleep and dreams in gifted adolescents. *Psychiatric Journal of the University of Ottawa, 7,* 56–76.

Porte, H. S., & Hobson, J. A. (1987). Bizarreness in REM and NREM sleep reports. *Sleep Research, 16,* 81.

Punamäki, R.-L. (1997). Determinants and mental health effects of dream recall among children living in traumatic conditions. *Dreaming 7,* 235–263.

Punamäki, R.-L. (1998a). Correspondence between waking-time coping and dream content. *Journal of Mental Imagery, 22,* 147–164.

Punamäki, R.-L. (1998b). The role of dreams in protecting psychological well-being in traumatic conditions. *International Journal of Behavioral Development, 22,* 559–588.

Punamäki, R.-L. (1999). The relationship of dream content and changes in daytime mood in traumatized vs. non-traumatized children. *Dreaming, 9,* 213–233.

Punamäki, R.-L., Ali, K. J., Ismahil, K. H., & Nuutinen, J. (2005). Trauma, dreaming, and psychological distress among Kurdish children. *Dreaming, 15,* 178–194.

Qouta, S., Punamäki, R.-L., & Sarraj, E. E. (2003). Prevalence and determinants of PTSD among Palestinian children exposed to military violence. *European Child & Adolescent Psychiatry, 12,* 265–272.

Revonsuo, A. (2000). The reinterpretation of dreams: An evolutionary hypothesis of the function of dreaming. *Behavioral and Brain Sciences, 23,* 877–901; discussion 904–1121.

Reynolds, C. F., Hoch, C. C., Buysse, D. J., Houck, P. R., Schlernitzauer, M., Pasternak, R. E., et al. (1993). Sleep after spousal bereavement: A study of recovery from stress. *Biological Psychiatry, 34,* 791–797.

Rofe, Y., & Lewin, I. (1982). The effect of war environment on dreams and dream habits. In N. A. Milgram (Ed.), *Stress and anxiety* (Vol. 8, pp. 67–79). Washington, DC: Hemisphere Publishing Corporation.

Ross, R. J., Ball, W. A., Dinges, D. F., Kribbs, N. B., Morrison, A. R., Silver, S. M., et al. (1994a). Rapid eye movement sleep disturbance in posttraumatic stress disorder. *Biological Psychiatry, 35,* 195–202.

Ross, R. J., Ball, W. A., Dinges, D. F., Kribbs, N. B., Morrison, A. R., Silver, S. M., et al. (1994b). Motor dysfunction during sleep in posttraumatic stress disorder. *Sleep, 17,* 723–32.

Ross, R. J., Ball, W. A., Sullivan, K. A., & Caroff, S. N. (1989). Sleep disturbance as the hallmark of posttraumatic stress disorder. *American Journal of Psychiatry, 146,* 797–707.

Ross, R. J., Ball, W. A., Sullivan, K. A., & Caroff, S. N. (1990). Sleep disturbance in posttraumatic stress disorder. *American Journal of Psychiatry, 147,* 374.

Schredl, M. (2003). Continuity between waking and dreaming: A proposal for a mathematical model. *Sleep & Hypnosis, 5,* 38–52.

Schredl, M., & Doll, E. (1998). Emotions in diary dreams. *Consciousness and Cognition, 7,* 634–646.

Schredl, M., & Hofmann, F. (2003). Continuity between waking activities and dream activities. *Consciousness and Cognition, 12,* 298–308.

Schredl, M., Kleinferchner, P., & Gell, T. (1996). Dreaming and personality: Thick vs. thin boundaries. *Dreaming, 6,* 219–233.

Schreuder, B. J., Kleijn, W. C., & Rooijmans, H. G. (2000). Nocturnal re-experiencing more than forty years after war trauma. *Journal of Traumatic Stress, 13,* 453–463.

Siegel, A. (1996). Dreams of firestorm survivors. In D. Barrett (Ed.), *Trauma and dreams* (159–176). Cambridge, MA: Harvard University Press.

Stein, M. B., Walker, J. R., Haze, A. L., & Forde, D. R. (1997). Full and partial post-traumatic stress disorder: Findings from a community survey. *American Journal of Psychiatry, 154,* 1114–1119.

Stewart, D. W., & Koulack, D. (1993). The function of dreams in adaption to stress over time. *Dreaming, 3,* 259–268.

Strauch, I., & Meier, B. (1996). *In search of dreams results of experimental dream research.* Albany, NY: State University of New York Press.

Terr, L. (1981). Psychic trauma in children: Observations following the Chowchilla school-bus kidnapping. *American Journal of Psychiatry, 138,* 15–19.

Terr, L. (1990). *Too scared to cry.* New York: Basic Books.

Trosman, H., Rechtschaffen, A., Offenkrantz, W., & Wolpert, E. (1960). Studies in psychophysiology of dreams IV: Relation among dreams in sequence. *Archives of General Psychology, 3,* 602–607.

Tulving, E. (1983). *Elements of episodic memory.* Oxford: Oxford University Press.

Valli, K., Revonsuo, A., Pälkäs, O., Ismahil, K. H., Ali, K. J., & Punamäki, R-L. (2005). The Threat Simulation Theory of the evolutionary function of dreaming: Evidence from dreams of traumatized children. *Consciousness & Cognition, 14,* 188–218.

Valli, K., Revonsuo, A., Pälkas, O., & Punamäki, R. (2006). The effect of trauma on dream content: A field study of Palestinian children. *Dreaming, 16, 63–87.*

van der Kolk, B. (1987). *Psychological trauma.* Washington, DC: American Psychiatric Press.

van der Kolk, B. (1997). The psychobiology of posttraumatic stress disorder. *Journal of Clinical Psychiatry, 58*(Suppl. 9), 16–24.

van der Kolk, B., Blitz, R., Burr, W., Sherry, S., & Hartmann, E. (1984). Nightmares and trauma: A comparison of nightmares after combat with lifelong nightmares in veterans. *American Journal of Psychiatry, 141,* 187–190.

van der Kolk, B., & Fisler, R. (1995). Dissociation and the fragmentary nature of traumatic memories. Overview and exploratory study. *Journal of Traumatic Stress, 8,* 505–525.

Wesley, H. S., Clark, P. M., & Monroe, J. L. (1978). Dream reports of subjects with high and low in creativity ability. *Journal of General Psychology, 99,* 205–211.

Wilmer, H. A. (1996). The healing nightmare: War dreams of Vietnam veterans. In D. Barrett (Ed.), *Trauma and dreams* (pp. 85–99). Cambridge, MA: Harvard University Press.

Wolfe, J. (1995). Trauma, traumatic memory, and research: Where do we go from here. *Journal of Traumatic Stress, 8,* 717–726.

Wright, J., & Koulack, D. (1987). Dreams and contemporary stress: A disruption-avoidance adaptation model. *Sleep, 10,* 172–179.

Yehuda, R. (1995). Conflict between current knowledge about posttraumatic stress disorder and its original conceptual basis. *American Journal of Psychiatry, 152,* 1705–1713.

Zadra, A. L., & Donderi, D. C. (2000). Nightmares and bad dreams: Their prevalence and relationship to well-being. *Journal of Abnormal Psychology, 109,* 273–281.

Zadra, A. L., O'Brien, S., & Donderi, D. C. (1997–1998). Dream content, dream recurrence and well-being: A replication with a younger sample. *Imagination, Cognition & Personality, 17,* 293–311.

Zeitlin, S. B., & McNally, R. J. (1991). Implicit and explicit memory bias for threat in post-traumatic stress disorder. *Behaviour Research & Therapy, 29,* 451–457.

Nine

Nightmares, Dreaming, and Emotion Regulation: A Review

Tore Nielsen and Jessica Lara-Carrasco

INTRODUCTION

A satisfactory explanation of nightmares remains elusive. Theorists since Freud have speculated on mechanisms that produce nightmares, but no single, widely accepted explanation has emerged (see Nielsen & Levin, 2007b; Levin & Nielsen, 2007). This continuing uncertainty stems, in part, from the fact that nightmares, like dreams more generally, are expressions of human emotional memory—which itself is a complex and intransigent phenomenon. The inner workings of emotional memory have yet to be completely decoded, and the transformations of emotional memory that produce nightmares are even less well understood. This chapter provides a brief survey of theories and empirical research that have addressed the notion that dreaming serves an emotional regulation function and that nightmares are expressions of this function. We further suggest new directions for exploring nightmares and propose that emotional function may be linked especially to the socioemotional imagery of dreaming.

In the clinical literature, the emotional nature of nightmares is emphasized as a defining criterion. Nightmares are described as emotionally disturbing and highly realistic mental experiences that arise from rapid eye movement (REM) sleep (and occasionally from Stage 2 sleep) and are clearly recalled (American Academy of Sleep Medicine, 2005; American Psychiatric Association, 2000). The emotional component of nightmares typically consists of anxiety, fear, or terror, although other dysphoric emotions such as anger and sadness also occur less frequently (Belicki & Cuddy, 1991; Zadra, Pilon, & Donderi, 2006). These emotions are typically embedded in contexts that portray imminent danger to the individual. Idiopathic nightmares, for which the specific causes are unknown, are now distinguished from posttraumatic nightmares, which contain and cause a very high degree of emotional distress and are frequently comorbid with posttraumatic stress disorder (PTSD) (American Academy of Sleep Medicine, 2005; American Psychiatric Association, 2000). In sum, the clinical severity of nightmares is closely linked to their emotional content.

Epidemiological studies (Belicki & Belicki, 1982; Bixler, Kales, Soldatos, Kales, & Healy, 1979; Haynes & Mooney, 1975; Levin, 1994; Ohayon, Morselli, & Guilleminault, 1997) indicate that nightmares occur weekly among 2 to 6 percent of the population. Contrary to popular belief, frequent nightmares are not prevalent among preschoolers (Simard, Nielsen, Tremblay, Boivin, & Montplaisir, 2006) but become more prevalent in later childhood and adolescence (American Psychiatric Association, 2000; Fisher, Pauley, & McGuire, 1989; MacFarlane, Allen, & Honzik, 1954; Mindell & Barrett, 2002; Nielsen, Laberge, Tremblay, Vitaro, & Montplaisir, 2000; Partinen, 1994; Salzarulo & Chevalier, 1983; Simonds & Parraga, 1982; Vela-Bueno et al., 1985). They are also not prevalent in elderly populations (Nielsen & Levin, 2005; Partinen, 1980, 1994; Salvio, Wood, Schwartz, & Eichling, 1992; Wood, Bootzin, Quan, & Klink, 1993). A genetic influence has been described (Hublin, Kaprio, Partinen, & Koskenvuo, 1999) and a substantial gender difference demonstrated, with females at all ages reporting nightmares more often than males (Claridge, Clark, & Davis, 1997; Feldman & Hersen, 1967; Hartmann, 1984; Hersen, 1971; Hublin et al., 1999; Levin, 1994; Nielsen & Levin, 2005; Nielsen et al., 2000; Ohayon et al., 1997; Schredl & Pallmer, 1998; Tanskanen et al., 2001). A large literature, not reviewed here (for reviews see Levin & Nielsen, 2007; Spoormaker, Schredl, & Bout, 2005), is consistent in demonstrating that both the frequency of nightmares and the distress caused by them are associated with a variety of pathologies, symptoms, and personality characteristics that share the common attribute of emotional distress.

Considered together, these findings support the prominent clinical view that nightmares are a common emotional disturbance. However, many nightmare theorists go further, considering them to be implicated in a functional system of emotional regulation.

THEORIES ABOUT NIGHTMARES AND EMOTION REGULATION

A majority of nightmare theories converge on the view that a principal function of dreaming is the regulation of emotion and that some alteration of this emotion regulation leads to nightmares. Freud (1900/1953) stimulated subsequent theorists to broaden their conception of the emotional function of dreaming by suggesting that nightmares constitute a masochistic variation of wish fulfillment, that is, the preservation of sleep by containment of libidinally linked anxiety. Although few neopsychoanalytic models (apart from Jones, 1951) reflected such a strictly sex-centric interpretation of his nightmare theory, most nevertheless did maintain Freud's emphasis on affect transformation. For example, adaptive functions of nightmares have been described as assimilating repressed anxiety (Fisher, Byrne, Edwards, & Kahn, 1970) or transforming shame into fear (Lansky & Bley, 1995). Nightmares have also been considered as emotionally maladaptive, for example, as failing to master trauma (Greenberg, Pearlman, & Gampel, 1972). The theme of emotion regulation recurs in models of nightmare etiology to the present day.

Charles Fisher and his colleagues at the Mount Sinai Hospital in New York (Fisher et al., 1970) examined such psychoanalytical speculations about emotion regulation by recording nightmare sufferers polysomnographically in the sleep laboratory. Their recordings revealed that nightmares occur primarily during REM sleep (very occasionally during Stage 2 sleep) and are accompanied by less autonomic activation than might be expected from subjects' accounts of the fear and anxiety they felt during the nightmares. To illustrate, twelve of twenty recorded nightmares involved mild, moderate, or marked levels of anxiety yet were associated with *no* concomitant increases in respiratory, cardiac, or eye movement indicators of autonomic activity (see Figure 9.1). Similarly low levels of activation were found in our study of nightmares that occurred spontaneously in the laboratory to otherwise healthy subjects (Nielsen & Zadra, 2005). This apparent separation of fearful dream imagery from its psychophysiological concomitants prompted Fisher and colleagues (1970) to propose a mechanism akin to the psychoanalytic conceptions popular at the time. He suggested that REM dreaming possesses a mechanism for modulating affect by "desomatizing" anxious dream imagery of its physiological concomitants (p. 770). Similar to Freud's sleep-preservation function, Fisher suggested that desomatization preserves REM sleep by diminishing the intensity of anxiety and its self-perpetuation (at times, to panic levels) and contributing to the mastery of traumatic experiences (Fisher et al., 1970). Severe nightmares thus occur when anxiety exceeds REM sleep's capacity to contain it, and the desomatization mechanism breaks down.

Speculations similar to these appeared sporadically in the literature shortly after publication of this landmark work; for example, a short note was published on a desensitization function of dreaming (Beavers, 1973) as well as an empirical study on a speculative anxiety-extinction function of

FIGURE 9.1

Levels of anxiety (ANX) and autonomic (ANS) activity in 20 laboratory recorded nightmares (11 subjects); 12 of the nightmares (white
bars) show no ANS activity despite mild to marked levels of anxiety
in the dream content—suggesting that anxious dream imagery may
be stripped of its autonomic correlates.

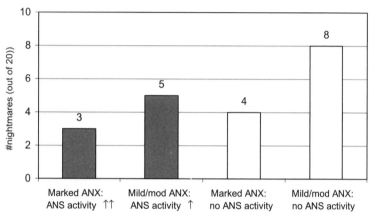

Source: Fisher et al., 1970.

nightmares (Haynes & Mooney, 1975). Haynes and Mooney proposed an
extinction function by which cognitive exposure to fear-inducing stimuli
during nightmares extinguishes fear responses over time in a manner similar
to implosion therapy. In a similar vein, a desensitization function was suggested for the eye movements of REM sleep (Shapiro, 1989; Stickgold,
2002) and for REM sleep muscle atonia (Nielsen, 1991; Nielsen, Kuiken, &
McGregor, 1989). Some evidence was also consistent with the notion that
dream emotion is inhibited by REM sleep processes related to the orienting
response (Nielsen et al., 1989). This notion was further expanded upon
(Perlis & Nielsen, 1993) with the suggestion that anxious dream imagery is
desensitized during REM sleep by the pairing of dysphoric dream imagery
and atonia of the musculature in a manner analogous to systematic desensitization therapy. From this perspective, nightmares reflect either interruptions of the desensitization process (producing waking sensitization and
distress) or amplification of it (producing an effect similar to flooding
therapy).

Investigation of an emotion regulation function for dreaming was under-
taken for several decades by Milton Kramer, then of the Bethesda Hospital
Sleep Center in Cincinnati (Kramer, 1991, 1993, 2006). Kramer characterized

the physiological profile of each REM sleep period as consistent with an affective "surge" unfolding over time, and the psychological accompaniment of dream content as a mechanism for adaptively regulating or "containing" this surge. The result is a measurable evening-to-morning improvement in mood. Functional containment of the affective surge consists of decreasing affect intensity and variability within a dream series that unfolds over successive REM periods of the night—a so-called "progressive-sequential" pattern of emotional problem-solving. This pattern is distinguished from a "repetitive-traumatic" pattern during which an emotional conflict is simply stated and restated but with no adaptive change in affect. Nightmares occur when the capacity of dreaming to assimilate the emotional surge in this fashion is exceeded.

Although the physiological description of REM sleep as surge-like remains debatable,[1] evidence that dreams are influenced by presleep thoughts and emotions (Kramer, 1993; Nielsen, Kuiken, Alain, Stenstrom, & Powell, 2004; Piccione, Thomas, Roth, & Kramer, 1976) and that dreams as related to waking state mood the next day (Kramer, 1982) is consistent with the claim that intervening dream activity regulates mood across the night. More specific evidence that dreaming is causally implicated in this regulation is still mixed. One pilot study (Kramer & Roth, 1973b) employing only two subjects each sleeping twenty nights (four awakenings for recall/night) demonstrated that evening-to-morning changes in Clyde Mood Scale (CMS) scores correlated significantly with Hall and Van de Castle ratings of the intervening dream content. Most (92 percent) of the fifty-four significant correlations uncovered implicated either ratings of non-self characters or scores on the CMS Unhappiness subscale; 26 percent of the correlations were specifically between character ratings and the CMS Unhappiness subscale. In contrast, CMS Sleepiness scores (but not Unhappiness scores) correlated significantly with intervening measures of sleep physiology, suggesting that dreaming, not sleep, is necessary for the regulation of affect across the night (whereas intervening sleep regulates sleepiness feelings). The findings were replicated in a larger study of twelve college students on the same twenty-night protocol (Kramer & Roth, 1980). In this case, a number of ratings of intervening dream content were again correlated with CMS subscale ratings, and again, a disproportionate number of the relationships was between character scale ratings and CMS Unhappiness subscale scores (Kramer, 1993). However, a further replication study by Kramer's group failed to replicate the same mood regulatory effect (Kramer, 1993).

Nonetheless, findings consistent with these were later reported by Cartwright and colleagues (Cartwright, 1991, 2005; Cartwright, Agargün, Kirkby, & Friedman, 2006; Cartwright, Luten, Young, Mercer, & Bears, 1998). One study (Cartwright, 1991) demonstrated that depressed, untreated divorcees who successfully adapted to their situations of divorce at follow-up one year later had more emotionally intense incorporations of their ex-spouse character in the REM dreams of their first laboratory night at intake than did divorcees who were later less successful in their adaptation. Cartwright concluded that this pattern of dreaming helped the successful patients "work through" their states of depression. A more recent study replicated and extended these results (Cartwright, 2005). Twenty depressed and ten control subjects, all living through a divorce, were studied for five months, including repeated assessments of current concerns and laboratory polysomnograms with REM sleep awakenings for dream reporting. The findings confirmed an apparent mediating role for non-self dream characters in that (1) degree of waking concern about the ex-spouse is associated with the number of dreams containing the ex-spouse as a character, and (2) subjects in remission at follow-up (versus those not in remission) have more dreams in which the ex-spouse character is associated with emotions and is linked to other memories within the dream. Furthermore, (3) remitted subjects in early stages of separation dream more about their children than do nonremitted subjects, and the number of these dreams is correlated significantly with the degree of waking concern subjects express about their children.

In other studies of divorced women (Cartwright, 1996; Cartwright, Newell, & Mercer, 2001; Cartwright, Young, & Mercer, 1998; Cartwright, Baehr, Kirkby, Pandi-Permual, & Kabat, 2003) and suicidal patients (Agargün & Cartwright, 2003), presleep emotional measures (for example, depression) were shown to be associated with altered patterns of both REM sleep and dreaming. For example, among subjects undergoing marital separation, a "progressive" pattern of more negative dreams occurring early versus later in the night predicts remission a year later compared with the opposite, more typical, pattern of positive dreams early and negative dreams late (Cartwright et al., 1998). Among depressed patients, a "progressive" pattern of increasing dreamlike quality from early to late in the night is also associated with a *lack* of suicidal tendency compared with the opposite pattern of decreasing dreamlike quality (Agargün & Cartwright, 2003). Although suicidal individuals also report a greater frequency of nightmares (Agargün et al., 1998, 2003; Bernert, Joiner, Cukrowicz, Schmidt, & Krakow, 2005; Liu, 2004; Tanskanen et al., 2001), relationships between nightmares and these altered dreaming patterns have not been studied.

Other findings for depressed subjects are consistent with the latter findings. The dreams of depressed but untreated college women contain less anger and fewer characters—fewer strangers in particular—than do the dreams of nondepressed women (Barrett & Loeffler, 1992). Similarly, patients in the grips of a depression have neutral to positive dream emotions, whereas those recovering from depression have negative dreams with much interpersonal conflict (Miller, 1969). Other studies of depression and dreams are consistent with the preceding in that they demonstrate similar alterations of either person imagery (Kramer, Baldridge, Whitman, Ornstein, & Smith, 1969; Langs, 1966) or emotions (Beck & Hurvich, 1959; Beck & Ward, 1961; Hauri, 1976; Kramer, Whitman, Baldridge, & Lansky, 1965).

Some studies of objective sleep measures are also consistent with these types of studies except that dreaming is implicated only indirectly. Studies of REM density are of particular interest because (1) eye movement density correlates positively with the active participation of subjects in their dreams (Rotenberg, 1988; Berger & Oswald, 1962), (2) patterns of eye movement across the night distinguish depressed subjects from controls (Wichniak, Antczak, Wierzbicka, & Jernajczyk, 2002), and (3) eye movement density increases as a function of recent learning (Smith, Nixon, & Nader, 2004). One study of evening-to-morning mood change revealed that eye movement densities increase across successive REM episodes on nights when mood improves but decrease on nights when mood deteriorates or stays the same (Indursky & Rotenberg, 1998). A second study (Germain, Buysse, Ombao, Kupfer, & Hall, 2003) found that presleep notification of having to give a speech in the morning (which presumably produces a deterioration of morning mood) leads to a decrease in eye movement density.

Together, the preceding findings support the notion that dreaming contributes to an emotion regulation function and that specific attributes of dream content may predominate in mediating this function. Presumably, the presence of emotions and characters depicting significant others mediate emotion regulation in the case of depressed subjects. Cartwright et al. (2006) link this mediating role to "image contextualization" or the interweaving of character images with many other memory elements (see next paragraph). However, evidence supporting a specific role for dream content is not yet definitive given the dearth and inconsistencies of replication studies. Nonetheless, the work achieved to date is strongly suggestive and lays out clear templates for experimental designs and methods that could serve in future studies.

Yet another variation of the emotion regulation function of dreaming was elaborated by Ernest Hartmann of Tufts University and the Newton Wellesley Hospital Sleep Disorders Center (Hartmann, 1996, 1998a, 1998b). His *image contextualization* model of nightmares proposes that emotional adaptation is facilitated when an individual's predominant emotional concerns are contextualized within a dream, that is, depicted in a visual context consisting of new associations (see Figure 9.2) that are conceptually linked to the

FIGURE 9.2

Two types of connectionist nets in cognitive functioning. Feed-forward nets process information unidirectionally from input, through layered connections, to output, and are characteristic of waking thought. Autoassociative nets process information through symmetric connections, with no input and output, but settling into more or less stable patterns, and are characteristic of dream mentation. The latter formation of broad connections underlies image contextualization.

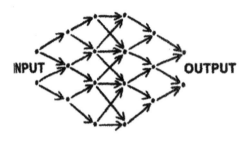 

A Feed-Forward Net   **An Autoassociative Net**

Source: Hartmann, 1998a, p. 85.

emotion (Hartmann, 1998a). These contextualizing images are fundamental to the dream narrative even though the events portrayed may be quite different from those that initially gave rise to the emotions. For example, a dream image of being swept up in a tornado may contextualize an individual's feelings of helplessness, fear, and foreboding that stem—not from a previous tornado experience—but from a previous physical assault. Hartmann's group demonstrated that such images are, in fact, more frequent after trauma (Hartmann, 1998a; Hartmann, Rosen, & Grace, 1998) and are related to a history of trauma (Hartmann, Zborowski, & Kunzendorf, 2001; Hartmann, Zborowski, McNamara, Rosen, & Gazells, 1999). Some features of the model were recently replicated by independent groups (Davidson, Lee-Archer, & Sanders, 2005; Levin & Basile, 2003). The claim that memory systems become hyperassociative and more flexible during REM sleep has also been supported by studies on sleep and learning (Stickgold, Scott, Rittenhouse, & Hobson, 1999; Walker, Liston, Hobson, & Stickgold, 2002), although no direct links to dream content have yet been reported. A general relationship between "insecurely attached" participants and the presence of more frequent and intense dream images that contextualize strong emotions has been reported (McNamara, Andresen, Clark, Zborowski, & Duffy, 2001). This model's emphasis on context formation during dreaming is also broadly consistent with recent suggestions that sleep-related changes in context-building functions of the hippocampus influence the consolidation of episodic memories (for review, see Nielsen & Stenstrom, 2005). For example, Hartmann's model predates the notion that a central function of REM sleep is to create contextual memories (Johnson, 2004, 2005), and recent research demonstrating that implicit contextual learning is facilitated during sleep (Spencer, Sunm, & Ivry, 2006).

From this perspective, nightmares are not necessarily dysfunctional. Rather, they are similar to dreams in that they constitute attempts to create image context for problematic memories. In fact, Hartmann considers nightmares to be exemplary instances of this regulatory function.

Most recently, Ross Levin of Yeshiva University in New York City and I proposed a model of nightmares that ascribes a very specific function to normal dreaming, that of *fear memory extinction.* We further suggest that various disturbances in the component processes of this function produce different types and degrees of disturbing dreams including, especially, bad dreams and idiopathic and posttraumatic nightmares (Levin & Nielsen, 2007; Nielsen & Levin, 2007a, 2007b). This model explains the emotion regulation mechanism of fear memory extinction at two levels: cognitive and neural.

Cognitive Level Explanation

At the cognitive level, fear extinction entails the activation of fear memory elements that are isolated and removed from their episodic (real-world) contexts, the recombination of these into novel "here-and-now" simulations of reality, the expression of alternate emotional reactions to this virtual context, and the production of new *fear extinction memories* (Davis, Myers, Chhatwal, & Ressler, 2006; Kim & Jung, 2006). The latter compete with and, if sufficiently maintained over time, supersede the original fear memories. In short, fear extinction during dreaming is achieved by the coupling of fear memory elements with nonaversive contexts, that is, virtual worlds that are emotionally incompatible with fear, to produce competing fear extinction memories.

This sequence of image-based processes is assumed to obey the widely accepted principles of fear memory learning and extinction described by Pavlov (1927) and elaborated in numerous recent animal and human studies (for reviews, see Barad, Gean, & Lutz, 2006; Bouton, Westbrook, Corcoran, & Maren, 2006; Hermans, Craske, Mineka, & Lovibond, 2006; Kim & Jung, 2006). The fact that the fear memories are replaced rather than eliminated altogether means that they may be reinstated under various conditions. Appropriate reinstatement of a fear memory is itself, in fact, a vital aspect of emotional adaptation. Nightmares occur as a result of dysfunctional activity in any of these processes. For example, if an entrenched fear memory resists recombination with new, incompatible contexts (as might be the case in a nightmare with recurrent themes), new extinction memories may not be formed. Or, if an extinction memory is not properly maintained, an old fear memory may return. Furthermore, an individual's temperament may interact with these basic extinction processes to attach varying levels of *affect distress* to the emotional responses produced (see next section).

Neuronal Level Explanation

At the neural level, fear extinction is supported by a network of four brain regions that control the representation and expression of emotions in both sleeping and waking states: the amygdala, the medial prefrontal cortex (MPFC), the hippocampal complex, and the anterior cingulate cortex (ACC). Each region can be roughly equated with a particular domain of processing in the fear extinction process (Table 9.1), although the normal functioning of these regions is more likely to be as interactive components in the larger integrated network.

During nightmares, the amygdala becomes increasingly responsive to fear-related memory elements portrayed in the dream, while processes in the

TABLE 9.1
Brain Regions Implicated in the Production of Dreams and Nightmares

Brain Region	Proposed Function	Sample References
Medial prefrontal cortex (MPFC)	Inhibition of fear memories (in the amygdala) via storage and recall of extinction memories	Kalisch et al., 2006; Milad et al., 2005; Phelps, Delgado, Nearing, & LeDoux, 2004
Hippocampus	Regulation of virtual simulation (context); evaluation of fear memory context to regulate extinction and reinstatement of fear memories (in the amygdala, MPFC)	Maren, 2005; Eichenbaum, 2004; Nielsen & Stenstrom, 2005
Amygdala	Activation of subjective and autonomic correlates of emotion	Maren & Quirk, 2004; McGaugh, 2004
Anterior cingulate cortex (ACC)	Regulation of affect distress (in autonomic NS)	Blumberg et al., 2000; Eisenberger & Lieberman, 2004; Kalisch et al., 2006; Whittle, Allen, Lubman, & Yucel, 2006

Sources: Adapted from Levin & Nielsen, 2007; Nielsen & Levin, 2007a.

MPFC, hippocampus, and ACC that normally downregulate amygdala activity are disrupted. The result is an abnormally high expression of fear. This aspect of the neural model is similar to empirically supported models of PTSD pathology (Nutt & Malizia, 2004; Rauch, Shin, & Phelps, 2006). However, the present model also explains the distress caused by nightmares as a result of a separate, trait-like factor (*affect distress*) thought to be controlled by the ACC. Affect distress is shaped by the emotional history of the individual (for example, childhood family stress) and is akin to the *negative affect* and *negative emotions* personality dimensions (Chorpita & Barlow, 1998; Watson & Pennebaker, 1989). Its role in the fear extinction mechanism derives from evidence linking the ACC to subjective distress associated with pain (Qiu et al., 2006, Rainville, 2002), social exclusion (Eisenberger & Lieberman, 2004; Eisenberger, Lieberman, & Williams, 2003; Panksepp, 2003), romantic separation (Najib, Lorberbaum, Kose, Bohning, & George, 2004), bereavement (Gundel, O'Connor, Littrell, Fort, & Lane, 2003), and caregiver separation (see review in Eisenberger & Lieberman, 2004; Lorberbaum et al., 2002), as well as evidence that dysfunctional connections between ACC and other regions of the proposed network underlie a negative affect temperament (Whittle et al., 2006) and difficulties with emotional expression (Mériau et al., 2006).

This is a new model whose assumptions have not yet been tested experimentally. Nonetheless, it is broadly consistent with the diverse literature on sleep, PTSD, fear memory learning and extinction, personality, and psychopathology, and it is amenable to empirical testing on a number of fronts.

Summary

Theoretical and empirical work on nightmares from Freud to the present day converges on and supports to some extent the notions that (1) emotion regulation is a function of dreaming and (2) nightmares are either exemplary expressions or psychopathological disturbances of this function. The work also brings to light several possible mechanisms that may be central to emotion regulation during dreaming, including desomatization, contextualization, progressive emotional problem-solving, and fear memory extinction. It also provides suggestive evidence that some aspects of dream content (for example, characters and emotions), and not simply the physiological state of REM sleep per se, are implicated in the emotion regulation function. However, the empirical support for the existence of an emotion regulation function for dreaming is still provisional, and many questions about the possible roles of specific dream and nightmare contents in such a function remain unanswered. Nonetheless, the territory that has been covered on the question of nightmares and dream function does hold clues as to where we might look next for evidence of emotion regulation.

WHERE TO LOOK NEXT: SOCIAL IMAGERY AND EMOTION REGULATION

Much of the previous research is consistent with the possibility that a prerequisite for emotion regulation during dreaming is the realistic simulation of *character-self interactions* (CSIs) and that nightmares reflect anomalies of this form of simulation. Of the many features of waking experience that are simulated during dreaming (Levin & Nielsen, 2007; Nielsen, Powell, & Cervenka, 1994; Revonsuo, 2000), CSIs are of particular interest for at least two reasons: (1) emotional concerns are largely social in nature (Cartwright et al., 2006; Klinger, 1977) and (2) one's predominant social relationships and conflicts continue to be portrayed during dreaming (Bilu, 1989; Cartwright et al., 2006; Eudell-Simmons, Stein, Defife, & Hilsenroth, 2005; McNamara, McLaren, Smith, Brown, & Stickgold, 2005; Popp et al., 1996). The fact that the predominant relationship themes that recur in dreams tend more often to be negative in nature than do themes in reports of waking experiences (Nielsen, Deslauriers, & Baylor, 1991b; Popp et al., 1996) and that dream emotions tend to turn from positive to negative significantly more often than they do the opposite (Merritt, Stickgold, Pace-Schott, Williams, & Hobson, 1994; Nielsen, Deslauriers, & Baylor, 1991a), suggests that the activation of negative emotions related to social relationships is privileged during dreaming—as would be expected if it played some role in regulating negative emotions.

But there is much more evidence that points in the direction of CSI simulation as a possible mediator of emotion regulation. Some attributes of dream characters are particularly apt to qualify them as mediators of emotion, including their consistent presence and stability, realism, apparent autonomy and ability to evoke reactions from the dream self, and reactivity to daytime socioemotional events and situations. These attributes are considered in turn.

Dream Characters are Consistently Present and Stable

Characters maintain a more or less constant presence in dream narratives. While they are as prevalent as the dream ego or as dream settings, appearing in over 95 percent of adult reports (Hall & Van de Castle, 1966), the average number of non-self characters in every dream is 2.6 to 3.7 for adults (Hall, 1951; Kahn, Stickgold, & Hobson, 2000) and 2.2 for children aged four to ten (Resnick, Stickgold, Rittenhouse, & Hobson, 1994). The self is usually active during dreaming, even in children (Resnick et al., 1994; although Foulkes, 1982b), engaging in some form of interaction with these non-self characters. In fact, social interactions are even more frequent in dream reports than they are in reports of randomly selected daytime experiences (McNamara et al., 2005). Characters are more often familiar than unfamiliar in both children's dreams (70 versus 30 percent, respectively) (Resnick et al., 1994) and adults' dreams (52 versus 48 percent) (Hall & Van de Castle, 1966; Kahn, Pace-Schott, & Hobson, 2002), although the proportion of unknown characters may be as low as 22 percent if "generic" characters, for example, "policeman," or "a friend" are separately tallied (Kahn et al., 2002).

Dreamed characters are spatially and temporally stable, especially in the lengthy dreams of REM sleep. Spatially, dream characters show a lower overall incidence of distortion relative to their waking state referents than do other features of dreams, like settings (Dorus, Dorus, & Rechtschaffen, 1971). Only 14 percent of characters reveal any sign of bizarreness (Kahn et al., 2000); nonetheless, over 60 percent of known characters deviate in some manner from their waking counterparts—usually in how they behave or in the feelings they evoke (Kahn et al., 2002). Temporally, characters from REM sleep dreams demonstrate less moment-to-moment variation relative to actions performed than do characters from non-REM sleep dreams (Foulkes & Schmidt, 1983). In fact, the longer a dream report from REM sleep, the less there is variation in character composition (Foulkes & Schmidt, 1983). Foulkes and Schmidt note a striking instance of a dream report from REM sleep in which the same character persists over fifteen episodes. These observations prompted the conclusion that characters ". . . are central, and generally highly concretely portrayed, features of REM dream narratives. . ." (Foulkes & Schmidt, 1983, p. 279).

The stability of character images in dreams is demonstrated also by the fact that their representation does not depend exclusively upon imagery of any particular sense modality—or of any sense modality whatsoever. Characters are usually identified by appearance, face, or behavior (Kahn et al., 2000) either visually or by sounds, speech content, and prosody (Heynick, 1983, Snyder, 1970), but in many instances (12 percent) are "just known" to be present (Kahn et al., 2002). Moreover, characters also occur frequently in the dreams of the blind (Kerr, Foulkes, & Schmidt, 1982; Kirtley & Sabo, 1984). Helen Keller, who was both deaf and blind, provided very vivid descriptions of the nonvisual, nonauditory character images pervading her dreams (Jastrow, 1900). In sighted subjects, the most vivid example of this type of dream character is the "sensed presence" that appears frequently during sleep paralysis episodes (Cheyne, 2001; Solomonova et al., 2007). The sensed presence does not depend upon visual, auditory, or other pseudosensory attributes for its recognition; rather, it appears to be a form of purely spatial character representation (Solomonova et al., 2007).

Dream Characters are Realistic and Engaging

Characters appear quite autonomous in dreams and tend easily to incite emotional reactions from the dreamed self. They evoke feelings in the dreamed self whether they are known (81 percent) or unknown (69 percent) to the dreamer, with feelings of caring and affection being the most frequently evoked (Kahn et al., 2002). Content analysis of aggressive and friendly social interactions in dreams (Hall & Van de Castle, 1966) indicate that among the aggressive encounters for which an initiator of the action can be identified, 68.2 percent are perpetrated by other characters—only 31.8 percent by the dreamed self. Friendly interactions are also frequently initiated by other characters (52.4 versus 47.6 percent). In the case of "attack nightmares," where the dream-ego is chased, threatened, or assaulted, the intention of the attacker is clearly apparent 59 percent of the time; moreover, 75 to 85 percent of the time, the dream ego does nothing to clearly incite the attack (Hall, 1955). The autonomy of characters may be at its highest during lucid dreams, when they appear to demonstrate independence of mind and feeling, separate perspectives, creative thoughts, and command of information that was previously "unknown" to the dreamer (Tholey, 1989).

Not only do dream characters appear to initiate emotional encounters with the dream-ego, they communicate their emotional meanings through channels that closely resemble those used by real individuals in the waking world. They display facial expressions and emotional gestures, express concerns in speech rich with inflection and prosody, and touch or manipulate the dreamed self in provocative and intimate ways. One study of 635 REM sleep dream reports (Snyder, 1970) found that almost every interaction between the self and another character involved talking (see also Foulkes, 1982a; Heynick, 1983). A second study (Heynick, 1983) found that 40.4 percent of verbal communications in dreams were produced by characters, and these communications were syntactically well formed, occasionally complex, and considered appropriate to the dream scenario; the majority (85.3 percent) were experienced as vocalized utterances that were completely "sayable" or "hearable" in waking life.

The simulated emotional expressions of dream characters appear to be as subtle or overt, direct or indirect, or simple or complex as the expressions that are used daily on the social stage. Moreover, these expressions appear to incite the dream self to react emotionally. Such reactions may be in sympathy with those of the character or they may be appropriately complementary, but rarely are they judged by subjects themselves to be inappropriate to the waking-state situation depicted by the dream (Foulkes, Sullivan, Kerr, & Brown, 1988).

Dream Characters are Affected by Daytime Socioemotional Events

While the consistency and stability of interactive characters are dream attributes that may be necessary for emotion regulation to exist as a function of dreaming, the plausibility of such a function would be increased if these characters proved to be influenced by the changing emotional concerns of the individual while awake. Evidence for such influence can, in fact, be found in a variety of different clinical and empirical studies.

Clinically, dreams are used regularly to clarify the nature of a patient's interpersonal relationships, for example, the quality of object relations and patient-therapist transference situations (Carlson, 1986; Hersh & Taub-Bynum, 1985). A patient's level of object representations can be identified in dream narratives as it can in other measures such as the Early Memories scale (Krohn & Mayman, 1974). Popp and colleagues (1996) used a validated system for content analysis of repetitive relationship patterns, the Core Conflictual Relationship Theme (CCRT) method (Luborsky, 1977), to demonstrate that that an individual's most frequent relationship patterns are expressed in their dreams as they are in their waking psychotherapy narratives. Emotionally negative themes are predominant in both types of report. In a similar vein (Eudell-Simmons et al., 2005), dream narratives can be assessed reliably using measures of interpersonal behavior on the Social Cognition and Object Relations Scale (SCORS; Westen, 1991); the SCORS categories of Affect and Relationships are rated with particularly high reliability. Furthermore, SCORS categories are significantly correlated with the degree of similarity between dreaming and waking experiences on the Zepelin Dream Distortion Scale (Winget & Kramer, 1979); less distorted dreams exhibit more complexity of self/other representations, fewer gaps in interpersonal narrative accounts, and more stability or coherence of self-representation.

Laboratory research is consistent with these clinical findings. McNamara and colleagues (2005) randomly sampled mentation in REM and NREM sleep (Nightcap procedure), as well as wakefulness (pager procedure) and scored the resulting reports with Hall and Van de Castle (1966) social interaction scales. REM sleep reports were twice as likely as waking state reports ($p < .04$) to simulate social interactions but were not different from NREM sleep reports. Also, REM sleep reports contained more aggressive interactions than did either waking state ($p < .02$) or NREM sleep ($p < .06$) reports.

Finally, a study of over 200 "encounter" dreams reported by Jewish and Arab preteens indicates that these children internalize the contents and affective tone of the Jewish/Arab conflict (Bilu, 1989). Children incorporated both stereotypical characterizations of the "other" and the aggression and violence of interactions with them.

In sum, assessments of dream content using a variety of validated measures of socioemotional dynamics reveal that such dynamics are present in dream reports with at least the same frequency as in waking state comparison reports. The fact that these comparison reports are, for the most part, descriptions of personally important relationships (core relationships, psychotherapy narratives, political events) attests to the extent to which dream characters reflect an individual's socioemotional concerns.

These findings are generally consistent with laboratory and home studies that have attempted to identify dream content related to an individual's current concerns (Hoelscher, Klinger, & Barta, 1981; Nielsen, Alain, Kuiken, & Powell, 2003; Nikles, Brecht, Klinger, & Bursell, 1998). First, daytime events identified in dreams (by judges working from subjects' written logs) are rated by subjects themselves to be more emotional than are nonincorporated events (Kramer, 2006; Piccione, Jacobs, Kramer, & Roth, 1977). Second, concern-related themes administered before sleep with suggestions to dream about them also influence dream content—largely the central imagery of dream content—more than either nonconcern themes or themes administered without suggestions (Nikles et al., 1998). Third, when subjects are asked to rehearse a statement about wishing to attain a desired personality attribute, the wished-for attributes are reflected in dreams to a greater extent that are nondesired attributes; in this study, both the self and other characters exhibited this effect (Cartwright, 1974). Fourth, verbal stimuli that are related to subjects' current concerns and presented during sleep influence dream content to a much greater extent than do stimuli that are not so related (Hoelscher et al., 1981). Finally, subjects who rate their recent dreams as having a high personal impact incorporate aspects of their waking experiences into dreams with a particular temporal pattern, for example, events occurring from one to two or five to seven days before the dream but not from days in between (Nielsen et al., 2003).

These findings stand in stark contrast to many laboratory attempts to influence dream content with emotion-provoking stimuli—primarily films—that have produced inconsistent or marginal results (see review in Arkin & Antrobus, 1991). It may be that the latter studies failed because the stimuli used did not resonate sufficiently with the emotional tenor of a subject's current concerns. In contrast, studies that were successful may have had just such an effect because of the more general relevance of the stimuli to a subject's concerns. For example, stimulation with an erotically arousing film produces more dreams with a reduced number of opposite sex characters and a higher frequency of only a single character (Cartwright, Bernick, Borowitz, & Kling, 1969). Or, when a painful stimulus is presented during REM sleep, that stimulus may be reflected in attributes of both the dream self and non-self characters (Nielsen, McGregor, Zadra, Ilnicki, & Ouellet, 1993).

The suggestion that an emotional film may have substantially less effect on subjects than an actual interpersonal encounter is consistent with findings from studies that have used emotional stimuli or situations that are more clearly interpersonally engaging. One such situation is the experience of sleeping in a laboratory—which for first-time subjects often constitutes a considerably intense, if not stressful, social encounter. Dreams collected from the first night of sleep in the laboratory contain more unknown than known characters, whereas the opposite is true for dreams collected from the second night (Dorus et al., 1971). This difference may have to do with the "first-night effect," which is known to affect REM sleep (Agnew, Webb, & Williams, 1966; Browman & Cartwright, 1980; Coble, Le Bon O. et al., 2001) and which likely reflects the social stress of encountering laboratory personnel in close quarters for the first time (the first-night effect is attenuated in home sleep recordings). Laboratory subjects regularly dream about the lab personnel; in late-night REM dreams, the proportion of lab characters is higher than it is in NREM dreams (Raymond, Nielsen, Bessette, Faucher, & Germain, 1999). In a related finding, dreams collected in the laboratory contain more characters and more aggressive character interactions than do dreams collected at home (Domhoff & Kamiya, 1964).

Other findings are consistent with the idea that dream characters and their interactions with the self are influenced by daytime emotional situations. Animal dream characters are a case in point. The presence of animal characters in dreams consistently decreases with increasing age, whether measured in a sleep lab (Foulkes, 1985; Foulkes, Hollifield, Sullivan, Bradley, & Terry, 1990) or at home (Resnick et al., 1994; Van de Castle, 1994) (see Figure 9.3). With increasing age, the frequency of generic animal characters and strangers diminishes while the frequency of familiar and family characters increases (Foulkes, 1985). However, in older children, the presence of dreamed animals is associated with social immaturity (Foulkes, 1985). The more predominant animal characters are in dreams, the greater the likelihood that these dreams also contain aggression (Van de Castle, 1994, p. 307; Seidel, 1984). In the dreams of 11- and 12-year-olds, aggression is present

FIGURE 9.3

Decrease in proportion of dreams with animal characters with increasing age.

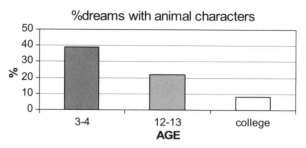

Source: Adapted from Van de Castle, 1994, p. 306.

more often when an animal character is also present (74 percent) than when no animal is present (44 percent; (Seidel, 1984)). In fact, children are four times as likely as adults to be victims of aggression in their dreams, and animal characters are the source of this aggression (Domhoff, 1993). These findings together suggest that the increasing differentiation of emotions and emotional control through childhood is accompanied by a consistent change in the nature of dream characters and how they relate to the dreamed self.

Dream characters and their associated emotions also vary with the symptoms of affective illness. The early dreams of paranoid schizophrenics contain both more strangers than familiar people and more aggressive themes (Kramer, Whitman, Baldridge, & Ornstein, 1970). Chronic schizophrenic's dreams are bland, sterile, and devoid of people and all but individual objects (Dement, 1955). Chronic hebephrenic schizophrenics off medications (and hallucinating) have more sadness, anger, and anxiety and less frequent friendly characters (Okuma, Sunami, Fukuma, Takeo, & Motoike, 1970). The dreams of depressed subjects more often represent family members, and less often strangers, than the dreams of schizophrenic subjects (Kramer & Roth, 1973a; Kramer et al., 1969). Together, such research indicates that dream characters may be responsive to varying emotional conditions induced by affective illnesses and, thus, may be implicated in the elevated need to regulate emotion in these cases.

Perhaps most telling are changes in dream characters that accompany transitional periods in emotional relationships with an important other person ("significant other"), for example, the death of a loved one, making and breaking of new friendships, conflict with family partners, birth of a child, and so forth. During these transitions, mechanisms for emotional regulation may also be in greater demand and, thus, in greater evidence in dream reports. It is also

FIGURE 9.4

Log frequency of nightmares in primi- and multiparous new mothers queried at 3, 6, and 12 weeks postpartum. Many reported nightmares depicted the infant in peril and were accompanied by enacting behaviors.

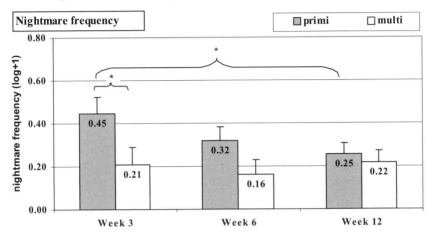

likely that when such transitions are quite severe, nightmares that reflect the social dynamics of the transition will occur. Some evidence linking dream changes with divorce and possible emotion regulation was already presented in an earlier section. Two other transitional periods are of particular interest. One of these is the postpartum period, when mothers report intense dreams and nightmares of their new infants. The other is the aftermath of a loved one's death, when bereavement dreams and nightmares are common.

In the case of postpartum dreams, results from our study of 220 new mothers (Nielsen & Paquette, 2004, 2006) show that of women who are able to recall a dream in the postpartum period, a sizeable number (55.8 percent) reported having had nightmares about the infant (see Figure 9.4). An even larger proportion (86.5 percent) reported dreaming about the new infant and, among those who responded to specific probe questions, 74.8 percent indicated that these dreams contained anxiety. The concern expressed toward the infant character is clear in the fact that, for 64.3 percent of the women, the infant is depicted as injured or in danger, and for 50.4 percent the infant is depicted as lost. In fact, the dreams are often so perceptually vivid that the women believe they are really taking place. Upon awakening, they may stay confused for a short time about whether or not their infants were, in fact, in peril. The dreams are also frequently (63.4 percent) accompanied by overt dream-enacting behaviors, such as motor activity of the limbs or trunk, speaking out loud, and expressing emotions.

The incorporation of the infant as a character into dreams is more apparent for primiparas, who are undergoing the transition to motherhood for the first time, than it is for multiparas, who have previous motherhood experience. More primiparas (87.4 percent) recall an infant dream than do multiparas (66.4 percent; $p = .0005$), and more primiparas also recall an infant nightmare (52.6 versus 34.6 percent; $p = .010$).

The most severe of these episodes, those involving dream-enacting behaviors, proved to be associated with psychopathological indicators. For the *Expressing Emotions* category of dream-enacting behaviors, relationships were found with low maternal affection scores on the Parental Bonding Instrument (PBI) ($p = .01$), with high PBI-maternal protection scores ($p = .002$), with high PBI-paternal protection scores ($p = .07$), and with high Symptom Check List (90 item) Revised General Symptom Index (SCL90-R-GSI) scores ($p = .04$). For the *Motor Activity* category, behaviors were associated with higher attachment instability ($p = .007$) and lower PBI-maternal affection ($p = .08$) and higher SCL90-R-GSI ($p = .08$) scores.

The observed relationships between infant dreams, sleep behaviors, and disturbed attachment are consistent with the possibility that postpartum infant dreams reflect emotional changes compelled by the arrival of the new infant and the new attachment imagery it entails. As the mother adjusts to the demanding presence of a new infant in her life, she is pressed to encode and consolidate stable, emotion-laden representations of this infant, representations that correspond in many ways to what have been termed *internal working models* of attachment figures (Cicchetti, Toth, & Lynch, 1995; Thompson & Raikes, 2003). The consolidation of such representations may well require sleep and dreaming processes (Nielsen & Germain, 2000) as do other types of learning (Stickgold, 2003). Specific links between emotional memory and sleep have, in fact, been made in some studies (Wagner, Hallschmid, Rasch, & Born, 2006; Wagner, Hallschmid, Verleger, & Born, 2003; Wagner et al., 2005). For example, implicit memory consolidation of human faces is dependent upon intact REM sleep (Wagner et al., 2003).

In the case of bereavement, vivid images of the deceased may persist for years as hallucinations, illusions, and intense dreams (Bowlby, 1980; Cookson, 1990). Dreams of a deceased love one occur in about half of widows and widowers, by whom they are experienced to be extremely vivid and realistic—much as is the sense of the deceased's presence during the waking state (Bowlby, 1980). One widow cited by Bowlby (1980, p. 97) recalled the following dream. "It was just like everyday life ... my husband coming in and getting his dinner. Very vivid, so that when I woke up I was very annoyed." The realness of the characters is part of what renders them so comforting, and a majority of subjects studied describe their dreams of the dead as comforting. By the same token, waking up to the harsh reality that the dream was only a dream can also bring back intense feelings of sadness and grief. Many subjects studied by Gorer (1965) reported that they tried to preserve their dreams in memory after they awakened but, being saddened by their fading, they would often end up weeping in the recounting of it. Even more intense reactions to such dreams may occur; in some cases, distressing aspects of the bereaved person's previous relationship with the deceased are depicted, and in others, the trauma of the deceased's illness or death are redramatized.

On the surface, both nightmarish dreams of the dead and sad awakenings from dreams of the dead as alive again may seem quite undesirable; however, they should be appreciated for their possible functional value. Such dreams may serve to help the individual accept the reality of their loss, to express appropriate emotions of loss as well as of renewal towards life, and to gain a sense of closure on the loss. In fact, the comforting nature of such dreams is widely appreciated by bereaved persons. The taking of comfort from dreams of the deceased seems so basic to the resolution of grief that it has prompted Bowlby (1980) to conclude that "Whether on balance a bereaved person finds his dreams comforting seems likely to be a reliable indicator of whether or not mourning is taking a favourable course" (p. 98).

A qualitative study of over 400 dreams about recently deceased persons (Garfield, 1996) identifies many features of dream characters that may be implicated in mediating these dreams' capacity to mitigate an adaptive response to death, for example, features of a character's face, expression, and clothing or their "message" for the dreamer. For example, a transformation in appearance may accompany a profound sense of reassurance (see also Morse, 1994). Embracing a departed dream character appears to be particularly comforting (Garfield, 1996). It is noteworthy that the most common "message" from characters in such bereavement dreams is that the dreamer should not worry, that the deceased is "okay." Feelings subsequent to such dreams are often intense and adaptive, as the following excerpts demonstrate.

> ... I felt so wonderful and happy; the pain in my heart had been kissed away, all my suffering gone; ... he came to say goodbye and it healed me; ... I felt better about his passing for I knew he was at last at peace.... (Garfield, 1995, p. 9)

Two different kinds of emotion regulation effect are illustrated in the following accounts. In the first, a dramatic turning point is achieved within the dream, with the dreamer obtaining an insight about compassion from a particular facial expression on his lost son's face. In the second, mood is enhanced whenever the dream recurs during times of stress.

(1) There he was! Walking toward me as if coming out of a mist. There he was—that lanky 17-year-old whose life I loved better than my own. He looked deeply into my eyes and with a grin on his face, the way he used to do when he was "buttering me up." Not a word was spoken, but everything was said that needed to be said for my turning point to come.

It was time to resume life. I would not be bitter, but in loving memory I would be better. I would live again because I knew that my boy lived again. My own Christian faith was to be retrofitted. It offered meaning and purpose within the shadow of my loss. (Klass, 1992, p. 256)

(2) My father died nine years ago but I often dream that he returns, especially at times of stress in my life. He looks older than he ever got to be in real life and very wise looking. I tell him problems I am having and sometimes he just listens and I feel better but usually he gives me advice, sometimes very clear, sometimes garbled. In the instances where it is clear, it is always good advice but things I already know I should do. But just seeing him and hearing it from him makes me feel better. (Barrett & Loeffler, 1992)

In sum, evidence from a variety of types of studies supports the notion of an emotion regulation function for dreaming and the more specific suggestion that dream characters and their emotion-laden interactions with the dream self may mediate this regulatory effect. Future progress in the testing of this perspective on dream function will clearly require targeted assessments of dream contents that include, but are not restricted to, the variety of character-self interactions that occur in dreaming during a variety of emotionally significant transitional states.

ACKNOWLEDGMENT

This work was funded by the Canadian Institutes for Health Research.

NOTE

1. In distinction to the within-period surges suggested by Kramer, a strong case can be made that an affective surge, indexed by a cross-night increase in cortisol, occurs across multiple REM periods of the same night and increasingly favors amygdala-related emotional memory consolidation (Born & Wagner, 2004; Payne & Nadel, 2004; Wagner, Degirmenci, Drosopoulos, Perras, & Born, 2005).

REFERENCES

Agargün, M. Y., & Cartwright, R. (2003). REM sleep, dream variables and suicidality in depressed patients. *Psychiatry Research, 119*, 33–39.

Agargün, M. Y., Cilli, A. S., Kara, H., Tarhan, N., Kincir, F., & Oz, H. (1998). Repetitive and frightening dreams and suicidal behavior in patients with major depression. *Comprehensive Psychiatry, 39*, 198–202.

Agargün, M. Y., Kara, H., Ozer, O. A., Selvi, Y., Kiran, U., & Ozer, B. (2003). Clinical importance of nightmare disorder in patients with dissociative disorders. *Psychiatry & Clinical Neurosciences, 57,* 575–579.

Agnew, H. W., Webb, W. E., & Williams, R. L. (1966). The first night effect: An EEG study. *Psychophysiology, 2,* 263–266.

American Academy of Sleep Medicine (2005). *International classification of sleep disorders: Diagnostic and coding manual* (2nd ed.). Chicago: American Academy of Sleep Medicine.

American Psychiatric Association (2000). *Diagnostic and statistical manual of mental disorders, 4th edition, text revision (DSM-IV-TR).* Washington, DC: American Psychiatric Association Press.

Arkin, A. M., & Antrobus, J. S. (1991). The effects of external stimuli applied prior to and during sleep on sleep experience. In S. J. Ellman & J. S. Antrobus (Eds.), *The mind in sleep* (2nd ed., pp. 265–307). New York: John Wiley & Sons, Inc.

Barad, M., Gean, P. W., & Lutz, B. (2006). The role of the amygdala in the extinction of conditioned fear. *Biological Psychiatry, 60,* 322–328.

Barrett, D., & Loeffler, M. (1992). Comparison of dream content of depressed vs nondepressed dreamers. *Psychological Reports, 70,* 403–406.

Beavers, T. L. (1973). A note on the function of dreams. *Psychology, 10,* 31–32.

Beck, A. T., & Hurvich, M. S. (1959). Psychological correlates of depression: Frequency of masochistic dream content in a private practice sample. *Psychosomatic Medicine, 28,* 50–55.

Beck, A. T., & Ward, C. H. (1961). Dreams of depressed patients: Characteristic themes in manifest content. *Archives of General Psychiatry, 5,* 462–467.

Belicki, D., & Belicki, K. (1982). Nightmares in a university population. *Sleep Research, 11,* 116.

Belicki, K., & Cuddy, M. A. (1991). Nightmares: Facts, fictions and future directions. In J. Gackenbach & A. A. Sheikh (Eds.), *Dream images: A call to mental arms* (pp. 99–115). Amityville, NY: Baywood.

Berger, R. J., & Oswald, I. (1962). Eye movements during active and passive dreams. *Science, 137,* 601.

Bernert, R. A., Joiner, T. E., Jr., Cukrowicz, K. C., Schmidt, N. B., & Krakow, B. (2005). Suicidality and sleep disturbances. *Sleep, 28,* 1135–1141.

Bilu, Y. (1989). The other as a nightmare: The Israeli-Arab encounter as reflected in children's dreams in Israel and the West Bank. *Political Psychology, 10,* 365–389.

Bixler, E. O., Kales, A., Soldatos, C. R., Kales, J. D., & Healy, S. (1979). Prevalence of sleep disorders in the Los Angeles metropolitan area. *American Journal of Psychiatry, 136,* 1257–1262.

Blumberg, H. P., Stern, E., Martinez, D., Ricketts, S., De Asis, J., White, T., et al. (2000). Increased anterior cingulate and caudate activity in bipolar mania. *Biological Psychiatry, 48,* 1045–1052.

Born, J. & Wagner, U. (2004). Memory consolidation during sleep: Role of cortisol feedback. *Annuals of the New York Academy of Sciences, 1032,* 198–201.

Bouton, M. E., Westbrook, R. F., Corcoran, K. A., & Maren, S. (2006). Contextual and temporal modulation of extinction: behavioral and biological mechanisms. *Biological Psychiatry, 60,* 352–360.

Bowlby, J. (1980). Attachment and loss. In *Loss, sadness and depression* (Vol. 3). New York: Basic Books.

Browman, C. P., & Cartwright, R. D. (1980). The first-night effect on sleep and dreams. *Biological Psychiatry, 15,* 809–812.

Carlson, R. (1986). After analysis: A study of transference dreams following treatment. *Journal of Consulting and Clinical Psychology, 54,* 246–252.

Cartwright, R. D. (1974). The influence of a conscious wish on dreams: A methodological study of dream meaning and function. *Journal of Abnormal Psychology, 83,* 387–393.

Cartwright, R. D. (1991). Dreams that work: The relation of dream incorporation to adaptation to stressful events. *Dreaming, 1,* 3–9.

Cartwright, R. D. (1996). Dreams and adaptation to divorce. In D. Barrett (Ed.), *Trauma and dreams* (pp. 179–185). Cambridge, MA: Harvard University Press.

Cartwright, R. (2005). Dreaming as a mood regulation system. In M. H. Kryger, T. Roth, & W. C. Dement (Eds.), *Principles and practice of sleep medicine* (4th ed., pp. 565–572). Philadelphia, PA: Elsevier Saunders.

Cartwright, R., Agargün, M. Y., Kirkby, J., & Friedman, J. K. (2006). Relation of dreams to waking concerns. *Psychiatry Research, 141,* 261–270.

Cartwright, R., Baehr, E., Kirkby, J., Pandi-Permual, S., & Kabat, J. (2003). REM sleep reduction mood regulation and remission in untreated depression. *Psychiatry Research, 12,* 159–167.

Cartwright, R. D., Bernick, N., Borowitz, G., & Kling, A. (1969). Effect of an erotic movie on the sleep and dreams of young men. *Archives of General Psychiatry, 20,* 262–271.

Cartwright, R., Luten, A., Young, M., Mercer, P., & Bears, M. (1998). Role of REM sleep and dream affect in overnight mood regulation: A study of normal volunteers. *Psychiatry Research, 81,* 1–8.

Cartwright, R., Newell, P., & Mercer, P. (2001). Dream incorporation of a sentinel life event and its relation to waking adaptation. *Sleep & Hypnosis, 3,* 25–32.

Cartwright, R., Young, M. A., & Mercer, P. (1998). Role of REM sleep and dream variables in the prediction of remission from depression. *Psychiatry Research, 80,* 249–255.

Cheyne, J. A. (2001). The ominous numinous. *Journal of Consciousness Studies, 8,* 133–150.

Chorpita, B. F., & Barlow, D. H. (1998). The development of anxiety: The role of control in the early environment. *Psychological Bulletin, 124,* 3–21.

Cicchetti, D., Toth, S. L., & Lynch, M. (1995). Bowlby's dream comes full circle. The application of attachment theory to risk and psychopathology. In T. H. Ollendick & R. J. Prinz (Eds.), *Advances in clinical child psychology* (Vol. 17, pp. 1–75). New York: Plenum Press.

Claridge, G. K., Clark, K., & Davis, C. (1997). Nightmares, dreams, and schizotypy. *British Journal of Clinical Psychology, 36,* 377–386.

Coble, P., McPartland, R. J., Silva, W. J., & Kupfer, D. J. (1974). Is there a first night effect? (A revisit). *Biological Psychiatry, 9,* 215–219.

Cookson, K. (1990). Dreams and death: An exploration of the literature. *Omega Journal of Death & Dying, 21,* 259–281.

Davidson, J., Lee-Archer, S., & Sanders, G. (2005). Dream imagery and emotions. *Dreaming, 15,* 33–47.

Davis, M., Myers, K. M., Chhatwal, J., & Ressler, K. J. (2006). Pharmacological treatments that facilitate extinction of fear: Relevance to psychotherapy. *Journal of the American Society for Experimental NeuroTherapeutics, 3,* 82–96.

Dement, W. (1955). Dream recall and eye movements during sleep in schizophrenics and normals. *Journal of Nervous & Mental Disease, 122,* 263–269.

Domhoff, B., & Kamiya, J. (1964). Problems in dream content study with objective indicators. I. A comparison of home and laboratory dream reports. *Archives of General Psychiatry, 11,* 519–524.

Domhoff, G. W. (1993). The repetition of dreams and dream elements: A possible clue to a function of dreams? In A. Moffitt, M. Kramer, & R. Hoffmann (Eds.), *The functions of dreaming* (pp. 293–320). Albany, NY: SUNY Press.

Dorus, E., Dorus, W., & Rechtschaffen, A. (1971). The incidence of novelty in dreams. *Archives of General Psychiatry, 25,* 364–368.

Eichenbaum, H. (2004). Hippocampus: Cognitive processes and neural representations that underlie declarative memory. *Neuron, 44,* 109–120.

Eisenberger, N. I., & Lieberman, M. D. (2004). Why rejection hurts: A common neural alarm system for physical and social pain. *Trends in Cognitive Sciences, 8,* 294–300.

Eisenberger, N. I., Lieberman, M. D., & Williams, K. D. (2003). Does rejection hurt? An FMRI study of social exclusion. *Science, 302,* 290–292.

Eudell-Simmons, E. M., Stein, M. B., Defife, J. A., & Hilsenroth, M. J. (2005). Reliability and validity of the Social Cognition and Object Relations Scale (SCORS) in the assessment of dream narratives. *Journal of Personality Assessment, 85,* 325–333.

Feldman, M. J., & Hersen, M. (1967). Attitudes toward death in nightmare subjects. *Journal of Abnormal Psychology, 72,* 421–425.

Fisher, B. E., Pauley, C., & McGuire, K. (1989). Children's Sleep Behavior Scale: Normative data on 870 children in grades 1 to 6. *Perceptual & Motor Skills, 68,* 227–236.

Fisher, C., Byrne, J., Edwards, A., & Kahn, E. (1970). A psychophysiological study of nightmares. *Journal of the American Psychoanalytic Association, 18,* 747–782.

Foulkes, D. (1982a). A cognitive-psychological model of REM dream production. *Sleep, 5,* 169–187.

Foulkes, D. (1982b). *Children's dreams: Longitudinal studies.* New York: John Wiley & Sons.

Foulkes, D. (1985). *Dreaming: A cognitive-psychological analysis.* Hillsdale, NJ: Lawrence Erlbaum Associates.

Foulkes, D., Hollifield, M., Sullivan, B., Bradley, L., & Terry, R. (1990). Children's dreams: A cross-sectional replication. In J. Horne (Ed.), *Sleep '90* (pp. 285–287). Bochum, Germany: Pontenagel Press.

Foulkes, D., & Schmidt, M. (1983). Temporal sequence and unit composition in dream reports from different stages of sleep. *Sleep, 6,* 265–280.

Foulkes, D., Sullivan, B., Kerr, N. H., & Brown, L. (1988). Appropriateness of dream feelings to dreamed situations. *Cognition & Emotion, 2,* 29–39.

Freud, S. (1953). *The interpretation of dreams* (J. Strachey, Trans.). New York: Penguin Books. (Original work published 1900)

Garfield, P. (1995). Dream messages from the dead. *ASD Newsletter, 12,* 4–9.

Germain, A., Buysse, D. J., Ombao, H., Kupfer, D. J., & Hall, M. (2003). Psychophysiological reactivity and coping styles influence the effects of acute stress exposure on rapid eye movement sleep. *Psychosomatic Medicine, 65,* 857–864.

Gorer, G. (1965). *Death, grief and mourning in contemporary Britain*. London: Tavistock Publications.

Greenberg, R., Pearlman, C. A., & Gampel, D. (1972). War neuroses and the adaptive function of REM sleep. *British Journal of Medical Psychology, 45*, 27–33.

Gundel, H., O'Connor, M. F., Littrell, L., Fort, C., & Lane, R. D. (2003). Functional neuroanatomy of grief: An FMRI study. *American Journal of Psychiatry, 160*, 1946–1953.

Hall, C. S. (1951). What people dream about. *Scientific American, 184*, 60–63.

Hall, C. S. (1955). The significance of the dream of being attacked. *Journal of Personality, 24*, 168–180.

Hall, C., & Van de Castle, R. I. (1966). *The content analysis of dreams*. New York: Appleton-Century-Crofts.

Hartmann, E. (1984). *The nightmare: The psychology and the biology of terrifying dreams*. New York: Basic Books.

Hartmann, E. (1996). Outline for a theory on the nature and functions of dreaming. *Dreaming, 6*, 147–170.

Hartmann, E. (1998a). *Dreams and nightmares: The new theory on the origin and meaning of dreams*. New York: Plenum.

Hartmann, E. (1998b). Nightmare after trauma as paradigm for all dreams: A new approach to the nature and functions of dreaming. *Psychiatry, 61*, 223–238.

Hartmann, E. L., Rosen, R., & Grace, N. (1998). Contextualizing images in dreams: More frequent and more intense after trauma. *Sleep, 21*(Suppl. 1), S284.

Hartmann, E., Zborowski, M., & Kunzendorf, R. (2001). The emotion pictured by a dream: An examination of emotions contextualized in dreams. *Sleep & Hypnosis, 3*, 33–43.

Hartmann, E. L., Zborowski, M., McNamara, P., Rosen, R., & Gazells, G. N. (1999). Contextualizing images in dreams: Relationship to the emotional state of the dreamer. *Sleep, 21*(Suppl. 1), S131.

Hauri, P. (1976). Dreams in patients remitted from reactive depression. *Journal of Abnormal Psychology, 85*, 1–10.

Haynes, S. N., & Mooney, D. K. (1975). Nightmares: Etiological, theoretical, and behavioral treatment considerations. *The Psychological Record, 25*, 225–236.

Hermans, D., Craske, M. G., Mineka, S., & Lovibond, P. F. (2006). Extinction in human fear conditioning. *Biological Psychiatry, 60*, 361–368.

Hersen, M. (1971). Personality characteristics of nightmare sufferers. *Journal of Nervous & Mental Disease, 153*, 27–31.

Hersh, J. B., & Taub-Bynum, E. (1985). The use of dreams in brief therapy. *Psychotherapy, 22*, 248–255.

Heynick, F. (1983). *Theoretical and empirical investigation into verbal aspects of the Freudian model of dream generation*. Helmond, Netherlands: Dissertatie Drukkerij Wilbro.

Hoelscher, T. J., Klinger, E., & Barta, S. G. (1981). Incorporation of concern and non-concern-related verbal stimuli into dream content. *Journal of Abnormal Psychology, 90*, 88–91.

Hublin, C., Kaprio, J., Partinen, M., & Koskenvuo, M. (1999). Nightmares: Familial aggregation and association with psychiatric disorders in a nationwide twin cohort. *American Journal of Medical Genetics, 88*, 329–336.

Indursky, P., & Rotenberg, V. (1998). The change of mood during sleep and REM sleep variables. *International Journal of Psychiatry in Clinical Practice, 2,* 47–51.

Jastrow, J. (1900). The dreams of the blind. In *Fact and fable in psychology* (pp. 337–370). Boston and New York: Houghton Mifflin Co.

Johnson, J. D. (2004). Episodic memory and the hippocampus: Another view. *Medical Hypotheses, 63,* 963–967.

Johnson, J. D. (2005). REM sleep and the development of context memory. *Medical Hypotheses, 64,* 499–504.

Jones, E. (1951). *On the nightmare.* New York: Liveright.

Kahn, D., Pace-Schott, E., & Hobson, J. A. (2002). Emotion and cognition: Feeling and character identification in dreaming. *Consciousness & Cognition, 11,* 34–50.

Kahn, D., Stickgold, R., E. F., & Hobson, J. A. (2000). Dreaming and waking consciousness: A character recognition study. *Journal of Sleep Research, 9,* 317–325.

Kalisch, R., Korenfeld, E., Stephan, K. E., Weiskopf, N., Seymour, B., & Dolan, R. J. (2006). Context-dependent human extinction memory is mediated by a ventromedial prefrontal and hippocampal network. *Journal of Neuroscience, 26,* 9503–9511.

Kerr, N. H., Foulkes, D., & Schmidt, M. (1982). The structure of laboratory dream reports in blind and sighted subjects. *The Journal of Nervous & Mental Disease, 170,* 286–294.

Kim, J. J., & Jung, M. W. (2006). Neural circuits and mechanisms involved in Pavlovian fear conditioning: A critical review. *Neuroscience & Biobehavioral Reviews, 30,* 188–202.

Kirtley, D. D., & Sabo, K. T. (1984). A content analysis of affiliative interactions in the dreams of the visually impaired. *International Journal of Rehabilitation Research, 7,* 333–335.

Klass, D. (1992). The inner representation of the dead child and the worldviews of bereaved parents. *Omega-Journal of Death & Dying, 26,* 255–272.

Klinger, E. (1977). *Meaning and void: Inner experience and the incentives in people's lives.* Minneapolis, MN: University of Minnesota.

Kramer, M. (1982). The psychology of the dream: Art or science? *Psychiatric Journal of the University of Ottawa, 7,* 87–100.

Kramer, M. (1991). The nightmare: A failure of dream function. *Dreaming, 1,* 277–285.

Kramer, M. (1993). The selective mood regulatory function of dreaming: An update and revision. In A. Moffitt, M. Kramer, & R. Hoffmann (Eds.), *The functions of dreaming* (pp. 139–196). Albany, NY: State University of New York.

Kramer, M. (2006). *The dream experience: A systematic exploration.* New York: Routledge.

Kramer, M., Baldridge, B. J., Whitman, R. M., Ornstein, P. H., & Smith, P. C. (1969). An exploration of the manifest dream in schizophrenic and depressed patients. *Diseases of the Nervous System, Supplement, 30,* 126–130.

Kramer, M., & Roth, T. (1973a). A comparison of dream content in laboratory dream reports of schizophrenic and depressive patient groups. *Comprehensive Psychiatry, 14,* 325–329.

Kramer, M., & Roth, T. (1973b). The mood-regulating function of sleep. In W. Koella & P. Levin (Eds.), *Sleep 1972* (pp. 536–571). Basel, Switzerland: Karger.

Kramer, M., & Roth, T. (1980). The relationship of dream content to night-morning mood change. In L. Popoviciu, B. Asigian, & G. Bain (Eds.), *Sleep 1978* (pp.621–624). Basel: S. Karger.

Kramer, M., Whitman, R. M., Baldridge, B., & Lansky, L. (1965). Depression: Dreams and defenses. *American Journal of Psychiatry, 122,* 411–419.

Kramer, M., Whitman, R. M., Baldridge, B. J., & Ornstein, P. H. (1970). Dream content in male schizophrenic patients. *Diseases of the Nervous System, Supplement, 31,* 51–58.

Krohn, A., & Mayman, M. (1974). Object representations in dreams and projective tests. *Bulletin of the Menninger Clinic, 38,* 445–466.

Langs, R. J. (1966). Manifest dreams from three clinical groups. *Archives of General Psychiatry, 14,* 634–643.

Lansky, M. R., & Bley, C. R. (1995). *Posttraumatic nightmares. Psychodynamic explorations.* Hillsdale, NJ: Analytic Press.

Le Bon, O., Staner, L., Hoffmann, G., Dramaix, M., San Sebastian, I., Murphy, J. R., et al. (2001). The first-night effect may last more than one night. *Journal of Psychiatric Research, 35,* 165–172.

Levin, R. (1994). Sleep and dreaming characteristics of frequent nightmare subjects in a university population. *Dreaming, 4,* 127–137.

Levin, R., & Basile, R. (2003). Psychopathological correlates of contextualized images in dreams. *Perceptual & Motor Skills, 96,* 224–226.

Levin, R., & Nielsen, T. A. (2007). Disturbing dreams, PTSD and affect distress: A review and neurocognitive model. *Psychological Bulletin.*

Liu, X. (2004). Sleep and adolescent suicidal behavior. *Sleep, 27,* 1351–1358.

Lorberbaum, J. P., Newman, J. D., Horwitz, A. R., Dubno, J. R., Lydiard, R. B., Hamner, M. B., et al. (2002). A potential role for thalamocingulate circuitry in human maternal behavior. *Biological Psychiatry, 51,* 431–445.

Luborsky, L. (1977). Measuring a pervasive psychic structure in psychotherapy: The core conglictual relationship theme. In N. Freedman & S. Grand (Eds.), *Communicative structures and psychic structures* (pp. 367–395). New York: Plenum.

MacFarlane, J. W., Allen, L., & Honzik, M. P. (1954). *A developmental study of the behavior problems of normal children between twenty-one and fourteen years.* Berkeley, CA: University of California Press.

Maren, S. (2005). Building and burying fear memories in the brain. *Neuroscientist, 11,* 89–99.

Maren, S., & Quirk, G. J. (2004). Neuronal signalling of fear memory. *Nature Reviews Neuroscience, 5,* 844–852.

McGaugh, J. L. (2004). The amygdala modulates the consolidation of memories of emotionally arousing experiences. *Annual Review of Neuroscience, 27,* 1–28.

McNamara, P., Andresen, J., Clark, J., Zborowski, M., & Duffy, C. A. (2001). Impact of attachment styles on dream recall and dream content: A test of the attachment hypothesis of REM sleep. *Journal of Sleep Research, 10,* 117–127.

McNamara, P., McLaren, D., Smith, D., Brown, A., & Stickgold, R. (2005). A "Jekyll and Hyde" within: Aggressive versus friendly interactions in REM and non-REM dreams. *Psychological Science, 16,* 130–136.

Mériau, K., Wartenburger, I., Kazzer, P., Prehn, K., Lammers, C. H., van der Meer, E., et al. (2006). A neural network reflecting individual differences in cognitive processing of emotions during perceptual decision making. *NeuroImage, 33,* 1016–1027

Merritt, J. M., Stickgold, R., Pace-Schott, E., Williams, J., & Hobson, J. A. (1994). Emotion profiles in the dreams of men and women. *Consciousness & Cognition, 3,* 46–60.

Milad, M. R., Quinn, B. T., Pitman, R. K., Orr, S. P., Fischl, B., & Rauch, S. L. (2005). Thickness of ventromedial prefrontal cortex in humans is correlated with extinction memory. *Proceedings of the National Academy of Sciences of the United States of America, 102,* 10706–10711.

Miller, J. B. (1969). Dreams during varying stages of depression. *Archives of General Psychiatry, 20,* 560–565.

Mindell, J. A., & Barrett, K. M. (2002). Nightmares and anxiety in elementary-aged children: Is there a relationship? *Child: Care, Health & Development, 28,* 317–322.

Morse, M. (1994). *Parting visions. Uses and meanings of pre-death, psychic, and spiritual experiences.* New York: Villard.

Najib, A., Lorberbaum, J. P., Kose, S., Bohning, D. E., & George, M. S. (2004). Regional brain activity in women grieving a romantic relationship breakup. *American Journal of Psychiatry, 161,* 2245–2256.

Nielsen, T. A. (1991). Affect desensitization: A possible function of REMs in both waking and sleeping states. *Sleep Research, 20,* 10.

Nielsen, T. A., Alain, G., Kuiken, D., & Powell, R. (2003). Temporal delays in dreaming about daytime events vary with the personal impact of recalled dreams. *Sleep, 26,* A90.

Nielsen, T. A., Deslauriers, D., & Baylor, G. (1991a). Non-random positive and negative affect sequences in dream and waking event reports. *Sleep Research, 20,* 163.

Nielsen, T. A., Deslauriers, D., & Baylor, G. W. (1991b). Emotions in dream and waking event reports. *Dreaming, 1,* 287–300.

Nielsen, T. A., & Germain, A. (2000). Post-traumatic nightmares as a dysfunctional state. *Behavioral & Brain Sciences, 23,* 978–979.

Nielsen, T. A., Kuiken, D., Alain, G., Stenstrom, P., & Powell, R. (2004). Immediate and delayed incorporations of events into dreams: further replication and implications for dream function. *Journal of Sleep Research, 13,* 327–336.

Nielsen, T. A., Kuiken, D. L., & McGregor, D. L. (1989). Effects of dream reflection on waking affect: Awareness of feelings, Rorschach movement, and facial EMG. *Sleep, 12,* 277–286.

Nielsen, T. A., Laberge, L., Tremblay, R., Vitaro, F., & Montplaisir, J. (2000). Development of disturbing dreams during adolescence and their relationship to anxiety symptoms. *Sleep, 23,* 727–736.

Nielsen, T. A., & Levin, R. (2005). Nightmare frequency by age, gender and 9/11: Findings from an internet questionnaire. *Sleep, 28*(Abstract Supplement), A52.

Nielsen, T. A. & Levin, R. (2007a). Nightmares: A new neurocognitive model. *Sleep Medicine Reviews.*

Nielsen, T. A., & Levin, R. (2007b). Theories and correlates of nightmares. In L. R. Squires (Ed.), *New encyclopedia of neuroscience.*

Nielsen, T. A., McGregor, D. L., Zadra, A., Ilnicki, D., & Ouellet, L. (1993). Pain in dreams. *Sleep, 16,* 490–498.

Nielsen, T. A., & Paquette, T. (2004). High prevalence of postpartum peril dreams and sleep behaviors. *17th Congress of the European Sleep Research Society, October 5–9, 2004, Prague, Czech Republic.*

Nielsen, T. A., & Paquette, T. (2006). A postpartum dream-enacting parasomnia. Manuscript submitted for publication.

Nielsen, T. A., Powell, R. A., & Cervenka, T. (1994, May). *Asleep in cyberspace? Investigation of the dreamlike nature of virtual reality.* Paper presented at CYBERCONF: The 4th International Conference on Cyberspace, Banff, Alberta.

Nielsen, T. A., & Stenstrom, P. (2005). What are the memory sources of dreaming? *Nature, 437,* 34–38.

Nielsen, T. A., & Zadra, A. L. (2005). Nightmares and other common dream disturbances. In M. Kryger, N. Roth, & W. C. Dement (Eds.), *Principles and practice of sleep medicine* (4th ed., pp. 926–935). Philadelphia, PA: Elsevier Saunders.

Nikles, C. D., Brecht, D. L., Klinger, E., & Bursell, A. L. (1998). The effects of current-concern- and nonconcern-related waking suggestions on nocturnal dream content. *Journal of Personality & Social Psychology, 75,* 242–255.

Nutt, D. J., & Malizia, A. L. (2004). Structural and functional brain changes in posttraumatic stress disorder. *Journal of Clinical Psychiatry, 65*(Suppl. 1), 11–17.

Ohayon, M. M., Morselli, P. L., & Guilleminault, C. (1997). Prevalence of nightmares and their relationship to psychopathology and daytime functioning in insomnia subjects. *Sleep, 20,* 340–348.

Okuma, T., Sunami, Y., Fukuma, E., Takeo, S., & Motoike, M. (1970). Dream content study in chronic schizophrenics and normals by REMP-awakening technique. *Folia Psychiatrica et Neurologica Japonica, 24,* 151–162.

Panksepp, J. (2003). Neuroscience. Feeling the pain of social loss. *Science, 302,* 237–239.

Partinen, M. (1994). Epidemiology of sleep disorders. In M. H. Kryger, T. Roth, & W. C. Dement (Eds.), *Principles and practice of sleep medicine* (2nd ed., pp. 437–452). Philadelphia, PA: WB Saunders Company.

Pavlov, I. P. (1927). *Conditioned reflexes.* New York: Dover.

Payne, J. D., & Nadel, L. (2004). Sleep, dreams, and memory consolidation: The role of the stress hormone cortisol. *Learning & Memory, 11,* 671–678.

Perlis, M. L., & Nielsen, T. A. (1993). Mood regulation, dreaming and nightmares: Evaluation of a desensitization function for REM sleep. *Dreaming, 3,* 243–257.

Phelps, E. A., Delgado, M. R., Nearing, K. I., & LeDoux, J. E. (2004). Extinction learning in humans: Role of the amygdala and vmPFC. *Neuron, 43,* 897–905.

Piccione, P., Jacobs, G., Kramer, M., & Roth, T. (1977). The relationship between daily activities, emotions and dream content. *Sleep Research, 6,* 133.

Piccione, P., Thomas, S., Roth, T., & Kramer, M. (1976). Incorporation of the laboratory situation in dreams. *Sleep Research, 5,* 120.

Popp, C. A., Diguer, L., Luborsky, L., Faude, J., Johnson, S., Morris, M., et al. (1996). Repetitive relationship themes in waking narratives and dreams. *Journal of Consulting & Clinical Psychology, 64,* 1073–1078.

Qiu, Y., Noguchi, Y., Honda, M., Nakata, H., Tamura, Y., Tanaka, S., et al. (2006). Brain processing of the signals ascending through unmyelinated C fibers in humans: An event-related functional magnetic resonance imaging study. *Cerebral Cortex, 16,* 1289–1295.

Rainville, P. (2002). Brain mechanisms of pain affect and pain modulation. *Current Opinion in Neurobiology, 12,* 195–204.

Rauch, S. L., Shin, L. M., & Phelps, E. A. (2006). Neurocircuitry models of posttraumatic stress disorder and extinction: Human neuroimaging research—present, and future. *Biological Psychiatry, 60,* 376–382.

Raymond, I., Nielsen, T. A., Bessette, P., Faucher, B., & Germain, A. (1999, July). Laboratory incorporations in the REM and stage 2 mentation reports of men and women. Paper presented at the 16th International Conference of the ASD, Santa Cruz, CA.

Resnick, J., Stickgold, R., Rittenhouse, C. D., & Hobson, J. A. (1994). Self-representation and bizarreness in children's dream reports collected in the home setting. *Consciousness & Cognition, 3,* 30–45.

Revonsuo, A. (2000). The reinterpretation of dreams: An evolutionary hypothesis of the function of dreaming. *Behavioral & Brain Sciences, 23,* 877–901.

Rotenberg, V. S. (1988). Functional deficiency of REM sleep and its role in the pathogenesis of neurotic and psychosomatic disturbances. *Pavlovian Journal of Biological Sciences, 23,* 1–3.

Salvio, M. A., Wood, J. M., Schwartz, J., & Eichling, P. S. (1992). Nightmare prevalence in the healthy elderly. *Psychology & Aging, 7,* 324–325.

Salzarulo, P., & Chevalier, A. (1983). Sleep problems in children and their relationship with early disturbances of the waking-sleeping rhythms. *Sleep, 6,* 47–51.

Schredl, M., & Pallmer, R. (1998). Geschlechtsspezifische Unterschiede in Angsttraumen von Schulerinnen und Schulern [Gender differences in anxiety dreams of school-aged children]. *Praxis der Kinderpsychologie und Kinderpsychiatrie, 47,* 463–476.

Seidel, R. (1984). The relationship of animal figures to aggression and ego immaturity in the dreams of eleven- and twelve-year-old children. Unpublished manuscript.

Shapiro, F. (1989). Efficacy of the Eye Movement Desensitization procedure in the treatment of traumatic memories. *Journal of Traumatic Stress, 2,* 199–223.

Simard, V., Nielsen, T. A., Tremblay, R. E., Boivin, M., & Montplaisir, J. Y. (2006). Longitudinal study of bad dreams in preschool children: Prevalence, demographic correlates, risk and protective factors. Manuscript submitted for publication.

Simonds, J. F., & Parraga, H. (1982). Prevalence of sleep disorders and sleep behaviors in children and adolescents. *Journal of the American Academy of Child & Adolescent Psychiatry, 21,* 383–388.

Smith, C. T., Nixon, M. R., & Nader, R. S. (2004). Posttraining increases in REM sleep intensity implicate REM sleep in memory processing and provide a biological marker of learning potential. *Learning & Memory, 11,* 714–719.

Snyder, F. (1970). The phenomenology of dreaming. In L.Madow & L. H. Snow (Eds.), *The psychoanalytic implications of the psychophysiological studies on dreams* (pp. 124–151). Springfield, IL: Charles Thomas.

Solomonova, E., Nielsen, T., Stenstrom, P., Simard, V., Frantova, E., & Donderi, D. (2007). Sensed presence as a correlate of sleep paralysis distress, social anxiety and waking state social imagery. Manuscript submitted for publication.

Spencer, R. M., Sunm, M., & Ivry, R. B. (2006). Sleep-dependent consolidation of contextual learning. *Current Biology, 16,* 1001–1005.

Spoormaker, V. I., Schredl, M., & Bout, J. V. (2005). Nightmares: From anxiety symptom to sleep disorder. *Sleep Medicine Reviews, 10,* 19–31.

Stickgold, R. (2002). EMDR: a putative neurobiological mechanism of action. *Journal of Clinical Psychology, 58,* 61–75.

Stickgold, R. (2003). Human studies of sleep and off-line memory reprocessing. In P. Maquet, C. Smith, & R. Stickgold (Eds.), *Sleep and brain plasticity* (pp. 41–63). New York: Oxford Universities Press.

Stickgold, R., Scott, L., Rittenhouse, C., & Hobson, J. A. (1999). Sleep-induced changes in associative memory. *Journal of Cognitive Neuroscience, 11,* 182–193.

Tanskanen, A., Tuomilehto, J., Viinamaki, H., Vartiainen, E., Lehtonen, J., & Puska, P. (2001). Nightmares as predictors of suicide. *Sleep, 24,* 845–848.

Tholey, P. (1989). Consciousness and abilities of dream characters observed during lucid dreaming. *Perceptual & Motor Skills, 68,* 567–578.

Thompson, R. A. & Raikes, H. A. (2003). Toward the next quarter-century: Conceptual and methodological challenges for attachment theory. *Development & Psychopathology, 15,* 691–718.

Van de Castle, R. L. (1994). *Our dreaming mind.* New York: Ballantine Books.

Vela-Bueno, A., Bixler, E. O., Dobladez-Blanco, B., Rubio, M. E., Mattison, R. E., & Kales, A. (1985). Prevalence of night terrors and nightmares in elementary school children: A pilot study. *Research Communications in Psychology, Psychiatry & Behavior, 10,* 177–188.

Wagner, U., Degirmenci, M., Drosopoulos, S., Perras, B., & Born, J. (2005). Effects of cortisol suppression on sleep-associated consolidation of neutral and emotional memory. *Biological Psychiatry, 58,* 885–893.

Wagner, U., Hallschmid, M., Rasch, B., & Born, J. (2006). Brief sleep after learning keeps emotional memories alive for years. *Biological Psychiatry, 60,* 788–790.

Wagner, U., Hallschmid, M., Verleger, R., & Born, J. (2003). Signs of REM sleep dependent enhancement of implicit face memory: A repetition priming study. *Biological Psychology, 62,* 197–210.

Walker, M. P., Liston, C., Hobson, J. A., & Stickgold, R. (2002). Cognitive flexibility across the sleep-wake cycle: REM-sleep enhancement of anagram problem solving. *Brain Research. Cognitive Brain Research, 14,* 317–324.

Watson, D., & Pennebaker, J. W. (1989). Health complaints, stress, and distress: Exploring the central role of negative affectivity. *Psychological Review, 96,* 234–254.

Westen, D. (1991). Social cognition and object relations. *Psychological Bulletin, 109,* 429–455.

Whittle, S., Allen, N. B., Lubman, D. I., & Yücel, M. (2006). The neurobiological basis of temperament: Towards a better understanding of psychopathology. *Neuroscience & Biobehavioral Reviews, 30,* 511–525.

Wichniak, A., Antczak, J., Wierzbicka, A., & Jernajczyk, W. (2002). Alterations in pattern of rapid eye movement activity during REM sleep in depression. *ACTA Neurobiologiae Experimentalis (Warszawa), 62,* 243–250.

Winget, C., & Kramer, M. (1979). *Dimensions of dreams.* Gainesville, FL: University Presses of Florida.

Wood, J. M., Bootzin, R., Quan, S. F., & Klink, M. E. (1993). Prevalence of nightmares among patients with asthma and chronic obstructive airways disease. *Dreaming, 3,* 231–241.

Zadra, A., Pilon, M., & Donderi, D. C. (2006). Variety and intensity of emotions in nightmares and bad dreams. *Journal of Nervous & Mental Disease, 194,* 249–254.

Ten

Anomalous Experiences and Dreams

Stanley Krippner

Reports of strange, extraordinary, and unexplained experiences related to dreams have been a topic of fascination to people throughout the millennia (Barrett, 2001; Krippner, 1990). For many Native American tribes, there was no distinction between nighttime dreams and daytime visions; either could portend the future or describe distant events (Krippner & Thompson, 1996). In modern times, these reports persist and have become controversial because they seem to transcend conventional notions of time and space, at least to highly educated members of Western society. However, in ancient eras, they were often attributed to divine forces and found their way into the sacred writings of various faiths.

The *Old Testament* relates the puzzling dream of an Egyptian pharaoh that was interpreted by his Israeli slave, Joseph, as forecasting seven years of plenty followed by seven years of famine. The pharaoh took Joseph's advice, naming the young man overseer of a network of storehouses that stocked extra food supplies that saved the country from starvation when the second part of the dream came to pass. In contemporary terms, we would say that the dream and its interpretation were "verified" and that the dream, if the account of it was accurate, provided a prediction that was subject to "falsification."

In many ancient religious traditions, the divinities were consulted through dreams. Tablets dating from the Assyrian, Babylonian, and Sumerian cultures in the third millennium BCE indicate that people distinguished between ordinary dreams and extraordinary dreams that demanded attention and interpretation by religious practitioners. These practitioners often distinguished between "divine" dreams that had to be interpreted and obeyed and "malevolent" dreams sent by demons. As far back as 2000 BCE, ancient Egyptians cited another category: some dreams were sent to earth by spirits of the dead (de Becker, 1965/1968).

The Babylonian *Talmud*, compiled between 200 BCE and 200 CE, contains some 270 references to dreams. Indeed, the word "dream" as a noun appears sixty-four times in the *Old Testament*, and only six of these were ordinary dreams. The verb "to dream" occurs twenty-eight times, of which only three were ordinary (Lavie, 1993). Dreams containing predictive or warning messages came to patriarchs, prophets, kings, and occasionally to ordinary people, such as Joseph. But the lack of important dreams was seen as a negative omen; before his downfall, King Saul lamented "God is departed from me and answereth me no more, neither by prophets nor by dreams" (*Samuel I*, 28:5). Unlike many other ancient people, the Hebrews had no technologies to induce predictive dreams; the source of their dreams was believed to be entirely external to the dreamers and out of their control (Ehrenwald, 1967).

A different perspective was taken in Tibetan Buddhism; "dream yoga" (now referred to as "lucid dreaming") was practiced by monks who held that conscious awareness while dreaming was a means to understanding and enlightenment (Weil, 1988). In Buddhism, Hindu, and several indigenous traditions, the etiology of dreams was believed to be a temporary separation of the earthly body from the spirit, providing the latter an opportunity to wander into subtle realms, often communicating with other spirits or with divinities. As an old Hindu proverb puts it, "If you conquer the mind, you have conquered the world." There are long passages about dreams in the *Upanishads* of India dating back to 1000 BCE, many of them containing specific instructions for interpreting dream images (Webb, 1990, p. 128).

When Alexander the Great was besieging the city of Tyre or *Tyros*, he reportedly dreamed about a satyr dancing on a shield. Aristander, a noted dream interpreter, was asked for the dream's meaning, and he focused on the Greek word for satyr, *satyros*. Aristander pointed out that *Sa Tyros* meant, "Tyre is yours." Encouraged by the dream, and by Aristander's interpretation, Alexander continued the battle with renewed vigor and captured the city. Again, Aristander had posited a falsifiable hypothesis, one that was verified, if indeed the story is an accurate account of what took place (Ullman & Krippner, with Vaughan, 2002, p. 5).

Alexander's tutor, Aristotle, did not doubt the occurrence of anomalous dreams but doubted their divine origin. He believed that some dreams were coincidental in nature, whereas others reflected the skill of the interpreter or became self-fulfilling prophecies. All three explanations could account for the longevity of some 300 ancient sleep temples devoted to the Greek divinity, Asclepius, who was said to diagnose and even heal clients while they slept in the sites. An adaptation of the Egyptian practices attributed to Imhotep, the legendary physician to several Pharaohs, special rituals were devised to "incubate" these healing dreams, a practice dating back to 2900 BCE. These incubation rituals were also instituted in Northern Africa and were adopted by the Romans (Kilbourne, 2000, p. 201).

The Roman orator Cicero (1947) warned against taking these types of dreams too seriously, attributing them to chance and selective attention. Rather than relying on "observations," Cicero asked whether these dreams can "be experimented on." In other words, he foresaw the necessity of introducing methods that could lead to the falsification or verification of soothsayers' claims. Without experimentation, Cicero warned that people would fall prey to "diviners," "superstition," and "endless imbecilities." Surprisingly contemporary perspectives on dreams were taken by Plato, Hippocrates, and Herodotus as well. The former held that dreams were generated internally rather than by external supernatural powers. Hippocrates' medical treatises dealt with dreams as physiological events, and in the fifth century CE, Herodotus posited that dreams reflected the waking concerns of the dreamer (Wheatland, 1993).

At the same time that Cicero, Herodotus, and other writers were positing naturalistic explanations of presumptively predictive and therapeutic dreams, Greek and Roman popular opinion held that dreams were of supernatural origin, and various "dream dictionaries" flourished. With the advent of Christianity, writers generally agreed with this perspective; Cyprian, an early bishop of Carthage, asserted that the councils of the church were guided by God through dreams and visions. St. Augustine described dreams as "gifts" from God, and Bishop Cynesium of Cyrene proclaimed "Dreams, more than any other thing, entice us toward hope" (Savary, Berne, & Williams, 1984, p. 39).

Shortly after this pronouncement, however, St. Jerome prepared a translation of the Bible in which he consistently mistranslated the Hebrew term "seeking guidance through dreams" as "witchcraft." This error stimulated prohibitions against working with dreams, unless church authorities believed they were divinely inspired. The popularity of St. Jerome's translation, with its apparently deliberate mistranslation, effectively blocked mainstream Christianity's interest in dreams for over one thousand years (Kelsey, 1974, p. 159). However, Greek and Roman treatises on dreams were saved and savored by the Muslim world. Indeed, the legitimacy of the Sunni Islamic sect often is attributed to a dream of Muhammad (Webb, 1981).

Nonetheless, some Muslims believe that it is incorrect to attribute the transcription of the *Holy Koran* to a series of dreams by the Prophet Muhammad, holding that Allah directly dictated it during a series of "night flights" by the Prophet (Barrett & Behbehani, 2003).

Dreams were resurrected during the European Renaissance. During the Elizabethan period in England, the works of Shakespeare were saturated with dream motifs. The dreams of *Richard III* are laden with guilt that proved to be predictive. The seventeenth century materialism of Bacon, Locke, and Hobbes caused a decrease in literary dream motifs, but dreams returned in nineteenth century Romanticism, especially in the works of Russian novelists including Tolstoy, Chekhov, and Dostoevsky (Wheatland, 1993). Interest in dreams, many of them at odds with conventional views of space and time, can be seen in Latin American "fantastic realism" and in such twentieth century European writers as Strindberg, Kafka, James Joyce, and Thomas Mann. The twenty-first century has brought dreams front and center not only in novels (for example, *The Lathe of Heaven,* and Divakarumi's *Queen of Dreams*) but in films ("Waking Life" and "Travelers and Magicians") and television dramas ("Six Feet Under" and "Earth II"), many of them reflecting a "post-modern" sensibility in which dream life and waking life are intertwined.

The emergence of the "grass roots dreamwork movement" is a reflection of postmodernism in dream interpretation. Stressing dream appreciation rather than dream interpretation, these groups do not rely an authoritative "leader," simply a facilitator who guides the group's discussion of members' dream reports (Hillman, 1990). These groups have provided many people the opportunity to discuss dreams that they would hesitate to share with friends, family members, or even their psychotherapists. These dreams bear such labels as "out-of-body dreams," "healing dreams," "telepathic dreams," "clairvoyant dreams," "precognitive dreams," "past life dreams," and "visitation dreams." As a group, they are often called "extraordinary dreams" (Krippner, Bogzaran, & de Carvalho, 2002) or the somewhat less value-laden term "anomalous dreams."

ANOMALOUS EXPERIENCES

The English word "anomalous" derives from the Greek *anomalos,* meaning "irregular, departing from the common." It contrasts with *homalos,* meaning "common" or "ordinary." Hence, an "anomalous experience" is one that is uncommon or rare (such as a detailed and accurate dream about an historical event) or one that may be reported by many people but deviates from ordinary experiences or from a society's explanations of reality (for example, a dream set in the future that actually occurs a few days later). Anomalous experiences might be accompanied by the subjective feeling that they reflect some aspect of reality, but under close scrutiny that feeling often proves to be illusory. Therefore, it is important to differentiate an "experience" from an "event," the latter term referring to something that occurs in consensual reality, in a definable time and place. "Anomalous dreams" are rarely "abnormal experiences," the latter term denoting psychopathology. Indeed, there is considerable evidence that most anomalous experiences do not serve as indicators of mental illness (Cardeña, Lynn, & Krippner, 2000, p. 4).

The disciplined examination of anomalous dreams can be attributed to two nineteenth century scholars, Alfred Maury and the Marquis d'Hervey de Saint-Denys. They devised self-awakening practices and utilized assistants as well. Maury made detailed records of his sleep awakenings and their content, conducting experiments to determine whether external stimuli could be incorporated into his dreams, a hunch later verified by several twentieth century investigators. Saint-Denys filled twenty-two volumes with his dream reports, self-observations, and hypotheses. Both scholars broke with church traditions by taking dreams seriously, studying their naturalistic origins, and noting dreams' creative and problem-solving capacities (Krippner, Bogzaran, & de Carvalho, 2002, pp. 11, 17).

In 1899, Sigmund Freud's *The Interpretation of Dreams* (1900/1953) went on sale; its publisher advanced the date on the book's title page to 1900, to herald the new century and to emphasize the book's importance. However, after six years, only 351 copies were sold, despite the fact that Freud had reinstated the importance of dreams for Western culture. In addition, Freud demonstrated how dreams could be used in the treatment of mental and emotional disorders.

Freud, who wrote several articles on purported telepathic dreams, was a member of the Society for Psychical Research, founded in London in 1882. Among the topics investigated by the society were hypnosis, multiple personalities, near-death experiences, reincarnation, lucid dreaming, out-of-body experiences, and so-called "psychic phenomena" that appeared to transcend the constraints of space, time, and energy. Most of these topics, including lucid dreaming, have passed into the scientific mainstream, even though their explanatory mechanisms are still a matter of conjecture (Krippner, 2005).

Freud's former colleague, Carl Jung, used anomalous dreams in his psychotherapeutic sessions, especially those denoting "synchronicity," an internal event (such as a dream) that matched a later external event (such as an unexpected occurrence of good or bad fortune). Montague Ullman drew inspiration from both Freud and Jung, and from their erstwhile colleague, Alfred Adler, who had little interest in anomalous dreams, focusing on the continuity between dreams and waking life.

LABORATORY STUDIES ON ANOMALOUS DREAMS

The first attempt to study telepathic dreams experimentally was reported by G. B. Ermacora (1895) in a publication of the Society for Psychical Research. Ermacora worked with an Italian medium who tried to influence the dreams of a child at a distance, an attempt that was deemed successful. Although amateurish by contemporary standards (evaluation procedures lacked rigor and the child was the medium's cousin), the attempt was of historical importance because Ermacora had placed an anomalous phenomenon into a controlled setting, attempting to falsify (refute) or verify (confirm) the medium's claims.

It was not until the middle of the twentieth century that telepathic dream studies were again investigated in a disciplined manner, this time using newly developed electroencephalographic technology to monitor the rapid eye movements and brain waves found to correspond with most periods of nighttime dreaming. This work was spurred by a collection of some 7,000 self-reported anecdotal telepathic experiences that had been collected by Louisa Rhine (1961); nearly two-thirds of them reputedly occurred in dreams. Rhine also collected presumptive precognitive dream reports, which allegedly forecast events that had not yet occurred, and clairvoyant dreams in which distant events are depicted. For example, at the end of World War II, a woman in Florida claimed that she awakened one night crying out between sobs that she had seen her soldier son die in the crash of a burning airplane. The next day, a cheerful letter arrived from her son, and the woman regained her composure. Five nights later, however, the same nightmare occurred, and she was sent to the psychiatric ward of a hospital for treatment. The next day a telegram arrived relaying the news that her son had been killed in an airplane crash on the night of her initial dream (Rhine, 1953, p. 105).

In his work as a psychoanalyst, Ullman (1969) often had patients reporting dreams that coincided with events in his personal life. Realizing that the correspondences could have been coincidental, or due to sensory clues or faulty memory, Ullman arranged for a "target picture," sealed in an envelope, to be selected once the research participant retired for the night. His first research participant was the celebrated medium Eileen Garrett, who agreed to have electrodes glued to her head and connected to an electrode box that was linked to an electroencephalograph (EEG), placed in another room. A clairvoyant task had been arranged, and one of the pictures was a color photo of the chariot race from the film *Ben-Hur*, currently in release. Garrett reported a dream concerning horses going uphill and associated the image with *Ben-Hur*, which she had seen two weeks previously (Ullman & Krippner, 1970, pp. 32–33).

In 1966, Ullman moved his operation into Maimonides Medical Center, Brooklyn, New York, where Stanley Krippner, who became director of the new laboratory, soon joined him. A protocol was devised in which a "telepathic transmitter" would interact with the research participant and then be separated for the night. The transmitter threw dice to select one envelope from a stack of double-sealed envelopes, taking this envelope to a distant room. Upon opening the envelope and discovering the identity of the target picture, the transmitter spent much of the night attempting to relate to the picture's contents through associations, enactments, and emotion. The participant, although virtually immobile in a sound-attenuated room, attempted to "reach out" and incorporate the picture's images into his or her dreams (Ullman & Krippner, with Vaughan, 2002).

An experimenter awakened the participant when the EEG tracings (and similar tracings that tracked eye movements and muscle tension) indicated that a dream had been in process, asking, "What has been going through your mind?" The dream report was tape-recorded for subsequent transcription. In the morning, the research participant was asked to provide associations for each dream report and then was shown copies of each picture in the "target pool," arranging them in order of correspondence to the dream reports. These selections provided statistical data that would verify or falsify the telepathy hypothesis on that particular night and for the experimental series as a whole. In the precognition dream studies, the target was selected randomly following the participant's night in the laboratory, typically while he or she was showering and dressing. The judging proceeded in the same way, with the research participant arranging the potential targets in order of closeness to his or her recalled dreams.

To evaluate whether or not the target/transcript correspondences were due to chance, the Maimonides team sent transcripts of the dream reports and postsleep associations to three outside judges who worked blind and independently. All judges had worked previously with dream reports and/or with "free response" parapsychological material (in which the variety of potential targets is unlimited rather than circumscribed). Each judge was sent copies or duplicate sets of the targets used in the study; no judge was sent the actual target that had been used because it might have been possible that a smudge or written note on the picture would have cued the judge that someone had been concentrating upon that particular item. The averages of the judges' evaluations were used as data for statistical analysis.

Outside consultants conducted the statistical evaluation; however, these consultants were not thoroughly experienced with the design problems presented in this type of research. The most serious difficulty arose when a judge, having been presented with a set of dream transcripts and a target pool, was asked to evaluate the similarity of each potential target with each transcript. The original instructions to the judges asked them to rank each target against a transcript, assigning a rank of #1 to the match that showed the closest correspondence, a rank of #2 to the match showing the next closest correspondence, and so on. The statistics used assumed that each judgment was independent of each other judgment. But if one target's content was close to a particular transcript's dream content, the judge may have been especially confident of having made a correct match. In this case, he or she could have minimized the similarity of the rest of the target pictures to that transcript, spending little time with them. The instructions presented to the judges explicitly urged them to avoid this error; nevertheless, any ensuing nonindependence would have altered variability and rendered inappropriate some standard tests of statistical significance.

When this problem became fully apparent, the Maimonides team altered the judging procedure and presented each target/transcript pair to a judge in a random order. This procedure, which minimized the independence problem, called for ratings (between 1 and 100) rather than rankings. Also, some studies avoided the independence problem by using a different target pool each night. In one instance when a different pool was used each night, a research participant judged the results himself the following morning. His results were highly significant, far more so than those of the judges who only worked with the eight pictures selected randomly as targets each of the nights of the study (Ullman & Krippner, 1969).

RETROSPECTIVE DATA ANALYSES

Many of the Maimonides target/transcript correspondences were quite striking on a *prima facie* basis. For example, when Degas's painting "School of the Dance" was the target picture, the dreamer had several dreams about a school; in one of them a young girl invited him to dance with her. However, in another instance the target pool included "Bijin by a Waterfall," a painting by Harunobu that portrays a Japanese woman with long hair, dressed in a robe, sitting by a waterfall. The research participant was a male college student whose dream reports included the following statements:

> Right now an association to "Japanese" comes to mind for some reason.... Women in kimonos with their hair ... tied up ... and the fancy picks or sticks that they put in their hair.

During another session of the same study, the research participant was a female college student, who reported dreaming,

> Suddenly the whole area is filled with girls, especially in bikinis.... Most of them were running around in bathing suits.... Somewhere along the line I got to Tokyo.... I remember somewhere in the crowd this very, very beautiful Japanese girl, like she was very special. She was in this outfit ..: and she paraded before us.

Although "Bijin by a Waterfall" was a target used in this study, it was not the target selected on the night that either of these two students served as research participants.

In other words, it is sometimes facile to find target correspondences in a night of dream reports, especially if there have been four or five lengthy reports during the session. An apologist can always make the excuse that "displacement" was at work, and that the research participant merely "displaced" his or her telepathy, identifying a different target in the pool. But this scenario has no value for serious investigators unless it is hypothesized in advance and worked into the experimental design.

In most of the Maimonides studies, dream transcripts tended to resemble the target pictures used on those nights more closely than they resembled other targets in the pool. Several of the studies that were free of the nonindependence problem (because different target pools were used each night) yielded significant results (for example, Krippner, Honorton, Ullman, Masters, & Houston, 1971). This eight-night study was statistically significant at the .001 level, using a "two-tailed test" (in which the direction of the results was not predicted).

Parapsychological experiments are often criticized on the grounds that the evidence they provide for psi phenomena is gleaned from very small effects detectable only when large bodies of data are amassed. However, Irwin Child (1985) points out that the Maimonides experiments are exempt from this criticism; significant results often resulted from only eight data points.

The rigor of statistical analysis stands in sharp contrast to other studies of external influence of dream content conducted in that era. Shortly before the initiation of the studies at Maimonides, a different team of New York investigators (Witkin & Lewis, 1967) showed research participants an emotionally threatening film before they went to sleep. For example, they were shown such anthropological documentary films as a monkey hauling her dead baby about by the limbs while nibbling at it, or of an Australian aboriginal puberty rite in which an incision is made across the surface of an initiate's penis with a sharp stone. The investigators observed that there were no direct incorporations of film content, but that their judges were able to find elements of the film in the dream reports, often in disguised "symbolic" form.

Had this been a parapsychological study, the researchers would never have been taken seriously. They would have been accused of possible cueing of the research participants' responses, of projecting their expectations while collecting the dream reports, and (since blind judging was not employed) of "reading" purported symbolism into the dream content. However, this study did not study anomalous phenomena; hence, a less than rigorous approach appears to have been permissible. In the case of parapsychology, however, it is often pointed out that claims of extraordinary phenomena require extraordinary proof; for parapsychological studies to be taken seriously, their data need to be scrupulously collected and carefully evaluated.

In another influential study, dream reports were collected from patients who were about to undergo surgery; the investigators claimed that the upcoming operation was featured symbolically in the patients' dreams (Breger, Hunter, & Lane, 1971). However, the investigators who collected the dream reports were well aware of the type of surgery each patient was facing. They easily could have found specific relationships between dream content and the scheduled operation, given the vagueness and variety of dream symbols. Again, this was not a parapsychological experiment and so there was little criticism of this study's obvious flaws.

In an investigation funded by the U.S. Institute of Mental Health, the Maimonides team exposed research participants to target material before they went to sleep, comparing the ensuing dreams to those in which they attempted to incorporate target events by means of telepathy (Honorton, Ullman, & Krippner, 1976). Attempted telepathic incorporation of target material produced chance results but the target-transcript matches in the presleep condition were highly significant. The materials utilized were some of the films (for example, the aboriginal puberty rites) that had been used in the earlier nonparapsychological studies that had not been analyzed statistically. By applying rigorous procedures of random target selection, blind judging, and statistical analysis, the Maimonides team accidentally verified the subjective judgments of the earlier study (Witkin & Lewis, 1967).

Over the years that the Maimonides laboratory was in operation, five professional magicians visited the premises to determine whether sleight of hand or fraudulent transmitter/participant collaboration could have accounted for the results. The magicians filed negative reports, stating that the only opportunities for fraud would have been on the part of the staff members who could have altered transcripts before mailing them to the statisticians or by the statisticians who analyzed the data. As a result of this suggestion, statistical analysis was carried out by outside experts who were never present during experimental sessions (Krippner, 1991, p. 47). Data given the statisticians included participants' scores, as well as scores given by three outside evaluators, none of whom had been present during the experimental sessions. In most cases, there were between eight and twelve target pictures (most of them art prints) in the target pool; evaluators matched every picture against the total transcript containing dream reports and the participants' associations to those reports.

Before the laboratory closed in 1978, Ullman and his team conducted thirteen formal experimental studies (eleven focusing on telepathy and two on precognition) and three groups of pilot studies in which telepathy, precognition, and clairvoyance were investigated. A meta-analysis of 450 nighttime dream sessions was conducted by Dean Radin (1997, pp. 71–72) who concluded that the overall confirmatory rate of 63 percent produced odds of 75 million to one against achieving such a result by chance. However, the studies cannot be considered conclusive because of the lack of replication, the loss of some early data, and the variation in evaluation procedures over the years (Child, 1985; Hyman, 1986; Krippner, 1991). On the other hand, both Child (1985) and Krippner (1991) have compiled a list of misrepresentations of the Maimonides experiments in the psychological literature, one of which contained no less than four errors (that is, Zusne & Jones, 1982, pp. 260–261).

Approximately two dozen attempts have been made by other laboratories to replicate the Maimonides work; however, it is difficult to make comparisons because many of them used different outcome measures, and most relied upon home dreams instead of on dream reports collected in the laboratory. Nevertheless, Simon J. Sherwood and Chris A. Roe (2003) made a valiant attempt, concluding that in both sets of studies "raters could correctly identify target materials more often than would be expected by chance using dream mentation" (p. 85). The Maimonides studies were seen to be "significantly more successful ... than post-Maimonides studies," but Sherwood and Roe stated, "We can be 95% confident that the true effect size is positive and therefore better than chance expectations for both sets of studies" (pp. 104, 106).

The first attempt at replication was conducted by Calvin Hall (1967), who reported data that seemed to be anomalous in nature, even though the data were too spare to allow for statistical analysis. Of those studies that were statistically analyzed, the results also were mixed. Inge Strauch (1970) served as both agent and experimenter for twelve research participants who each slept three nights in a dream laboratory. The judges' evaluations did not attain statistical significance. David Foulkes and his associates conducted two eight-night telepathy experiments, each with one of the research participants whose sessions at Maimonides yielded significant results. In neither of these attempted replications were the judges' evaluations significant (Belvedere & Foulkes, 1971; Foulkes, Belvedere, Masters, Houston, Krippner, Honorton, et al., 1972). The research participant in one of these studies criticized the target selection; although a different pool was used each night, he claimed that there was a lack of contrast among targets, making the judging process difficult (Van de Castle, 1989).

Because lack of replication and the absence of an exploratory mechanism were the major obstacles to mainstream science's serious consideration of dream telepathy and associated phenomena, Michael Persinger and Krippner (1989) explored the geomagnetic ambience during the first night each research participant engaged in an experimental session at Maimonides. A significant difference was observed between "high" and "low" scoring nights, the former being linked to the absence of electrical storms and sunspots. Krippner and Persinger (1996) repeated this analysis with a participant who spent more nights at Maimonides than any other participant, again attaining significant results. These data may indicate that the telepathic and clairvoyant capacities of the human brain are sensitive to geomagnetic activity, which could interfere with the dreaming participant's ability to transcend customary time and space constraints. A continuation of work along these lines might lead both to an increase in reliability and an understanding of explanatory mechanisms of these types of anomalous dreams.

OUT-OF-BODY DREAM EXPERIENCES

When individuals have out-of-body experiences during wakefulness, they often report a rush of energy, bodily paralysis and vibrations, and strange sounds. To the dream researcher, these symptoms resemble sleep paralysis, which typically takes place when someone is waking up from or falling into rapid eye movement (REM) sleep. Out-of-body experiences during sleep were linked to lucidity 9 percent of the time in a study involving 107 lucid dreams (Levitan & LaBerge, 1991).

One of the Maimonides research participants was a medical student who claimed to have occasional out-of-body experiences, purportedly as a result of correspondence courses taken with the Order of the Rosicrucians, a school in San Jose, California. A four-night pilot study was designed in which there was a telepathic transmitter in a distant room, as well as a randomly selected clairvoyant target resting in an open box near the ceiling of the sound-attenuated room where the participant spent the night. Care was taken so that the clairvoyant target was taken from its envelope and placed in the box in such a way that the experimenter did not observe the images on the target.

On the final night of the study, the clairvoyant target was a postcard-sized reproduction of Berman's painting, "View in Perspective of a Perfect Sunset." The participant's dream reports read, in part, "It was dark outside and light inside.... It was dusk.... It was just getting dark. Sunset. Very hazy. It was hazy. It wasn't a clear sunset.... It reminds me of a chilly or cold winter's day which is coming to an end. A day which has been cloudy all day long and the sun in just beginning to go down." In his morning interview, the participant reported having had an out-of-body experience during one of the dreams. An inspection of the EEG record disclosed an un-usual pattern of slow brain waves in the theta and delta frequencies, inter-rupting REM sleep shortly before he was awakened for his final dream report. The EEG records were shown to several sleep experts who com-mented that the interruption of REM sleep by slow brain wave activity is unusual but not unknown.

According to the norms reported in *A Content Analysis of Dreams* (Hall & Van de Castle, 1966), sunsets appear in less than 1 out of every 500 male dreams. In 1968, Charles Tart reported a study in which a sleep laboratory participant correctly identified a five-digit numeral, placed on a ledge above her bed. Tart went to great lengths to identify possible flaws with this study, and the Maimonides study attempted to avoid each of the defects pointed out by Tart. When the outside raters matched the telepathic and the clair-voyant targets against each night of dreams, sheer chance results were obtained for the telepathic condition. The clairvoyant matches were more numerous; there was only a 1 in 10 chance that they would have occurred by coincidence. Although not statistically significant, it must be recalled that this study was limited to four nights because of the participant's medical school schedule (Krippner, 1996).

Out-of-body experiences by themselves are not considered to be parapsy-chological phenomena, because there are several plausible psychophysiologi-cal explanations for the phenomena, such as their association with vestibular sensations and body schema disorders associated with temporal-parietal dys-function (Blanke, Landis, Spinelli, & Seeck, 2004; Blanke, Ortigue, Landis, & Seeck, 2002; Persinger, 1995). Nonetheless, they sometimes contain anomalies such as the "sunset" dream report of the medical student investigated in the Maimonides laboratory. As for the possible link between parapsychological-related dreams and the geomagnetic field, Persinger (1989) proposed two interpretations. The first is that such anomalies as telepathy are geomagnetic field correlates; solar disturbances and electrical storms may disrupt this connection. Second, the geomagnetic field affects the brain's receptivity to such phenomena as telepathy, which remains constant. In the latter speculation, telepathy, precognition, and clairvoyance are always present, waiting to be accessed by emotions, crises, or optimal laboratory conditions. Geomagnetic activity and other yet-to-be discovered correlates might affect the detection capacity of the brain for this information, especially the neural pathways that facilitate the consolidation and conscious access to this information. Without the geomagnetic activity, awareness of the anomalous stimuli might not be as likely. Persinger adds that temporal lobe activity exists in equilibrium with the global geomagnetic condition. When there is a sudden decrease in geomagnetic activity, there could be an enhancement of processes that facilitate telepathy and related phenomena. Such proposals, and those like them (for example, Laszlo, 2004; Ryback, 1986; Sheldrake, 2006), can lead to experiments that would verify or refute these speculations.

NONLABORATORY ANOMALOUS DREAM REPORTS

Laboratory studies focus on verifying or refuting hypotheses, determining whether reports are subjective experiences or objective events, examining the conditions under which those events can be observed, and determining the variables that are helpful in explaining the mechanisms that trigger and sustain those events. Despite the data that has been collected regarding such anomalies as telepathic, clairvoyant, and precognitive dreams, mainstream science refuses to place them in the "events" category because of their ephemeral nature, their resistance to appearing on demand, and their lack of satisfactory explanatory mechanisms. As a result, they remain in the "reports" category, while advocates struggle with the replication and explanation issues that prevent their acceptance as "events."

Even so, anomalous dream reports can be extremely useful to science; the identification of such variables as gender, age, and cross-cultural differences can assist investigators understand the roles that dreams play in human development. Stanley Krippner and Laura Faith (2001) looked for "exotic dreams" (that is, anomalies) in a collection of 910 dream reports from women and 756 from men. Krippner had collected all reports in seminars presented in six different countries between 1990 and 1998. Seminar participants were simply asked to volunteer a recent dream, and only one dream per participant was utilized in the analysis. When a dream report was not written in English, a native speaker of that language translated it. Krippner and Faith made no pretense that the dream reports were representative of the general population of the countries investigated. Scoring guidelines were applied to the dreams, and when a report fell into more than one category, half a point was given for each category. Two raters scored each of the 1,666 dreams; interrater reliability was .95; in other words, the scoring guidelines were clear with minimal overlap. The categories used were those described in the book *Extraordinary Dreams* (Krippner, Bogzaran, & de Carvalho, 2002).

There were no statistically significant differences between genders; 8.5 percent of all female dreams were anomalous versus 7.7 percent of male dream reports. The country with the highest number of anomalous dreams was Russia (12.7 percent), followed by Brazil (10.9 percent), Argentina (8.6 percent), Japan (8.1 percent), Ukraine (5.9 percent), and the United States (5.7 percent). The only categories that surpassed 1 percent of all dream reports were lucid dreams (1.7 percent), out-of-body dreams (1.4 percent), visitation dreams (1.1 percent), and precognitive dreams (1.1 percent). To be scored as a visitation dream, a deceased person or an entity from another reality provided counsel or direction that the dreamer felt of comfort or value. For example, a Ukrainian woman reported

> In this dream, I am afraid of dying because my neighbors start to die, one by one. I think of what a short period of time it took for so many of them to die, both men and women. I would like to live a more spiritual life, but the conditions around me do not permit it, so I must work very hard each day. Then one of my dead neighbors comes to see me and tells me that I can lead a spiritual life through my work.

Of course, the existence of the deceased neighbor cannot be verified, but the dream assisted the dreamer in resolving an existential dilemma in her life.

Fariba Bogzaran related a dream by one of her clients, an illustrator named "Louise" (in Krippner, Bogzaran, & de Carvalho, 2002, pp. 109–110).

> I am racing about in a distant city, trying desperately to reach a friend. The nature of the urgency is unclear; I only know that I must find her. I awake feeling frantic and distraught. I then return to dreaming. I hear a woman's voice repeating, "It was the worst pain—terrifying. I thought I was dying." There is no accompanying imagery. I awake confused with the bizarre thought that I am having someone else's dream.

That morning, Louise woke up puzzling over this dream and decided to give her friend a call. The friend told Louise that her timing was remarkable. The night before, at the time of Louise's dream, the friend had been rushed to the hospital in excruciating pain. Her friend repeated the exact words Louise had heard in her dream. She had thought she was dying, but the doctors had denied Louise's friend any pain reliever until the nature of her condition had been determined.

Louise told Bogzaran that there was now an explanation for the sense of urgency in her dream. She had been looking for her friend who was being rushed to the hospital. This dream not only connected Louise more closely to her friend, but also prepared her for the worst—the possibility of her friend's death. Again, the anomalous elements in this dream may have been coincidental; however, in retrospect the dream served a useful purpose.

Not all anomalous dreams are intentional in nature. Some serve no apparent purpose but, at best, are mere curiosities; others can have unforeseen maladaptive consequences. In 1980, Steve Linscott was awakened by a dream in which a man had approached a young woman with a blunt object in his hand. In a second dream, this man "was beating her on the head.... She was on her hands and knees ... and didn't resist.... Blood flying everywhere." Linscott went back to sleep, but later that day he noticed police cars two doors away from his house. A young woman had been brutally beaten and murdered in a nearby apartment building. He told the dream to his wife and two colleagues at the Christian halfway house in the Chicago suburb where he worked. They all persuaded Linscott to tell his dream to the police, and he complied with their suggestions.

A few weeks later, Linscott was charged with the murder of the young woman. The dreams, according to the police, included too many accurate details to be coincidental. Linscott was convicted and sentenced to forty years in prison. The prosecution finally dropped the case after several appeals by defense attorneys. Apparently, the police department did not consider the possibility that the dreams might have represented anomalies, nor did they realize that coincidental "matches" frequently occur in dreams (Krippner, 1995).

Past-life dreams occur most frequently where the doctrine of reincarnation forms a basic part of a society's religions and philosophies. Many Asian, Australian aboriginal, tribal African, Pacific Island, and Native American cultural groups have adopted this perspective. The concept is an appealing one; it satisfies the hope for immortality and assures eventual justice as right actions in one's current life are rewarded in the next one. The "return" of a deceased person is often "announced" in a dream; shortly after this announcement, a pregnant woman might adopt food preferences that match those of the person who is "returning," and preparations are made for the event. However, there are cultural differences; "announcements" generally occur in the final months of pregnancy in Alaskan Tlinget groups but shortly before conception in rural Burmese families where the "returning" person requests permission to be reborn there (Matlock, 1990).

Bogzaran reported the case of "Antonia" who had been suffering from acute neck pains that had not yielded to conventional medical treatment (Krippner, Bogzaran, & de Carvalho, 2002, pp. 132–134). During a psychotherapy session, she related a recent dream:

> I am a seamstress in France, and a revolution has just taken place. I am taken before a tribunal and am called an enemy of the people because I worked for a countess. I protest my innocence, but to no avail. I am condemned to death, and taken to the guillotine where I am beheaded.

The psychotherapist had Antonia associate each salient word or phrase in the dream and divide the dream into scenes. In the first scene, Antonia is a hard worker engaged in a feminine occupation where she carries out detailed work during a time of momentous challenge in a setting that is imperious. In the second scene, neither her employer's power nor her own protest is a match for the male tribunal that condemns her. In the third scene, Antonia "gets it in the neck."

Antonia applied these scenarios to her everyday life, observing that she worked very hard, providing basic necessities for her family and mediating disputes between her husband and their children. Despite her husband's high-paying job, he would frequently be drunk upon his arrival home, throwing the household into disarray; Antonia's feminine skills were no match for his demands and accusations. His abuse was verbal rather than physical, but Antonia would still suffer neck pains after each of his temper outbursts. The psychotherapist viewed the dream narrative as metaphorical, but Antonia became convinced that it represented an actual past life. Once she announced this conviction, her neck pain disappeared; within a few years, Antonia's husband entered psychotherapy and reduced his alcohol consumption and abusive behavior.

Did Antonia's dream reflect reality or create it? There were not enough historical details in the dream report to verify the possibility of a past life; nevertheless, the dream report served a useful purpose, thanks to the therapist's willingness to spend time discussing it and to refrain from making a judgment concerning the dream's veridicality.

CONCLUSION

It is tempting to ignore or dismiss dreams that simply do not "fit" mainstream scientific concepts of time, space, and energy. Nevertheless, psychiatrists such as Ullman and psychologists such as Bogzaran have used unusual dreams advantageously in psychotherapy. Alfred Adler, Calvin Hall, and other dream theorists have traced the connection between dreams and waking life; these connections usually are apparent even in anomalous dream reports.

Writers who dismiss or belittle anomalous dreams often assume that the universe operates in a linear, cause-and-effect manner that precludes consideration of such phenomena as telepathy or precognition. But what if the universe is nonlinear, at least in part, and if interactions between people do not always follow linear causality? These propositions have been considered by nonlinear dynamical theory or "chaos theory," and the resulting model of dreaming may allow for the operation of anomalous effects. Stanley Krippner and Allan Combs (2000) observed that those parts of the brain ordinarily involved in practical activity based on working memory are less active during the night, giving other brain centers the opportunity to organize dream content, much of which is generated randomly by the brain's internal mechanisms. As a result, many of the resulting dream stories are bizarre, marked by abrupt transitions, quick changes of scene, and actions that seem illogical in daily life.

At the same time, dreams provide "networks of meaning" that reflect "emotional intelligence," assisting dreamers to understand emotional relationships and their own personal feelings (Hardy, 1998). Dreams often reflect conflicts between two or more "chaotic attractors," for example, between activity and passivity or between authenticity and superficiality. Christine Hardy (1998) described a dreamer whose reliance on social interactions based on authority and hierarchy was undermined by a powerful dream focusing on cooperation and synergy, leading him to adopt a new set of values. This clash between chaotic attractors provides the opportunity for anomalous dream content to emerge and to find its niche in the resulting synthesis.

Krippner and Combs proposed that there are two other important qualities of the sleeping brain that make people sensitive to subtle influences. The first of these is the brain's susceptibility to what chaos theorists call the "butterfly effect"; very small alternations in the present condition of the weather or the stock market can lead to major variations in its future status. A small shift in the brain's neurochemistry can introduce a new image into an ongoing dream narrative, and the integration of this element into someone's dream demonstrates the brain's creative potential, even though the result may seem illogical, irrational, or unrealistic upon awakening.

The second remarkable quality of the sleeping brain is its capacity to respond to signals so tiny that they would not otherwise affect the brain. Known to chaos theorists as "stochastic resonance," this effect has been noted in electronic circuits, as well as in nerve cells. The quality of this type of resonance keeps a system in motion; the signal follows the path of least resistance, rather than disappearing or getting trapped. As a result, small emotional residues of the day's experience may return during a dream or nightmare on the given night or later in the week (Hartmann, 1998). Examples would be a dramatic scene from a movie, an intriguing face in the crowd, a sarcastic comment from an e-mail, or a poignant phrase from an overheard conversation.

In other words, chaotic attractors, the butterfly effect, and stochastic resonance are qualities of the sleeping brain that make it susceptible to anomalous interactions, especially if geomagnetic and other environmental conditions provide a suitable milieu. Emotion in dreams may provide a network that assists self-organization of diverse images, memories, and even some events distant in space and time that are attracted to the dream's formulating emotional vortex.

Ernest Hartmann (1998) described how the brain's neural networks are open to greater novelty and emotional impact during sleep than during wakefulness and notes that anomalous dreams often involve someone close to the dreamer with whom there is an emotional connection. In this manner, the self-organizing dream creates order from chaos, resulting in a unique narrative. The story may be a review of daily events, an attempt to resolve a life trauma, an inventive technological or artistic product, a metaphorical solution to a psychological problem, or a preview of an oncoming event in the dreamer's life.

Dreams appear to be the creative product of an adaptive process that is crucial to the development of human communication (McNamara, 2004). Anomalous dreams, whatever their explanations, suggest that there are profound interconnections and entanglements among human beings, as well as between humans and the rest of nature (Ullman, 1999). Perhaps these linkages can help to mend the torn social and ecological fabric of the current era. Working with dreams is one way of reweaving this tattered tapestry, and anomalous dreams may represent a resource that could play a vital role in addressing the imbalance between humans and their environment.

ACKNOWLEDGMENT

The preparation of this paper was supported by the Chair for the Study of Consciousness, Saybrook Graduate School and Research Center, San Francisco, California.

REFERENCES

Barrett, D. (2001). *The committee of sleep*. New York: Crown.
Barrett, D., & Behbehani, J. (2003). Post-traumatic nightmares in Kuwait following the Iraqi invasion. In S. Krippner & T. M. McIntyre (Eds.), *The psychological impact of*

war trauma on civilians: An international perspective (pp. 135–141). Westport, CT: Greenwood.

Belvedere, E., & Foulkes, D. (1971). Telepathy and dreams: A failure to replicate. *Perceptual & Motor Skills, 33*, 783–789.

Blanke, O., Landis, T., Spinelli, I., & Seeck, M. (2004). Out-of-body experience and autoscopy of neurological origin. *Brain, 127*, 243–258.

Blanke, O., Ortigue, S., Landis, T., & Seeck, M. (2002). Stimulating illusory own-body perceptions. *Nature, 419*, 269–270.

Breger, L., Hunter, I., & Lane, R. (1971). Effects of stress on dreams. *Psychological Issues, 7* (No. 3, Monograph 27).

Cardeña, E., Lynn, S. J., & Krippner, S. (Eds.). (2000). *The varieties of anomalous experience: Examining the scientific evidence.* Washington, DC: American Psychological Association.

Child, I. L. (1985). Psychology and anomalous observations: The question of ESP in dreams. *American Psychologist, 40*, 1219–1230.

Cicero. (1947). Argument against taking dreams seriously. In R. L. Woods (Ed.), *The world of dreams* (pp. 203–204). New York: Random House.

de Becker, R. (1968). *The understanding of dreams and their influence on the history of man* (M. Heron, Trans.). New York: Bell. (Original work published 1965)

Ehrenwald, J. (1967). Precognition, prophecy, and self-fulfillment in Greco-Roman, Hebrew, and Aztec antiquity. *International Journal of Parapsychology, 9*, 22.

Ermacora, G. B. (1895). Telepathic dreams experimentally induced. *Proceedings of the Society for Psychical Research, 22*, 345–308.

Foulkes, D., Belvedere, E., Masters, R. E. L., Houston, J., Krippner, S., Honorton, C., et al. (1972). Long-distance "sensory-bombardment" in dreams: A failure to replicate. *Perceptual & Motor Skills, 35*, 731–734.

Freud, S. (1953). *The interpretation of dreams.* London: Hogarth Press. (Original work published 1900)

Hall, C. S. (1967). Experiments with telepathically influenced dreams. *Zeitschrift fur Parapsychologie und Grenzgebiete der Psychologie, 10*, 18–47.

Hall, C. S., & Van de Castle, R. L. (1966). *The content analysis of dreams.* New York: Appleton-Century-Crofts.

Hardy, C. (1998). *Networks of meaning: A bridge between mind and matter.* Westport, CT: Praeger.

Hartmann, E. (1998). *Dreams and nightmares: The new theory on the origin and meaning of dreams.* New York: Plenum.

Hillman, D. (1990). The emergence of the grassroots dreamwork movement. In S. Krippner (Ed.), *Dreamtime and dreamwork: Decoding the language of the night* (pp. 13–20). New York: Jeremy P. Tarcher/Putnam.

Honorton, C., Ullman, M., & Krippner, S. (1976). Comparison of extrasensory and pre-sleep influences on dreams. In J. D. Morris, W. G. Roll, & R. L. Morris (Eds.), *Research in parapsychology 1976* (pp. 154–155). Metuchen, NJ: Scarecrow Press.

Hyman, R. (1986). Maimonides dream-telepathy experiments. *Skeptical Inquirer, 11*, 91–92.

Kelsey, M. T. (1974). *God, dreams and revelations.* Minneapolis: Augsburg.

Kilbourne, B. (2000). Ancient and native peoples' dreams. In S. Krippner (Ed.), *Dreamtime and dreamwork: Decoding the language of the night* (pp. 194–203). New York: Jeremy P. Tarcher/Putnam.

Krippner, S. (1990). Tribal shamans and their travels into dreamtime. In S. Krippner (Ed.), *Dreamtime and dreamwork: Decoding the language of the night* (pp. 185–193). New York: Jeremy P. Tarcher/Putnam.

Krippner, S. (1991). An experimental approach to the anomalous dream. In J. Gackenbach & A. A. Sheikh (Eds.), *Dream images: A call to mental arms* (pp. 31–54). Amityville, NY: Baywood.

Krippner, S. (1995). A psychic dream? Be careful who you tell! *Dream Network, 14,* 35–36.

Krippner, S. (1996). A pilot study in ESP, dreams, and purported OBEs. *Journal of the Society for Psychical Research, 61,* 88–93.

Krippner, S. (2005). Psychoneurological dimensions of anomalous experience in relation to religious belief and practice. In K. Bulkeley (Ed.), *Soul, psyche, brain: New directions in the study of religion and brain-mind science* (pp. 61–92). New York: Palgrave/Macmillan.

Krippner, S., Bogzaran, F., & de Carvalho, A. P. (2002). *Extraordinary dreams and how to work with them.* Albany, NY: State University of New York Press.

Krippner, S., & Combs, A. (2000). Self-organization in the dreaming brain. *Journal of Mind & Behavior, 21,* 399–412.

Krippner, S., & Faith, L. (2001). Exotic dreams: A cross-cultural study. *Dreaming 11,* 73–82.

Krippner, S., Honorton, C., Ullman, M., Masters, R. E. L., & Houston, J. (1971). A long-distance "sensory-bombardment" study of ESP in dreams. *Journal of the American Society for Psychical Research, 65,* 468–475.

Krippner, S., & Persinger, M. A. (1996). Evidence for enhanced congruence between dreams and distant target material during periods of decreased geomagnetic activity. *Journal of Scientific Exploration, 10,* 487–483.

Krippner, S., & Thompson, A. (1996). A 10-facet model of dreaming applied to dream practices of sixteen Native American cultural groups. *Dreaming, 6,* 71–96.

Laszlo, E. (2004). *Science and the Akashic field: An integral theory of everything.* London: World Scientific.

Lavie, P. (1993). Religion and dreaming. In M. A. Carskadon (Ed.), *Encyclopedia of sleep and dreaming* (pp. 496–497). New York: Macmillan.

Levitan, L., & LaBerge, S. L. (1991). Mind in body or body in mind? *NightLight, 3,* 1–3.

Matlock, J. G. (1990). Past life memory case studies. In S. Krippner (Ed.), *Advances in parapsychological research* (Vol. 6, pp. 184–267). Jefferson, NC: McFarland.

McNamara, P. (2004). *An evolutionary psychology of sleep and dreams.* Westport, CT: Praeger.

Persinger, M. A. (1989). Psi phenomena and temporal lobe activity: The geomagnetic factor. In L. A. Henkel & R. E. Berger (Eds.), *Research in parapsychology 1988* (pp. 121–156). Metuchen, NJ: Scarecrow Press.

Persinger, M. A. (1995). Out-of-body-like experiences are more probable in people with elevated complex partial epileptic-like signs during periods of enhanced geomagnetic activity: A non-linear effect. *Perceptual & Motor Skills, 80,* 563–569.

Persinger, M. A., & Krippner, S. (1989). Dream ESP experiments and geomagnetic activity. *Journal of the American Society of Psychical Research, 83,* 101–106.

Radin, D. (1997). *The conscious universe: The scientific truth of psychic phenomena*. New York: Harper Collins.

Rhine, J. B. (1953). *New world of the mind*. New York: William Sloane.

Rhine, L. E. (1961). *Hidden channels of the mind*. New York: William Sloane.

Ryback, D. (1986). Future memory as holographic process: A scientific model for psychic dreams. *Journal of Creative Behavior, 20,* 283–295.

Savary, L. M., Berne, P. H., & Williams, S. K. (1984). *Dreams and spiritual growth*. New York: Paulist Press.

Sheldrake, R. (2006). Morphic fields. *World Futures: The Journal of General Evolution, 62,* 31–41.

Sherwood, S. J., & Roe, C. A. (2003). A review of dream ESP studies conducted since the Maimonides dream ESP programme. In J. E. Alcock, J. E. Burns, & A. Freeman (Eds.), *Psi wars: Getting to grips with the paranormal* (pp. 85–109). Charlottesville, VA: Imprint Academic.

Strauch, I. (1970). Dreams and psi in the laboratory. In R. Cavanna (Ed.), *Psi favorable states of consciousness* (pp. 46–54). New York: Parapsychology Foundation.

Tart, C. T. (1968). A psychophysiological study of out-of-the-body experiences in a selected subject. *Journal of the American Society for Psychical Research, 62,* 3–27.

Ullman, M. (1969). Telepathy and dreams. *Experimental Medicine & Surgery, 27,* 19–38.

Ullman, M. (1999). Dreaming consciousness: More than a bit player in the search for an answer to the mind/body problem. *Journal of Scientific Exploration, 13,* 91–112.

Ullman, M., & Krippner, S. (1969). A laboratory approach to the nocturnal dimension of paranormal experience: Report of a confirmatory study using the REM monitoring technique. *Biological Psychiatry, 1,* 259–270.

Ullman, M., & Krippner, S. (1970). *Dream studies and telepathy: An experimental approach*. New York: Parapsychology Foundation.

Ullman, M., & Krippner, S., & Vaughan, A. (2002). *Dream telepathy: Experiments in Nocturnal extrasensory perception* (3rd ed.). Charlottesville, VA: Hampton Roads.

Van de Castle, R. L. (1989). Appendix C. In M. Ullman, S. Krippner, & A. Vaughan (Eds.), *Dream telepathy: Experiments in nocturnal ESP.* (Rev. ed., pp. 209–216). Jefferson, NC: McFarland.

Webb, W. (1981). A historical perspective on dreams. In B. B. Wolman (Ed.), *Handbook of dreams* (pp. 3–19). New York: Van Nostrand.

Webb, W. (1990). Historical perspectives: From Aristotle to Calvin Hall. In S. Krippner (Ed.), *Dreamtime and dreamwork: Decoding the language of the night* (pp. 175–184). New York: Tarcher/Perigree.

Weil, P. (1988). Tibetan dream yoga. In M. A. Descamps, C. M. Bouchet, & P. Weil (Eds.), *The transpersonal revolution in dreams* (61–97). Paris: Editions Trismegiste.

Wheatland, T. (1993). Sleep and dreams in literature. In M. A. Carskadon (Ed.), *Encyclopedia of sleep and dreaming* (pp. 332–335). New York: Macmillan.

Witkin, H., & Lewis, H. (1967). *Experimental studies of dreaming*. New York: Random House.

Zusne, L., & Jones, W. H. (1982). Anomalistic psychology: A study of extraordinary behavior and experience. Hillsdale, NJ: Erlbaum.

Eleven

Lucid Dreaming

Stephen LaBerge

In the course of everyday life, most people do not ordinarily think about the fact that they are awake. Likewise, generally most people are not usually aware of the fact that they are dreaming while they are dreaming. However, there is a significant exception to this generalization: at times, more often for some than others, while dreaming we are cognizant of the fact that we are dreaming. The experience of *lucid dreaming*, as this phenomenon is termed (van Eeden, 1913), is exceptional in several ways to be discussed below. The term *lucid* is used in the psychiatric sense, indicating a condition of clear insight and correct orientation to reality in opposition to the clouded insight and deluded disorientation of the delirious.

Just as there are degrees of delirium, there are degrees of lucidity (Barrett, 1992; Kahan & LaBerge, 1994; LaBerge, 1985a; LaBerge & DeGracia, 2000). In the best of conditions, lucid dreamers claim to be fully in possession of their cognitive faculties: they report being able to reason clearly, to remember the conditions of waking life, and to act voluntarily upon reflection or in accordance with plans decided upon before sleep. At the same time, they remain soundly asleep, experiencing a dream world that can seem vividly real.

The usual definition of lucid dreaming is simply *dreaming while knowing that one is dreaming* (Green, 1968; LaBerge, 1985a). Some researchers (for example, Tart, 1984; Tholey, 1988) consider this minimal criterion too broad and argue that the term lucid dreaming should require, in addition, correct memory for the circumstances of waking life, and a degree of control over the dream. However, there are compelling reasons for preferring the simpler, minimalist definition. For example, in laboratory studies of lucid dreaming, memory for the fact that one is sleeping in the laboratory is relevant and essential (LaBerge, 1990), but in other lucid dreams, the location where one is sleeping may be entirely irrelevant. Moreover, although dream control and dream awareness are correlated, neither requires the other (Kahan & LaBerge, 1994), and there is no requirement for a fully lucid dreamer to exercise control over the dream at all; one might, for instance, choose to lucidly observe the events of the dream without interference (LaBerge, 1985a).

The concept of "conscious sleep" can seem so self-contradictory and paradoxical that some theoreticians have considered lucid dreams impossible and even absurd (for example, Malcolm, 1959). Before the empirical studies reviewed later established the physiological basis of lucid dreaming, most sleep researchers were reasonably skeptical, supposing that lucid dreams were "not typical parts of dreaming thought, but rather brief arousals" (Hartmann, 1975, p. 74; Berger, 1977). Schwartz and Lefebvre (1973) noted that frequent transitory arousals were common during REM sleep and proposed these "microawakenings" as the physiological basis for lucid dream reports. Although no one had put forward any evidence for this mechanism, it seems to have been the orthodox opinion (for example, Foulkes, 1974) up until the last few years.

In the late 1970s, research began to accumulate suggesting that lucid dreams occur during rapid eye movement (REM) sleep. Based on standard sleep recordings of two subjects who reported a total of three lucid dreams upon awakening from REM periods, Ogilvie, Hunt, Sawicki, and McGowan (1978) cautiously concluded that "it may be that lucid dreams begin in REM" (p. 165). However, no proof was given that the reported lucid dreams themselves had in fact occurred during the REM sleep immediately preceding the awakenings and reports. What was needed to unambiguously establish the physiological status of lucid dreams was some sort of behavioral response signaling to the experimenter the exact time the lucid dream was taking place.

LUCID DREAMING VERIFIED BY VOLITIONAL SIGNALING

Earlier studies found that the directions of eye movements recorded during REM sleep sometimes exactly corresponded to the directions in which subjects reported they had been looking in their dreams (for example, Roffwarg, Dement, Muzio, and Fisher 1962). I reasoned that if lucid dreamers can in fact act volitionally, they should be able to prove it by making a prearranged eye-movement signal marking the exact time they became lucid. Using this approach, my colleagues at Stanford and I (LaBerge, Nagel, Dement & Zarcone, 1981) reported that the occurrence of lucid dreaming during unequivocal REM sleep had been verified for five subjects. After being instructed in the method of lucid dream induction (MILD) described by LaBerge (1980b), the subjects were recorded from two to twenty nights each. In the course of the thirty-four nights of the study, thirty-five lucid dreams were reported subsequent to spontaneous awakening from various stages of sleep as follows: REM sleep, 32 times; NREM Stage 1, twice; and

FIGURE 11.1
A signal-verified lucid dream (SVLD) initiated 24.5 min into REM period #5. Three channels of standard sleep physiological data (brainwaves, from left central [EEG], C3–A2, Horizontal eye movement [EOG], and chin muscle tone [EMG]) are shown. Upon awakening, the subject reported having made five eye movement signals (labeled 1–5 in figure). The first signal (1, LRLR) marked the onset of lucidity. Skin potential artifacts can be observed in the EEG at this point. During the following 90 seconds, the subject "flew about" exploring his dream world until he believed he had awakened, at which point he made the signal for awakening (2, LRLRLRLR). After another 90 seconds, the subject realized he was still dreaming and signaled (3) with three pairs of eye movements. Realizing that this was too many, he correctly signaled with two pairs (4). Finally, upon awakening 100 seconds later, he signaled appropriately (5, LRLRLRLR). Calibrations are 50 μV and 5 seconds.

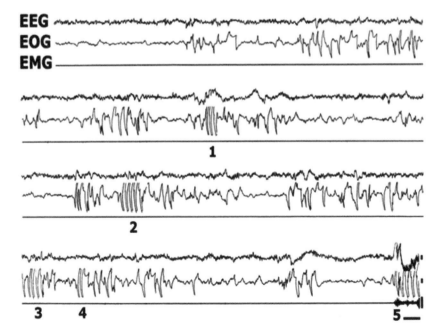

during the transition from NREM Stage 2 to REM, once. The subjects reported signaling during thirty of these lucid dreams. After each recording, the reports mentioning signals were submitted along with the respective polysomnograms to a judge uninformed of the times of the reports. In twenty-four cases (90 percent), the judge was able to select the appropriate 30-second epoch on the basis of correspondence between reported and observed signals. All signals associated with lucid dream reports occurred during epochs of unambiguous REM sleep scored according to the conventional criteria (Rechtschaffen & Kales, 1968).

A later analysis extending these data with two additional subjects and twenty more lucid dreams produced identical results (LaBerge, Nagel, Taylor, Dement, & Zarcone, 1981), supporting the conclusion that stable lucid dreams usually (though perhaps not exclusively) occur during REM sleep.

Ogilvie et al. (1983) reported the physiological state preceding fourteen spontaneous lucidity signals as unqualified REM in twelve (86 percent) of the cases; of the remaining two cases, one was "ambiguous" REM and the

FIGURE 11.2
A SVLD occurring during the first 30 sec of REMP #1. Note the sleep spindles and elevated EMG indicating NREM Stage 2, with sharp transition to REM stage (EMG supression, saw-tooth waves, and rapid eye movements). Six channels of physiological data (EEG from left and right central locations, [C3–C4]; midline occipital, [Oz], [EOG] right and left outer canthus, ROC and LOC), and chin muscle tone [EMG]). Calibrations are 50 μV and 5 seconds.

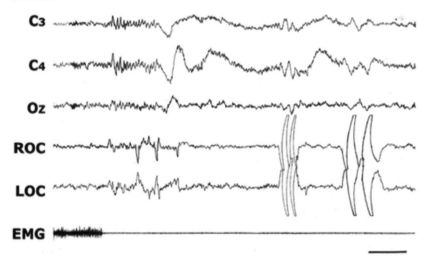

other appeared to be wakefulness. Keith Hearne and Alan Worsley collaborated on a pioneering study of lucid dreaming in which the latter spent fifty nonconsecutive nights in the Hull University sleep lab while the former monitored the polygraph. Worsley reported signaling in eight lucid dreams, all of which were described by Hearne (1978) as having occurred during REM sleep.

The basic methodology establishing the association of lucid dreaming with REM sleep has been repeatedly replicated in at least a dozen different studies and laboratories around the world (Brylowski, Levitan, & LaBerge, 1989; Dane, 1984; Erlacher, Schredl & LaBerge, 2003; Fenwick et al., 1984; Hearne, 1978; Hickey, 1988; Holzinger et al., 2006; Kueny, 1985; LaBerge et al., 1981a, 1981b, 1986; Ogilvie, Hunt, Kushniruk, & Newman, 1983).

The evidence is clear: lucid dreaming is an experiential and physiological reality; though perhaps the most paradoxical phenomenon of "paradoxical sleep," it is undeniably a feature of REM sleep.

PHYSIOLOGICAL CHARACTERISTICS OF LUCID DREAMING

Tonic versus Phasic REM

The preceding studies showed that lucid dreams typically occur in REM sleep. However, REM sleep is a heterogeneous state exhibiting considerable variations in physiological activity, of which two distinct phases are ordinarily distinguished. In its most active form, REM is dominated by a striking variety of irregular and short-lived events such as muscular twitching, including the rapid eye movements that give the state one of its most common names. This variety of REM is referred to as "phasic," while the relatively quiescent state remaining when rapid eye movements and other phasic events temporarily subside is referred to as "tonic." On first thought, one might expect lucid dreams to be associated with decreased phasic activity (Pivik, 1986). However, research by the Stanford group, detailed below, has shown lucid dreaming to be associated with, on the contrary, increased phasic activity.

Physiology of Lucid Dream Initiation

LaBerge, Levitan, and Dement (1986) analyzed physiological data from seventy-six signal-verified lucid dreams (SVLDs) of thirteen subjects. The polysomnograms corresponding to each of the SVLDs were scored for sleep stages, and every SVLD REM period was divided into thirty-second epochs aligned with the lucidity onset signal. For each epoch, sleep stage was scored and rapid eye movements (EM) were counted; if scalp skin-potential responses were observable as artifacts in the electroencephalogram (EEG), these were also counted (SP). Heart rate (HR) and respiration rate (RR) were determined for SVLDs recorded with these measures.

For the first lucid epoch, beginning with the initiation of the signal, the sleep stage was unequivocal REM in seventy cases (92 percent). The remaining six SVLDs were less than thirty-seconds long and hence technically unscorable according to the standard methodology (Rechtschaffen & Kales, 1968). For these cases, the entire SVLD was scored as a single epoch; with this modification, all SVLDs qualified as REM. The lucid dream signals were followed by an average of 115 seconds (range: 5 to 490 seconds) of uninterrupted REM sleep. Physiological comparison of EM, HR, RR, and SP for lucid versus nonlucid epochs revealed that the lucid epochs of the SVLD REM periods had significantly higher levels of physiological activation than the preceding epochs of nonlucid REM from the same REM period.

Physiological data (EM, RR, HR, and SP) were also collected for sixty-one control nonlucid REM periods, derived from the same thirteen subjects, to allow comparison with SVLDs. Mean values for EM and SP were significantly higher for REM periods with lucid dreams than nonlucid control REM periods (RR and HR did not differ).

Temporal Distribution of Lucid Dreams Within REMPs

Given the finding that lucid dreams reliably occur during activated (phasic) REM, measures of central nervous system (CNS) activation, such as eye movement density, should contribute something to the pattern of lucid dream distribution. Because it was previously observed that eye-movement density starts at a low level at the beginning of REM periods and increases until it reaches a peak after approximately five to seven minutes (Aserinsky, 1971), we (LaBerge, 2004) hypothesized that lucid dream probability should follow a parallel development and accordingly found that mean eye-movement density correlated positively and significantly with lucid dream probability ($r = .66$; $p < .01$).

The Distribution of REM Lucid Dreams as a Function of Circadian Phase

Lucid dreams have been frequently reported to occur most commonly late in the sleep cycle (Green, 1968). LaBerge et al. (2004) tested this hypothesis by first determining for each of their twelve subjects the time of night that divided their total REM time into two equal parts. All but one of the subjects had more lucid dreams in the second half of their REM time than in the first half (binomial test; $p < .01$). For the combined sample, relative lucidity probability was calculated for REM periods 1 through 6 of the night by dividing the total number of lucid dreams observed in a given REM period by the corresponding total time in stage REM for the same REM period. A regression analysis clearly demonstrated that relative lucidity probability was a linear function of ordinal REM period number ($r = .98$; $p < .0001$).

Dream-initated versus Wake-initiated Lucid Dreams

There are two distinct ways in which lucid dreams are initiated. In the usual case, subjects report being in the midst of a dream when a bizarre occurrence causes sufficient reflection to yield the realization that they are dreaming. In the other, less frequent case, subjects report briefly awakening from a dream and then falling back asleep directly entering the dream with no (or very little) break in consciousness (Green, 1968; LaBerge, 1985a). Here is an example of a wake-initiated lucid dream:

> I was lying awake in bed late in the morning listening to the sound of running water in the adjoining bathroom. Presently an image of the ocean appeared, dim at first like my usual waking imagery. But its vividness rapidly increased while, at the same time, the sound of running water diminished; the intensity of the internal image and external sound seemed to alter inversely (as if one changed a stereo balance control from one channel to the other). In a few seconds, I found myself at the seashore standing between my mother and a girl who seemed somehow familiar. I could no longer hear the sound of the bath water, but only the roar of the dream sea.... (LaBerge, 1980a, p. 85)

Note that the subject is continuously conscious during the transition from wakefulness to sleep. This fact suggests that Foulkes (1985) is overstating the case by claiming that it is "... a necessary part of the experience we call 'sleep' that we lose a directive and reflective self. You can't fall asleep, or be asleep, if your waking self is still regulating and reflecting upon your conscious mental state" (p. 42).

Because lucid dreams initiated in these two ways ought to differ physiologically in at least one respect (that is, an awakening preceding one but not the other), the SVLDs were dichotomously classified as either "wake-initiated" (WILD) or "dream-initiated" (DILD), depending on whether or not the reports mentioned a transient awakening in which the subject consciously perceived the external environment before re-entering the dream state.

Fifty-five (72 percent) of the SVLDs were classified as DILDs and the remaining 21 (28 percent) as WILDs. For all thirteen subjects, DILDs were more common than WILDs (binomial test; $p < .0001$). As expected, compared to DILDs, WILDs were more frequently immediately preceded by

FIGURE 11.3

A SVLD initiated following a transient awakening during REM (WILD). Six channels of physiological data (left and right temporal EEG [T3 and T4], left and right eye-movements [LOC and ROC], chin muscle tone [EMG], and electrocardiogram [ECG]) from the last 3 min of a 14 min REM period are shown. The subject awoke at 1 and after 40 s returned to REM sleep at 2, and realized he was dreaming 15 s later and signaled at 3. Next he carried out the agreed-upon experimental task in his lucid dream, singing between signals 3 and 4, and counting between signals 4 and 5. This allowed comparison of left and right hemisphere activation during the two tasks (LaBerge and Dement, (1982b)). Note the heart-rate acceleration-deceleration pattern at awakening (1) and at lucidity onset (3), and the skin potential potential artifacts in the EEG (particularly T4) at lucidity onset (3). Calibrations are 50 microV and 5 s.

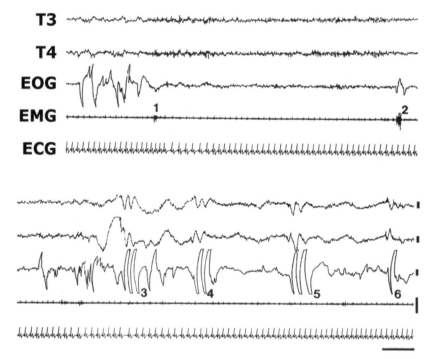

physiological indications of awakening ($\chi^2 = 38.3$; 1 degree of freedom; $p < .0001$) establishing the validity of classifying lucid dreams in this manner. Figure 11.3 illustrates a WILD; all the other lucid dream records shown in this chapter are DILDs.

As mentioned earlier, momentary intrusions of wakefulness occur commonly during the normal course of REM sleep, and it had been proposed by

Schwartz and Lefebvre (1973) that lucid dreaming occurs during these microawakenings. However, LaBerge et al.'s (1981a, 1981b, 1986) data indicate that while lucid dreams do not take place during interludes of wakefulness within REM periods, a minority of lucid dreams (WILDs) are initiated from these moments of transitory arousal, with the WILDs continuing in subsequent undisturbed REM sleep.

High CNS Activation Required for Lucidity

To summarize, an elevated level of CNS activation seems to be a necessary condition for the occurrence of lucid dreams. Evidently, the high level of cognitive function involved in lucid dreaming requires a correspondingly high level of neuronal activation. In terms of Antrobus's (1986) adaptation of Anderson's (1983) ACT model of cognition to dreaming, working memory capacity is proportional to cognitive activation, which in turn is proportional to cortical activation. Becoming lucid requires an adequate level of working memory to activate the presleep intention to recognize that one is dreaming. This level of cortical and cognitive activation is apparently not always available during sleep, but normally only during phasic REM.

PSYCHOPHYSIOLOGICAL RELATIONSHIPS DURING REM SLEEP

The Psychophysiological Approach

Psychologists attempting to apply rigorous scientific methodology to the study of such phenomena as mental imagery, hallucinations, dreaming, and in general, conscious processes face a major challenge: The most direct account available of the private events occurring in a person's mind is his or her own subjective report. But, unfortunately, subjective reports are difficult to objectively verify, and introspection is far from an unbiased and direct process of observation. There are two strategies likely to increase our confidence in the reliability of subjective reports: (1) use highly trained (and in the context of dream research, lucid) subjects who are skillful reporters and (2) use the psychophysiological approach, which makes use of the fact that the convergent agreement of physiological measures and subjective reports provides a degree of validation to the latter (Stoyva and Kamiya, 1968).

A New Strategy for Dream Research

Indeed, the psychophysiological approach was responsible for the Golden Age of dream research in the decades following the discovery of REM sleep (Aserinsky and Kleitman, 1953) and the subsequent association of REM with dreaming (Dement and Kleitman, 1957). Although the psychophysiological paradigm of dream research yielded an abundant harvest for many years (see Arkin, Antrobus, & Ellman, 1978), it possessed a fatal flaw: as long as the subjects are nonlucid, the researcher has no way of making certain that the subjects will dream about what the researcher might like to study. Presleep manipulations producing reliable effects on dream content have not been highly successful (Tart, 1988). One can only wait and hope that eventually a dream report will turn up what one is looking for. This is really no better than a shot-in-the-dark approach, and some researchers have been calling for abandoning the psychophysiological method in favor of a purely psychological approach. An influential researcher has written that "... psychophysiological correlation research now appears to offer such a low rate of return for effort expended as not to be a wise place for dream psychology to continue to commit much of its limited resources" (Foulkes, 1985). This conclusion might well be justified, but only insofar as it refers to the psychophysiological approach as traditionally practiced, using nonlucid subjects. The use of lucid dreamers overcomes the basic difficulty of the old methodology and may revitalize the psychophysiological approach to dream research.

The fact that lucid dreamers can remember to perform predetermined actions and signal to the laboratory suggested to a new paradigm for dream research (LaBerge, 1980a): Lucid dreamers, I proposed, "could carry out diverse dream experiments marking the exact time of particular dream events, allowing the derivation of precise psychophysiological correlations and the methodical testing of hypotheses" (LaBerge, Nagel, Dement, & Zarcone, 1981, p. 727). This strategy has been put into practice by the Stanford group in a series of studies summarized in the following section.

Dream Time

How long do dreams take? This question has intrigued humanity for many centuries. A traditional answer was that dreams take very little or no time at all, as in the case of Maury's famous dream in which he had somehow gotten mixed up in a long series of adventures during the French Revolution, finally losing his head on the guillotine, at which point he awoke to find the headboard had fallen on his neck. He supposed, therefore, that the lengthy dream had been produced in a flash by the painful stimulus. The idea that dreams occur in the moment of awakening has found supporters over the years (for example, Hall, 1981).

We have been able to address the problem of dream time very directly by asking subjects to estimate ten-second intervals (by counting, "one thousand and one, one thousand and two, and so on") during their lucid dreams. Signals marking the beginning and end of the subjective intervals allowed

FIGURE 11.4

Dream time estimations. Subjects estimated ten-second intervals by counting, "one thousand and one, one thousand and two, etc." during their lucid dreams. Eye-movement signals marking the beginning and end of the subjective intervals allowed comparison with objective time. In all cases, time estimates during the lucid dreams were very close to the actual time between signals.

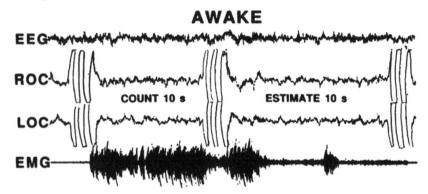

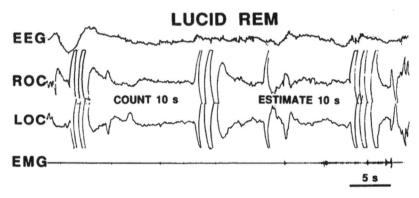

Sources: LaBerge, 1980a, 1985b.

comparison with objective time. In all cases, time estimates during the lucid dreams were very close to the actual time between signals (LaBerge, 1980a, 1985). However, this finding does not rule out the possibility of time distortion effects under some circumstances.

Smooth Tracking Eye Movements

The data reported by LaBerge, Nagel, Dement, and Zarcone (1981) and LaBerge, Nagel, Taylor, Dement, and Zarcone (1981) indicate that there is a very direct and reliable relationship between gaze shift reported in lucid dreams and the direction of polygraphically recorded eye movements. The results obtained for lucid dreams (see also Dane, 1984; Fenwick et al., 1984; Hearne, 1978; Ogilvie, Hunt, Tyson, Lucescu, & Jeakins, 1982) are much stronger than the generally weak correlations obtained by previous investigators testing the hypothesis that the dreamer's eyes move with his or her hallucinated dream gaze, who had to rely on the chance occurrence of a highly recognizable eye-movement pattern that was readily matchable to the subject's reported dream activity (for example, Roffwarg, Dement, Muzio, & Fisher, 1962).

In a related experiment (LaBerge, 1986), two subjects tracked the tip of their fingers moving slowly left to right during four conditions: (1) awake, eyes open; (2) awake, eyes closed mental imagery; (3) lucid dreaming; and (4) imagination ("dream eyes closed") during lucid dreaming. The subjects showed saccadic eye movements in the two imagination conditions (2 and 4), and smooth tracking eye movements during dreamed or actual tracking (conditions 1 and 3). A replication with six subjects and circular tracking (LaBerge & Zimbardo, 2000) had similar results. Mean eye movement velocity, allowed the correct classification in 95 percent of the cases, strongly supporting the hypothesis that as far as the visual vividness dimension is concerned, dreaming consciousness is nearly identical to waking perceptual consciousness, and just as distinct from imagination as imagination is distinct from perception (see Figure 11.5).

Respiration

In another study, LaBerge and Dement (1982a) demonstrated the possibility of voluntary control of respiration during lucid dreaming. They recorded three lucid dreamers who were asked to either breathe rapidly or to hold their breath (in their lucid dreams), marking the interval of altered respiration with eye movement signals. The subjects reported successfully carrying out the agreed-upon tasks a total of nine times, and in every case, a judge was able to correctly predict on the basis of the polygraph recordings which of the two patterns had been executed (binomial test; $p < .002$).

Other Muscle Groups

Evidence of voluntary control of other muscle groups during REM was found by LaBerge, Nagel, Dement, and Zarcone (1981) while testing a variety of lucidity signals. They observed that a sequence of left and right

FIGURE 11.5

Smooth tracking eye-movements discriminate both dreaming and perception from imagination. (A) Circle tracking compared in three states. (B) Mean values of standardized eye-movement velocities (EMVZ) as a function of state. The gray boxes contain 50 percent of the data, with median values, 75th and 25th percentiles marked.

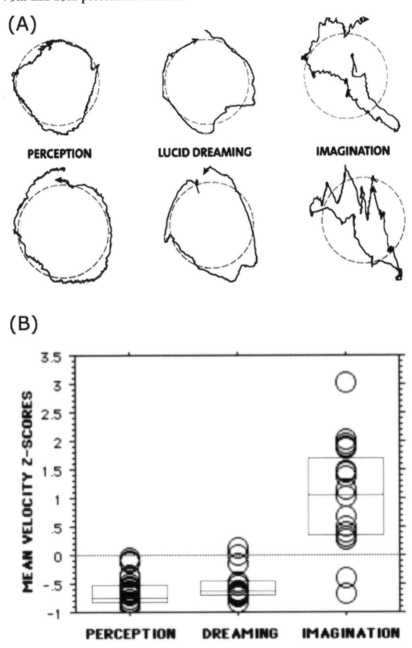

Source: LaBerge and Zimbardo, 2000.

dream-fist clenches resulted in a corresponding sequence of left and right forearm twitches as measured by an electromyogram (EMG). However, the amplitude of the twitches bore an unreliable relationship to the subjective intensity of the dreamed action.

The results of the studies just reviewed are consistent with the view that bodily movements dreamed during REM sleep generate motor output equivalent at the supraspinal level to the patterns of neuronal activity that would be generated if the corresponding movements were actually executed. Most voluntary muscles are, of course, paralyzed during REM, with the notable exceptions of the ocular and respiratory muscles. Hence, the perfect correspondence between dreamed and actual movements for these two systems (Figures 11.1 to 11.6), and the attenuated intensity (but preserved spatio-temporal pattern) of movements observed in Figure 11.6.

FIGURE 11.6
Morse code communication from the lucid dream. Evidence of voluntary control of other muscle groups during REM was found by LaBerge, Nagel, Dement, and Zarcone (1981) while testing a variety of lucidity signals. We observed that a sequence of left and right dream-fist clenches resulted in a corresponding sequence of left and right forearm twitches as measured by EMG. Here the subject (the author) sends a Morse code signal with left and right fist clenches corresponding to dots and dashes, respectively. Hence the message translates as "SL," the subject's initials. Note that the amplitude of the twitches bore an unreliable relationship to the subjective intensity of the dreamed action.

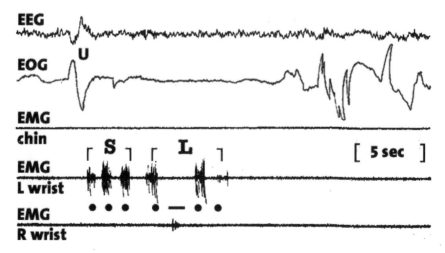

Cognitive Task Dependency of EEG Laterality

Following reports of cognitive task dependency of lateralization of EEG alpha activity in the waking state by many researchers, LaBerge and Dement (1982b) undertook a pilot study demonstrating the feasibility of similar investigations in the lucid dream state. The two tasks selected for comparison were dreamed singing and dreamed counting, activities expected to result in relatively greater engagement of the subjects' left and right cerebral hemispheres, respectively. (Figure 11.3 shows a lucid dreamer carrying out these two tasks.)

Integrated alpha band EEG activity was derived from electrodes placed over right and left temporal lobes while four subjects sang and estimated ten seconds by counting in their lucid dreams (marking the beginning and end of each task by eye movement signals). The results supported the hypothesized lateralization of alpha activity: the right hemisphere was more active than the left during singing; during counting, the reverse was true. These shifts were similar to those observed during actual singing and counting. In contrast, a control condition with imagined singing and counting showed no significant laterality shifts (though statistical power was limited by the small sample size).

LaBerge and Dement noted an important implication of their results on the interpretation of EEG alpha activity during REM sleep. Because continuous alpha activity occurs when a subject awakens, sleep researchers have assumed that increased alpha activity in the context of sleep is always a sign of wakefulness or relative cortical activation. The findings just discussed suggest the contrary: alpha activity during REM sleep is, as in waking, inversely related to cortical activation. When a person awakens from a vivid dream to a dark room, his cortical (occipital, at least) activation has decreased, not increased, with the resultant appearance of elevated alpha power.

In this view, it is a straightforward prediction that occipital alpha power during REM sleep will correlate negatively with subsequently reported dream vividness. This could provide the proper explanation for the finding that awakenings following REM periods with high levels of alpha activity are more likely to yield "thinking" reports than awakenings from low-alpha REM periods which yield more "dreaming" reports (Antrobus, Dement, & Fisher (1964). A pilot study of motor area activation during dreamed hand-clenching supports the inverse alpha-cortical activity interpretation (Erlacher, Schredl, & LaBerge, 2003).

IMPLICATIONS FOR RESEARCH ON SLEEP AND COGNITION

"Awake" versus "Asleep": A Procrustian Dichotomy

Fenwick et al. (1984) showed that a subject was able to perceive and respond to environmental stimuli (electrical shocks) without awakening from his lucid dream. This result raises a theoretical issue: if we take perception of the external world to be the essential criterion for wakefulness (LaBerge et al., 1981a; see previous section), then it would seem that Worsley must have been at least partially awake. On the other hand, when environmental stimuli are incorporated into dreams without producing any subjective or physiological indications of arousal, it appears reasonable to speak of the perception as having occurred during sleep.

Furthermore, it may be possible, as LaBerge (1980c) has suggested, for one sense to remain functional and "awake" while others fall "asleep." Similarly, Antrobus, Antrobus and Fisher (1965) argued

> ... that the question—awake or asleep—is not a particularly useful one. Even though we have two discrete words—sleep and wakefulness—this does not mean that the behavior associated with the words can be forced into two discrete categories.... not only do sleeping and waking shade gradually into one another but there is only limited agreement among the various physiological and subjective operations that discriminate between sleeping and waking. At any given moment, all systems of the organism are not necessarily equally asleep or awake. (pp. 398–399)

As long as we continue to consider wakefulness and sleep as a simple dichotomy, we will lie in a Procrustian bed that is bound at times to be most uncomfortable. There must be degrees of being awake just as there are degrees of being asleep (that is, the conventional sleep stages). Before finding our way out of this muddle, we will probably need to characterize a wider variety of states of consciousness than those few currently distinguished (for example, "dreaming," "sleeping," "waking," and so on).

Developmental Perspective

It may be helpful to consider lucidity from a cognitive developmental perspective. According to Piaget (1926), children pass through three stages of understanding of the concept "dream." In the first stage, they believe that dreams take place in the same external world as all other experiences. In the second stage, children treat dreams as if they were partially external and partially internal. This transitional stage gives way to the third stage, in which children recognize the dream is entirely internal in nature, a purely mental experience.

These foregoing developmental stages refer to how children think about dreams when they are awake. While asleep and dreaming, children, and also adults, tend to remain at the first stage—implicitly assuming that the dream events are external reality. Out-of-body experiences (LaBerge, Levitan,

Brylowski & Dement, 1988; Levitan, LaBerge, DeGracia, & Zimbardo, 1999), with a contradictory mixture of material and mental (external and internal), may provide examples of the second stage. In the fully lucid dream, the dreamer attains the third stage, realizing that the dream world is distinct from the physical world.

Foulkes (1982, 1985) emphasized the idea that the growth of mind whether dreaming or awake shows parallel degrees of development

> . . . there are "stages" of dream development which individual children reliably pass through one after the other, and that the precise age at which they reach a new stage is at least partially predictable from independent measures of their waking mental development. (1985, p. 137)

Lucid Dreaming a Learnable Ability

Lucid dreaming represents in this view what ought to be a normal ability in adults. If this is correct, why are lucid dreams so rare, especially in cases such as nightmares, where lucidity should be extremely helpful and rewarding? I think a partial answer can be seen by comparing lucid dreaming with another learnable cognitive skill, namely, language. All normal adults speak and understand at least one language. But how many would do so if they were never taught? Unfortunately, in this culture, with few exceptions, we are not taught to dream.

LaBerge (1980b) has demonstrated that it is possible to learn to have lucid dreams volitionally, that is to say, essentially on demand (LaBerge, 1985b). Concentration, motivation, and prospective memory are required for best results. The Stanford group has experimented with methods for helping dreamers to realize that they are dreaming by means of external cues applied during REM sleep, which if incorporated into dreams, can remind dreamers that they are dreaming (LaBerge, 1980a). They have tested a variety of stimuli, including tape recordings of the phrase "This is a dream," (LaBerge, Owens, Nagel & Dement, 1981) conditioned tactile stimuli, (Rich, 1985) olfactory stimuli, and light (LaBerge, Levitan, Rich & Dement, 1988). The most promising results so far have been with light stimuli.

There are other procedures that can favorably influence lucid dreaming frequency. For example, interruptions of the sleep cycle with thirty to sixty minutes of wakefulness strongly facilitates lucidity in subsequent sleep (LaBerge, 2004).

The Experiential Reality of Dreams

The psychophysiological studies reviewed previously all support the following picture: During REM dreaming, the events we experience (or seem to) are the results of patterns of CNS activity that produce in turn effects on our autonomic nervous system and bodies to some extent modified by the specific conditions of active sleep, but still homomorphic to the effects that would occur if we were actually to experience the corresponding events while awake.

This conclusion may need further qualification and explanation. Although the events we appear to perceive in dreams are illusory, our feelings in response to dream content are real. Indeed, most of the events we experience in dreams are real; when we experience feelings, say, anxiety or ecstasy, in dreams, we really do feel anxious or ecstatic at the time. When we think in dreams, we really do think (whether clearly or not is another matter). If we think in our dreams that Monday comes before Sunday, it is not the case, as some philosophers (for example, Malcolm, 1959) assert, that we have only dreamed we thought; we may have thought incorrectly (to the usual way of thinking), but thought nonetheless.

If we were to vividly imagine a detailed sequence of movements, say, walking around the room, it is probable that motor areas of the brain would be activated in the same pattern as involved in actually walking. However, they would presumably be less activated than when walking. Otherwise, what would prevent us from actually walking when we imagined doing so?

In REM sleep there is a spinal paralysis that causes the muscles of locomotion and vocalization to fail to completely execute the action orders programmed by the brain. Thus, in REM, unlike the waking state, there is no impediment to the brain issuing sequences of motor commands at normal levels of activation, and this probably contributes to the experienced reality of dreamed action.

As for the afferent side of the equation, there is empirical evidence suggesting that imagery uses the same neural systems as perception in the corresponding sensory mode (see for example, Farah, 1988; Finke, 1980). In this view, the essential difference between a perception and a corresponding image is how the identical neural system acquires sufficient activation to produce a conscious experience. In the case of perception, neural excitation (and the resultant experience) is generated by external input, driving activation of the particular schema to-be-perceived in a largely bottom-up process. In the case of imagining (likewise, hallucinating, or dreaming) the experienced image is generated internally by top-down processes activating the appropriate neural network (schema).

Imaginations and perceptions are normally distinguishable by the fact that images are usually much less vivid than perceptions. Normally, perceptions seem real and images seem—imaginary. How real something appears depends mainly on its relative vividness, and experienced vividness is probably a function of intensity of neural activation. Thus, we may conjecture that images usually involve a lesser degree of neural activation than the corresponding perceptions, and this results in a lesser degree of experiential reality for imagination. At least two factors contribute to this state of affairs: one is that while we are awake, sensory input produces much higher levels of activation than imaginary input. Imagination interferes with perception in the same modality (Perky, 1910; Segal, 1971), and we may suppose the reverse is true as well. Another more speculative factor favoring perceptual processes over imagination in the waking state is the existence of a neural system to inhibit the activation (vividness) of memory images while perception is active. Evolutionary considerations make such a system likely; it would obviously be extremely maladaptive for an organism to mistake a current perceptual image of a predator for the memory of one (LaBerge, 1985a). Mandell (1980) has proposed a serotonergic system that normally inhibits vivid images (hallucinations), but is itself inhibited in REM sleep, allowing dreamed perceptions (that is, images) to appear as vividly real as perceptions. In REM, also, sensory input is actively suppressed preventing competition from perceptual processes.

Perhaps this explains in part why we are so inclined to mistake our dreams for reality: To the functional systems of neuronal activity that construct our experiential world (model), dreaming of perceiving or doing something is equivalent to actually perceiving or doing it.

Finally, lucid dreaming provides a perspective from which to ask what does it mean to be conscious?

WHAT DOES IT MEAN TO BE "AWAKE"?

I remember going to bed with mind peacefully composed and full of a quiet joy. The dream during the night that followed was at the beginning quite irrational, though perhaps more keenly followed than usual. I seemed to move smoothly through a region of space where, presently, a vivid sense of cold flowed in on me and held my attention with a strange interest.

I believe that at that moment the dream became lucid. Then suddenly, . . . all that up to now had been wrapped in confusion instantly passed away, and a new space burst forth in vivid presence and utter reality, with perception free and pin-pointed as never before; the darkness itself seemed alive. The thought that was then borne in upon me with inescapable conviction was this: "I have never been awake before." (Whiteman, 1961, p. 57)

REFERENCES

Anderson, J. R. (1983). *The architecture of cognition*. Cambridge, MA: Harvard University Press.

Antrobus, J. S. (1986). Dreaming: Cortical activation and perceptual thresholds. *Journal of Mind & Behavior, 7*, 193–212.

Antrobus, J. S., Antrobus, J. S., & Fisher, C. (1965). Discrimination of dreaming and nondreaming sleep. *Archives of General Psychiatry, 12,* 395–401.

Antrobus, J. S., Dement, W., & Fisher, C. (1964). Patterns of dreaming and dream recall: An EEG study. *Journal of Abnormal & Social Psychology, 69,* 244–252.

Arkin, A., Antrobus, J., & Ellman, S. (Eds.). (1978). *The mind in sleep.* Hillsdale, NJ: Lawrence Erlbaum Associates.

Aserinsky, E. (1971). Rapid eye movement density and pattern in the sleep of young adults. *Psychophysiology, 8,* 361–375.

Aserinsky, E., & Kleitman, N. (1953). Regularly occurring periods of eye motility and concomitant phenomena during sleep. *Science, 118,* 273–274.

Barrett, D. (1992). Just how lucid are lucid dreams? *Dreaming: The Journal of the Association for the Study of Dreams, 2,* 221–228.

Berger, R. (1977). *Psyclosis: The circularity of experience.* San Francisco, CA: W. H. Freeman & Co.

Brylowski, A., Levitan, L., & LaBerge, S. (1989). H-reflex suppression and autonomic activation during lucid REM sleep: A case study. *Sleep, 12,* 374–378.

Dane, J. (1984). An empirical evaluation of two techniques for lucid dream induction. Unpublished doctoral dissertation, Georgia State University.

Dement, W., & Kleitman, N. (1957). Cyclic variations in EEG during sleep and their relation to eye movements, body motility, and dreaming. *Electroencephalography & Clinical Neurophysiology, 9,* 673–690.

Erlacher, D., Schredl, M., & LaBerge, S. (2003). Motor area activation during dreamed hand clenching: A pilot study on EEG alpha band. *Sleep & Hypnosis, 5,* 180–185.

Farah, M. J. (1988). Is visual imagery really visual? Overlooked evidence from neurophysiology. *Psychological Review, 95,* 307–317.

Fenwick, P., Schatzman, M., Worsley, A., Adams, J., Stone, S., & Baker, A. (1984). Lucid dreaming: Correspondence between dreamed and actual events in one subject during REM sleep. *Biological Psychology, 18,* 243–252.

Finke, R. A. (1980). Levels of equivalence in imagery and perception. *Psychological Review, 87,* 113–132.

Foulkes, D. (1974). Review of Schwartz & Lefebvre (1973). *Sleep Research, 3,* 113.

Foulkes, D. (1982). A cognitive-psychological model of dream production. *Sleep, 5,* 169–187.

Foulkes, D. (1985). *Dreaming: A cognitive-psychological analysis.* Hillsdale, NJ: Lawrence Erlbaum.

Green, C. (1968). *Lucid dreams.* London: Hamish Hamilton.

Hartmann, E. (1975). Dreams and other hallucinations: an approach to the underlying mechanism. In R. K. Siegal & L. J. West (Eds.), *Hallucinations* (pp. 71–79). New York: J. Wiley & Sons.

Hearne, K. M. T. (1978). Lucid dreams: An electrophysiological and psychological study. Unpublished doctoral dissertation, University of Liverpool.

Hickey, D. A. (1988). The validation of lucid dreams in school age children. *Sleep Research, 17,* 114.

Holtzinger, B., LaBerge, S., & Levitan, L. (2006). Psychophysiological correlates of lucid dreaming. *Dreaming, 16,* 88–95.

Kahan, T., & LaBerge, S. (1994). Lucid dreaming as metacognition: Implications for cognitive science. *Consciousness & Cognition, 3,* 246–264.

Kueny, S. (1985). Auditory cuing in REM sleep for the induction of lucid dreaming. Unpublished doctoral dissertation. Pacific Graduate School of Psychology, Menlo Park, CA.

LaBerge, S. (1980a). Lucid dreaming: An exploratory study of consciousness during sleep. Doctoral dissertation, Stanford University, 1980. University Microfilms International No. 80-24,691.

LaBerge, S. (1980b). Lucid dreaming as a learnable skill: A case study. Perceptual & Motor Skills, 51, 1039–1042.

LaBerge, S. (1980c). Induction of lucid dreams. Sleep Research, 9, 138.

LaBerge, S. (1985a). Lucid dreaming. Los Angeles, CA: J. P. Tarcher.

LaBerge, S. (1985b). The temporal distribution of lucid dreams. Sleep Research, 14, 113.

LaBerge, S. (1990). Lucid dreaming: Psychophysiological studies of consciousness during REM sleep. In R. R. Bootsen, J. F. Kihlstrom, & D. L. Schacter (Eds.), Sleep and cognition (pp. 109–126). Washington, DC: American Psychological Association Press.

LaBerge, S. (2004). Lucid dreaming: A concise guide. Boulder, CO: Sounds True.

LaBerge, S., & DeGracia, D. J. (2000). Varieties of lucid dreaming experience. In R. G. Kunzendorf & B. Wallace (Eds.), Individual differences in conscious experience (pp. 269–307). Amsterdam: John Benjamins.

LaBerge, S., & Dement, W. C. (1982a). Voluntary control of respiration during REM sleep. Sleep Research, 11, 107.

LaBerge, S., & Dement, W. C. (1982b). Lateralization of alpha activity for dreamed singing and counting during REM sleep. Psychophysiology, 19, 331–332.

LaBerge, S., Levitan, L., Brylowski, A., & Dement, W. (1988). "Out-of-body" experiences occurring during REM sleep. Sleep Research, 17, 115.

LaBerge, S., Levitan, L., & Dement, W. C. (1986). Lucid dreaming: Physiological correlates of consciousness during REM sleep. Journal of Mind & Behavior, 7, 251–258.

LaBerge, S., Levitan, L., Rich, R., & Dement, W. (1988). Induction of lucid dreaming by light stimulation during REM sleep. Sleep Research, 17, 104.

LaBerge, S., Nagel, L., Dement, W. C., & Zarcone, V., Jr. (1981a). Lucid dreaming verified by volitional communication during REM sleep. Perceptual & Motor Skills, 52, 727–732.

LaBerge, S., Nagel, L., Taylor, W., Dement, W. C., & Zarcone, V., Jr. (1981b). Psychophysiological correlates of the initiation of lucid dreaming. Sleep Research, 10, 149.

LaBerge, S., Owens, J., Nagel, L., & Dement, W. (1981). "This is a dream": Induction of lucid dreams by verbal suggestion during REM sleep. Sleep Research, 10, 150.

LaBerge, S., & Zimbardo, P. G. (2000). Smooth tracking eye-movemtns discrimate both dreaming and perception from imagination. Toward science of consciousness conferencere IV, Tuscon, April 10, 2000. Abstract available from: http://lucidity.com/Tucson2000abs.html

Levitan, L., LaBerge, S., DeGracia, D. J., & Zimbardo, P. G. (1999). "Out-of-body experiences," dreams, and REM sleep. Sleep & Hypnosis, 1, 186–196.

Malcolm, N. (1959). Dreaming. London: Routledge.

Mandell, A. J. (1980). Toward a psychobiology of transcendence: God in the brain. In J. M. Davidson & R. J. Davidson (Eds.), The psychobiology of consciousness (pp. 379–464). New York: Plenum Press.

Ogilvie, R., Hunt, H., Kushniruk, A., & Newman, J. (1983). Lucid dreams and the arousal continuum. Sleep Research, 12, 182.

Ogilvie, R., Hunt, H., Sawicki, C., & McGowan, K. (1978). Searching for lucid dreams. *Sleep Research, 7,* 165.

Ogilvie, R., Hunt, H., Tyson, P. D., Lucescu, M. L. & Jeakins, D. B. (1982). Lucid dreaming and alpha activity: A preliminary report. *Perceptual & Motor Skills, 55,* 795–808.

Perky, C. W. (1910). An experimental study of imagination. *American Journal of Psychology, 21,* 422–452.

Piaget, J. (1926). *The child's conception of the world.* New York: Harcourt, Brace & Co.

Pivik, R. T. (1986). Sleep: Physiology and psychophysiology. In M. G. H. Coles, E. Donchin, & S. Porges (Eds.), *Psychophysiology: Systems, processes, and applications.* (pp. 378–406) New York: Guilford Press.

Rechtschaffen, A., & Kales, A. (Eds.). (1968). *A manual of standardized terminology, techniques and scoring system for sleep stages of human subjects.* Bethesda, MD: HEW Neurological Information Network.

Rich, R. (1985). The induction of lucid dreams by tactile stimulation during REM sleep. Unpublished honors thesis.

Roffwarg, H., Dement, W. C., Muzio, J., & Fisher, C. (1962). Dream imagery: Relationship to rapid eye movements of sleep. *Archives of General Psychiatry, 7,* 235–238.

Schwartz, B. A., & Lefebvre, A. (1973). Contacts veille/P.M.O. II. Les P.M.O. morcelees [Conjunction of waking and REM sleep. II. Fragmented REM periods.]. *Revue d'Electroencephalographie et de Neurophysiologie Clinique, 3,* 165–176.

Segal, S. J. (1971). Processing of the stimulus in imagery and perception. In S. J. Segal (Ed.) *Imagery: Current cognitive approaches* (pp. 73–100). New York: Academic Press.

Stoyva, J., & Kamiya, J. (1968). Electrophysiological studies of dreaming as the prototype of a new strategy in the study of consciousness. *Psychological Review, 75,* 192–205.

Tart, C. (1984). Terminology in lucid dream research. *Lucidity Letter, 3,* 4–6.

Tart, C. (1988). From spontaneous event to lucidity: A review of attempts to consciously control nocturnal dreaming. In J. Gackenbach & S. LaBerge (Eds.), *Conscious mind, dreaming brain* (pp. 67–103). New York: Plenum Press.

Tholey, P. (1988). A model for lucidity training as a means of self-healing and psychological growth. In J. Gackenbach & S. LaBerge (Eds.), *Conscious mind, sleeping brain* (pp. 263–287). New York: Plenum.

Van Eeden, F. (1913). A study of dreams. *Proceedings of the Society for Psychical Research, 26,* 431–461.

Whiteman, J. H. M. (1961). *The mystical life.* London: Faber & Faber.

Index

The letters following page numbers in the index refer to tables (*t*) and figures (*f*) in the book.

About the Editors and Contributors

DEIRDRE BARRETT, PhD, is a clinical psychologist and Assistant Professor of Psychology at Harvard Medical School. She is Past President of the Association for the Study of Dreams, author of three trade books including *The Committee of Sleep* (Random House, 2001) and editor of *Trauma and Dreams* (Harvard University Press, 1996). She is Editor-in-Chief of the journal *Dreaming* and a Consulting Editor for *Imagination, Cognition, and Personality* and the *International Journal for Clinical and Experimental Hypnosis*. She is President of American Psychological Association's Division 30, the Society for Psychological Hypnosis. Dr. Barrett has published dozens of academic articles and chapters on dreaming, imagery, and hypnosis.

Dr. Barrett's commentary on dreams has been featured on *Good Morning America*, *The Today Show*, CNN, Fox, The Discovery Channel, and Voice of America. She has been interviewed for dream articles in the *Washington Post*, the *New York Times*, *Life*, *Time*, and *Newsweek*. Her own articles have appeared in *Psychology Today*, and her film review column "The Dream Videophile" is published in the magazine *Dream Time*. Dr. Barrett has lectured on dreams at Esalen, the Smithsonian, and at universities across the United States and in Russia, Kuwait, Israel, England, and Holland.

PATRICK McNAMARA, PhD, is Director of Evolutionary Neurobehavior Laboratory, in the Department of Neurology at the Boston University School of Medicine and the Veterans Administration New England Healthcare System. Upon graduating from the Behavioral Neuroscience Program at Boston University in 1991, he trained at the Aphasia Research Center at the Boston VA Medical Center in neurolinquistics and brain-cognitive correlation techniques. He then began developing an evolutionary approach to problems of brain and behavior and currently is studying the evolution of the frontal lobes, the evolution of the two mammalian sleep states (REM and NREM), and the evolution of religion in human cultures.

Mehmet Yücel Agargün is Professor of Psychiatry at Yuzuncu Yil University. He is head of the Department of Psychiatry and Neuroscience Research Unit. He is interested in dreams, hypnosis, and dissociation. Dr. Agargün is editing a new book *Dreams, Islam, and Psychotherapy*, and he is also the editor of *Sleep and Hypnosis*.

Mark Blagrove obtained his BA in Natural Sciences from Cambridge University and then his PhD on the relationships between dreaming and waking life thinking from Brunel University. He then worked on the effects of sleep deprivation at Loughborough University sleep laboratory. Since 1991, he has lectured at Swansea University, in Wales, teaching a course on sleep and dreaming and a course on consciousness while also running the university's sleep laboratory. He is on the editorial advisory board of the *Journal of Sleep Research*, is a consulting editor for the journal *Dreaming*, and is a past-president of the International Association for the Study of Dreams. His research interests are the etiology of nightmares, relationships between personality and dreaming, functions of REM sleep, and the effects of the anesthetic ketamine on dreaming.

G. William Domhoff is a Research Professor at the University of California, Santa Cruz, where he has taught since 1965. He holds degrees in psychology from Duke University, Kent State University, and the University of Miami. He is the author of *The Mystique of Dreams* (University of California Press, 1985), *Finding Meaning in Dreams* (Plenum, 1996), and *The Scientific Study of Dreams* (APA Books, 2003), as well as numerous articles on dream content.

Roar Fosse is a Clinical Psychologist and obtained his PhD in Cognitive Neuroscience from the University of Oslo in 2002. He completed his postdoctorate at the Laboratory of Neurophysiology at Harvard Medical School in 2002–2003. Since 2004, he has been the Director of Research and Development at the Regional Center of Traumatic Stress and Suicide Prevention in East Norway.

Clara E. Hill earned her PhD at Southern Illinois University in 1974. She started as an Assistant Professor in the Counseling Psychology Program at the Department of Psychology, University of Maryland, where she is currently a Professor and Co-Director of the Counseling Psychology Program. She has been the President of the Society for Psychotherapy Research, Editor of the *Journal of Counseling Psychology and Psychotherapy Research*, winner of the Leona Tyler Award from Division 17 of the American

Psychological Association (APA), the Distinguished Psychologist Award from Division 29 of APA, and the Outstanding Lifetime Achievement Award from the Section on Counseling and Psychotherapy Process and Outcome Research of Division 17 of APA. Her major research interests are dream work, psychotherapy process and outcome, training novice therapists in helping skills, and qualitative research. She has published seven books and over 170 journal articles and chapters in books.

Stanley Krippner, PhD, is the Alan Watts Professor of Psychology, Saybrook Graduate School and Research Center, San Francisco, California, where he has designed several graduate level courses on the psychology of dreams and dreaming. A former president of the International Association for the Study of Dreams and the former director of the Dream Laboratory at Maimonides Medical Center, Brooklyn, New York, he is the editor of *Dreamtime and Dreamwork,* the co-editor of *Dreamscaping,* and the co-author of *Dream Telepathy* (with Montague Ullman), *Dreamworking, Extraordinary Dreams and How to Work with Them,* and *The Varieties of Anomalous Experience,* which was published by the American Psychological Association (APA). He was the 2002 recipient of APA's Award for Distinguished Contribution to the International Advancement of Psychology, is a Fellow of five APA Divisions, and a former president of two APA Divisions. He has authored and co-authored over 1,000 articles, several of them on anomalous dream reports, cross-cultural aspects of dreams, the use of dreams by tribal shamans, and a chaos theory approach to the neuropsychology of dreams and dreaming. Dr. Krippner was the 2003 recipient of the Ashley Montague Peace Award, and co-edited *The Psychological Effects of War Trauma on Civilians.*

Stephen LaBerge received his PhD in Psychophysiology in 1980 from Stanford University where he studied consciousness, dreaming, and waking for 25 years. He has taught courses on sleep and dreaming, psychobiology, and altered states of consciousness at Stanford University, the California Institute of Integral Studies in San Francisco, and San Francisco State University. In addition to numerous scientific articles on lucid dreaming, he has published several popular books on the topic, which have been translated into eighteen languages and widely read. He continues his research and writing as an independent scholar based in California and Hawaii.

Jessica Lara-Carrasco is a doctoral student in Psychology at the Université de Montréal and a research assistant in the Dream and Nightmare Laboratory of the Hôpital du Sacré-Coeur in Montreal. She has won numerous bursaries from the Canadian Institutes of Health Research, the Quebec Health Research Fund, the National Bank, and the J.A. DeSève

Foundation. She is presently conducting research on the emotional adaptation functions of REM sleep and dreaming.

Tore Nielsen is a Full Professor in the Department of Psychiatry at the Université de Montréal and Director of the Dream and Nightmare Laboratory at the Sacré-Coeur Hospital since 1991. He received a PhD in Experimental Psychology from the Department of Psychology, University of Alberta, Canada, in 1986. He was a Research Scholar of the Canadian Institutes of Health Research (CIHR) from 1993–1998 and both Junior and Senior Research Scholar of the Quebec Health Research Fund from 1998–2003. His research is currently funded by the CIHR, the Natural Sciences and Engineering Research Council of Canada (NSERCC), and the Social Sciences and Humanities Research Council of Canada (SSHRCC). Research topics include: Nightmares and PTSD, Covert REM sleep and NREM Dreaming, Sensed Presence and Social Anxiety, Introspection and Dream Reporting, Virtual Reality Exposure Effects on Dream Content, Emotional Functions of Dreaming, and Dreaming Among New Mothers. He has authored numerous scientific chapters and papers; most recently in *Behavioral and Brain Sciences* (2000), *The Principles and Practice of Sleep Medicine*, 4th Edition (2005) *Nature* (2005) and *Psychological Bulletin* (2007). He is a licensed psychologist in the province of Québec.

Raija-Leena Punamäki is a psychologist and professor in University of Tampere, Finland. She specializes in child development and mental health in conditions of war and military violence. The specific topics are resiliency, symbolic processes like dreaming and playing, family dynamics, and adult attachment in traumatized populations.

Currently, her research activities focus on effectiveness prevention and intervention programs for war-traumatized children, and mother-child interaction in life-endangering conditions. She is a member of the Finnish Psychologist for Social Responsibility and a board member of European Society for Study Traumatic Stress and the Academy of Finland Research Council for Culture and Society.

Michael Schredl, PhD, is Research Director of the Sleep Laboratory at the Central Institute of Mental Health, Mannheim, Germany. He received a diploma in electrical engineering and psychology. Since 1990, his research has focused on different aspects of dreams and nightmares. He has published numerous articles, chapters, and four books on a variety of topics, including factors of dream recall, nightmare treatment, the continuity between waking and dreaming, the effect of dreams on waking-life, and nightmares in children. He is on the Editorial Board of the journals *Dreaming* and *Sleep and Hypnosis*, founded the Dream section in the German Sleep Society, and lectures on dream research at the University of Mannheim.

Patricia Spangler is a doctoral student in the Counseling Psychology program in the Department of Psychology at the University of Maryland, College Park. Her current research interests include dream work in psychotherapy and therapist dreams about clients.